Critical Theory and Democracy

This book focuses on Andrew Arato's democratic theory and its relevance to contemporary issues such as processes of democratization, civil society, constitution-making, and the modern executive.

Andrew Arato is – both globally and disciplinarily – a prominent thinker in the fields of democratic theory, constitutional law, and comparative politics, influencing several generations of scholars. This is the first volume to systematically address his democratic theory. Including contributions from leading scholars such as Hubertus Buchstein, Dick Howard, and János Kis, this book is organized around three major areas of Arato's influence on contemporary political and social thought. The first section offers a comprehensive view of Arato's scholarship from his early work on critical theory and Western Marxism to his current research on constitution-making and its application. The second section shifts its focus from the previous, comprehensive approach, to a much more specific one: Arato's widespread influence on the study of civil society in democratization processes in the Americas. The third section includes Arato's previously unpublished work, "Conceptual History of Dictatorship (and its Rivals)," one of the few systematic interrogations on the meaning of a political form of fundamental relevance in the contemporary world.

Critical Theory and Democracy will be of interest to political and social theorists, and all Arato scholars.

Enrique Peruzzotti is Professor in the Department of Political Science at Di Tella University, and Researcher at CONICET, Argentina.

Martín Plot is Full-Time Faculty of the Aesthetics and Politics Program at the CalArts' School of Critical Studies, USA.

Routledge innovations in political theory

1. **A Radical Green Political Theory**
   Alan Carter

2. **Rational Woman**
   A feminist critique of dualism
   Raia Prokhovnik

3. **Rethinking State Theory**
   Mark J. Smith

4. **Gramsci and Contemporary Politics**
   Beyond pessimism of the intellect
   Anne Showstack Sassoon

5. **Post-Ecologist Politics**
   Social theory and the abdication of the ecologist paradigm
   Ingolfur Blühdorn

6. **Ecological Relations**
   Susan Board

7. **The Political Theory of Global Citizenship**
   April Carter

8. **Democracy and National Pluralism**
   Edited by Ferran Requejo

9. **Civil Society and Democratic Theory**
   Alternative voices
   Gideon Baker

10. **Ethics and Politics in Contemporary Theory**
    Between critical theory and post-Marxism
    Mark Devenney

11. **Citizenship and Identity**
    Towards a new republic
    John Schwarzmantel

12. **Multiculturalism, Identity and Rights**
    Edited by Bruce Haddock and Peter Sutch

13. **Political Theory of Global Justice**
    A cosmopolitan case for the world state
    Luis Cabrera

14. **Democracy, Nationalism and Multiculturalism**
    Edited by Ramón Maiz and Ferrán Requejo

15. **Political Reconciliation**
    Andrew Schaap

16 **National Cultural Autonomy and Its Contemporary Critics**
Edited by Ephraim Nimni

17 **Power and Politics in Poststructuralist Thought**
New theories of the political
Saul Newman

18 **Capabilities Equality**
Basic issues and problems
Edited by Alexander Kaufman

19 **Morality and Nationalism**
Catherine Frost

20 **Principles and Political Order**
The challenge of diversity
Edited by Bruce Haddock, Peri Roberts and Peter Sutch

21 **European Integration and the Nationalities Question**
Edited by John McGarry and Michael Keating

22 **Deliberation, Social Choice and Absolutist Democracy**
David van Mill

23 **Sexual Justice/Cultural Justice**
Critical perspectives in political theory and practice
Edited by Barbara Arneil, Monique Deveaux, Rita Dhamoon and Avigail Eisenberg

24 **The International Political Thought of Carl Schmitt**
Terror, liberal war and the crisis of global order
Edited by Louiza Odysseos and Fabio Petito

25 **In Defense of Human Rights**
A non-religious grounding in a pluralistic world
Ari Kohen

26 **Logics of Critical Explanation in Social and Political Theory**
Jason Glynos and David Howarth

27 **Political Constructivism**
Peri Roberts

28 **The New Politics of Masculinity**
Men, power and resistance
Fidelma Ashe

29 **Citizens and the State**
Attitudes in Western Europe and East and Southeast Asia
Takashi Inoguchi and Jean Blondel

30 **Political Language and Metaphor**
Interpreting and changing the world
Edited by Terrell Carver and Jernej Pikalo

31 **Political Pluralism and the State**
Beyond sovereignty
Marcel Wissenburg

32 **Political Evil in a Global Age**
Hannah Arendt and international theory
Patrick Hayden

33 **Gramsci and Global Politics**
Hegemony and resistance
Mark McNally and John Schwarzmantel

34 **Democracy and Pluralism**
The political thought of William E. Connolly
Edited by Alan Finlayson

35 **Multiculturalism and Moral Conflict**
Edited by Maria Dimova-Cookson and Peter Stirk

36 **John Stuart Mill – Thought and Influence**
The saint of rationalism
Edited by Georgios Varouxakis and Paul Kelly

37 **Rethinking Gramsci**
Edited by Marcus E. Green

38 **Autonomy and Identity**
The politics of who we are
Ros Hague

39 **Dialectics and Contemporary Politics**
Critique and transformation from Hegel through post-Marxism
John Grant

40 **Liberal Democracy as the End of History**
Fukuyama and postmodern challenges
Chris Hughes

41 **Deleuze and World Politics**
Alter-globalizations and nomad science
Peter Lenco

42 **Utopian Politics**
Citizenship and practice
Rhiannon Firth

43 **Kant and International Relations Theory**
Cosmopolitan community building
Dora Ion

43 **Ethnic Diversity and the Nation State**
National cultural autonomy revisited
David J. Smith and John Hiden

44 **Tensions of Modernity**
Las Casas and his legacy in the French Enlightenment
Daniel R. Brunstetter

45 **Honor: A Phenomenology**
Robert L. Oprisko

46 **Critical Theory and Democracy**
Civil society, dictatorship, and constitutionalism in Andrew Arato's democratic theory
Edited by Enrique Peruzzotti and Martín Plot

Critical Theory and Democracy

Civil society, dictatorship, and constitutionalism in Andrew Arato's democratic theory

Edited by Enrique Peruzzotti and Martín Plot

Includes Andrew Arato's 'Conceptual History of Dictatorship (and its Rivals)'

Routledge
Taylor & Francis Group
LONDON AND NEW YORK

First published 2013
by Routledge
2 Park Square Milton Park Abingdon Oxon OX14 4RN

Simultaneously published in the USA and Canada
by Routledge
711 Third Avenue, New York, NY 10017

Routledge is an imprint of the Taylor & Francis Group, an informa business.

British Library Cataloguing in Publication Data
A catalogue record for this book is available from the British Library

Library of Congress Cataloging in Publication Data
A catalog record has been requested for this book

ISBN: 978-0-415-66555-1 (hbk)
ISBN: 978-0-203-08321-5 (ebk)

Typeset in Times New Roman
by Wearset Ltd, Boldon, Tyne and Wear

Printed and bound in the United States of America by Publishers Graphics, LLC on sustainably sourced paper.

Contents

Notes on contributors

Andrew Arato is the Dorothy Hart Hirshon Professor in Political and Social Theory at the New School for Social Research. He has also taught at the Ecole des hautes etudes, Sciences Po in Paris, and the Central European University in Budapest. He had a Fulbright teaching grant to Montevideo in 1991, and was Distinguished Fulbright Professor at the Goethe University in Frankfurt. Professor Arato served as a consultant for the Hungarian Parliament on constitutional issues from 1996 to 1997, and as US State Department Democracy Lecturer and Consultant (on constitutional issues) for Nepal in 2007. He has been reappointed by the State Department in the same capacity for Zimbabwe. He was also appointed Honorary Professor, and Bram Fischer Visiting Scholar at the School of Law, University of Witwatersrand Johannesburg, South Africa, from June 2010 to June 2011. In Spring 2012 he was an invited professor at the College de France. Andrew Arato's research is widely recognized and conferences and sessions have been organized around his work: at the University of Glasgow Law School in Spring 2009, and Koc University, Istanbul, in December 2009, as well as at the Faculty of Law University of Witwatersrand Johannesburg, in August 2010. *Democracy and Critical Theory* is the first volume dedicated to discussing Andrew Arato's political and social thought.

Leonardo Avritzer is Professor of Political Science at the Federal University of Minas Gerais. He is the author of several books on democracy and participation, among them *Democracy and the Public Space in Latin America* (Princeton University Press, 2002) and *Participatory Institutions in Democratic Brazil* (Johns Hopkins University Press, 2009).

Hubertus Buchstein is Professor for Political Theory and the History of Political Ideas at Greifswald University, Germany, and Fellow at the Wissenschaftskolleg Berlin in 2012–13. From 1995 until 2003 he was teaching at the New School for Social Research. From 2009 to 2012 he was President of the German Political Science Association. His research interests are focused on theories of democracy, in particular on political procedures; the history of political science as a discipline; and critical theory. His recent publications include *Demokratie und Lotterie* (Campus Verlag, 2009), 'Randomizing Europe – The Lottery as a Decision Making Procedure for Policy Creation in the EU' (in *Critical Policy Studies* 3:29–58), *Demokratiepolitik* (Nomos Verlag, 2010) and 'The Argumentative Turn toward Deliberative Democracy: Habermas' Contribution and the Foucauldian Critique' in Frank Fischer and Herbert Gottweis' *The Argumentative Turn Revisited* (Duke, 2012).

Maria Victoria Crespo (Ph.D., New School for Social Research, 2011, Albert Salomon Award in Sociology) is a Research Associate at El Colegio de México. She works in the fields of political and historical sociology. She recently co-edited *Estado y sociedad en el Morelos posrevolucionario y contemporáneo* (Congreso del Estado de Morelos, 2010) and has written several book chapters and journal articles on Latin American politics and history. Her book *Del rey al presidente. Poder ejecutivo, formación del estado y soberanía en la Hispanoamérica revolucionaria, 1810–1826* (El Colegio de México Press) is forthcoming.

Carlos de la Torre is Professor of Sociology and Director of International Studies, University of Kentucky, Lexington. His most recent books are *Populist Seduction in Latin America* (Ohio University Press, 2010); *The Ecuador Reader: History, Culture, Politics*, co-edited with Steve Striffler (Duke University Press, 2008); *El Retorno del Pueblo*, co-edited with Enrique Peruzzotti (FLACSO, 2008). He has been a fellow of the John Simon Guggenheim Memorial Foundation, the Woodrow Wilson International Center for Scholars, and a New Century Fulbright Scholar.

Dick Howard is Distinguished Professor Emeritus at Stony Brook University. Among Dick Howard's fifteen books is *The Unknown Dimension: European Marxism since Lenin* (Basic Books, 1972), in which Andrew Arato published his first essay on Lukács. The title of that volume suggests the path Howard has followed for forty years, from an edition of *Selected Writings of Rosa Luxemburg* (Monthly Review Press, 1971) to his most recent book, *The Primacy of the Political: A History of Political Thought from the Greeks to the French Revolution* (Columbia University Press, 2011). Along the way came books such as *The Politics of Critique* and *Defining the Political*, as well as historical studies of *Les origines de la pensée politique américaine*, themselves relayed by books of commentary and present-day radio commentaries on US politics. His commentaries on contemporary politics are found at his website: www.dickhoward.com.

János Kis is University Professor and Professor of Philosophy and Political Science at Central European University and Global Professor of Law and Global Distinguished Professor of Philosophy at New York University. In the 1970s, he was a leading figure of the democratic opposition to the Communist regime in Hungary. He was also Founder and first President of the Alliance of Free Democrats, Hungary's left-liberal party. His books include *L'Égale Dignité* (Seuil, 1989), *Political Neutrality* (in Hungarian, Atlantisz, 1997), *Constitutional Democracy* (CEU Press, 2002), and *Politics as a Moral Problem* (CEU Press, 2008).

Nicolás Lynch (Ph.D. in Sociology, New School for Social Research, 1992) is Professor of Sociology at the National University of San Marcos in Lima, Perú. He has worked extensively in social movements and political parties in Latin America and also in the theory and practice of populism. He has been Peruvian Minister of Education and he is currently the Peruvian Ambassador in Argentina. He is the author of numerous books, including *La transición conservadora* (Lima, El zorro de abajo ediciones, 1992) and *Política y Antipolítica en el Perú* (Lima, Desco 2000).

Alberto J. Olvera is Professor-Researcher at the Instituto de Investigaciones Histórico-Sociales, Universidad Veracruzana, Mexico (of which he was Director, 2001–2006). He has worked as invited professor in universities of Brazil, Colombia, the United States, and Mexico. He has written extensively on civil society, citizen participation, and democratic innovation in Mexico and Latin America, and is editor and co-author of several books, and author of numerous book chapters and articles published in Mexico, Brazil, Colombia, Argentina, Spain, and the United States. He has been a civic activist for thirty years and is an op-pages collaborator in Mexico's main newspapers.

Enrique Peruzzotti is Professor in the Political Science Department of Di Tella University and a researcher at CONICET, Argentina. His work on accountability politics, democratic innovation, and civil society has appeared in *Global Governance*; *Human Rights Quarterly*; *Citizenship Studies*; *Journal of Democracy*; *Journal of Third World Studies*; *Journal of Latin American Studies*; and *Constellations*: *An International Journal of Critical and Democratic Theory*. He has co-edited *Enforcing the Rule of Law: Social Accountability in Latin America* (Pittsburgh University Press, 2006) and *Participatory Innovation and Representative Democracy in Latin America* (Johns Hopkins University Press, 2009).

Martín Plot (Ph.D., New School for Social Research, 2004) teaches at the CalArts' School of Critical Studies and its Graduate Program in Aesthetics and Politics. He has published *El kitsch político* (Prometeo, 2003), *La carne de lo social* (Prometeo, 2008), and *Indivisible* (Prometeo, 2011). He has also edited several books and published in many journals and reviews, including: *Constellations: An International Journal of Critical and Democratic Theory*; *Continental Philosophy Review*; *Theory and Event*; *International Journal of Communication*; *Umbrales*; *Punto de Vista*; and *Le monde diplomatique*.

Ulrich K. Preuss is Professor Emeritus of Law and Politics at the Freie Universität Berlin and at the Hertie School of Governance in Berlin. He worked as Professor for Public Law at the University of Bremen from 1972 to 1996. From 1989 to 1990, he co-authored the draft of the constitution as a participant of the Round Table of the German Democratic Republic, and in 1992–1993 he advised the Thuringian Parliament on the conception of a new constitution. He has taught at, among others, Princeton University, New School University, New York, and the University of Chicago. From 1992 until 2011 he was a judge of the Staatsgerichtshof (State Constitutional Court) of Freie Hansestadt Bremen.

Uri Ram is Professor of Sociology and Chair of the Department of Sociology and Anthropology at Ben Gurion University of the Negev in Israel. He graduated in 1992 in the Department of Sociology and the Committee on Historical Studies, at the Graduate Faculty of the New School for Social Research, under the mentoring of Andrew Arato. His recent books include *The Globalization of Israel: McWorld in Tel Aviv, Jihad in Jerusalem* (Routledge, 2007) and *Israeli Nationalism: Social Conflicts and the Politics of Knowledge* (Routledge, 2011).

Introduction

The political and social thought of Andrew Arato

Enrique Peruzzotti and Martín Plot

Andrew Arato's scholarship transited, over the past decades, several facets and interrogated different political and social phenomena. His first years of work were devoted to the Frankfurt tradition of critical theory and to what has come to be known as "Western Marxism." A young Hungarian, he was then also close to the Budapest School, whose central figures were Agnes Heller, Ferenc Fehér, and Mihály Wajda, among others. During these years, Andrew Arato co-wrote and co-edited two still unmatched volumes. The first one remains the most authoritative and comprehensive book – in America and elsewhere – on the social, cultural, and political theorizing of the Frankfurt School: *The Essential Frankfurt School Reader* (Arato and Gebhardt 1982). The second volume also remains un-substitutable, offering a unique analysis of Györy Lukács' work, one still indispensable to those working on the historical and conceptual beginnings of Western Marxism and critical theory: *The Young Lukács and the Origins of Western Marxism* (Arato and Breines 1979). In the 1980s, Arato started to shift his theoretical inquiry in the analytical and interpretive direction that would end up shaping his characteristic intellectual style – that of rendering theory empirically relevant and empirical research theoretically prolific. His first area of theoretically informed social and political research had the late Soviet-type societies at its center. Arato was certainly one of the leading figures in the sociological and comparative analysis that provided a unique view of the social processes and political institutions and actors that immediately preceded and followed the 1989 collapse of the Eastern European old regimes. Books such as *Gorbachev: The Debate* (Fehér and Arato 1989) and *Crisis and Reform in Eastern Europe* (Fehér and Arato 1991) are both fundamental documents of that exceptional period of political innovation and theoretical reflection.

However, it was in the 1990s that Arato became the globally known social and political theorist he is today. The two books published early in the decade – *Civil Society and Political Theory* (Cohen and Arato 1992) and *From Neo-Marxism to Democratic Theory* (Arato 1993) – became the central influence, and therefore the obligatory reference, in the field of theorization and social research that turned the question of civil society into the critically informed perspective that dominated the analysis and interpretation of the transitions to democracy in Latin America and Eastern Europe during the 1990s. Many of us, contributors and editors of this volume, have been formed as political and social theorists, sociologists, or comparative political scientists, as a consequence of our first encounter with these two volumes. During the 1990s, Arato continued conducting research and writing in the field of democratic theory from the perspective of a social and political thought of late Frankfurtian inspiration. In particular, these years were closely related to Arato's engagement with Jürgen Habermas' discourse-ethical project. Several of his essays of the period expanded his research by explicitly intertwining his intellectual interests with those of Habermas and other democratic theorists indentified with critical theory and social-philosophical perspectives. His co-edited book, *Habermas on Law and Democracy: Critical Exchanges* (Rosenfeld and Arato 1998), stands as one of the central compilations in the field. Finally, the just described dimensions of Arato's scholarship – from the Western Marxist reflections on historical processes and emancipatory normative models, to the communicative rationality of its Habermasian contemporary manifestation and the study of civil society and democratic legitimacy – have more recently converged in his studies on transitions from authoritarian rule, emergency regimes, and postsovereign constitution making. During the past ten years, Arato has published two exemplary models of the aforementioned *empirically relevant theory* and *theoretically prolific empirical research*. Engaging directly the thought of crucial twentieth century political theorists such as Hannah Arendt and Carl Schmitt, he has become one of the leading scholars in the analysis and interpretation of the two most significant processes of political foundation and constitution making of the turn of the century: the "self-limited revolutions" of the 1990s in Eastern Europe and the "externally imposed revolution" attempted by the Bush Administration during the invasion and occupation of Iraq.

Although the two political processes just mentioned could not be, at first sight, more different from each other, the continuity between the two volumes published during this period – *Civil Society, Constitution, and Legitimacy* (2000) and *Constitution Making Under Occupation* (2009) – is simply astonishing. The first book engages in a detailed analysis of the constitution, both in its political and legal/juridical senses, of the new Eastern European regimes. Masterfully relying on that analytical precedent – originally articulating the questions of transitions to democracy, self-limited revolutions, and democratic constitution making – Arato recently published the most serious and theoretically groundbreaking interpretation of the consequences of the neoconservative externally imposed revolution in the Middle East during the Bush Administration. This analysis, moreover, will no doubt become obligatory reference for those trying to understand the set of processes triggered by the so-called "Arab Spring." In both volumes, his theoretical approach reactivates the explicit and implicit debate between Schmitt and Arendt on questions such as sovereignty, constituent power, and revolution, giving it a renewed life in the context of developing conceptual tools for interpreting post 9/11, globally relevant political processes. In a way unique to his work – but undoubtedly initiating a path to be transited by many others – Arato has shown how the largely successful foundational political experiences of Southern European (Spain, Portugal, Greece), Latin American (from Argentina to México), Central and Eastern European, and finally South African transitions from authoritarian rule and constitution making, have developed crucial theoretical perspectives from where to launch the most solid critique of the misguided ideology of militarily imposed social change that has so far dominated America's vision in the new century.

In short, Arato's work has always been characterized by a recurrent gesture towards *deprovincializing* the theoretical implications of contemporary political processes. His work has developed the farthest reaching and most sophisticated learning from political phenomena, from the 1970s' and 1980s' crisis of the Soviet-type societies to the transitions "from authoritarian rule" in Latin America, and from the "self-limiting revolutions" of Eastern Europe to the post-sovereign model of constitution making under the devastating conditions created by the neoconservative, American destruction of the Iraqi state. The cases are particular – and most of the literature developed around them tend to remain such – but Arato's intellectual project is indeed that of thinking through their particularities and into their common implications, their "elective afinities" and their shared, overlapping, but also contrasting, contributions to political and social thought. It is in this way that Arato has no doubt become *the* political and social theorist of self-limiting democratic foundations and postsovereign constitution making of our time.

Theorizing the break with the revolutionary model

In his first important work, *The Young Lukács and the Origins of Western Marxism*, Arato, writing with Paul Breines, establishes himself as a young scholar exploring the theoretical conditions under which the breakdown of the Marxist, revolutionary model of social transformation could lead to a democratic turn in critical theory's emancipatory project. The work, an immanent criticism of Lukács' *oeuvre* in general, and of *History and Class Consciousness* in particular, defines the latter as "a groundbreaking manifesto of critical, humanistic Marxism," while at the same time a work that "provided a philosophy of the dogmatic and totalitarian Marxism it sought to avert" (Arato and Breines 1979: ix). For those familiar with Arato's scholarship, it should be both unsurprising and curious that this early work's central concept of Western Marxism came straight from a French's philosopher's book – Maurice Merleau-Ponty's *Adventures of the Dialectic* – since it was in the latter that the notion was used for the first time to describe the uniqueness of Lukács' position vis-à-vis Marxist thought. Unsurprising, we say, because the book (Merleau-Ponty 1973) was one of the most sophisticated inaugural gestures in the post-Marxist embracement of democracy (Plot 2012), and the principled and philosophical critique of the revolutionary formula – "a no that is a yes" in the words of Merleau-Ponty – an absolute rejection of a given order that becomes an absolute affirmation of the new one once victorious (Plot 2009a). Revolution became, for the Merleau-Ponty of *Adventures of the Dialectic*, simply the preannouncement of dictatorship – an insight that would never abandon Arato's concerns. This early influence, although curious because Arato's main intellectual interlocutors have not usually come from French phenomenology or existential (post)Marxism, was nonetheless very significant. Proving the basic relevance of this early influence, over a decade later Arato again tells us that

> Western Marxism [was] Maurice Merleau-Ponty's name for a post-social-democratic, post-Bolshevik, primary philosophical tradition of Marx interpretation in Europe and America. … Initially a philosophical justification of the October Revolution whose Eastern self-understanding did not meet either West-European theoretical criteria or political needs, and hence a form of Left Communism, since 1940 at least, Western Marxism has become a critical theory of all contemporary forms of domination including the societies of the Soviet type.
>
> (Arato 1993: 84)

We have already implied but not yet made explicit what we see as Arato's major intellectual enterprise: the critique of any kind of "mythical" belief in a single, absolute source of either (legitimate) political power or (definitive) social knowledge. His method of choice for this critical enterprise – immanent criticism – turned him into the most loyal of readers, one that is never afraid of taking his intellectual interlocutors seriously, an attitude that necessarily led him to identifying the elements of their conceptual apparatus that fall prey to the myth of totality. The exercise he inaugurated with Lukács was successively replicated in his readings of Habermas, Schmitt, Arendt, Preuss, Ackerman and others. Arato was, of course, never "Lukácsian," but thus he was never just "Habermasian," "Schmittian," or "Arendtian" either. Arato could be described – again borrowing from Merleau-Ponty, this time we being the borrowers – with the words the latter used for describing Machiavelli: "a difficult thinker without idols" (Merleau-Ponty 1964). Arato is a thinker who does not underestimate the subjects of his critiques, therefore one who learns as much as could possibly be learned from their work, but who is also not afraid of parting company with them in those turns of their thought in which they can no longer be followed.

Arato and Breiner's book on Lukács identifies, of course, what has always made *History and Class Consciousness* a crucial moment in the history of modern philosophy: a work that offered a reading of the central Hegelianism of Marx's ideas even before the texts that would prove such a generative influence had been made available. Their book, however, adds to this interpretation of Lukács' work the thick web of sociological references that makes it truly intelligible. Georg Simmel and Max Weber are also there, adding another, fundamental aspect that made Lukács the axis of a tradition of critical theory that put the sociological critique of culture at the center of its concerns. Finally, it is a third dimension of the development of Lukács' thought that made Arato's immanent critique of his work an indication of the latter's future research. "According to Lukács," he said,

> even progressive movements – he mentions social democracy explicitly – become conservative when their institutions become ends in themselves. On the other hand, a Kantian or Fichtean primacy of ethics in politics guarantees a constant revolutionary thrust against *all* institutions (even revolutionary institutions), a "permanent revolution" aiming at the concrete, empirical realization of the categorical imperative forbidding the instrumentalization of men.
>
> (Arato and Breiner 1979: 73)

Why is this third dimension the one that renders visible how Arato's earlier immanent critique is an indicator of future concerns? Because it shows how Arato had already understood at the time the failure of the revolutionary project's crucial dimension: that of a dream of total discontinuity with a given order, the dream of *ex-nihilo* creating a society fully transparent to itself, fully "democratic" in its aim at coinciding entirely with itself; and that such a dream, a revolutionary dream, is not an emancipatory but an authoritarian one:

> The deep-seated antinomy of Lukács' own theory, flowing from the innermost sources of his project, was in summation this: a relentless critique which, sparing neither Engels nor, implicitly, Marx or the Bolsheviks, pointed beyond the Marxian tradition itself; *and* a philosophy of history that sought to discover the macrosubjects capable of anticipating and achieving a society of absolute freedom and transparency. It is this antinomy … what made his early work the origin of "Western Marxism." [It] is [also] what made his synthesis unacceptable to both the Bolsheviks and to any future tradition of revolutionary thought.
>
> (Arato and Breiner 1979: 160)

As the final line of this quote makes clear, Arato was (in 1979) still unwilling to completely abandon the general umbrella of "revolutionary thought" under which to inscribe the future of the emancipatory project. It should be also clear though, that the tradition that will no longer have a use for Lukács was not the revolutionary one but that of the democratic theory of post-Marxist origin that would dominate a significant part of continental political theory for the following three decades.

There is one notion that appears in all of Arato's works, from the early critique of Lukács to the most recent *Constitution Making Under Occupation* – the notion of *myth*. Of course, it is hardly possible to claim that Arato is a theorist of myth or mythology; Arato is neither an anthropologist nor a semiotician. The reason this word is crucial is because it migrates from his critique of the revolutionary model of *ex-nihilo* social creation to the critique of the Jacobin, "democratic" myth of the sovereign *pouvoir constituant*. The notion of *myth* first appears used in the following context: Lukács, say Arato and Breiner, "points out that Hegel's conceptual *mythology* negates history and historical practice. [The] result is either extreme voluntarism (practice is completely free) or extreme determinism (there is no practice in the sense of praxis, that is, subject-object dialectic)" (Arato and Breiner 1979: 129, our emphasis). The problem, however, is that "in the face of the opacity and density of history, in the face of reification" (Arato and Breiner 1979: 130), Lukács' thought itself became mythological, since he ended up developing "a totally utopian, mythologized view of the Communist Party" (Arato and Breiner 1979: 156). The problem at stake here is not secondary, since Arato's work should indeed be regarded as a multilayered, multidisciplinary theory of political and social transformation[s] that consistently avoid the mystification of agents, actors, and even procedures. Therefore, the notion of myth first appeared associated with the Lukácsian mythological embracement of the Bolshevik Party as a radically representative agent embodying (but also giving existence to) the proletariat in its revolutionary task of bringing to being the classless society. Once the hope of a more organic, dialectical advent of Communism was abandoned, the question of how is it that the figure of an egalitarian, socially emancipated world could emerge from a background of domination and hierarchy, the answer has become, again and again, mythical: the proletariat, the Party, the people-as-sovereign *pouvoir constituant* – something, anything must be able to become the standard-bearer for what seems to always be lacking, the actual democratic subject capable of *ex-nihilo* constituting itself and society at large. In the first appearance of such a mythical entity in Arato's work, "as Merleau-Ponty … pointed out … official Communist theory 'placed the knowing subject (ultimately the Party itself) outside the tissue of history and accorded it access to absolute being, freed from the duty of autocritique…" (Arato and Breiner 1979: 182). And it is in this context, as we have already suggested, that the fundamental question, the one that will remain the long lasting interrogation driving Arato's research, made its appearance: Whenever dealing with a revolutionary or radically transformative political process, the question to be posed is clear: "are we dealing with an emancipatory or an authoritarian utopia?" (Arato and Breiner 1979: 159).

Indeed, it is as early as his book on Lukács that Arato was already a thinker of transitions, political transformations, and "regime change." The ground that he covered in his displacement from this early critique of the revolutionary model to his current work on postsovereign constitution making (Arato 2009) was his theorizing of the notion of civil society as the realm of social plurality and publicity capable of resisting the colonizing tendencies of the systems – in the Habermasian sense – of the state and the economy. Arato, in his work with Jean Cohen, offered the notion of civil society as an improvement of that of Habermas' lifeworld – itself borrowed from Husserl. In Arato's own words: "[As] the decade of the eighties progressed I came to believe that the cornerstone of a critical theory of modern society should be a democratic theory built around the concept of civil society, rather than any, even the most, 'self-critical' Marxism" (Arato 1993: x). And he continued, "I use the concept of civil society for a critical theory of the 'transition from state socialism'" (Arato 1993: xi). Arato's reading of the break with the revolutionary model was thus a faithful expression of his early empirically relevant theorizing. In becoming one of the central interpreters and analysts of the collapse of Soviet-type societies and the advent of new, largely liberal-democratic regimes in Eastern Europe, on the other hand, Arato offered his first massive project of theoretically prolific empirical research.

The crucial articulation between his earlier concern with neo- or post-Marxist emancipatory critical theory and his later work on the theory and practice of civil society was the notion of *self-limitation*. What Arato found in – and heard from – a number of the dissident social and political actors of the regimes in the east was the abandonment of the horizon of a total revolution or an absolute discontinuity with the old regimes. For them, as Arato would put it years later in *Civil Society, Constitution, and Legitimacy*, it became clear that "the new can be built without total rupture with the past" (Arato 2000: xiv). It was thus the round-table negotiations, the taking seriously the previously just decorative constitutional amendment rules, the radically changing the political order without forcing explicit legal discontinuity, in short, the Central and Eastern European "widespread rejection of the tradition and of the semantics of modern revolutions" (Arato 2000: 12) and "of utopian narratives and the hubris of making history" (Arato 2000: 15) that triggered Arato's research at the time:

> To be sure, from various conservative points of view the project of reconstructing civil society under the aegis of self-limitation could be accused of hypocrisy: What was declared to be self-limitation in principle could be thus unmasked as self-limitation due to weakness; interest in civil rights, free associations and alternative publics, and social movements, could be denounced as temporary replacement for the real motivation, namely taking state power; a principled postrevolutionary stance could be declared to be only prerevolutionary mystification.
>
> (Arato 1993: 296)

Although later on, at the time of *Civil Society, Constitution, and Legitimacy* Arato was going to worry about the revolutionary threats coming this time from the right – from the neoconservative and nationalist ideologies he called "neorevolutionary" (Arato 2000: 69) – to the consolidation of liberal democracies in Central and Eastern Europe (Arato 2000: 106–121) it was first the time of theorizing the organizing principle of his social and political thought at the time: civil society.

Arato's theory of civil society

The concept of civil society will become for Arato and Jean L. Cohen the cornerstone of an ambitious project for the reformulation of critical theory. In their view, the development of a critical theory that could adequately account for existing social conditions and serve as a normative guidance for emancipatory political struggles demanded a different social and political theory from the one that had developed from the classical work of a critical theory of Luckàsian and Frankfurtian inspiration. According to Arato and Cohen, the move away from classical critical theory called for two significant tasks at theoretical reformulation. In the first place, it was imperative to disentangle critical theory from some Marxist and neo-Marxist presuppositions that prevented an adequate recognition of the institutional achievements of modernity. A post-Marxist theory of civil society had to be predicated on a sophisticated theory of social differentiation that could properly account for the dynamics of structurally differentiated societies.

The starting point for such a conceptual reconstruction was the recognition that the differentiation between state and society represents a crucial accomplishment of political modernity and that any attempt to reverse it can only lead to an authoritarian regression.[1] Yet, a mere dualist model of state and society was, in the eyes of Arato and Cohen, still insufficient as an analytical framework to understand the phenomena of social differentiation in contemporary societies. Following some insights from the theories of Antonio Gramsci, Talcott Parsons, and Jürgen Habermas, they introduced a tripartite social framework predicated on the existence of three central institutional complexes (state, market, and civil society) as well as on a considerable number of mediating structures among them, to respectively move away from Marxist and liberal dichotomous models of state/society as well as from the different strands of fusion or societal de-differentiation arguments (Cohen and Arato 1992: chapter 9).

In the second place, the reconstruction of critical theory called for breaking with the Frankfurt School's diagnosis of the gradual consolidation of a "one dimensional society" that had successfully managed to suppress social conflict and radical politics from the landscape of contemporary societies. The goal of a reformulated critical theory is to find the loci of emancipatory struggles in present-day political processes to evaluate their potential contribution to the democratization of existing societies. In a historical context marked by the spread of struggles against different forms of authoritarianism in several places of the world, it was necessary to expand the concerns of critical theory beyond the confines of advanced Western democracies. This meant paying particular attention to the events that were taking place in regions like Eastern and Central Europe and Latin America. Arato thus found in the political use of the concept of civil society by dissident movements in authoritarian contexts the seeds of what he considered to be a significant transformation in radical democratic politics. The forms of self-understanding of dissident movements in places like Poland and Brazil – which called for a strategy of reconstruction of an autonomous civil society – insinuated an important paradigm shift (and democratic orientation) in radical politics. Their project of reconstruction of civil society reoriented politics both in a post-statist and a post-revolutionary direction. The idea of political self-limitation that was initially developed by the Polish opposition, Arato argued, not only grew out of strategic limitations but also out of a normative concern to avoid the negative experiences of radical revolutions:

> The contemporary revolution can end the age of revolutions only if it refuses to be so like the modern revolutions as to repeat their logic, but to be enough like them to be able to accomplish a full transformation of existing regimes.
>
> (Arato 2000: 15–16)

This is why he and Cohen claimed in *Civil Society and Political Theory* that the current discourse of civil society is "at the heart of a sea change in political culture" (Cohen and Arato 1992: 3).

The goal of critical theory is to interpret those discourses, identifying common strands and differences as well as conceptual misunderstandings in order to theoretically reconstruct the concept of civil society to show its normative relevance for all types of contemporary societies. As we have already discussed above,

> at an earlier stage, the task of Western Marxism was to deepen Marxian social philosophy by a return to philosophical roots and to reveal the connections of a re-Hegelianized Marx to some very specific works in non-Marxist philosophy and social theory: to Max Weber, Georg Simmel, Benedetto Croce, and Sigmund Freud among others. ... Reviving the concept of civil society was apparently an analogous move, since its presence in the young Marx justified a critical reexamination and appropriation of ideas of yet another series of non-Marxist thinkers from Alexis de Tocqueville to Hannah Arendt.
>
> (Arato 2000: 43)

This was one of the central missions that Cohen and Arato set for themselves in *Civil Society and Political Theory*. The aim of the book, they stated, was to develop a systematic theory of civil society adequate for contemporary conditions in order to demonstrate the relevance of the concept to political theory and to existing democratic struggles (Cohen and Arato 1992: vii). In this way, they hoped to shed light on the relation between the normative intentions of democratizing projects and the structure, institutions, and dynamics of civil society, showing the "possibilities and constraints of action" that a plurality of political initiatives in Latin America, Eastern Europe, and the West were confronting while attempting to carry out a project of reconstruction of civil society (Cohen and Arato 1992: 3).

The reformulation of radical politics entailed challenging the authoritarian legacy of the revolutionary tradition which had been historically hostile to the idea of a democratic and autonomous civil society. Radical revolutionary processes, Arato argued, are at odds with any project of reconstructing a democratic civil society for all major revolutions demobilized and suppressed the very forms of social organization that carried them, establishing dictatorial conditions to prevent the eventual self-reorganization of such forces or of any other form of autonomous social and political life. The end result of revolutionary politics is the consolidation of statist regimes that claim sovereign dictatorial powers over society, suppressing all those constitutional guarantees that make possible the existence of an institutionalized civil society. That is the great novelty that Cohen and Arato saw behind the notions of "self-limiting revolution" or "radical reform from below" that were respectively coined by Jacek Kuron and Adam Michnik in Poland. While there were clear strategic motives to renounce a revolutionary project from below in the geopolitical context of Soviet-type societies given the experience of Hungary in 1956, there was also a normative concern behind such a project of reconstituting and strengthening from below an autonomous, organized, and mobilized civil society: to shift the locus of the project of democratization from the state to civil society in order to avoid the statist reconstitution of sovereignty that would risk the very survival of a self-organized civil society in the new regime. The latter move represented, in Arato and Cohen's view, a major break with the Rousseaunian/Jacobin interpretation of constituent power as an unbound foundational force promoting a total rupture with the past (Arato 2000: 48; Cohen and Arato 1992: 624; Preuss 1995: 76). Such notion of constituent acts as an exercise of unmediated political action by a people that liberates politics from its constitutional containment was thus substituted by a theory in which the constituent and constituted dimensions of politics are conceptually reconciled.

The notions of full-fledged sovereignty and of an absolute break predicated on to the *myth* of a non-institutionalized unified people that is directly present to itself as a subject of constituent action (Lindhal 2008) is replaced by a new theory of democratic constitutionalism that presupposes legal continuity and that promotes a method of constitution making based on civil society and the public sphere (Arato 2000: 132). "It is the democratic amending process, 'always under the law,' that should be the model for a dedramatized understanding of constitution making" (Arato 2000: xiv). Arato saw in the institutional innovation of Round Tables in Eastern Europe a path to constitution making that was able to promote radical change without the threat that a radical legal discontinuity with the past model always opens for freedom. Paradoxically, it was the self-limitation exhibited by those movements and organizations that had become the carrier of political transformation in relation to the constitutional rules of the previous regime, and this had allowed the "...continuation of their social role and influence beyond the constituent and into the constituted phase" (Cohen and Arato 1992: 16). The method of constitution making through Round Tables is at odds with the idea of a monolithic people expressing the unmediated power of a unified *pouvoir constituant*. Rather, the participants of the Round Tables view themselves as representatives of a plurality of heterogeneous citizens whose diversity could not be absorbed into the fiction of a unified will (Preuss 1995: 95; 77–78). The Eastern Europeans "have responded to the normative 'perplexities of founding a new regime' by resolutely avoiding the legal state of nature that Arendt linked to the logic of revolution and dictatorship" (Arato 2000: 173). Only through this path to regime change – Arato believed – can constitutional transformation guarantee limitations on state power without constraining democratic forms of power (Arato 2000: 133).

Behind Arato and Cohen's notion of civil society lies a new interpretation of the nature and linkages between constituent (*pouvoir constituant*) and constituted power (*pouvoir constitué*). The latter is perhaps the most innovative element of their theory of civil society. Their theory, unlike others, focuses as much on actors (in the words of Arato, the active dimension) as it does on institutions (the passive dimension). Modern civil societies, Cohen and Arato argue, can only develop in an institutional setting that guarantees basic rights. Consequently, there is an intimate relationship between civil society and constitutionalism: constitutionalism provides the institutional soil for the flourishing of a civil society and the latter provides a social setting amenable to democratic constitutionalism. Modern constitutionalism cannot be reduced to the liberal notion of limited government but plays a double "constituting" role for it presupposes a simultaneous process of juridification of both politics and society which institutionalizes the state as a legal state and the social as a civil society (Cohen and Arato 1992; Peruzzotti 1997). Certainly, the concept of civil society cannot be solely reduced to its institutional dimension: the vitality of any civil society depends on the forms of social life that emerge within it, on the existence of a public sphere that can serve as a resonance box to the claims and arguments of different groups, movements and publics, as well as on the existence of adequate bridging mechanisms between civil society, state, and market (what Cohen and Arato respectively define as political and economic society) (Cohen and Arato 1992).

Another central tenet of Arato's intellectual project is – it can be perceived already – formulating a democratic theory of popular sovereignty that could properly account for the interdependencies and tensions between instituted (or constituted) and instituting (or constituent) power. As Arato himself summarizes the theoretical move in *Civil Society, Constitution, and Legitimacy*, he and Cohen had already distinguished in their work between

> civil society as movement and civil society as institution. [They] did this because the differentiation is a fluid one: Mobilization always seeks at least some institutionalization … and institutionalization is the precondition for new movements and initiatives. [The] distinction is rooted in Cornelius Castoriadis' dualism of *société instituante* and *société instituée*.[2]
>
> (Arato 2000: 71)

In this reconstruction, Arato wants to move the analysis away from what he considers two controversial interpretations: the first one, present in revolutionary and populist models of politics, which tends to privilege constituent over constituted politics, and a second one – clearly exemplified by mainstream democratic theory – that relies on a purely institutional account of political dynamics in which the creative dimension of constituent power simply disappears.

In *Civil Society and Political Theory*, Cohen and Arato challenged existing elitist, participatory, and populist models of democracy to present a democratic theory predicated on a dynamic articulation of constituent and constituted politics that makes productive use of the inevitable tensions that exist between them.

Rather than attempting to conceptually dissociate constituent from constituted power – as the political fundamentalism of radical democracy and the elitism of realist models of democracy do – the program of a self-limiting radical democracy should revolve around the question of how to productively connect both dimensions of politics. This inevitably reorients democratic theory into a query about the proper linkages or mediations between state and civil society. While social movements and publics in civil society are, in their view, what keep a democratic political culture alive, they should not be considered a substitute for the institutional arrangements of representative democracy (Cohen and Arato 1992: 19–20). Rather, the central question that contemporary democratic theory should address is that of creating and strengthening mediating structures that could guarantee a proper influence of civil over political society (Cohen and Arato 1992: 563).

As a fundamental contribution to this task, Cohen and Arato moved to the dynamics and politics of a democratic civil society. This problematic is mostly dealt with in the third part of *Civil Society and Political Theory*, where Cohen and Arato develop a democratic theory organized around the concept of civil society. The latter openly confronts the tradition of democratic elitism and calls for a program of democratization of existing liberal democracies. Here the discussion largely focuses on the shortcomings of existing Western democracies. Following Habermas, they argue that the historical development of Western societies resulted in a selective pattern of modernization that distorted the dynamics and potential of civil society (Cohen and Arato 1992: 442). In their view, the "utopian horizon of civil society" that their theoretical reconstruction postulates seeks a reflexive continuation of the project of the welfare state based on the principle of political self-limitation. The latter entails, in the Western context, the need to protect the boundaries between the different subsystems and a lifeworld threatened by the paternalist logic of welfare bureaucratization. It is the task of civil society to defend the resource of social solidarity against the reifying impulses of the welfare state and of market commodification. This task entails setting and strengthening institutional barriers to protect the lifeworld and civil society from the colonizing impulses of market and state while simultaneously building adequate bridging mechanisms between civil society and the economic and political subsystems (Cohen and Arato 1992: 472, 478). At the same time, the idea of boundary preservation that is behind their project of political self-limitation means restricting the principle of communicative coordination of action to the institutional space of civil society (Cohen and Arato 1992: 456).

Lastly, Cohen and Arato returned to the dialectic between constituent and constituted power in their discussion about civil disobedience. In their view, the full institutionalization of a democratic civil society does not presuppose the end of such dialectic: all forms of democracy are always subject to further democratization. And since civil society is always the locus of both democratic legitimacy and rights, a conflict should not be ruled out between the constituent and the constituted as expressed in the strategy of civil disobedience. Civil disobedience, they claimed, is a form of "non-institutional political action specific to citizens of modern civil society" that appeals to the utopian horizon of the democratic ideal (Cohen and Arato 1992: 566). Acts of civil disobedience are "examples of self-limiting radicalism par excellence" which define the outer limits of radical politics under constitutional democracy (Cohen and Arato 1992: 567). They entail a reawakening of constituent power by actors who – by engaging in self-limiting acts of civil disobedience – "assume the original rights of the sovereign" to denounce a breach of democratic legitimacy on the part of existing laws and institutions (Cohen and Arato 1992: 601–602).

From civil society to postsovereign constitution making

Seen from a broad perspective, Arato's work can be read, as we have already suggested, as a theoretical reflection on radical political transformations: his work is that of a theorist of the strains and challenges that specific political conjunctures introduce in the relationship between constituent and constituted power. Throughout the years, his analyses have focused on the challenges that specific political situations posed on such interaction in three distinctive moments: (1) the reconstitution of civil society under authoritarian settings (or the reawakening of constituent power); (2) the risks and challenges of regime change (or how to promote it without severing the connection between constituent and constituted power), and (3) the question of the role of an institutionalized civil society in a consolidated democracy (or how to maintain a productive tension between constitutive and constituent power under democracy).[3]

As we have just described, the first moment that drew Arato's attention was that of the reconstruction of a civil society. In a series of works produced between 1982 and 1991 Arato thus focused on the challenges that different movements were confronting in authoritarian settings that had suspended or eliminated those institutions that could stabilize the social as civil society (Arato 1981, 1982, 1984, 1985, 1990, 1991; Fehėr and Arato 1991). The structures of Soviet-type regimes and of bureaucratic authoritarianism were inimical to the idea of an institutionalized civil society given their de facto suppression of constitutional guarantees and the prevalence of a repressive environment. In the absence of institutions that could stabilize the social as civil society, the latter only expressed itself as a movement. Civil society, Cohen and Arato argued, consisted of a social movement attempting to organize and institutionalize itself (Cohen and Arato 1992: 75). Civil society as a movement represents, as Alberto Olvera highlights in his chapter in this volume, an intermediary stage between a depoliticized society of latent networks of social life and a fully institutionalized civil society. It represents a moment of awakening or reconstitution of the *pouvoir constituent* in which social networks and other forms of social ties leave their latent stage and begin developing a plurality of independent and public initiatives. Those independent movements and publics set the social into motion – awakening the constituent power of society from its latent stage – with the ultimate goal of reconstructing civil society and transforming the existing political regime. The central question of this period was that of launching the transition from civil society as a movement to civil society as an institution. Arato's analyses largely centered on the different forms of political self-understanding that inspired the projects for the reconstruction of civil society in Eastern and Central Europe, and particularly in the idea of a self-limiting revolution or radical reformism. In his view, the latter political strategy was the more adequate one for developing and strengthening those autonomous networks of solidarity, publics, and other forms of independent cultural and social life that would provide the associational foundations of a future democratic civil society in the region.[4]

The second stage of his theoretically prolific empirical research was that of regime change or democratic transitions[5] (Arato 1993, 1994a, 1994b, 1994c, 1995). In this dimension of his work, the central question is no longer how to reconstitute a constituent power but how to articulate the two dimensions of *pouvoir constituant* and *pouvoir constitué* in such a way as to simultaneously ensure regime change and the future institutionalization of civil society and a vibrant democratic polity. This is also the moment in Arato's thought in which he shifts from a concern on civil society to one on constitutional politics. Since then, he has engaged in a critical analysis of the most important transition theories that were in vogue at the time, which in his view blatantly neglected the role of civil society in the development of the emergent constitutional designs as well as on the policy-making process (Arato 2000: ix). Arato's shift to constitutionalism did not represent a break with his previous concern with the reconstitution of civil society, however. Rather, the turn itself was determined by his preoccupation of how to best secure a transition from civil society as a movement to civil society as an institution, which in his view is the only way to ensure a future and permanent role for the latter in a consolidated democracy. The fate of the reconstituted civil society was intimately connected in his opinion to "the establishment and survival of constitutionalism in the midst of radical democratic transformations in the countries of the former Soviet imperium" (Arato 2000: x).

In his analysis of the most relevant cases in the Eastern European constitutional processes, he arrives at the conclusion that the maintenance of the rule of law throughout the transition was an essential condition for its success, as it was building a democratic legitimacy for the new constitutional arrangements. Arato warned about the dangers posed by the possibility of a revolutionary hiatus inspired in an old notion of the *pouvoir constituant*; a movement that could lead to the rejection and suppression of all constituted legality and thus put the recently organized civil society at the mercy of a new discretionary power. Quoting from the Constitutional Court of Hungary Resolution No. 11/1992, Arato states: "A rule of law state cannot be created by violating the rule of law" (Arato 2000: 102). The Court therefore asserted

> the compatibility of using the amendment rules of the old system and creating an entirely new one. Thus the self-limiting revolution limits itself, its desire for substantive justice in particular, by submitting to the rule of law. It is this self-limitation in fact that inaugurates a new legal order, the rule of law, that could not emerge in any other way.
>
> (Arato 2000: 103)

This model of social and political change is

> both less revolutionary and more radical than a radical revolution could be. It is less revolutionary because it presupposes legal continuity. But it is more radical because it breaks with legal nihilism immediately, while a radical revolution could only produce, in the short term at least, a "legal" condition outside the law.
>
> (Arato 2000: 103)

The novelty he thus saw in some of the forms of constitution making in the Eastern European transitions was a method that replaced such questionable notions of the *pouvoir constituant* with a pluralist understanding to a large extent rooted on the concept and institutions of civil society. Drawing on the interpretation of such processes offered by Ulrich Preuss, Arato highlighted the innovative features of such method of constitution making:

> In Preuss' analysis, one can detect two interrelated devices by which the East European revolutions sought to avoid the logic of permanent revolution, one leading to dictatorship. First, the protagonists acted as if there was no need to abolish an existing form of sovereignty. [Thus] in effect the regimes were treated as if their claim to represent a particular version of popular sovereignty was somehow valid. [The] second, and more important, device, was to renounce, at least implicitly, the model of unitary sovereignty, and the corresponding idea of its undivided representation by a constituent assembly bound by no rules, a sovereign dictator possessing revolutionary legitimacy. [In Preuss' presentation,] the process of constitution making is not in the state of nature for two fundamental reasons: It assumes the constitutional rules of the previous system and refers back not to the unified but unstructured people, but to the organized groups, bodies, and institutions of civil society. [In] Preuss's depiction, civil society becomes the stand-in for the *pouvoir constituant* and the alternative framework to a unitary sovereignty.
>
> (Arato 2000: 38–39)

By adopting a non-revolutionary legitimacy (and thus rejecting the authoritarian idea of a unified constituent power that claims full sovereignty) Eastern European societies managed to create something new on a method that maintained institutional continuity:

> The old written constitutions were only fictionally the constitutions of Soviet-type societies. … At the moment the rules of the old formal constitution were used for the first time for real, a break in the actual structure of constitutionality has arguably occurred.
>
> (Arato 2000: 143)

This is why Arato considers that the process of regime change in Eastern Europe followed on the footsteps of the American rather than the French revolution – although this legacy carried unresolved problems that required further self-reflective theorization. Let us quote now in its entirety the paragraph that most precisely defines the task of constitutional theorizing under the new circumstances:

> Many years after the dramatic events of 1989 let us recall the outcome of Hannah Arendt's analysis of revolutions. According to her, in modern times, the history of revolution was dominated by the antinomy paradigms of a permanent revolution that fails to make a new beginning of freedom and a conservative revolution that forgets its very origins, or converts them into mere tradition. This diagnosis has certainly not lost its power. It is no longer too early to speak of outcomes in East Europe, and specially of the self-interpretations of the actors themselves who, whether or not they used the term *revolution*, have reproduced the very antinomy Arendt analyzed. This time it was elements of a new nationalist right who clamored for a total break with the past and the indefinite prolongation of radical revolution, while the liberals and the remnants of a democratic left, who have done far more to change the earlier regime, now affirmed continuity and the rule of law. Once again a third possibility, a combination of revolution and constitutionalism, of public freedom and fundamental rights, seems to have been excluded. The leading slogans were "restoration" for the revolutionaries and "imitation" for the liberals, with very few people recognizing the necessity or even the possibility of innovation, of new historical creation.
>
> (Arato 2000: 129)

And Arato became indeed one of the main theorists of such innovation. As we have pointed out early in this section, a third stage of theoretical concerns for Arato was the institutional conditions needed for a revival of civil society, and thus of democratic vitality, in the context of the Western democracies (Arato 2000: 44). These two areas of political and social research – becoming the theorist of the innovations in *democratic constitutionalism* springing from the transitions from authoritarian rule in Eastern Europe and investigating the conditions for a *democratization of the really existing democracies* in the West – were at the center of Arato's work at the turn of the decade. Without having significantly changed, however, those concerns found renewed relevance after the 9/11 terrorist attacks and during the "war on terror" with which the Bush Administration decided to respond to them.

There have been two areas of research and writing that have dominated the past ten years of Arato's scholarship – emergency regimes and constitutional politics – and both found their contexts of application in the world born in the wake of 9/11. It was already after the consecutive constitutional crises of President Clinton's impeachment in 1998 and the contested presidential elections of 2000, that Arato started focusing explicitly on the notorious shortcomings of the American constitution. The attempt to remove President Clinton from office for having lied about sex under oath had been, of course, a scandalous abuse of the Constitutional Convention's original intent for the remedy of impeachment. (Arato 1999) Having sought to protect the republic against the threats of tyranny, treason, bribery, and similarly politically dangerous crimes, the framers were surely not expecting the "remedy" to be used against a widely popular president without any tyrannical or traitorous temptations that had committed a private infidelity and wanted to keep it so – i.e., private. Somehow even more serious was, however, the Supreme Court's partisan and indefensible ruling stopping in its tracks the Florida statewide recount in December of 2000; a ruling that the Supreme Court itself claimed should set no precedent for future, similar cases. ... It was in response to these two consecutive constitutional crises that Arato published in *Constellations*, right before the infamous events of September 11, 2001, the following premonitory lines:

> Again, after a severe crisis [Gore vs. Bush] the Constitution has been pronounced, consensually, the only real winner. ... Many more such triumphs for the Constitution are likely to be extremely dangerous or even fatal. Those of us who dream of changing or replacing it are therefore in a paradoxical position. We know that given the sacralization of the American constitutional tradition, no serious change is likely to come without crisis. The only times in the past the Constitution was significantly altered were during disruptions and emergencies. Perhaps we should welcome one, more ... many constitutional crises. But presidential systems are very risky for freedom and democracy precisely in crisis moments. ... Presidentialism is very hard to contain within constitutional limits.
>
> (Arato 2001: 289)

Premonitory, we say, for reasons that should be obvious: the crisis immediately came. Arato reacted to the terrorist attacks of September of 2001[6] with a series of fundamental – though sadly yet unpublished in book format – texts on the sequences of threats triggered by the event and its subsequent constitutional crisis. An early, "aphoristic" response called "*Minima Politica* after September 2001" (Arato 2002) was followed by analyses of the emergency regime generated by the war on terror (e.g., Arato 2005). This is the context in which the previously unpublished, outstanding manuscript included in this volume "Conceptual History of Dictatorship (and its Rivals)" was written. Parallel to Arato's concern for the "specter of dictatorship" in the United States (Plot 2005; 2009b), moreover, Arato immediately realized that the American invasion and occupation of Iraq had created new political and social conditions that could benefit from the constitutional learning that emerged from the transitions from authoritarian rule in Southern Europe, Latin America, Eastern Europe, and South Africa. The results of these investigations have been recently published as *Constitution Making under Occupation: The Politics of Imposed Revolution in Iraq* (2009).

The book introduced itself as "part of a rescue operation: an attempt to redeem the still redeemable" (Arato 2009: vii). What it sought to redeem was the democratic paradigm of constitution making that had emerged in Spain in the 1970s, spread throughout Eastern Europe during the early 1990s, and had finally found its most accomplished version in the South African postsovereign, two-stage constitutional process of 1993–7. The reason why this novel method of constitution making was in need of redemption was very clear. On the one hand, it needed redemption because, although somehow luckily for the Iraqis, the method became the one reluctantly used in the aftermath of the Americans' invasion, occupation, and "revolutionary destruction" of the Iraqi state – but it was used in such a distorted way that the process was ultimately unsuccessful. More importantly though, the method was in need of redemption because, unluckily for the paradigm of postsovereign constitution making itself, it was at risk of ending up buried under the rubble of the American disaster in Iraq, associated as it could become mostly with neoimperial Americans trying to impose an obedient "democratic" regime in the aftermath of an illegal and illegitimate war of aggression.

The method of postsovereign constitution making is – it should be stressed – in an astonishing continuity with Arato's early critique of the revolutionary myth of pure, *ex-nihilo* beginning discussed in the first sections of this Introduction. The new method's central features are that in it "first, the constituent power is not embodied in a single organ or instance with the plenitude of power, and second, that all organs participating in constitutional politics are brought under legal rules" (Arato 2009: vii). The reasons why these features are relevant and, from a democratic theory point of view, should be seen as a normative improvement, are also twofold. On the one hand, the method addresses one of the most fundamental perplexities of democratic politics: how to begin a democracy democratically when there is no democracy to begin with. On the other hand, in institutionalizing two stages of constitution making with a variety of political and social actors participating in both of them, the method comes to terms with the need of a "plurality of democracies," since "given the exclusionary implications of any type of formal democratic procedure, combining a plurality of forms has important compensating effects" (Arato 2000: 252). The method is, in short, "the democratic alternative to revolutionary constitution making, which all too easily can step over the threshold of dictatorship" (Arato 2009: viii).

The book is unique in its combination of constitutional theorizing (fundamentally in Chapters 1, 2, and the Conclusion) and a virtuoso political interpretation of the conflicts, bargaining, principled politics, and maneuvering and outmaneuvering triggered by the American invasion of Iraq (fundamentally in Chapters 3 to 5). In his intertwining of analysis and interpretation, Arato reveals the conditions under which the method of postsovereign constitution making made itself available and almost unavoidable: being the desired method of none of the two dominant political actors, it became the outcome of the clash between their favored strategies. The American occupiers, resembling executive powers elsewhere attempting a top-down imposition of a favored, self-serving constitutional design, encountered the democratic populist opposition of the Grand Ayatollah Sistani, who out of both self-interest – he was the main representative of the Shia demographic majority – and principle – he consistently advocated the European model of *pouvoir constituant* – forced the Americans to implement a (distorted-because-imposed) version of the two-stage method. As Arato puts it, however, his overall argument should not be misunderstood, since far from recommending invasion, occupation, state destruction, imposition (you name it) as an originating context for constitution making, his analysis fundamentally "presupposes that the window of opportunity for democratization in Iraq was very small to begin with, and it was only slightly widened by the method of constitution making that was adopted" (Arato 2009: ix). The constitutional and political learning from the neoconservative misadventure in Iraq and the Middle East are clear though. In a masterful summary of them, Arato writes:

> The first lesson is: don't invade or occupy when you are the aggressor. (The United States did and was.) If you have fully justifiable reasons to invade, get full international support. (The United States didn't and didn't.) If, for some reason, through no fault of your own, you could not succeed at your goals of regime change or the imposition of a democratic government, hand over the occupied country to international authority and withdraw as soon as possible. (It was the fault of the United States, and it didn't.) If you did not hand the country over to international authority, then include all possible social forces in the country in political bargaining, defer to them, and then withdraw. (The United States didn't and didn't.) And so on.
>
> (Arato 2009: x)

It takes a relentless and normative commitment to democracy for, in the context of such calamitous conditions as those created by the radical neoconservative ideology, and its subsequent neoimperial policies, to nonetheless attempt to think what the options were, for the Iraqis, to make the best out of the mess. The attitude is counterintuitive, to say the least. For most in the Left, both in the US and in the entire planet, the intuition could easily go the other way: to hell with the Americans, let them be swallowed by the swamp of their own creation, even if in the process it is the Iraqis too that go down with the occupiers; there is no point in trying to "redeem the unredeemable" (Arato 2003: 408). A democrat, however, ought not to let him or herself be seduced by this train of thought. As Arendt would have put it, what is at stake is the world, not ourselves and our egos – and the world, for Arato, would be much better off if more peoples around the globe could live under their own democratic rule.

Critical theory, civil society, and constitutional politics today

The essays in this book offer a comprehensive picture of the current state of Arato's ongoing influence on the theoretical and empirical research in the fields of constitutional politics, emergency regimes, and the critical and comparative study of civil and political society. The five chapters that compose the first section of this volume focus on the widespread theoretical relevance of Arato's current and lifelong concerns. The book kicks off with Dick Howard's text, a warm, half-biographical, and half-theoretical genealogy of critical theory's commitment to politics and democracy. Howard is one of Arato's fellow travelers – not in the famous French sense, of course, that of those marching next, but not inside, the Communist Party, but in the sense of those that, having understood the incompatibility between democratic aspirations and the revolutionary model, decided to also reject the opposite, easy elitist, or "pragmatist" denunciation *in toto* of the emancipatory project. Howard's text is, in a way, a second introduction to the volume and to Arato's critical project, one that chooses to tell their shared story first, in order to then offer his own general theoretical interpretation of their shared learning.

Ulrich Preuss is another, more recent Arato fellow traveler – it is the work on the democratic normative dimensions of constitutional theory that they share. In the limited company of probably only Ackerman, Schmitt, and Arendt, Preuss is one of Arato's central interlocutors of the last decade and a half. In his contribution to this volume, Preuss focuses on the difficult task of thinking about both the viability and integrative role of a constitutionalism for ethnically, culturally, socially, and religiously fragmented societies. The text offers a careful and detailed genealogy and analysis of constitutional history, moving from an understanding of constitutionalism as protection of rights and limitation and separation of powers to one that emphasizes its *constituting function*. Further exploring other dimensions of Arato's contribution to modern constitutional theory, Hubertus Buchstein's text critically explores the relevance of the concept of "self-binding" for a democratic understanding of constitutionalism, reaching the conclusion that "it leads to a theoretical impasse in modern constitutional theory." Self-binding may be at first sight associated with the potential constitutional relevance of what Arato has once called "the great democratic art of political self-limitation" (Arato 2000: 80). The notion of self-binding, however, more closely associated to the neoliberal, rational-choice, and even deliberative than to the more "realistic," liberal-democratic tradition – the latter being the one he associates with Arato's constitutional thought – fails to persuade Buchstein of its desirability. He lists seven objections to the application of the notion of self-binding to constitutional practice, reaching the conclusion that they "are strong enough to abandon the idea … as a theoretical way of justifying the normative validity of modern constitutions" (Buchstein, in this volume).

The chapter by János Kis intends to show on abstract analytic grounds the limitations and problematic aspects of the idea of popular sovereignty that historically served as a theoretical and philosophical justification of foundational processes of constitution making. Kis agrees with Arato on the historical relevance of the recent paradigm shift within constitutionalism that is taking place within the contemporary world and from the later evaluation of such transformation as resulting in the development of a postsovereign model of constitution making. In fact, the chapter's main argument aims at showing that sovereign constitution making was never a reality and proposes a new interpretation of the idea of popular sovereignty adequate to the contemporary model of democratic constitutionalism. In the fifth and last chapter of Part I, Uri Ram explores the negative, straightforwardly antidemocratic effects of an ethnic approach to constitutionalism and state formation in Israel. An advocate of a universalist and egalitarian understanding of citizenship and political identity, Ram critically analyzes the history of Israeli constitutional history, focusing in particular on the Palestinian-Arab citizens' several demands for democratic constitutional change, materialized in a series of recent "constitutional documents" that he carefully interprets. The need for transcending "the ethnic principle of the Israeli polity" if a democratic state is to be built is thus here theoretically backed and forcefully defended – a defense that even requires the critique of the aforementioned "constitutional documents" themselves, since they also tend to fall into the trap of an ethno-nationalist perspective.

The five chapters that make up Part II of this volume further explore the interpretive and practical implications of Arato's work, this time focusing on the different ways in which it has influenced social and political theory in Latin America. *Civil Society and Political Theory* had a profound effect on a new generation of scholars who used the theoretical tools of Cohen and Arato's theory to analyze the different processes of democratization that were taking place in the continent.[7] The crisis of military rule and the emergence of a social cry for democracy and the rule of law prompted a significant process of intellectual and political reflection throughout the region by a generation of intellectuals and activists that had been formerly influenced by the Marxist paradigm of revolutionary politics. As Olvera argues in his chapter, Cohen and Arato's book was a timely and important influence on an intellectual milieu which was undergoing a dramatic normative shift, a shift that the title of an influential article of the time adequately synthetized in the formula "from revolution to democracy" (Lechner 1990).[8] In such a context, Arato and Cohen's work offered a novel and sophisticated theoretical framework for grounding a new type of radical democratic politics that questioned not only the normative assumptions of revolutionary politics but also those that were hiding behind the 'realism' of the various strands of democratic minimalism and elitism that had influenced most of the academic production on transitions from authoritarianism and of democratic consolidation at the time. Inspired by the work of Arato, a younger generation of social scientists began developing a critical theory of the Latin American democratization processes built around the notion of civil society. The chapters by Avritzer and Olvera present an illuminating overview of the central tenets of such a project.

The chapter by Olvera engages with a discussion with some aspects of Cohen and Arato's framework. In his view, the project of an institutionalized democratic civil society poses significant challenges in a region where large sectors of the population live a very precarious and informal existence that seldom or intermittently interacts with the formal institutions of the market and of the democratic state. A project of construction of a democratic civil society should take notice of the peculiarities of Latin American modernization's selective pattern and the resulting systemic deficit both in the economy and political system (Peruzzotti 1999a). A pure politics of civil society would be, in Olvera's eyes, ineffective under such circumstances: what is also required is the parallel construction of a strong democratic state and of a viable market economy that could integrate the mass of the population into it.

After acknowledging the contribution of Arato's thinking to a democratic theory of civil society, Leonardo Avritzer proceeds to reconstruct the origins of civil society in the region tracing it back to the mid 1970s (Avritzer 2002; Oxhorn 1995; Peruzzotti 2002). In his view, the original concern for establishing an organizational and politically autonomous civil society was eventually displaced in more recent years by a concern for the linkages of the former with the state. Once the institutional autonomy of civil society was secured due to democratic institutionalization, the focus moved to the question of establishing appropriate channels of communication that could ensure a strong influence of the former over the political system. Yet, Avritzer considers that a mere politics of influence was insufficient in the light of the dramatic inequalities that pervaded Latin American societies. There was a need to complement classical representative channels with a new set of institutions that could organize stronger publics, particularly at the level of the poor. If Olvera stressed the relevance of a democratic state as a basic institutional framework that could provide the conditions for the effective exercise of citizenship rights in civil society, Avritzer focuses on the question of state–society linkages, stressing the novelty of what he considers is a new form of articulation. Largely inspired by the institutional innovations that the Partido dos Trabalhadores (PT) introduced in Brazil (participatory budgeting, participatory urban planning, policy councils, etc.), he analyzes the democratizing impact of a novel sort of hybrid space where civil society participates on an equal standing with state representatives in the debate, formulation, and implementation of public policies. In his view, the Brazilian project of institutional innovation broadened civil society's repertoire by introducing a form of engagement that goes beyond the self-limiting nature of the politics of influence that informed Arato's project. Institutionalized forms of participation, Avritzer concludes, are part of a more offensive strategy at state democratization aimed at establishing a more open, deliberative, and participatory form of public administration.

The chapters by Carlos de la Torre and Nicolás Lynch, while they do not directly engage with core aspects of Arato's theory, address an issue that has been a constant concern of the latter: the conceptual and political challenges that the phenomenon of populism poses to a radical agenda of political and social change. Despite their disagreement over the normative and conceptual value of populism for understanding current political dynamics, de la Torre and Lynch nevertheless agree on the relevance of the concept for an understanding of the historical development of the selective Latin American pattern to democratization. Lynch privileges a historically delimited definition of populism to indicate the type of inclusionary regimes that emerged in Latin America during the post-World War II period. In his view, those regimes inaugurated the era of democratic politics in the region and thus should be considered as a first and fundamental democratizing wave which would be respectively followed by two other significant democratizing moments: the one that followed the crisis of military authoritarianism in the late 1970s and the current one characterized by the arrival of leftist administrations in Argentina, Bolivia, Brazil, Ecuador, and Venezuela. It is misleading, he argues, to analyze current political developments as populist. By pejoratively branding those regimes as populist, the media and their political opponents want to divert attention from the democratizing agenda that inform their projects and their efforts to establish a more inclusionary and socially just order.

The recent turn in Latin American politics is also at the center of de la Torre's concerns, whose chapter focuses on the nature of the emerging democratic regimes of Bolivia, Ecuador, and Venezuela. He wonders to what extent are those administrations instituting a novel form of democratic regime that could address some of the historical deficits of the region. His evaluation of those experiences is less enthusiastic than the one made by Lynch. What particularly troubles de la Torre are the threats to democratic constitutionalism and political pluralism that a substantive understanding of democracy poses. Inspired by Arato's criticism of the revolutionary forms of political self-understanding, he sees in the blending of revolutionary and democratic identities that characterizes contemporary forms of populism the seeds of a potential authoritarian reorganization of power, especially in the cases of Ecuador under Correa and the Venezuela of Chávez. De la Torre nevertheless acknowledges the democratizing contribution of such political experiments as expressed in the expansion of rights, the empowerment of indigenous people and the poor, and their sustained efforts at overcoming the tragic legacy of neoliberal economic policies.

Finally, as a quite appropriate final chapter for both the section and the volume at large, Maria Victoria Crespo, a former student of Arato, successfully completes the field of inquiry on the modern republican executive developed by the latter in recently published texts with notes and manuscripts from her experience as a student in the courses and seminars at the New School for Social Research that first addressed the issue. In this way, Crespo manages to systematize Arato's conception of the presidency, analyzing the complex theoretical question of the embodiment of popular sovereignty and linking it to his theorizing of the modern notion of dictatorship.[9] The text closes with a powerful analysis of the relevance of these investigations for a comparative study of contemporary American and Latin American politics.

Notes

1 Even Soviet-type societies – especially in its post-Stalinist forms – Arato argued, presuppose significant processes of societal differentiation despite the attempts at de-differentiation carried out during the totalitarian period. It was precisely the failure of the latter at eliminating an independent sphere that eventually allowed in societies like Poland or Hungary for the emergence of a social movement for the reconstitution of civil society (Arato 1993: 275–277).

2 A distinction itself rooted, we may add, in Merleau-Ponty's theorizing of the notion of "institution" as an alternative to the Kantian, constituting model of social transformation he attributed to the revolutionary project (Merleau-Ponty 2010).

3 The proposed periodization does not necessarily follow the academic production of Arato in a chronological way.
4 The production of this period is best represented by the articles compiled in part II of Arato 1993.
5 Arato's work on Iraq can be subsumed under this preoccupation despite his recognizing that the former "regime transition" was not the result of an endogenous autonomous movement but an external neoimperial imposition of the Bush government. As he states at the beginning of *Constitution Making under Occupation*, the book is "an attempt to redeem the still redeemable" by steering the process of constitution making away from Bonapartism or populism to a postsovereign method that could launch a democratic transformation in a context of state collapse (Arato 2009: 263–264).
6 Arato lives at walking distance from "Ground Zero" and thus experienced the devastation of the attacks from very close. Quoting from memory our conversations regarding the difficulties introduced by the "war" discourse dominating the aftermath of 9/11, he once said: "it may not *be* a war, but it certainly *looks* and *smells* like one."
7 See Avritzer 1997, 2002, 2009; Avritzer and Olvera 1992; Dagnino 2002; Dagnino *et al*. 2006; Isunza Vera and Olvera 2010; Lynch 1997; Olvera 1997, 1999, 2003; Panfichi 2002; Peruzzotti 1997, 1999a, 1999b; Peruzzotti and Smulovitz 2006; Seele and Peruzzotti 2009.
8 For an English review of those debates see Barros 1986. For a criticism of Latin American neo-Gramscianism from the perspective of Cohen and Arato see Peruzzotti 1999b.
9 See "Conceptual History of Dictatorship (and its Rivals)" in Part III of this volume.

References

Arato, A. (1981) "Civil Society vs. the State: Poland 1980–81," *Telos*, 47 (Spring 1980–81), pp. 23–47 (republished in Arato 1993).

Arato, A. (1982) "Empire vs. Civil Society: Poland 1981–82," *Telos*, 50 (Winter 1981–82), pp. 19–48 (republished in Arato 1993).

Arato, A. (1984) "The Democratic Theory of the Polish Opposition: Normative Intentions and Strategic Ambiguities," Working Paper Number 15, Kellogg Institute, University of Notre Dame (republished in Arato 1993).

Arato, A. (1985) "Some Perspectives of Democratization in East Central Europe," *Journal of International Affairs*, 38, pp. 321–335 (republished in Arato 1993).

Arato, A. (1990) "Thinking the Present: Revolution in Eastern Europe, Revolution, Civil Society and Democracy," *Praxis International*, 1 & 2, pp. 24–38 (republished in Arato 1993).

Arato, A. (1991) "Social Theory, Civil Society, and the Transformation of Authoritarian Socialism," in Fehér and Arato (eds.), *Crisis and Reform in Eastern Europe*, New Brunswick: Transaction Publishers.

Arato, A. (1993) *From Neo-Marxism to Democratic Theory: Essays on the Critical Theory of Soviet-Type Societies*, Armonk and London: M. E. Sharpe.

Arato, A. (1994a) "Constitution and Continuity in the Transitions," *Constellations: An International Journal of Critical and Democratic Theory*, 1:1.

Arato, A. (1994b) "Constitution and Continuity in the Transitions," *Constellations: An International Journal of Critical and Democratic Theory*, 1:2.

Arato, A. (1994c) "Revolution, Restoration and Legitimation: Ideological Problems of the Transition from State Socialism," in Kennedy, M. (ed.) *Envisioning Eastern Europe*, Ann Arbor: University of Michigan Press.

Arato, A. (1995) "Forms of Constitution-Making and Theories of Democracy," *Cardozo Law Review*, 17, pp. 191–225.

Arato, A. (1999) "Impeachment or Revision of the Constitution?" *Constellations: An International Journal of Critical and Democratic Theory*, 6:2, pp. 145–156.

Arato, A. (2000) *Civil Society, Constitution, and Legitimacy*, Lanham, MD: Rowman & Littlefield Publishers.

Arato, A. (2001) "Congressional or (Weak) Presidential Government: The Results of the Election Crisis of 2000," *Constellations: An International Journal of Critical and Democratic Theory*, 8:3, pp. 289–303.

Arato, A. (2002) "Minima Politica after September 2011," *Constellations: An International Journal of Critical and Democratic Theory*, 9:1, pp. 46–52.

Arato, A. (2005) "Post-Election Maxims," *Constellations: An International Journal of Critical and Democratic Theory*, 12.2, pp. 182–193.

Arato, A. (2009) *Constitution Making under Occupation: The Politics of Imposed Revolution in Iraq*, New York: Columbia University Press.

Arato, A. and Breines, P. (1979) *The Young Lukács and the Origins of Western Marxism*, New York: Seabury Press.

Arato, A. and Gebhardt, E. (eds.) (1982) *The Essential Frankfurt School Reader*, New York: Continuum.

Avritzer, L. (1977) Guest Editor and "Introduction, Special Section on Civil Society in Latin America," *Constellations: An International Journal of Critical and Democratic Theory*, 4:1, pp. 88–93.

Avritzer, L. (2002) *Democracy and the Public Space in Latin America*, Princeton: Princeton University Press.

Avritzer, L. (2009) *Participatory Institutions in Democratic Brazil*, Washington DC and Baltimore: The Woodrow Wilson Press/The John Hopkins University Press.

Avritzer, L. and Olvera, A. J. (1992) "El concepto de Sociedad Civil en el Estudio de la Transición Democrática," *Revista Mexicana de Sociología*, LV, 4:92, pp. 227–248.

Barros, R. (1986) "The Left and Democracy: Recent Debates in Latin America," *Telos*, 68, pp. 49–70.

Cohen, J. L. and Arato, A. (1992) *Civil Society and Political Theory*, Cambridge, MA: The MIT Press.

Dagnino, E. (coord.) (2002) *Sociedad Civil, Esfera Pública y Democratización en América Latina: Brasil*, México DF: Fondo de Cultura Económica.

Dagnino, E., Olvera A. J., and Panfichi, A. (coords.) (2006) *La Disputa por la Construcción Democrática en América Latina*, México DF: Fondo de Cultura Económica.

Fehér, F. and Arato, A. (eds.) (1989) *Gorbachev: The Debate*, Atlantic Highlands: Humanities Press International.

Fehér, F. and Arato, A. (eds.) (1991) *Crisis and Reform in Eastern Europe*, New Brunswick: Transaction Publishers.

Isunza Vera, E. and Olvera, A. J. (coords.) (2010) *Democratización, Rendición de Cuentas y Sociedad Civil. Participación Ciudadana y Control Social*, México: Miguel Angel Porrúa Editores.

Lechner, N. (1990) "De la Revolución a la Democracia," in Lechner, N., *Los Patios Interiores de la Democracia*, Mexico: Fondo de Cultura Económica.

Lindhal, H. (2008) "Constituent Power and Reflexive Identity: Towards an Ontology of Collective Self-hood," in Loughlin, M. and N. Walker (eds.) *The Paradox of Constitutionalism: Constituent Power and Constitutional Form*, Oxford: Oxford University Press, pp. 9–26.

Lynch, N. (1997) "New Citizens and Old Politics in Peru," *Constellations: An International Journal of Critical and Democratic Theory*, 4:1, pp. 124–140.

Merleau-Ponty, M. (1964) *Signs*, Evanston, IL: Northwestern University Press.

Merleau-Ponty, M. (1973) *Adventures of the Dialectic*, Evanston, IL: Northwestern University Press.

Merleau-Ponty, M. (2010) *Institution and Passivity, Course Notes from the College de France (1954–1955)*, Evanston, IL: Northwestern University Press.

Olvera, A. J. (1997) "Civil Society and Political Transition in Mexico," *Constellations: An International Journal of Critical and Democratic Theory*, 4:1, pp. 105–123.

Olvera, A. J. (ed.) (1999) *La Sociedad Civil: de la Teoría a la Realidad*, México: El Colegio de México.

Olvera, A. J. (ed.) (2003) *Sociedad Civil, Esfera Pública y Democratización en América Latina: México*, México DF: Fondo de Cultura Económica.

Oxhorn, P. (1995) *Organizing Civil Society: The Popular Sectors and the Struggle for Democracy in Chile*, University Park: The Pennsylvania State University.

Panfichi, A. (coord.) (2002) *Sociedad Civil, Esfera Pública y Democratización en América Latina: Andes y Cono Sur*, México DF: Fondo de Cultura Económica.

Peruzzotti, E. (1997) "Civil Society and the Modern Constitutional Complex: The Argentine Experience," *Constellations: An International Journal of Critical and Democratic Theory*, 4:1, pp. 94–104.

Peruzzotti, E. (1999a) "Modernization and Juridification in Latin America: A Reassessment of the Latin American Developmental Path," *Thesis Eleven*, 58, pp. 59–82.

Peruzzotti, E. (1999b) "Constitucionalismo, Populismo y Sociedad Civil: Lecciones del caso argentino," *Revista Mexicana de Sociología*, 61:4, pp. 149–172.

Peruzzotti, E. (2002) "Towards a New Politics: Citizenship and Rights in Contemporary Argentina," *Citizenship Studies*, 6:1, pp. 77–94.

Peruzzotti, E. and Smulovitz, C. (eds.) (2006) *Enforcing the Rule of Law: Social Accountability in the New Latin American Democracies*, Pittsburgh: Pittsburgh University Press.

Plot, M. (2005) "Democracy and Terror," *Constellations: An International Journal of Critical and Democratic Theory*, 12:2, pp. 173–181.

Plot, M. (2009a) "The Democratico-Political," *Theory and Event*, 12:4, E-ISSN: 1092–311X.

Plot, M. (2009b) "*Divided Power in Space and Time*," *Constellations: An International Journal of Critical and Democratic Theory*, 16:2, pp. 280–294.

Plot, M. (2012) "Our Element. Flesh and Democracy in Merleau-Ponty," *Continental Philosophy Review*, 45:2, pp. 235–259.

Preuss, U. K. (1995) *Constitutional Revolution: The Link between Constitutionalism and Progress*, New Jersey: Humanities Press.

Rosenfeld, M. and Arato, A. (1998) *Habermas on Law and Democracy: Critical Exchanges*, Berkeley: University of California Press.

Seele, A. and Peruzzotti, E. (eds.) (2009) *Participatory Innovation and Representative Democracy in Latin America*, Washington DC and Baltimore: Woodrow Wilson Center/Johns Hopkins University Press.

Part I

From critical theory to constitution making

The contemporary relevance of Arato's democratic theory

1 Politics and anti-politics

Dick Howard

Recalling my first meeting with Andrew Arato more than forty years ago, I am struck by a continuity in our concerns in spite of the different subjects we have studied. We met in 1970, at a time when the New Left knew that it had to be more than a counter-cultural movement, and that it could not simply mobilize the resentment of those who might be drafted into the vain and vainglorious anti-communist crusade in Vietnam. "From Resistance to Revolution" was the vague slogan of those who began to call themselves "comrades" as they abandoned what they called their bourgeois liberalism for one or another variant of Marxism (a few Stalinists, more Trotskyists, still more Maoists and of course the Castrist-Guevarist). For all their differences, these groups shared an orthodoxy built around the legacy of Lenin. It was in this context that Karl Klare and I decided to co-edit a volume called *The Unknown Dimension: European Marxism Since Lenin*.[1] Our goal was to show that critical political thought had not ceased after 1917; a radical tradition that was critical, curious and above all anti-dogmatic had continued. We thought that this hidden tradition could help the New Left to understand what was truly "new" about it, how its goals related to those of the classical "left" and how it belonged in fact to a deeper tradition of critical thought. Karl and I asked Andrew Arato to write the chapter on Lukács, who stood at the origins of what Merleau-Ponty, looking for the roots of critical political thought, had called "Western Marxism."[2]

Our collaboration continued in the journal *Telos*, whose editorial board Andrew joined with issue nine, in the fall of 1971. That journal was a kind of privileged place in which a few young multi-lingual American leftists had the luxury of, so to speak, getting our education in public thanks to the extraordinary dedication of the journal's editor, Paul Piccone. Looking back through its early issues, *Telos* and its young editors passed from leftist versions of Husserlian phenomenology mixed with a dose of Gramsci to Lukács and Korsch, and then onward, beyond the then-popular Herbert Marcuse to the various co-stars of the Frankfurt School. No orthodoxy could hold back the editors' curiosity or prevent their forward movement. There was a brief pause – but only for a moment – when editors hesitated to publish the openly *anti-Marxist* work of Claude Lefort and Cornelius Castoriadis.[3] Could we be leftists while criticizing Marxism?

By 1975, after the U.S. withdrawal from Vietnam and the accompanying decline of the anti-war movement, the goal of remaining on the left became unfortunately a rather academic matter. A kind of intellectual orthodoxy crept into the pages of *Telos* – or so it appeared to me at the time. The journal became a kind of academic project with a good conscience. What other options existed? No one really knew, until the emergence of *Solidarnosc* in 1980, whose importance was made clear by the brilliant editorial work of Andrew Arato, and by his own interpretative essays. The heady days of the old political adventure returned; *Telos* did not join the liberal chorus of anti-communism but sought to give voice to the new movement that was emerging. The twin themes of democracy and civil society became leitmotifs of the journal's quest for something like an "unknown dimension" of left-wing political thought and action. In spite of the well-earned label of "European intellectuals," some of us began to see that these themes could be found also in American history, a theme that we had neglected in the early years. But others in the circle around Paul Piccone had other ideas; *Telos* was increasingly drawn toward Carl Schmitt and turned, so to speak, from red to brown. Andrew could not hold back the tide; he left, as did others and I.

For my part, forty years later, the search for an "unknown dimension" that can fructify radical political reflection and prevent its dogmatic stagnation, remains a lodestar. Whether it can fulfill the old Marxist – and more specifically Lukácsian – goal of uniting theory and praxis is another question, and probably not the right one. The analysis which follows leaves behind the old vocabulary but does not abandon the goals that I have shared with Andrew and others over these four decades.

1 Defining the political

What is politics? What is the goal that defines it? The classical answer since Plato is justice; the modern definition borrowed from Machiavelli is power. Today, the fact that we use the word in a variety of disparate contexts reflects a flattening of the concept. We speak of office politics, family or gender politics, racial or class politics, domestic or foreign politics. We may express our disdain for someone by saying that he is just "playing politics." At the university, professors are sometimes accused of trying to advance their careers through "academic politics." The term politics seems to act like a sponge, soaking up adjectives that qualify it while having no substance of its own; what was the sun around which social life turned has become the moon that at best reflects it.

In its contemporary uses, politics cannot be separated from forms of power; but it cannot simply be reduced to these. Power is a means which cannot define the end for which it is used. Yet political power is not the same thing as material force, which is imposed on others without their consent. Although material force may be used, it will bring diminishing returns as those subjected to it resist (actively or passively). Successful political power must have legitimacy in the eyes of those subject to it. Such legitimate power generates authority to which members of a society implicitly or explicitly consent. They do not feel that they are obeying someone else's wishes but are carrying out their own freely chosen projects, exercising their own will to achieve ends that they have rationally chosen. The source of the legitimacy of power will differ in different societies: the kinds of authority on which it depends may be secular or sacred, rational or customary, institutional or charismatic. Its basis may be strength, knowledge or wealth, each of which will in turn be defined according to historical conditions. *Each of these sources of legitimate power and authority is an example of what I am calling the political.* The members of any society that is not governed by brute force share a basic, minimal, set of values that provide meaning to *all* the aspects of their lives, not only to those that concern government.[4] This shared meaning is defined by the political, which concerns not only social institutions but also the character of the men and women in the given society.

This general definition of the political provides a framework for the analysis of concrete political choices. The journalists' "first draft of history" describes the *particular* facts; but to evaluate them, it is necessary to fit them into a more *general* framework. That is why anyone who is interested in politics must be concerned with political theory. Without the help of some theory, the student of politics is lost, in the thicket of discrete events; the parts don't fit together into a whole. However, just as the word "politics" seems to function like a sponge that can absorb multiple, even contrary, meanings, the same is true of theory. Its claims are universal; they eliminate factors that are due to accident, subjective bias or contingent events. The social sciences offer many such theories, some at a macro-, others at a micro-level. But then, seemingly out of nowhere, history seems to take a new turn: *Solidarnosc* emerges, the Berlin Wall falls, the Arab Spring spreads rapidly. Theory's ability to put into perspective particular choices has clay feet. Social theory cannot explain the political. The universality of its claims blinds it.

Part of the problem is that social science looks at its object from outside of it, as if it were using a telescope or a microscope to study something that remains constant. It sees differences among individuals and groups, some natural, others cultural. Which ones count? The scientist describes differences of economic wealth, social status or political power; he then charts ethnicity, gender, religion or levels of education; finally, he looks for a correlation among them. But correlation is not causation. What is missing is the standpoint of the participants, for it is they who give meaning to the differences described. The participants determine which factors lead a person to complain about the injustice of her lot, and why she thinks that others will support her grievance. That is why some social differences are accepted even though they give advantages to one group or person over others. *This meaning-giving aspect of social relations is an expression of the political.* It defines legitimate power; and in so doing, it draws the line between the licit and the illicit, the just and the unjust, the known and the unknown. It establishes a shared background of values and meaning that leads the participants to treat certain differences as salient whereas others are considered normal.

This interpretation of the nature and role of the political owes more to continental thought than to the reigning Anglo-American approach. Rather than focus on the facts that *are* the case, that theoretical orientation is concerned to establish what *ought* to be the case. Since the publication of John Rawls' *Theory of Justice* (1971), this kind of normative theory has become dominant. In its original version, normative theory attempted at once to legitimate liberal political values while criticizing those practices that were inconsistent with them, most particularly social arrangements that distorted the possibility of realizing the values of the liberal creed. In the intervening decades, the Rawlsian version of normative theory has been criticized in particular for its assumption that free, rational individuals exist *before* they come together rationally to form a community. That appears to put the part before the whole. It would seem politically more accurate to examine first the bonds that tie together the community, since there are no individuals who do not belong to some sort of community. Whether one agrees with this general criticism or not, both sides share the goal of explaining the rational *reasons* that lead men and women to consider their social relations as legitimate.[5]

Normative theory makes no moral assumptions about the nature of the good; rather, it sets out to determine what duties and rights a person ought to agree to in a society that all its members would agree is just, whatever their effect on their own particular lives. In this way, normative theory is a modern reformulation of the social contract theories that try to show how and why men leave their natural, pre-political conditions to form political society. It asks what natural rights can be legitimately surrendered to the political state, and what that state owes (or not) to the members who accept the bargain. What freedoms are given up to the state; and what obligations does it have toward its members? Citizens of a political society must be equal to one another (at least as concerns their political rights); but they must also retain at least some of their natural liberty (which can lead to differences among them). What makes the normative theory effective is that its account of the relation between equality and liberty is political in a limited but important sense insofar as it is concerned only with the public activity of the members of society – not with their private moral beliefs – while at the same time its normative force binds the individual with a subjective force similar to the way a moral imperative affects a private person. In this way, normative theory claims to explain the existence of a political unity that leaves room for moral diversity, permitting believers in different gods, followers of different cults, agnostics and unbelievers to live together in public harmony in spite of their private differences.

2 The political and the moral

The attractiveness of normative political theory lies in its attempt to take into account the perspective of the actors in society. This permits it to study the way in which political action becomes the basis of legitimate power rather than the exercise of brute force. Although it claims to be indifferent to the personal moral values of the members of society, normative theory is ultimately a moral rather than a political theory. In the most simple terms, the difference between moral and political claims is that moral relations concern only two participants whereas political action takes place among three (or more) actors, one of whom is affected only indirectly by the behavior of the other two who must, however, take into account his perspective in making their choices. This fundamental distinction needs to be carefully explained.

Relations between two persons are direct and immediate; they are governed by a code of morality. In a dyadic relation, the participants can look one another in the eye; they can directly challenge the claims of the other both as to their veracity and to the sincerity with which the speaker emits the claim. The moral actor is never alone; but he is never in mixed company. When he asks what *ought* to be done in a given situation, the question is directed to himself, to his self as if it were another, the representative of moral humanity. If I resolve to act in a moral manner, it is because I have to continue to live with myself, and I don't want to have to spend my time with an amoral opportunist or an immoral evildoer. I look at my actions through the eyes of an other who is, however, identical with me. This is the other with whom, in the normative theory, all individuals as identical participants agree to participate in a contract that defines the political nature of their society. This other is at once like me and yet – at least in principle – different from me. If he were me, there would be no reason to inquire about his judgment of my behavior. But if he were completely other, there would be no reason for me to worry about his opinion, which wouldn't matter to me. What this second party through whose eyes I look at my own actions represents is my better self, the one whom I *should* become in order to truly be myself, an other who is sufficiently similar to me that I want to act together with him. In principle, there is no reason why I cannot achieve this goal, becoming what I am by joining with him in order to become a fully human self. In this sense, morality has a political dimension because it affects individual character; but it cannot be identified with the political, which concerns participants whose difference from one another is more important than their shared morality.

Relations among three (or more) persons depend always on the mediation of a third party whose relation to the other two can never be made fixed or permanent because any of the participants can in principle take the role of the Third. The Third can be another person, a group of people, or even an institution. It stands outside of the relation that the other two establish to one another; their accord was based on moral considerations and is in principle the private, subjective relation of two individuals. The Third threatens the unity of purpose sought by the dyad because it sees the public, objective character of their relation denying its claim to moral justification. As a result, one of the members of the dyad, feeling the critical gaze of the Third, may try to draw it into complicity with their couple; but the danger is that the previous partner will resent the lost immediacy of the dyad, looking jealously at the attempts by its former partner to widen their entente. This jealous former partner may become a Third in whose eyes the new partners have acquired an intimacy that seems to exclude his/her participation. At this point, the emerging new dyad may react by attempting to eliminate the former partner, who has become a Third. But in taking this action, the newly formed dyad violates its own moral structure, which was based on the immediacy of mutual recognition; it treats the new Third as foreign, other and inassimilable. The new Third, in turn, denounces as a private conspiracy what the new dyad conceived of as a moral protest against the refusal of the Third to respect its rights. The dyad replies to the accusation by denouncing the Third for "politicizing" their relation for its own benefit. In short, full political unity as moral fusion can never be achieved; but the quest for moral unity constantly renews the dynamic of political relations. While the political is not distinct from morality, it cannot be identified with morality, which is based on dyadic relations.

The distinction between morality and politics can be made more concrete by showing how and why there is always a temptation to replace the political by theories of morality. Moral values are justified by claims to universal validity; what is good for you is good for me and for all others as individuals. There may be difficulties in determining how to apply moral principles in specific situations; but the principle of universalizability is unchanging. For its part, the political deals with conditions that are always particular; solutions that have worked at one time will be inadequate just because the previous success has changed the conditions in which the new action must take place. In the previous example, the attempt to integrate the Third led to the perception by one member of the previously successful dyad that the assimilation of the outsider is a threat to its formerly stable position. Its suspicious reaction has the effect of cementing the new dyad, which now perceives the former partner as a threat. The result is a dynamic that feeds on and reproduces instability; the participants know that they must take into account not only the effects of their action on their immediate partner but also the way in which their action *appears* in the eyes of the Third. In this sense, "public opinion" becomes the Third whose allegiance is at once sought after but fickle.

The attempt to formulate a normative political theory fails to recognize the distinction between the creative potential of the political and the stabilizing role of morality. It does not recognize that the existence of the Third means that *particularity* rather than universality is the essential characteristic of the political. The normative theory imagines a sort of contract made between what might be called universal individuals, persons who are like one another in all public aspects (although differing in other, private, ways). There appears to be a virtue in a theory that treats everyone as equal to all others; but such a theory deals with the rule rather than the exception; it cannot deal with particular cases – which is the task of the political. For this reason, the implications of normative theory, and the various types of moral theory to which it appeals, are *anti-political.*

If politics is based on the legitimate presence of the Third, *anti-politics* can be defined as the attempt to eliminate that disturbing particular who stands outside the moral unity and shared values that makes a people or nation what it is. Anti-politics seeks to eliminate the need for the political. The twentieth century offered two stark illustrations of the attraction of anti-politics in the forms of communism and fascism. In both cases, democratization and capitalism were replacing aristocratic societies that left no room for particularity. The idea of individual rights and the possibility of social mobility legitimated conflicts that threatened a hierarchical world in which everyone and every thing had its proper place. The promise of communism was to overcome class divisions, economic exploitation and political injustice by creating a classless society in which private property would be eliminated and the state would wither away. The promise of Hitler's fascism was to insure the unity of the German *Volk* by exterminating the parasites that were threatening its purity while conquering the territories needed to incorporate all Germans into one *Reich* whose thousand-year life would put an end to change. One remarkable aspect of these twin totalitarianisms was the expansionist megalomania that resulted from their anti-political projects whose goal of eliminating particularity meant that they were unable to recognize any limits – since to do so would be to admit the legitimacy of particularity. Equally remarkable is the degree to which they found willing supporters who joined not (only) because of the material rewards they expected but because they were supporting a *moral* cause. In their eyes, totalitarianism was a legitimate form of power because it was being used to eliminate the particular interests that threatened social unity.

The fact that totalitarianism appealed to moral motivations calls attention to the fact that the temptation of anti-politics is not an aberration; it expresses a very human desire to insure social unity, whatever the cost. Totalitarianism is the most extreme form of anti-politics. But particularity can also be denied without its being exterminated, as can be seen in the case of capitalism. At first glance, capitalism constantly produces new products; and the free market can work only because new needs are constantly created, along with new commodities to satisfy them. But the magic of the market makes this particularity into a form of universality insofar as the new products are no more different from one another than one brand of laundry detergent from another.[6] Particularity here is illusory, a mere appearance, and a difference that makes no difference. Whatever novelty appears in the world of commodities is engulfed into the universality of the market where it is homogenized by the "invisible hand" working behind the backs of the players to arrange an outcome that insures the good of all. Capitalism too makes a moral appeal; but its principle of individual liberty ignores the debilitating effects of unbound liberty on social relations that are supposed to be based on an equality of rights.

The fact that capitalism is anti-political poses the question of its compatibility with democracy. After all, the two general types of totalitarianism that illustrate the way anti-politics functions were attempts to overcome what they took to be the immoral effects of democracy and the threat to social unity that it represented. Is capitalism therefore comparable to the other totalitarianisms, as some critics of economic globalization maintain today? This question, which cannot be answered here, makes clear the need to distinguish among the types of anti-politics.

3 The necessity of the political

It is time to ask: What *is* the political? Every society has to have a political dimension. Without it, men and women who co-exist in a given space and time would be no different than a random mix of entities which now-and-then make contact only to move on, and on, and on. ... Just as the members of an athletic team are united by what is often called a team "spirit" that transcends the particular or private concerns of any one of them, so too are citizens joined together by a shared framework of meaning and values that unite them in spite of their particular or private differences. People may belong to many social organizations, each of which is defined by the particular goals that it seeks. The political is the principle that organizes the relations among these particular groups (which themselves have their own organizing principles). It establishes a hierarchy among these groups, which can be challenged and replaced if it loses its ability to maintain the unity binding this diversity. In this way, the political can be said to define the grammar and the syntax that govern relations among the members of society. Just as there are some things that cannot be said, some expressions that cannot be understood, and some sounds that cannot be heard, so too in any political society there are things that cannot be done, actions that no one will join, and projects that no one could imagine.

The political must be distinct from the social relations that it organizes; but its legitimacy depends on its being perceived by the members of society as the expression of their own will. How can it be both without and within, transcendent and yet immanent? That is the paradox of the political, to which the consent of the governed is the modern solution.[7] Even if only implicit, such consent distinguishes political power from brute force. If the political becomes too far separated from the society that it governs, it appears foreign, either constraining obedience or encouraging rebellion, or sullen indifference. Respect for the law is lost, and with it disappears the solidarity that binds individuals into a whole. Conversely, if society recognizes itself wholly in the political, this will destroy the transcendent character of authority that makes power legitimate. Social relations are then governed solely by material force, and the law is degraded to a tool of the powerful. The members of such a society are bound by nothing more than personal interest; they are incapable of governing themselves in unexpected conditions because they are not able to transcend their immediate concerns and see themselves as a whole.

The history of the political is the story of the attempts to maintain this paradoxical structure. The principle that gives the political its authority cannot become wholly external to society; but the attempt to insure that it is recognized by the consent of the members cannot be assumed to be fully immanent to their social relations. The authority of the political may be based on nature or reason, on gods or God, on tradition or science. In each case, the principle is at once external to social relations and yet reflected in them. Nature's lawfulness is beyond men's power; yet they make use of its laws in their social relations and their modes of production. Reason is never fully present in human society; yet a wholly irrational society could never maintain itself. The gods or God govern the behavior of men; yet they can never deny them the freedom to choose to obey or to rebel. The same paradoxical structure holds for the ideas of tradition and science; they are transcendent principles that are also present within human society. The danger in each case, however, is that the tension can be broken; immanence or transcendence become absolute. The gods desert the universe, nature is seen as mere stuff, reason a romantic dream. Or, from the other side, nature is divinized, reason rationalized and religion replaced by science. The result will be anti-politics.

This same paradoxical structure can be observed at a more directly political level in the forms of monarchy, aristocracy or democracy. These are political principles which must be at once incarnated in the actual monarch, aristocrat or democrat, while retaining their value as principles that are not entirely realized in any present or past society. Monarchy, the rule of a single person (*monos*), realizes the overriding need for unity of action in any society; there must exist, somewhere, a source of ultimate decision. But of course some monarchs play this role better than others; and none can claim perfection. The monarch at times incarnates the transcendent principle of unity; at other times, he is the voice of the people, its representative, and the best it can offer. But the rule of one can become arbitrary; or a weak-willed monarch may fear to take initiatives. The resulting anti-political government will eventually be replaced by a political structure that is open to all of the best (the *aristoi*). Once again, the now familiar paradoxes reappear. How does this "best-ness" manifest itself? Is the aristocrat the most brave, or wise, or strong? Those are tangible qualities. But what of those with the best judgment, the most experience, the greatest piety? These qualities are harder to measure. Nonetheless, in today's representative democracies, we consider that those whom we elect are "the best" – or, at least, better than any other candidate. They have convinced us that they are sufficiently like us, and yet better than we. But if they fail to maintain this equality and equidistance, the political dynamic can become anti-political, in the form of either government by technocracy or a demagogic populism.

This political tension reaches its most acute form in a democracy. The name means literally that it is a form of power (*kratos*) by the people (*demos*). It appears at first that this rule by the people over itself eliminates the difference between the political and the social. The qualification "over" suggests that the difference in principle of the two domains remains. Self-rule is not simply the rule of the immediate desires of the self. Self-rule, moreover, is a form of freedom that is not arbitrary or capricious but the expression of autonomy in which the self (*autos*) gives itself its own law (*nomos*). In spite of this affirmation of freedom, the laws that a people gives to itself nonetheless *govern* the relations of those who are subject to them. The concept of *ruling* remains; democracy is not anarchy, the absence of rule (*arche*). The difference of the people as governing themselves and the people as governed (by themselves) remains; in the one case the citizens are active, in the other they are passive. The active citizen makes rules that apply to himself in his non-political life in society as a producer, family member or participant in the marketplace. In the one case, the citizen is a public person; in the other, he is a private individual. The greatest danger in a democracy is that the private interests come to dominate over the public good; when that happens, immanence destroys the regulative role of the principle of democracy, the "virtue" of the citizen who knows how to sacrifice his private interests. On the other hand, there are times when such transcendent values do return to the democratic stage, often expressing themselves under the concept of a republic (the *res publica*, the public thing or commonwealth). Was this not the "hope" that some felt with the emergence of *Solidarnosc*, the fall of the Berlin Wall, and now the "Arab Spring" of 2011?

The fundamental principle of democracy is not self-evident. The source of the legitimation that distinguishes the authority of power from the imposition of sheer force has always been situated in a transcendent power *outside* of society, in ideas such as gods or God, nature or natural law, tradition or reason. Relations within society were structured by this transcendent principle but the two levels were not considered to be identical to one another. In this way, a dynamic could develop because the distinction between the two levels meant that either the existing form of social relations could be challenged as not being adequate to the transcendent principle that made them legitimate; or the adequacy of the present interpretation of that transcendent principle could be put into question by the fact that it contradicted the actual relations among the members of society. Thus, a bad monarch did not destroy the principle of monarchy, nor a corrupt aristocracy that of a government of the best. For the same reason, the distinction between the two levels made it possible to insure that society remained plural, open to particular claims and to a diversity of interests. However, the distinction between the two levels did not make this political dynamic necessary. More often than not, the tension between the political principle and the society that it structured flew apart; politics went into abeyance while anti-politics triumphed.

Democracy's uniqueness is the result of the fact the fact that the source of its political legitimacy is *immanent* to the society. Put paradoxically, the transcendent source of authority is immanent in democracy; and yet it must continue to perform the political role that it played when it remained a transcendent principle. Sovereignty belongs to the people; but the people are also subject to the sovereign authority over them. When the political is located wholly within society, the social and the political have in principle become identical; the separation that had existed in previous forms of the political is overcome. When the social has thus become the political, the political appears to be "realized." But, by the same token, and in the same movement, the political has been destroyed, replaced by anti-politics. The political has lost the critical distance that permitted it to articulate social relations as a whole, and to criticize them for not being adequate to their own principle. Now these relations themselves have become the principle of their own self-criticism. This double movement illustrates both the strength and the weakness of democracy. It identifies the political with the actual competition among the interests that make up society. Democracy's strength is its realism; it need not look outside itself to justify the actions it takes and the legislation it proposes. But as a result, it may lose sight of the whole, which is more than the sum of the diverse interests in a pluralistic society. With this movement, the history of political philosophy comes to an apparent end; the great political thinkers of the nineteenth century are *social philosophers*: Karl Marx, Max Weber and Émile Durkheim. They recognized the necessity of the political, but they could only describe its effects not its origin.

The political paradox of democratic self-governance explains a fundamental aspect of modern political life. The essential difference between the people as active and self-governing and the people as passive and governed expresses the fact that society is essentially divided. Marx called this "class division," insisting in the *Communist Manifesto* that "all history is the history of class struggle." He was right, as an empirical sociologist; but he couldn't explain what he described because he treated the political as dependent on (rather than the foundation of) social conditions.[8] Marx did not see that in fact the division of rulers and the ruled exists in every society because social relations are always structured by the political. The challenge today is not to eliminate political division but to invent forms of the political that promote the autonomy that produces the general welfare. Max Weber recognized the centrality of the problem of the political, but his cross-cultural studies of the sources of its legitimacy culminated only in a reformulation of its paradoxical foundation. To the rational-legal grounds of authority typical of modern times, and the authority of custom and tradition, Weber added a type of authority that he called charismatic. This third type of authority, which redefines the political, can appear in any historical moment; but Weber recognized that once the prophet has faded away, his followers must "routinize" the magic if it is to be preserved. The tragic result, Weber knew, is an anti-politics, from which only a new "god" can save us. For his part, Émile Durkheim, Weber's French contemporary, also recognized the problem of social division. But rather than seeking to overcome what he called the "social division of labor," he tried to show that this division was functional to the maintenance of a modern type of social solidarity. As opposed to traditional societies that were held together by a mechanical solidarity in which all members were interchangeable parts of the whole, modern societies are organic; like a biological organism, their parts contribute to and strengthen the whole. One of those parts is the political, conceived of as just another organ among the many that co-exist in society. But if the political is simply another part of the social structure, it cannot perform its properly political function of giving meaning to the whole.

4 Recovering political thought

The title of this concluding paragraph refers to one aspect of the work that Andrew Arato and I (and others) began more than four decades ago. Each has taken a different path, sometimes more empirical than theoretical, sometimes more engaged with actual problems, and others more concerned with historical analogies or with fundamental principles. Parts of the preceding analysis were written as a draft of the Introduction to my own book, *The Primacy of the Political: A History of Political Thought from the Greeks to the French and American*

Revolutions.[9] That project is only one way of developing the insights that have guided four decades of thinking about politics that has been marked by a basic intuition, that there is a need to analyze the "unknown dimension" of political life to both understand it and to help change it. That journey continues.

Notes

1 (New York: Basic Books, 1971). In addition to the essay by Arato, the volume contained essays by Stanley Aronowitz, Robin Blackburn, Martin Jay, Bertell Ollman and Alfred Schmidt, among others.
2 C.f., Maurice Merleau-Ponty, *The Adventures of the Dialectic*, translated by Joseph Bien (Evanston, IL: Northwestern University Press, 1973).
3 Lefort was published in Number 22, Winter, 1974–75; Castoriadis appeared in Number 23, Spring 1975.
4 An assemblage of people governed by brute force is a "society" only in a metaphoric sense.
5 Evaluating these debates is not my concern; they all share a normative orientation, whether in Michael Sandel's original challenge to Rawls, *Liberalism and the Limits of Justice* (1982), or in more recent work such as Virginia Held's feminist ethics of "care."
6 This is the process that Marx called the "fetishism of commodities." Goods that are produced as use values are transformed by the market process into exchange values; use values that were qualitative are considered by the market only in terms of their exchange value.
7 The classical form of the paradox can be seen in Plato's *Republic* which insists on the correlation of types of individual souls to institutional forms. An early modern variant is found in Montesquieu's insistence on the types of virtue required by different political regimes.
8 *The Communist Manifesto* begins with the announcement that "A specter is haunting Europe, the specter of communism." Titling his pamphlet a "manifesto" suggested to Marx that he was not making a political claim; his intent was to make manifest, to uncover and explain, what was already present in existing social relations. I have criticized this aspect of Marx's work in a book titled *The Specter of Democracy* (New York: Columbia University Press, 2002), suggesting that Marx was describing the advent of democracy but was unable to recognize the political nature of this new era.
9 (New York: Columbia University Press, 2010).

2 Constitutionalism in fragmented societies

The integrative function of constitutions

Ulrich K. Preuss

There are rare cases where a political scientist has enriched and refined the understanding of constitutionalism and constitutional law – obviously Andrew Arato is one of them. Strongly inspired by the transformations of the formerly communist societies of Central and East Europe of which he has a deep knowledge and subtle understanding he has raised new questions which deal with the thorny issue of the sustainability of these countries' path towards a constitutional mode of governance which they started off only twenty years ago. After all, the state of democratic affairs in Bulgaria, Hungary, Poland, Rumania, let alone Russia gives rise to serious concerns: corruptive structures and networks which pervade many areas of society have furthered political apathy and cynicism and encouraged the renaissance of nationalist, xenophobic, and anti-Semitic tendencies which may no longer remain limited to the fringes of society and undermine citizens' trust in the capacity of democratic institutions to cope with the manifold conflicts of modern societies. As in all revolutionary changes of truly historical dimensions the societies which underwent these changes and at the same time actively pushed them forward simply did not have the time for reflections about the development to which at least their active parts should commit themselves. Such an undertaking requires the passion for making the world better and at the same time the capacity for intellectual objectivity and truthfulness. Obviously Andrew Arato is a prime example of this kind of political intellectual. The secular revolutions in East and Central Europe in the 1980s and 1990s lured his interest and spirited erudition in the field of social and political philosophy into the area of constitutional politics. Here he delved into what Hannah Arendt called the "perplexities of the beginning," developing and sharpening the conceptual tools for the understanding and eventually shaping of social, cultural, and institutional change.

However, as Arato's publications show,[1] he is by no means a mere regional specialist of Central and East Europe. His expertise stretches from West, Central, and East Europe, through Latin America, to the conflict-ridden Middle East. In his involvement in practical issues of constitution-making as an adviser in Central and East Europe and in Iraq he unites in a truly exceptional manner the highest standard of the state of the art of constitutionalism in its philosophical, legal, and political dimensions. This, then, gives rise to open a conversation with him about the force of constitutionalism and constitution-making under precarious conditions, namely in deeply divided societies. These are politics in which profound conflicts among the members of society undercut their motives to engage in durable schemes of social cooperation and thwart the genesis of trust in the beneficial effects of institutions. These conflicts may have socio-economic, religious, cultural, ethnic, or historical roots – what poses a threat to the stability of society is the underlying premise that institutions, and constitutions in particular, cannot contribute to the solution or mitigation of these conflicts. The stability and orderly functioning of institutions presuppose a minimally consolidated order of society, or so is a widely held assumption both on the right and the left side of the political spectrum. It is uncertain whether this idea fully grasps the relationship between society and constitutionalism. In the following – admittedly quite sketchy – reconstruction of this relationship we may find arguments that paint a more differentiated picture. It is, of course, not by accident that at the end of these reflections Arato's idea of a postsovereign understanding of constitutionalism will be taken up.

I

The most succinct definition of a constitution was laid down by the framers of the French Declaration of the Rights of Man and of the Citizen of 1789. Its legendary Article 16 reads: "A society in which the guarantee of rights is not assured, nor the separation of powers defined, has no constitution at all." This definition became the forefather of all minimalist concepts of the constitution according to which a constitution does not need more than a bill of rights, stipulations about the machinery of government and amendment rules. In the 1970s a distinguished US-German constitutional theorist condensed the essence of constitutionalism even more, into two words: "Limited Government."[2] In fact, the function of a constitution to limit state power – both through the separation of powers and the guarantee of individual spheres which were closed to any kind of state intervention – was the key concern of the forces which at the end of the eighteenth century struggled for a constitution in France and in the newly independent American states. The reason is easy to understand: in France the members of the Third Estate had suffered from the omnipresence and omnipotence of the royal bureaucracy that had suffocated the frail beginnings of civil autonomy. In the former British colonies of North America the fear of royal despotism and of any kind of autocracy, even one based upon democratic elections, motivated them to think first and foremost of the restraining attributes of a constitution.

However, we must not misunderstand this time-dependent concept of the constitution as the definitive fixing of its inherent meaning and rationale. Rather, the concept which predominated at the end of the eighteenth century must be comprehended as the first instance of the historical experience that constitutions mirror and process the key societal and political conflicts of any particular historical epoch. Either the text or its interpretation, or both, undergo changes in which each generation tries to find an appropriate institutional solution for the most relevant societal and political problems of the time. Thus, in the dawn of modern constitutionalism, at the end of the eighteenth century, the key political issue was the struggle of the emerging bourgeois class against dynastic absolutism. Its power-sensitive agenda entailed its imprint as liberal constitutionalism. During much of the nineteenth century, after the demise of absolutism and the establishment of the constitutional state as a system of bourgeois class domination, it was the battle of broad segments of the excluded inferior classes for their recognition as citizens through the extension of suffrage.[3] In some European countries this was not achieved until after World War I, when – as a new challenge to liberal constitutionalism – the organized working class claimed their "entry into the arena of national politics" (Bendix) and set off the epoch of mass democracy.[4] In each of these developmental stages constitutionalism changed its character, its institutions, and the legal instruments for coping with new challenges. The changing meaning of the concept of citizenship is the most significant indicator of this development.[5]

Hence, we can trace back the different dimensions of our contemporary concept of constitutionalism to the different historical constellations of social and political conflict. As we have seen, the basic and original function of constitutionalism – the *limitation of power* – must be assigned to the beginning of modern constitutionalism when it was a forceful weapon of the emerging bourgeois class in its power struggle with the old regime. In the US, where the successful struggle for independence of the former colonies had bonded the people, the main issue of the constitution was to find appropriate institutional devices for constituting the multitude of individuals – largely freedom-loving settlers – as "we the people," i.e., as a sovereign polity in the first place. At the same time the constitution had to protect the individuals' liberty against the power of the collective will of that very sovereign polity, the unified people. Obviously this was the central theme of the Federalist Papers of the founders of the USA.[6]

The US example points to the *constitutive function* of the constitution and the need to find a balance with its freedom-protecting function. This is the starting point of what Stephen Holmes has called the Janus face of the constitution.[7] Above and beyond its originally purely negative and defensive dimension it also plays a positive role in that it constitutes the unorganized multitude of people as a political body by establishing basic institutions of self-rule. The constitutive function plays a central role in constitutions which are primarily concerned with the creation and maintenance of the integrity of a democratic state power. In the case of the US the framers were worried about the construction of a superior power of a centralized authority, the Union. In the continental European context of the nineteenth century where popular sovereignty had still to be gained by strenuous efforts – where, in other words, political power was effectively organized, if in an undemocratic mode – the key problem of constitutionalism was the *legitimation of the existing political authority*. Of course, since the French Revolution the only legitimizing principle of modern constitutions has been the principle of popular sovereignty. But political realities were not up to this political principle. As a result, in addition to the aforementioned struggle for the extension of the suffrage different devices of power-sharing between the traditional monarchical power and the newly emancipated social classes surfaced. Incidentally, power-sharing was also the constitutional solution of some of the social and political conflicts of the twentieth century in cases where the principle of popular sovereignty could not be realized due to the continuing power of an old regime. The Round Table agreement, which the then communist government of Poland concluded with the Solidarity movement in 1989, is an obvious illustration. The National Peace Accord of South Africa, a multiparty agreement signed in September 1991, which started the negotiations about a peaceful transition to a non-racial democratic political system, is another case in point.

II

These examples lead us to the *integrative function* of many modern constitutions, the focus of this paper. It deals with the question of whether constitutions do not only organize the machinery of government and establish basic rights but, beyond that, create a sense of commonness, mutuality, and civic solidarity among citizens. In other words, the question is whether a constitution has the capacity to unite a society which is raven by manifold cleavages – economic, social, cultural, religious, ideological, and political – into a nation. The German constitutional lawyer Rudolf Smend first put the idea of an integrative function of the constitution forward in 1928 with respect to the Weimar Constitution of Germany.[8] Smend argued against a purely liberal understanding of the constitution as a system of limitations and demarcations of state competences. He maintained that the Weimar Constitution, rather, embodied the national spirit of the German people and its will to live together and to form a political community, frequently labeled as a "community of fate." However, this claim was by no means a descriptive account of the function of the Weimar Constitution. On the contrary, it was a kind of normative cry of help and an attempt to mitigate the troubled situation of the Weimar Republic, which was strongly polarized along class divisions, confessional cleavages, and ideological schisms.

It is a matter of debate whether the appeal to the people's national feelings as such is an effective remedy against deep social divisions. But constitutions can contain elements that encourage integrative effects, especially by the invocation of aspirations, values, and basic convictions commonly held by its members and which bind them together. In this case a constitution may serve as a kind of secular catechism. The US constitution played this role at least in the first decades of its existence.[9] Today the most apparent property of constitutions which have been designed with the aim to fulfill an integrative function is their more or less detailed catalogue of state goals and the concomitant guarantee of social and economic rights (such as the rights to education, to health, to shelter, to labor). Many of the new constitutions in the post-communist countries of East and Central Europe exhibit these attributes.[10]

It is not by accident that the issue of the alleged or actual integrative force of constitutions came up in the twentieth century. It was no earlier than in the twentieth century that constitutions embraced the whole of society, which means: the complexity of a modern differentiated and cleaved society. In the early periods of constitutionalism, constitutions presupposed the unity and homogeneity of the polity because the polity consisted basically only of one social class, the taxpayers, i.e., of the members of the bourgeoisie. Women and the inferior classes were excluded and did not count as members of the polity – they were considered unable to enjoy the status of citizenship. Hence, the constitution did not have to cope with the problem of social integration and disintegration. In the nineteenth century, as mentioned, the main constitutional struggles were connected to the claim of the hitherto excluded segments of the population into the polity; the issue was how to draw the lines between those who qualified for citizenship and those who did not. The issue was not yet the capacity of the constitution to sustain a polity in which all nationals have acquired citizenship. This situation was only reached in most European countries after World War I.

Despite the triumphant procession of constitutionalism since the end of the eighteenth century it was not the only pattern of political order. There were two powerful rivals that challenged its legitimacy – socialism and nationalism. The former was based on the theories of Karl Marx and Friedrich Engels who regarded constitutionalism as a subtle means of bourgeois class domination (what was not entirely wrong for the early periods of constitutionalism). They envisioned a world in which the solidarity of the working class would provide the appropriate principles of political order beyond legal institutions and render constitutions superfluous. The latter claimed that the commonness of ethno-national belonging should be the basis of political organization which, too, could dispense with a constitution. As constitutionalism embodies the principle of equal citizenship irrespective of ethnic affiliation, in the view of nationalists it had to be rejected offhand.

Note that each of these two contenders of constitutionalism included an implicit program of social integration of their own: socialism in its Marxist version relied on working class solidarity (during the period of the struggle for the classless society); nationalism claimed the inherent social solidarity based upon ethnic sameness and homogeneity of all members of the society. Both ideological strands were incompatible with the universalist axioms of constitutionalism: a political system in which the collective goals of a classless society or, respectively, of ethno-national homogeneity are the highest values cannot respect a polity which is governed according to the rule of law and the recognition of each individual's dignity and freedom.

After World War I, when the entirety of the society became politically organized by constitutions, constitutionalism came under pressure from powerful and militant social movements identified with the communist and nationalist-fascist ideology respectively. Obviously most of the European constitutional states could not withstand these pressures in the inter-war period and fell prey to some kind of authoritarian or totalitarian regime. Their constitutions were simply not up to the dynamics of social conflicts propelled by those movements. The collapse of the Weimar Constitution in Germany mentioned above and the rise to power of Nazism has proved the most dramatic and momentous result of this development. Must we assume that constitutions are only appropriate institutional devices for societies which are largely consolidated?

III

There is a long and venerable history of political reasoning which claims that economic development is an important, perhaps even indispensable precondition for the sustainability of democracy. "Democracy" in this context means "constitutional democracy," i.e., a system of popular rule embedded in a constitutional framework.

In 1959 Seymour Martin Lipset published his seminal article in which this paradigm was elaborated for the first time. According to a statistical survey of the countries of that time he concluded that "the factors of industrialization, urbanization, wealth, and education, are so closely interrelated as to form one common factor. And the factors subsumed under economic development carry with it the political correlate of democracy."[11] As Lipset explicitly admitted exception to this correlation, his theory is still today widely accepted. Needless to say, modifications are necessary which, however, do not concern me here. But there is one recent analysis of particular interest for our topic of the integrative function of constitutions. Its subject is a comparison of the capacity of the democratic systems of the US, Canada, and India to cope with deep social divisions.[12] This comparison is relevant for our topic because its author selected these three countries not because they were particularly significant or typical of the division between poor and rich, but because they are marked by divisions which are "formed by birth and are, for the most part and for most persons, inerasable: race, ethnicity, religion, and native language."[13] In the US, it is "the racial divide that has been so central to its history; Canada by the founding division between Francophone and Anglophone; and India by grave divisions in caste, religion, and language."[14] Obviously India is of special interest because this country, in addition, its immense economic progress in the last decade notwithstanding is still "a poor country, and yet it is a well-established democracy."[15]

In fact, when we speak of a country's divisions we must distinguish between the socio-economic rift between poor and rich and the one which pertains to issues of identity, which Glazer calls inerasable and which I call identity conflicts. Conflicts arising from those deep divides tend to be particularly intense and uncompromising. While pursuant to a well-known liberal line of argument in the social sciences, conflicts have a positive effect upon the social coherence of societies, this can hardly be said with respect to identity conflicts.[16] The American political economist Albert O. Hirschman offers an important distinction. In his view not all conflicts further coherence in all kinds of societies; rather, he claims, social conflicts have only positive effects in democratic market societies, and even this may be true only for a certain genre of conflicts.

> Many conflicts of market society are over the distribution of the social product among different classes, sectors, or regions. Highly varied though they are, they tend to be divisible; they are conflicts over getting more or less, in contrast to conflicts of the either-or, indivisible category that are characteristic of societies split along rival ethnic, linguistic, or religious lines.[17]

These conflicts, which Hirschman labels as categorical and which I call absolute, are disputes about the moral, legal, and political status of members of ethnic minorities or religious communities, about philosophical truths or political ideologies. By contrast, conflicts about the appropriate policies for the whole polity, including distributional conflicts, are relative conflicts characteristic of pluralist societies.

Thus, we should distinguish conflicts about how a country should be governed from disputes about who belongs to the polity and who is qualified and entitled to rule over the people. Conflicts about the former question are usually settled within the framework of liberal constitutionalism. They are disputes about the direction of political action, about the right options among alternative policies, or about what justice requires in a given situation – they are largely conflicts about the right pattern of distribution both of fundamental rights and liberties and of economic and social benefits (in the Rawlsian sense).[18] The basic institution is equal citizenship: all individuals are integrated into a polity irrespective of their sex, birth, language, ethnic and social origin, faith, religion, or political opinion, let alone socio-economic status. Obviously the concept of equal (national) citizenship is blind, if not hostile towards any claim to the recognition of a distinct identity of individuals in the public sphere. This is due to its strong commitment to the universalist principle that each individual has an equal value (dignity) as a human being and merits equal respect irrespective of his or her particular attributes. Moreover, since the inerasable properties of individuals which form their identity have most of the time in many countries been the reason for severe forms of discrimination, liberal constitutionalism is particularly suspicious of any kind of recognition of identity as a constituent element of the polity.

Indeed, were the constitutional state prepared to recognize the identity of individuals or of groups as a relevant parameter of the cohesion of the polity, it might open Pandora's box. While obviously it would have to make the demand upon its citizens to recognize each other as equally constituent parts of the polity, the official acknowledgment of the significance of their differences may impede rather than facilitate these demanded acts of civic recognition. What follows from the incidence of, say, a deeply rooted antipathy, disdain, and distrust of major segments of the population against certain minorities whom they deny the quality to belong to the polity? A society in which major conflicts exist about the morally justified belonging of certain classes of individuals to the political community as equal citizens and about the question of who is morally entitled to rule is a fragmented or deeply divided society. On this view the US society in which the moral right of the Afro-American part of the population to rule the country has long being called into question was a fragmented society for a long period of time, perhaps up until our days. In many East and Central European states ethnic and national conflicts dominated the political discourse since their very foundation at the beginning of the twentieth century and have remained the main causal factor of their contemporary divisions. In Western Europe, where the ideal of equal national citizenship prevailed and where during the twentieth century the confessional conflicts subsided in the wake of developing secularization, the pluralist mode of political integration prevailed after World War II and became an integral element of their stability and socio-economic success. However, there are now signs for their fragmentation as well.

Ideally, the entirety of the citizens of a polity constitute the nation – the nation is the community of citizens[19]; this is an equivalent term for the nation-state (*état-nation*). Membership in the civic nation (or in the nation-state) – which is tantamount to being a citizen – is the source of a sense of pride and self-esteem; it is the symbol of successful integration into the polity. Citizenship is a status implying recognition and esteem because the owner of this status participates actively in the rule of the polity, in contrast to individuals who are mere passive subjects. The source of a citizen's self-esteem is not his or her personal, prepolitical quality – in other words: his or her identity – but the fact that he or she has left the subaltern status of passive subjecthood and has entered into the role of somebody who rules his and her equals and is ruled by his and her equals.[20] Citizenship means to share a valuable experience with one's fellows. Thus, the ideal concept of citizenship as it was revived in the French Revolution amounted to the paradox that being one's equal is a status of distinction. Conversely, all particularities which constitute an individual's identity – race, ethnicity, origin, native language, membership in extra-political communities like religious communities and the like – are banned from the public sphere because their representation would undermine the coherence and the unity of the political body.

Consequently, when the politics of integration into the civic nation (or nation-state) is under study people do not normally refer to the question of how to include members of ethnic groups, religious dissenters, or national minorities in the polity. In this concept of nation these identity-defined categories simply do not exist; the refusal of the French Republic to ratify the "European Charter for Regional or Minority Languages," sponsored and promoted by the European Council and adopted by some twenty European states in 1992, is an obvious example for the inherent incompatibility of the identity-blind civic nation and the claim of individuals or groups that their particular identity be recognized as constituent elements of the polity.

IV

Today, however, cleavages resulting from cultural and ethnic differences have acquired a new relevance. There are several reasons for that. Let me just mention one which is of special relevance for the relations between the United States and

Germany. I mean the fact of mass immigration into many of the OECD – and the EU – countries. It has sharpened the sense of ethnic differences and strained the feelings of solidarity in many of the host countries. The members of immigrant communities tend to emphasize their identity as members of their ethnic or religious community for the reason that the host state denies them a status of recognition as equals. Conversely, the citizens of the host state frequently sense the alienage of the immigrants, their different habits, and cultural imprint as a threat to their traditional way of life and have a propensity to conceive of their polity as of a culturally homogeneous and exclusive community. But even if a country – e.g., traditional immigration countries like the US, Canada, or Australia – grant immigrants the status of equal national citizenship in a quite straightforward manner this does not necessarily keep many of them from defining themselves primarily through their ethnic belonging. Even more and more indigenous citizens of the host society identify more with a particular community whose members share certain characteristics – e.g., gender, sexual orientation, age, physical handicaps, origin in a particular region and the like – than with the seemingly abstract nation-state. For many equal citizenship has lost its distinctive quality because the price of this status has been the polity's indifference, even hostility towards his or her particular attributes, which the individual regards as identity-engendering. In the view of these citizens the status of equal citizenship has become a symbol of the polity's disrespect for their individuality. For them this is all the more obnoxious since membership in extra-political communities – religious, political, ethnic, or social – frequently gives the individual the motives and the power to make use of his or her civic rights. Thus, the quest for recognition of one's particularity, i.e., of one's otherness, has become one of the most important challenges to the traditional constitutional state and its essential premise of equal citizenship.

Obviously this is a challenge to the difference-blindness of civic institutions. According to this principle each individual has the *right to equal treatment*; but the fulfillment of this right may not satisfy, or even violate another right of the individual, namely the *right to treatment as an equal*.[21] This latter right does not aim at "the same distribution of some burden and benefit," e.g., obligations and rights, but at the right "to be treated with the same respect and concern as anyone else."[22] This points to the identity-shaping characteristics of the individual. If these characteristics are group-specific like ethnicity, race, or religion, the recognition of the respective group as an equally constituent part of the polity is an appropriate means to fulfill their members' right to be treated as equals.

This, then, suggests a modification of the traditional structure of modern constitutions and its principle of equal citizenship in the spirit of recognition of group identities. Kymlicka and Norman rightly state that,

> while difference-blind institutions purport to be neutral amongst different ethnocultural groups, they are in fact implicitly tilted towards the needs, interests, and identities of the majority group; and this creates a range of burdens, barriers, stigmatizations, and exclusions for members of minority groups.[23]

Of course, there are very diverse groups in the various countries of the world, and there is no ready-made constitutional pattern for all.[24] But first and foremost the politicians and constitutional theorists of contemporary constitutional states have to take into consideration the fact that only very few countries do *not* have major minorities as a relevant part of the polity. Almost four decades ago Walker Connor counted that of the total of then 132 only 12 (9.1 percent) could be described as essentially homogeneous from an ethnic viewpoint.[25] Even today, after the disintegration of the Soviet Union and of Yugoslavia and the increase of the number of states to almost two hundred this portion has hardly raised since the new states, which arose from the disintegration of the aforementioned multinational states, were by no means ethnically homogeneous.

If ethnic, cultural, and religious diversity has become a trait of contemporary states, the integration of minorities has become an inescapable objective of constitutions. After all, constitutions are supposed to embody the basic legal order of a polity, which requires the inclusion of all portions of the population as its constituent elements. Obviously the partition of a country or the secession of a minority are not options in the search for an appropriate constitutional design for a polity, and the same applies both to forced mass-population transfers and to forced assimilation.[26] From the viewpoint of constitutionalism and its inherent axiom of treating all human beings as equals only methods of managing, not suppressing diversity can come into consideration. To give a few examples which merit reflection:[27]

- federalizing a country to the effect that territorially concentrated minorities enjoy a certain degree of self-determination within a territorial subunit of the state;
- granting autonomy to territorially dispersed minorities in certain domains of special interest like family law or religious traditions;
- special representation of groups or their members within government or other public/semipublic institutions (e.g., mass media, school boards);
- granting exceptions from the general laws of the land for members of minorities (like, e.g., the dispensation from the obligation to wear helmets of Sikh motorcyclists in Canada, or the exemption from the prohibition of ritual slaughter for Islamic butchers in mainly Christian countries); and
- facilitating the access to the labor market for members of disadvantaged minorities.

This is not to say that the realization of these options is a guarantee of a decrease of tensions and conflicts resulting from ethnic, cultural, or religious diversity. It may well be that largely symbolic gestures of recognition of minority groups as constituent parts of a diverse polity (like, e.g., bi- or trilingual names for villages and cities of a region with considerable minorities) have a more integrative effect than for instance policies of affirmative action mentioned in the last bullet point.

In sum, the traditional constitutional pattern of the nation as the community of equal citizens has to be advanced towards a doctrine providing institutional devices for polities that more and more metamorphose into ethnically and culturally divided communities. As the example of India, the largest and most diverse constitutional democracy of the world shows,[28] cultural, religious, or ethnic diversity as such is not inherently incompatible with the idea of constitutionalism – the foundation of the polity upon the principle of equal respect and concern for all members of the society. Thus, despite new kinds of conflicts at the beginning of the twenty-first century there is no reason for defeatism. However, the viability of constitutionalism cannot be taken for granted. It requires an understanding of the political as a sphere of human life in which the libidinal and aggressive energies of human nature are domesticated and civilized through institutions which operate according to the principle of equal respect for all members of the community. While it is sometimes next to impossible that members of diverse groups which are deeply at enmity with each other are able to develop the moral capacity to recognize each other as equals it seems easier to convince them that the integrity of institutions may neutralize their mutual hatred and afford them the opportunity to find common ground in the recognition of genuinely neutral institutions.

V

Admittedly, we can hardly imagine cases where the question of whether an institution and its decision are neutral will not be contested. But this fact does not undermine the viability of constitutionalism in deeply divided societies. An indispensable element of constitutions are constitutional principles (as distinct from constitutional rules): vaguely specified legal standards of constitutional rank which, first, differ qualitatively from rules because their application requires balancing (as distinct from subsumption), and, second, differ from collective goals or policies because they follow a logic of appropriateness, which means: the criteria of what is right and proper for the self-esteem of the political We of the polity, rather than the calculus of anticipated consequences.[29] A striking case of the political significance of constitutional principles is the process of constitution-making in South Africa in the years between 1990 and 1996. For Arato, this process was a paradigm of what he called a postsovereign mode of constitution-making in that "the constituent power is not embodied in a single organ or instance with the plenitude of power," and that "all organic participating in constitutional politics are brought under legal rules."[30] As a matter of fact, in South Africa the process of constitution-making was not guided by rules in the strict sense of the concept, but by principles. This distinction played a significant role in the peaceful management of the transition from the apartheid regime to constitutional democracy.

Obviously South Africa was a deeply divided country even after the abolition of the apartheid system. When in February 1990 the then government of the Republic of South Africa announced its willingness to engage in negotiations with the liberation movements very soon the issue of a new constitution for the country came up. Both sides agreed that a constitution could not simply be negotiated but had to be created by an elected body mandated to do so. But they could not be certain that the final outcome of the deliberations of the elected constituent assembly would properly reflect the ideas of the negotiators and take into account the anxieties and expectations of the constituencies represented in the negotiations.[31] The South African Constitutional Court summed up the solution to this problem as follows:

> Instead of an outright transmission of power from the old order to the new, there would be a programmed two-stage transition. An interim government established and functioning under an interim constitution agreed to by the negotiating parties, would govern the country on a coalition basis while a final constitution was being drafted. A national legislature, elected (directly and indirectly) by universal adult suffrage, would double as the constitution-making body and would draft the new constitution within a given time. But – and herein lies the key to the resolution of the deadlock – that text would have to comply with certain guidelines agreed upon in advance by the negotiating parties. What is more, an independent arbiter would have to ascertain and declare whether the new constitution indeed complied with the guidelines before it could come into force.

The guidelines were attached to the negotiated Interim Constitution, which referred to them in its preamble as "a solemn pact recorded as Constitutional Principles." The list of those Principles included thirty-four items, ranging from a common South African citizenship, a "democratic system of government committed to achieving equality between men and women and people of all races" (No. 1) through the recognition of "all universally accepted fundamental rights, freedoms and civil liberties, which shall be provided for and protected by entrenched and justiciable provisions in the Constitution" (No. 2), the "separation of powers between the legislature, executive and judiciary, with appropriate checks and balances to ensure accountability, responsiveness and openness" (No. 6) to "representative government embracing multi-party democracy, regular elections, universal adult suffrage, a common voters' roll, and, in general, proportional representation" (No. 8) and the "determination of criteria shall be applied in the allocation of powers to the national government and the provincial governments" (No. 21).

As we know, the South African Constitutional Court served as this independent arbiter and performed the certification task in two proceedings.[32] The pre-formation of a constitution by a list of constitutional principles is a rather unique method of constitution-making. Certainly it is due to the particular situation of a profound political transformation in which new actors entered the political arena. After the collapse of the Soviet Union this happened in most East and Central European countries as well, and in most of them also Round Table talks and negotiations were conducted.[33] However, none of them chose the two-stage- and two-level method of South Africa, which, by standards of traditional constitutional theory, is a paradox. The political elites of South Africa acknowledged and stuck to the idea of a constituent power of the nation, which means the recognition of a constituent assembly as the supreme and sovereign source of political authority. At the same time they established an institutional device subjecting the constituent assembly to a monitoring procedure, thus seemingly denying its supremacy and sovereignty.

Actually, this was not the case. What happened was the setting up of a common ground of the various antagonistic political forces, which was broad enough as to allow all, or at least the politically most significant ones, to feel represented in the determinations of the thirty-four Constitutional Principles. Each of them is, of course, open to very divergent interpretations, depending not only on the situations where they apply, but also on the values, visions, and interests of the involved political forces and institutional actors. Think, for instance, of the principle of "universally accepted fundamental rights, freedoms and civil liberties" (No. 2) or of the principle that minority political parties can participate in the legislative process in a manner consistent with democracy (No. 14). It is the particularity of principles that their invocation and application requires interpretation, i.e., a mindset of discourse, not of violence.

So two qualities of principles rendered the South African experience possible: first, due to their semantic wideness and vagueness they encouraged the involvement and commitment of very diverse political forces to participate in the process of transforming the country into a polity based on equal national citizenship; second, by agreeing on principles even the most antagonistic forces were lured into a situation where their disagreement and conflict was transformed into a discursive process about the appropriate interpretation of the principles and their translation into the constitution. In other words, the prior agreement on principles for the constitution created a situation where the realization of the potentiality of a civil war could be avoided – and, to repeat that, only the vague character of principles made that prior agreement possible. So at least in the case of South Africa it is justified to speak of the integrative function of constitutional principles.[34]

As I said, the South African constitution-making process and the role of principles in that process are quite unique. After all, one is tempted to say that in this case principles were sort of super-constitutional. They did not embody the constitution proper simply because principles do not reach the degree of specificity and certainty which is a defining element of a legal text. Still, many constitutional texts contain principles, especially those aspiring to further a sense of common belonging and political identity among citizens that cannot presuppose it offhand. It is certainly not by accident that principles play a prominent role in constitutions of countries having to cope with the problems of the transition from authoritarian to democratic rule. An incomplete list of cases includes the French constitution of 1946, the Italian constitution of 1946, the German Basic Law of 1949, the Hungarian constitution (in its amended post-communist version of 1989), the Bulgarian constitution of 1991, and the Polish constitution of 1997. Constitutional principles embody the undisputed or least disputed values and objectives of a polity – a fact that has two paradoxical implications. First, in order to be undisputed, principles must be vague and open to very diverse, even opposite interpretations. Second, by that very openness to interpretation they open the door for dispute and political struggle. But, and this is the cunning of reason inherent in the concept of constitutional principles, these struggles are conducted in the field of constitutional interpretation. Constitutional principles are standing invitations to the actors in the polity to get involved in the process of their concretization. They guide the political antagonists away from the brink of civil war, and transform politics by luring the involved parties into a mode of institutionalized, discursive and, consequently, civilized conflict management.

This is not to say that constitutionalism is a panacea for each and every deeply divided society. Constitution-making cannot replace politics and diplomacy. But it creates an incentive to all political actors to explain their claims and to solicit support by way of argumentation. It has the potential to trigger political dynamics which may profoundly change the character of deep political conflicts. This is no promise, just a modest hope – but sometimes conflicts are so hopelessly bogged down that even a modest hope can encourage people to seek a political compromise rather than killing each other. Perhaps this is the most significant implication of "postsovereign constitutionalism."

Notes

1 See, e.g., Arato, Andrew (2000) *Civil Society, Constitution, and Legitimacy*. Lanham; Boulder; New York; Oxford, Rowman & Littlefield Publishers, Inc.; idem (2004) "Interim Imposition." *Ethics & International Affairs* 18(3): 25–50; idem (2009) *Constitution Making Under Occupation: The Politics of Imposed Revolution in Iraq*. New York, Columbia University Press; idem (2010) "The Constitutional Reform Proposal of the Turkish Government: The Return of Majority Imposition." *Constellations* 17(2): 345–350.

2 Friedrich, Carl J. (1974) *Limited Government: A Comparison*. Englewood Cliffs, NJ, Prentice-Hall.

3 Bendix, Reinhard (1996) *Nation-building and Citizenship: Studies of our Changing Social Order*. New Brunswick, NJ, Transaction Publishers.

4 Offe, Claus (1983) "Competitive Party Democracy and the Keynesian Welfare State: Factors of Stability and Disorganization." *Policy Sciences* 15(3): 225–246.

5 Marshall, T. H. (1964) *Class, Citizenship, and Social Development*. Garden City, NY, Doubleday.

6 Cf. Hamilton, Alexander, James Madison, and John Jay (1961 [1788]) *The Federalist Papers* (ed. Clinton Rossiter). New York and Scarborough, The New American Library.

7 Holmes, Stephen (1988) "Precommitment and the Paradox of Democracy." In: J. Elster and R. Slagstad, eds. *Constitutionalism and Democracy*. Cambridge, Cambridge University Press, pp. 195–240.

8 Smend, Rudolf (1928) *Verfassung und Verfassungsrecht*. München und Leipzig, Verlag von Duncker & Humblot.

9 Cf. Preuss, Ulrich K. (1995) *Constitutional Revolution: The Link Between Constitutionalism and Progress*. Atlantic Highlands, NJ, Humanities Press, pp. 25 et seq.

10 Elster, Jon, Claus Offe, and Ulrich K. Preuss (1998) *Institutional Design in Post-communist Societies: Rebuilding the Ship at Sea*. Cambridge, Cambridge University Press.

11 Lipset, Seymour Martin (1959) "Some Social Requisites of Democracy: Economic Development and Political Legitimacy." *The American Political Science Review* 53(1): 69–105 [80].
12 Glazer, Nathan (2010) "Democracy and Deep Divides." *Journal of Democracy* 21(2): 5–19.
13 Ibid, p. 5.
14 Ibid., p. 8.
15 Ibid.
16 See the overview of the literature in Albert O. Hirschman, "Social Conflicts as Pillars of Democratic Market Societies" in idem (1995) *A Propensity to Self-Subversion*. Cambridge, MA; London, Harvard University Press, pp. 231–248 [236ff.].
17 Ibid., p. 244.
18 Rawls, John (1978) *A Theory of Justice*. Cambridge, The Belknap Press of Harvard University Press, pp. 195 et seq.
19 Schnapper, Dominique (1994) *La communauté des citoyens. Sur l'idée moderne de nation*. Paris, Gallimard.
20 Pocock, J. G. A. (1995) "The Ideal of Citizenship Since Classical Times." In: Ronald Beiner, ed. *Theorizing Citizenship*. Albany, State University of New York Press: S. 29–52.
21 This distinction was introduced by Dworkin, Ronald (1978) *Taking Rights Seriously*. Cambridge, Harvard University Press, p. 227.
22 Ibid.
23 Kymlicka, Will and W. J. Norman, eds. (2000) *Citizenship in Diverse Societies*. Oxford; New York, Oxford University Press, p. 3.
24 See the typology of groups in ibid., pp. 18 et seq.
25 Connor, Walker (1972) "Nation-building or Nation-destroying?" *World Politics: A Quarterly Journal of International Relations* 24(3): 319–355 [320].
26 Cf. Kymlicka/Norman, *Citizenship in Diverse Societies*, p. 12.
27 See also ibid., pp. 24 et seq.
28 See the account of Glazer, "Democracy and Deep Divides" (Note 12), pp. 14; see also Lerner, H. (2011) *Making Constitutions in Deeply Divided Societies*. Cambridge, Cambridge University Press, p. 109 et seq.
29 See the debate about the structure of constitutional principles in Dworkin, *Taking Rights Seriously* (Note 21), pp. 22 et seq.; Alexy, R. (2000) "On the Structure of Legal Principles." *Ratio Juris* (3): 294–304; Schauer, Frederick (2010) "Balancing, Subsumption, and the Constraining Role of Legal Text." *Law & Ethics of Human Rights* 4(1): 34–45; see also the overview of Ulrich K. Preuss, "Philosophical Perspectives on Principles in Constitutional Law." Paper presented at the VIIIth World Congress of the International Association of Constitutional Law, 5–10 December 2010 in Mexico City.
30 Arato, *Constitution Making Under Occupation* (Note 1), pp. vii, 63 et seq.
31 See Constitutional Court of South Africa, Case CCT 23/96 (Certification of the Constitution, 6 September 1996), para 12.
32 Case CCT 23/96 (1st proceeding) and Case CCT 37/96 (2nd proceeding, 4 December 1996).
33 Cf. Elster, Jon (1996) *The Roundtable Talks and the Breakdown of Communism*. Chicago, University of Chicago Press.
34 A similar conclusion is drawn by Jakab, András (2010) "Re-Defining Principles as 'Important Rules.' A Critique of Robert Alexy." In: *On the Nature of Legal Principles. ARSP-Beiheft* 119. Baden-Baden, Franz Steiner Verlag – Nomos, 145–159 [159], p. 159.

3 The concept of "self-binding" in constitutional theory

Hubertus Buchstein[1]

> Das ist der edelste Vorzug des Edeln, dass er sich selbst bindet. Ketten sind für das rohe Geschlecht, das sich selbst nicht zu fesseln weiß.
>
> Johann Wolfgang von Goethe[2]

Introduction

Andrew Arato's impressive academic work of the last four decades can be read from different perspectives. One perspective points to his move from an early scholar of Georg Lukács and the traditional Frankfurt School to a defender of modern liberal capitalist democracy. Another way of reconstructing his intellectual journey follows its main topics – from his early interest in questions of class conflicts in Western societies and oppositional movements in Central and Eastern Europe to the topics of civil society and finally to democratic theory, constitutionalism and institutions. Yet another way of understanding his work focuses on his active political interventions and his reform proposals. In this article, however, I will take a different perspective on Andrew Arato's academic work: I will use the analytical and historical richness of his reflections as a source for a critical investigation of one of the main justifications for constitutionalism in modern democratic theory.

This justification borrows heavily on the metaphor of "self-binding." The idea of transferring the concept of "self-binding," binding oneself or precommitment – the three terms are mostly used synonymously – into the context of constitutional theory dates back to the eighteenth century. According to its basic argument, political constitutions in modern democracies should be understood as a form of collective self-paternalism. A classical formulation can be found in a statement by John Potter Stockton in a debate about the Ku Klux Klan Act of 1871: "Constitutions are chains with which men bind themselves in their sane moments that they may not die by a suicidal hand on the day of their frenzy."[3]

When we briefly look back into the history of political ideas, the first explicit mention of this idea in connection with a constitution can be found in Spinoza's *Tractatus Politicus*, where he already uses *Ulysses* as an illustration (Spinoza 1677: 106–109). However, his idea has always been controversial. In the eighteenth century Rousseau already rejected it as a logical impossibility, but it was up to David Hume to do so explicitly. Hume had argued in his political writings for institutional mechanisms of coercion "by which I may impose a restraint upon myself, and guard against this weakness" (Hume 1739: 382). Rousseau, on the other hand, argued that "it is consequently against the nature of the body politic for the Sovereign to impose on itself a law which it cannot infringe" (Rousseau 1762: 25).

Concerning the reception of the concept of self-binding in our days, the renaissance of the idea began in the field of moral philosophy on the topic of the phenomenon of *akrasia* (weakness of will), and how to overcome it.[4] A second strand of this renaissance took place in the field of decision theory. It was in particular Thomas C. Schelling who coined the term "egonomics" in order to deal with the limitations of making rational choices (see Schelling 1978, 1984; Beckmann 2007). A third strand can be seen in the work of neoclassic economic theorists such as Friedrich August Hayek, who pointed out the economic efficiency of a society governed by constitutional rules. Hayek also is the author who famously cited the saying that a constitution is a tie imposed by Andrew when sober on Andrew when drunk (Hayek 1960: 176–192).

The most influential transfer of the concept of "self-binding" to modern constitutional thought, however, must be attributed Jon Elster and his writings about the limits of rationality. After Elster's "rediscovery," the formula became prominent among a number of constitutional theorists in the 1980s and 1990s in their search for new or additional normative justifications for constitutional democracy during the political transformations in Eastern and Central Europe. More recently, the concept of self-binding has become a favorite way for neo-liberal economists to justify their proposals for more rigidity in monetary policy.[5]

As far as I am familiar with Andrew Arato's extensive academic work, he has always avoided the language of "self-binding" in connection with constitutional theory.[6] Some of his colleagues (and close friends), however, have been less reluctant. When we look back at the debates in the field of constitutional theory from the perspective of today, two main lines of argument can be identified in this theoretical field. The first one is a liberal model of constitutional self-binding which can be found in the work of Stephen Holmes. In the liberal interpretation, self-binding has the function of a guarantor of political neutrality. The second line of argument can be coined the "critical" or "deliberative" model of constitutional self-binding and can be found in the work by Claus Offe, Ulrich K. Preuss or Cass Sunstein. Today, the intense discussion about the adequacy of the self-binding formula for constitutional theory has died out. But the term – used in a metaphorical or even literal meaning – is alive today more than ever. It can be found in statements of leading constitutional judges as well as in the recent literature in constitutional law and theory.[7]

In the following, I would like to begin with a brief reminder of Elster's rediscovery of the concept of "self-binding" for modern political theory (1). In the next section I discuss the liberal and the deliberative models of self-binding in constitutional theory with the help of four analytical distinctions (2). In the third section some of Andrew Arato's critical observations and analyses in the field of constitutional theory will be used as a source and starting point for some objections to both the liberal and deliberative models of self-binding in constitutional theory (3). If one really wants to keep the concept of self-binding as a strong legitimizing formula for modern constitutional democracy, one has to be able to refute not just one or two, but all the objections listed above. My own view is negative: the concept of self-binding leads to a theoretical impasse in modern constitutional theory (4).

1 Sailing with Ulysses to safe constitutional ground: Jon Elster

Jon Elster's theory of self-binding was presented in a famous part of his book *Ulysses and the Sirens* (1979), where he undertakes a rational analysis of Ulysses' strategy for dealing with his desire to listen to the sound of the sirens. Since then, Elster has referred to this topic repeatedly.[8] According to the story of Homer in *The Odyssey*, Ulysses told his comrades to bind him to a mast and to put wax in their ears, which allowed him to listen to the sirens' wonderful singing without giving in to their temptations. Whereas Theodor W. Adorno and Max Horkheimer interpreted this episode of Homer in their *Dialectic of Enlightenment* as the birth of modern instrumental rationality, Elster uses it as an early illustration for intelligent self-management techniques. Elster defines self-binding in the following way: "to bind oneself is to carry out a certain decision at time t_1 in order to increase the probability that one will carry out another decision at time t_2" (Elster 1979: 39).

According to Elster's early writings on the topic, self-binding is the "main technique for achieving rationality by indirect ways" (37)[9] because it is the installation of a "causal mechanism being set up in the external world" (ibid.) at time t_1 which restricts one's own actions at time t_2. By employing such a strategy we delegate our will to an external structure for a period of time, thereby establishing a causal process that "after some time returns to its source and modifies our behavior" (43).

In certain situations, self-binding may even emerge as "acting upon one's preferences" (77). It places the actor in a position to "take an active or strategic attitude towards his own preferences" (ibid.). Self-binding is a mechanism of intentional self-control. The best-known and intuitively plausible example of such a process is that of smokers who inform all their friends of their decision to stop smoking so that they can utilize their jibes to apply additional pressure to their later behavior in the event that they contravene their own decision. Or to use another example: Take Andrew Arato's strategy of parking his car in the limited parking zone in front of the old New School GF Building on Fifth Avenue in order to force himself to leave the building in time – a real challenge for him.

If we disregard the general question of whether describing certain behavioral phenomena as the expression of "lack of willpower" might not be an error in philosophical categories,[10] strategies of self-binding appear to be theoretically unproblematic as long as only a single actor is involved (for example, if I place my alarm clock so far from my bed that after waking up in the morning I must get out of bed to turn it off). Things are different if additional people are involved.[11] The questions Elster discusses in this context are about the authenticity of preferences. Under what conditions should a person I ask free me from the mast again (105)? How should that person know whether the meta-rule or the request uttered later to take back the meta-rule articulates my preferences authentically (44)? Perhaps I have undergone a learning process and would genuinely prefer to revise my original request? The same holds the other way around for me as well, as the person who set the mechanism of self-binding in motion: "How can I know that my bright line is not constantly displacing itself 'behind my back' so as to justify, *ex post facto*, any exception to the rule?" (110) How in the world can I differentiate adaptive preferences (sour grapes) from real learning processes? So in some cases it even "may be reasonable to precommit yourself against precommitments" (89).

In spite of these misgivings, Elster presents a list of various cases in which he considers the transfer of self-binding to collective actors as a promising option. Some examples: the establishment of an independent central bank in order to "remove monetary policy from the political sphere" (61, 90); the autonomy of various countries' foreign ministries; the model of BBC radio; finally, the holding of periodic elections as "the electorate's method of binding itself and of protecting itself against its own impulsiveness" (91).

The most intriguing case, however, is the constitution. According to Elster, despotism and radical democracy are both distinguished by the fact that they lay claim to the right to intervene in all political matters at any time. By contrast, constitutional democracy is founded on a number of stable institutions which can no longer be disposed of once they have been established (93). The role of the constituent assembly is, of course, singular in this regard. It is the constitutional convention which "lays down the ground rules to be followed by all later generations" (ibid.). In this regard, "only the constituent assembly really is a political actor, in the strong sense of *la politique politisante*; all later generations are restricted to *la politique politisée*, or the day-to-day enactment of the ground rules" (94). According to Elster, the "nation," too, can bind itself through the constituent assembly "by entrusting certain powers of decision to the judiciary branch" (ibid.). Following Elster, this leads to the "paradox of democracy" (ibid.): each generation wants to be free to bind its successors, while not being bound by its predecessors (ibid.).

Elster's academic interests in constitutionalism led him in the same direction as Andrew Arato. Both began to analyze the processes of constitution-making and constitutional change in Central and Eastern Europe after 1990. In his more recent writings, the "democratic paradox" has led Elster to the conclusion that constitutional orders have to be seen most of all as fragile. In the end, there is nothing that can hinder a political community from getting rid of a constitution, even if the text claims eternity for some of its principles (as in the German case). In a society, Elster admits, "there is nothing external" and thus "societies cannot make themselves unable to renege on their precommitment" (Elster 2003: 1760).

In the following, I neither wish to discuss Elster's work on constitutionalism in Eastern and Central Europe[12] nor do I want to go deeper into the theoretical problems of his underlying theory of rationality.[13] Instead, I would like to follow and discuss the two ways in which the concept of self-binding was adapted among theorists of constitutional democracy in the late 1980s and early 1990s. As I mentioned at the beginning of this article, the term "self-binding" – used both in a metaphorical and in its literal meaning – has become prominent today among leading theorists in constitutional law and theory and deserves a closer critical look.

2 The liberal and the deliberative models of collective self-binding

Elster's notion in his early writings of connecting the concept of "self-binding" on the collective level with the constitution was widely accepted and often quoted among constitutional theorists. In the metaphorical language of Elster's *Ulysses*: They are the rowers on Ulysses' boat who now try to rationalize the distribution of labor on their boat. However, only a few scholars in constitutional theory have developed the concept further and dealt with its theoretical flaws.

Looking back at the heydays of this discussion in the late 1980s and 1990s, one can identify two general variants of reception. The first is the liberal model of constitutional self-binding, which was paradigmatically formulated by Stephen Holmes (2.1). The second line of argument connects the concept of self-binding with the theory of deliberative democracy and can be found in the work of Claus Offe, Ulrich K. Preuss and Cass Sunstein (2.2). In the following, I will compare the two models along four analytical distinctions in order to discuss both the liberal and the deliberative model of self-binding in constitutional theory more systematically (2.3).

2.1 The liberal model: Stephen Holmes

The liberal conception of self-binding is best elucidated in an essay written by Stephen Holmes two decades ago. According to Holmes, self-binding is one of the basic features of Western democracies: "Like 'self-binding' in general, tongue-tying may be one of constitutionalism's main gifts to democracy" (Holmes 1988: 21). It is true both of individuals and groups that they are able "to … gag themselves" (22). The idea of such "strategic self-censorship" (ibid.) corresponds to John Rawls's method of avoidance (Rawls 1992): "like individuals … organizations and collectivities can leave selected topics undiscussed for what they consider their own advantage" (Holmes 1988: 21). Topics whose potential for triggering conflict is too high are to be kept out of the non-controversial sector of political culture. Holmes goes so far as to claim that "the shape of democratic politics is undoubtedly determined by the strategic removal of certain items from the democratic agenda" (24/25).[14] In light of this sense of voluntary self-gagging, Holmes's practice-oriented question is: "Under what cultural and psychological conditions ... can gag rules be adhered to successfully?" (58). These conditions include proving that the mechanisms of self-gagging are legitimate. Holmes attempts to provide this proof of legitimacy using the example of constitutions. Constitutions are not the only mechanisms based on gag rules; other examples include private taboos or keeping secrets. Constitutions, by contrast, are highly formalized. Precisely for this reason, Holmes considers them to be the most important practical case of gag rules in modern political systems. Holmes begins with the normative question: "Why should a constitutional framework ... have such enormous power over our own lives today?" (21). His strategy for answering the question involves rejecting the juxtaposition of democracy and constitution in the first step. He asserts that their relationship to one another must be described as a positive conditional relationship rather than as one of competition: "constitutionalism and democracy are mutually supportive" (197). Medieval "constitutions" such as the Magna Carta were a contract between the king and the Estates; but today, "rather than being presented as an exchange of promises between separate parties, modern constitutions are typically styled as frameworks which 'we the people' give ourselves" (209). Following Madison, Holmes's line of argumentation holds that "bonds are not necessarily a form of bondage; constraints can promote freedom" (215). The American constitution, for example, "was not disabling, but enabling" (215) for democracy. His hypothesis can be summed up as saying that instances of self-binding in the form of guaranteeing institutional mechanisms are necessary to make democracy possible in the first place: "the constitution is an instrument of self-government, a technique whereby the citizenry rules itself" (239). Constitutionalism is "a cluster of techniques for collective self-management" (236). Holmes coins the term "autopaternalism" for this relationship (235). Important for Holmes's liberal thrust is that he uses the concept of autopaternalism to derive the validity of existing constitutional bindings for future generations as well:

> If we can take for granted certain procedures and institutions fixed in the past, we can achieve our present goals more effectively than we could if we were constantly being side-tracked by the recurrent need to establish a basic framework for political life. An inherited constitution can be democracy-enabling as well as democracy-stabilizing. It is not only and not essentially a hedge against arbitrary government. Because it is relatively hard to change, a constitution can disencumber, that is, emancipate the present generation. Thus it cannot plausibly be characterized as an oppressive force, an autocratic attempt by the past to enthrall the future. Precommitment is justified because it does not enslave but rather enfranchises future generations. (216)

According to Holmes, the problem lies not in self-binding per se; in his view, a problem of legitimacy emerges only if the rules of binding themselves contravene liberal ideas in that they lock in substantive provisions for the future which would better be left open.

Holmes's argument is problematic for two reasons. The first objection relates to the normative status of the "gag rules." As in Rawls's method of avoidance, they are supposed to limit the realm of legitimate intervention by the state a priori by guaranteeing differences and divergences in broad areas of political life. In this way, the accusation of paternalism can be avoided from the beginning, that is, when defining the subject of deliberations. The legitimation problem for institutions that protect the method of avoidance lies in the fact that their binding effect can extend only to actors who have already taken on some components of liberal thought.

As Brian Barry aptly puts it, dogmatic individuals are not distinguished by the fact that they champion a dogma, but above all by the fact that they do so dogmatically (see Barry 1990). In other words, even the liberal form of self-binding must insist on a certain position as good (in this case: the value of liberal tolerance) when grappling with opposing fundamentalist positions. The second objection is also fundamental in nature. The strategy of keeping silent about controversial topics makes sense as long as it involves questions in which no subjective rights clash with one another. In principle, however, gagging the state comes up against its limits where two incompatible individual rights oppose each other. Any attempt to depoliticize such a conflict by constitutionally mandated restraint effectively supports one of the two legal positions one-sidedly, and thus tends to have the opposite of a pacifying effect: the attempt, for instance, to solve the dispute about the question of abortion – where one side represents the rights of the woman and the other those of an unborn life – by leaving the decision to the woman mobilizes abortion opponents because they rightly consider the gagged state to be taking sides (see Preuss 1991: 17). Liberal self-binding on the part of the state is categorically overburdened when dealing with controversies having this structure.

2.2 The deliberative model: Claus Offe, Ulrich K. Preuss and Cass Sunstein

Andrew Arato in one of his polemical comments rightly observed that the label "deliberative democracy" today "often simply attempts to dress up a moribund council communism in Habermasian terms" (Arato 1996b). This observation may be true for a number of scholars, but surely not for Claus Offe, Ulrich K. Preuss and Cass Sunstein, who have always been aware of the fragility of complex institutions in modern democracies.

Following Elster, it was first Claus Offe who employed the concept of self-binding in an innovative way in the German-speaking world. Offe first used it in the context of political discussions about the best strategic orientation of Green parties in modern societies. In this context, self-binding became a central issue for Offe after he had redefined the task of leftist politics anew: In his view, a new political project of the Left had taken the place of the global goal known by the name socialism:

> namely the enterprise of guaranteeing minimums instead of realizing maximums, and of curbing and fettering the destructive effects of the technological, military, economic, bureaucratic and ecological dynamics of modernization by means of appropriate procedures and institutions so that principles of responsible self-restraint are brought to bear.
>
> (Offe 1989: 747)

In this context self-binding becomes a formula for reacting to "second-order modernization problems" (see Offe 1986). In Offe's reconstruction of Ulysses' options, to return to Elster's point of departure, Ulysses basically had three options to act: (i) he could react adaptively and even celebrate his unchecked abandon to the sirens as a learning process; (ii) he could try to react in an especially virtuous and moral way in order to resist temptation with all the means of self-discipline; between opportunism and excessive moral demands lies (iii) the "middle ground" (Offe 1989: 749) where he himself sees to it "that the undesired course of action becomes impossible by virtue of external circumstances" (ibid.). In doing so, he intentionally exposes himself to conditions that "accommodate his moral will" (749).

According to Offe, two reciprocal objections can be raised against the last strategy. For one thing, it might be possible that Ulysses had had exaggerated concerns regarding the quality of the sirens' singing and his reactions to it; in this case, he would have unnecessarily subjected himself and his men to the costs of self-binding. Or, and this is the point which had already been made by Elster, the person carrying out the actions has good reasons for dissolving the commitment that had been made – be it that the initial external conditions under which the order was given have changed; be it that a learning process has resulted in different preferences. The person in fetters, however, is not in a position to break free from the self-imposed binding mechanism. To repeat the problem already addressed by Elster: how should the person requested to dissolve the commitment be able to tell whether there are good reasons to do so in the particular case or whether the reasons for which self-binding occurred in the first place apply? Offe concludes from these difficulties that self-binding is obviously "not a problem of maximization, but of optimization" and that accordingly, "self-restraint is in order when it comes to the practice of self-restraint" (750).

But what does this mean in concrete terms? According to Offe, the problem of optimization cannot be solved by clever behavior alone. Instead, it requires "reference to emerging ideas of justice to which no direct path leads from the subjective sphere of the rationality of human action" (ibid.). Again following Elster's line of argument, Offe then introduces a differentiation between "hazardous" (758) and "adequate" (758) kinds of self-binding. The latter are characterized by the fact that "one can justify the actions that follow from them in anticipated retrospect as well," which Offe considers to be the content-related, social and temporal validation of actions and series of actions. Especially the highly differentiated societal systems of modernity are distinguished by an additional need for responsibility; if the political institutions of modernity are not to fail through constantly expecting too much of their citizens' good qualities, they need to be redesigned to ensure increased capability for moral self-binding (760f.). In the end, Offe remains unclear about the exact institutional form of "responsible" self-binding, despite his calls for strengthening of public discourse and democratization of parties and associations, and his argument becomes an appeal:

> The concept of an enlightened will of the people apparently includes the idea that it musters the strength to place itself under an "auto-paternalistic" caveat, thereby forgoing the opportunity to make its voice heard at all times and on all topics in the legislative process.
>
> (Offe 1992: 141)

Ulrich K. Preuss, another German legal theorist in the tradition of the Frankfurt School, distinguished two characteristics in his reception of the concept of self-binding: first, it functions as a building block in a context concerning justification of constitutional rules by means of theory of democracy, and second, it is infected to an even greater extent with moral goals than is Offe's. Concerning the democracy-theoretical aspect, Preuss states that considering self-binding to be the rationale for constitutions is a recent development, because in the long history of the constitutional state "all energies aiming for its establishment and justification [had] focused on the opposites of freedom and power" (Preuss 1990: 77). In the final analysis, Preuss's deliberations mean that the constitution is maneuvered out of the position of being a theoretical opposite of democracy and can be interpreted as being compatible with the concept of the sovereignty of the people, following Holmes's formula of "autopaternalism" (ibid.). Regarding the second aspect, Preuss's hypothesis is that Ulysses' autopaternalism has taken on a new role since the simple paradigm of progress has abdicated its position in light of the manifold risks and destructions of modern societies. The difference is so distinct that by now, its original form can be considered at most as a "precursor of a paradigm of reflexive rationality" (ibid.). Preuss speaks of a precursor "because this concerns a morally undemanding variant of individual self-instrumentalization that does not necessarily include the self-constraint to principled action" (ibid.). According to Preuss, societies are subject to the "coercion to reflect" (78) to an even greater extent than are individuals. In particular in modern experimental thinking in the tradition of the natural sciences, second-order reflexive thinking has not kept up with current developments at the first order level (85). In this context, self-binding means that "power" must be used in order to create and preserve the societal space and its institutions with the goal of "'forcing' experiences with oneself" (87). "Morally reflexive constitutionalism," Preuss's catchy programmatic formula, has a precise idea of what modern constitutions are supposed to achieve: they are to create certain institutional conditions that can "exert benevolent coercion to self-rationalization and 'self-improvement' on society" (73).

For Preuss's variety of self-binding, it is quite significant *to what* the self is to be bound. Not every causal mechanism can create what matters to Preuss. The goal of Preuss's coercion is the possibility of unhindered experience, in other words: learning. Means such as punishment or veto alone are hardly suitable for setting such a learning process in motion. The most suitable means is self-binding of the political process to public discourse. Of course, this goal has little more to do with Ulysses' actual concern, as portrayed by Elster. In the situation t_2, Ulysses wanted to enjoy the song of the sirens with relish, however immoral it might be, without desiring to improve himself in any way, whereas in t_1 he thought only how he could outwit his foreseeable *akrasia*; in other words, his concern was the stability of given preferences. For Preuss, in contrast, what one is to think about above all at the time t_1 is through which means of self-deception existing preferences will have acquired sufficient moral qualifications at the time t_2; in other words, his concern is changing given preferences.

It is apparent that Preuss's approach results in different proposals in practical politics than does the liberal model of neutrality. The consequences in terms of constitutional theory become more distinct when we consider the points where the responsible option of self-binding is linked to the new American discussion of liberalism and constitutionalism. Along with Frank Michelman, Cass Sunstein above all is relevant here.

Sunstein's attack – formulated with recourse to the republican tradition – on the liberal teachings concerning the inviolability of private preferences and on the political model of the aggregation of private interests derived from those teachings jumps in where he can point out that preferences are not always stable, but are subject to endogenous processes of change: "preferences are shifting, and endogenous rather than exogenous, and as a result are a function of current information, consumption patterns, legal rules, and general social pressure" (Sunstein 1991: 11). For Sunstein this means that the task of democracy is not only in satisfying existing preferences "but also, and more fundamentally, in the process of preference formation" (12). Government policy can be necessary to increase the autonomy of preference formation, if not, in some cases, even to bring that autonomy into existence in the first place. Self-binding measures can be derived from this, measures that aim not only at redistributing the chances of autonomous preference formation but in some cases, such as alcohol or cigarettes, extend to a rigid policy of bans.[15] The argument goes: precisely because the law has always not only restricted the actions of actors externally, but has interfered even in the processes of preference formation, democracy can and must take control. If it does not, it delivers itself up defenselessly to the egoistic and moral-free programming of preferences.

As for the mode of self-binding, Sunstein's plea results in an odd constellation. On the one hand, self-binding is supposed to legitimize the "cleansing" of preferences; at the same time, if a society desires to avoid developing totalitarian tendencies, it must respect its citizens' autonomy, thus binding itself inasmuch as it limits itself to exerting influence only if "welfare or autonomy will thereby be promoted" (24). It is a paradoxical task that is related here to the idea of self-binding.

2.3 The two concepts of self-binding in comparison

The modes of self-binding sketched out above can be differentiated according to four aspects:

- *Negative self-binding and positive self-binding.* Negative self-binding aims at refraining from or prohibiting certain actions, positive self-binding at mandating them. An example of positive self-binding is state goals such as the postulate of a welfare state, or environmental protection. An example of negative self-binding is the classical liberal basic rights of freedom of opinion and religion. Positive self-binding is considered a structure for enabling certain actions, negative self-binding as a bulwark against them. For this reason, the two varieties require different styles of politics.
- *Procedural self-binding and substantial self-binding.* Procedural self-binding is distinguished by binding regulations about procedural details as well as the actors who must be involved in decisions. The classic example of the latter is the separation of powers, an example of the former the required number of readings of bills in parliament. Substantial self-binding discriminates in terms of content in such a way that it blocks access to the procedures for certain content (example: the Federal Republic of Germany's "militant democracy"). In doing so, it takes sides on certain ideas about what is good. A constitution can codify the dignity of man or the privileges of an ethnic group; it can proclaim a state religion or quite concrete political goals. The procedural and the substantial aspects differ in their need for legitimacy. Procedural self-binding is legitimate if it possesses a maximum of neutrality, which means that it produces no filter effects at any stage of political processes. The requirements for legitimacy are different in the case of substantial self-binding: it is required to filter out all those positions that contradict the norms laid down at t_1, and in the process, it necessarily conflicts with the requirement that procedural self-binding be neutral. There is no meta-rule for deciding such conflicts; dissenters in terms of substance will always claim their procedural rights, which the mainstream will deny them posthaste. It appears reasonable to assume that decisions will be in favor of substantial goals, especially in critical situations. In the German context, this assumption corresponds with the critical diagnosis that the law has become independent of the democratic process of law-making inasmuch as the constitution, in the manner it is dealt with by the Federal Constitutional Court, is no longer considered to be primarily a system of rules of the game, but has itself become a catalog of various correct contents.
- *Rigid self-binding and flexible self-binding.* Instances of self-binding can have differing degrees of rigidity. As to the rule of law, the constitution cannot claim to be exclusive; rather, modern political systems display three levels of rigidity on a scale ranging from rigid self-binding to flexible self-binding. The first case is the unconditional constitutional provision which is to be valid for eternity. In the case of the Federal Republic of Germany,

Article 79, 3 of the Basic Law defines which constitutional provisions claim such eternal validity; if society desired to change them, this would amount to a revolution and the abolition of the existing constitutional order. If we follow the authors of the German Basic Law, mistrust due to the susceptibility of the democratic sovereign, the German people, to what they considered seduction was an important motive for the postulate of eternal validity. The conflict between constitutionalism and the sovereignty of the people appears in its sharpest form in such rigid cases of self-binding. For the normative status of such eternally valid constitutional provisions, this means that they must be able to refer back to foundations that are as universal as possible, not merely to particularistic motives arising from the prevailing circumstances of the day. The second case, placed roughly in the middle of the scale, concerns legal provisions that can be changed only under considerably more difficult conditions (a qualified majority). The purpose of making such changes difficult is obviously that short-term political majorities should not be placed in a position that would enable them to change fundamental political structures at their convenience. In addition, society employs this difficulty to protect it from itself, as it makes it harder to give in directly to impulsive changes of preferences straight away. Nonetheless, it remains open to longer-term changes of preferences. The form of self-binding that is easiest to handle in terms of its flexibility is the simple law or administrative regulation which can be adapted to altered circumstances with little effort within the framework of the two restrictions mentioned first, and which therefore displays the lowest degree of self-binding. Its lower degree of convincing normative foundation correlates with its lower degree of self-binding.

- *Self-binding of action and self-binding of deliberation.* Instances of self-binding can also be differentiated according to what they are supposed to bind. In the liberal case, as with Ulysses, it is about self-binding of the future ability to act. The means of costs and coercion (employing mechanisms constructed by institutional designers trained in rational choice theory) are to hinder actors from carrying out certain actions. Forms of self-binding that are designed to influence the interests of the actors themselves go much further. They use input filters rather than liberal output filters. Because actions are, as a rule, first desired – or must have at least entered the realm of being imaginable – before they can be carried out, this approach is particularly effective. For individual actors, a strategy based on thinking would follow the following logic: as it is possible that the consumption of certain pornographic films would modify my sexual preferences so much that I would then desire things which I now desire that I will never desire (example: child pornography), to be on the safe side I will not subject myself to such influences at all. Censorship and bans are conventional methods of stifling "dirty preferences." The difficulty begins with the question which preferences fulfill this incriminating criterion. In the final analysis, the verdict which preferences can be considered dirty and which clean can only be made with recourse to a substantial idea of what is good.

Constitutions are not only institutions of society acting upon itself as well as forms of societal self-organization; they also constitute the forms in which societies perceive themselves. The alternative to liberal self-binding takes up the provision mentioned last. Located between the variants of action- and thought-oriented self-binding, it could be called rationalist self-binding. This is where the positions of Offe and Preuss would be placed, which rely on coercing people and institutions into reflecting. This approach targets the "throughput" of the political process by institutionalizing reflection loops, thereby intervening via deliberations (with oneself or with others) in the process of preference formation itself.

These four differentiations are useful for giving the differences between the liberal and the deliberative concepts of self-binding more distinct contours. We can make the following attributions:

Against the background of these four differentiations it becomes apparent that mutual accusations of paternalism contribute little to bringing light to the controversies. Both concepts offer gateways for using the concept of self-binding paternalistically, which can result in political abuses. In the case of the liberal position, it is its rigidity which draws the criticism of being paternalistic in terms of the law; in the case of the deliberative position, it is the expansion of self-binding to future preferences that provokes accusations such as manipulation and totalitarianism. Each side accusing the other of paternalism is nothing more than an indicator of the actually important question which the concept of self-binding has to answer (and which Elster and Offe mentioned quite clearly): How can good reasons for dissolving self-binding arrangements be differentiated sufficiently clearly from bad reasons, the reasons because of which the arrangements were entered into in the first place, without making additional metaphysical assumptions?

The answer to this question given by the political system of the Federal Republic of Germany may be understood as the installation of a series of loops of self-binding. This means that, although the responsibility of acting as "*Hüter der Verfassung*" ("custodian of the constitution") resides with the Federal Constitutional Court, in conflicts considered to be particularly serious, the possibility of a haphazard result, as can occur in the case of simple majority decisions, is ruled out: a two-thirds majority is required in banning political parties, setting aside basic rights, or impeaching the president or a judge. Putting such a series of controls in place certainly makes sense politically speaking, but it does not provide a conclusive answer to a basic theoretical question: the question

Table 3.1 The liberal and the deliberative concepts of self-binding

Liberal concept	*Deliberative concept*
negative	positive
procedural	substantial
rigid	flexible
action	thinking

whether the formula of self-binding helps to solve basic problems of modern constitutional theory.

3 Problems of the concept of self-binding in modern constitutional theory

How convincing are these variants of the concept of self-binding for a theoretical justification of constitutions in general and of a certain constitution in particular? Although Andrew Arato has not discussed this issue explicitly, some of his analytical and historical reflections on constitutionalism can serve as a helpful source and intriguing starting point for a critical investigation of both the liberal and the deliberative models of collective self-binding. It turns out, however, that the differences between these two models are not worth being discussed too deeply because both models share the same theoretical flaws. These flaws are so serious that I suggest we should give up the notion of self-binding altogether for the context of constitutional theory.

The presentation of my list of objections against the use of self-binding in constitutional theory is inspired by some major and some marginal arguments in Andrew Arato's work of the last two decades in the field of constitutional theory and constitutional politics. The list includes seven main points.

3.1 Internal changes: autonomous learning processes

In his article "Slouching toward Philadelphia?" Andrew Arato discusses competing theoretical options for constitutional reform in the US. He describes the rigidity of the current way of constitutional reform and reminds the reader of Thomas Jefferson's preferred option of a periodic convention. Arato's next move is to interpret Article V of the US Constitution as a formula in this Jeffersonian sense. According to Arato, such an interpretation of Article V has the potential to lead to a second and hitherto entirely unused method of constitutional revision: he mentions Sanford Levinson's proposal of calling a national constitutional convention to amend the constitution (Arato 1996a: 233–234, 241; Levinson 1996). Arato's discussion about opportunities to free the American people from the rigidity of its constitutional provisions for revising the constitution leads to a general question in modern constitutional theory: Under what circumstances may "the people" claim that they have "learned" autonomously and thus should be enabled to free themselves from constitutional mechanisms that are too rigid?

Any successful self-binding requires not only being restricted at time t_2, but also the projection of "the day after" (t_3), when on looking back one is happy and thankful to have been bound, albeit grudgingly, by a meta-rule at time t_2. But what if the original rule has fallen out of favor at times t_3 to t_n? The criticism of "legal paternalism" leveled against liberalism stems mainly from the accusation that in cases of doubt it opts for the original binding formula and against the new preferences. Any attempt to establish a meaningful opposing view is confronted by the question how authentic learning processes – be they on the part of the bound or the binding party – that have led to altered preferences can be differentiated from merely adapted or manipulated preferences. Self-binding mechanisms by definition neglect the idea of such a learning process which may provide good reasons to break with old rigid rules.

3.2 External changes: new conditions

Significant renovations and constitutional reforms in the US political system – as Andrew Arato has pointed out time and again (Arato 1996a: 226–228; 1999: 152–154; 2000a: 229–256) – were produced by "the least dangerous branch," the Supreme Court. Most of these revisions had been responses to certain challenges and changes in the societal environment of the constitutional order. But the number of constitutional changes is rare in comparison to the changes in the environment of the constitution. The American constitution was written more than two hundred years ago, at a time when Benjamin Franklin invented the lightning rod. Since then, technology, the economy and society in the US have undergone tremendous changes. The old constitution of 1788 is situated today in an environment the framers could not have been able to think of.

This observation poses another very general question to the defenders of the self-binding theory: Some environmental changes of the constitution may be so tremendous that the measure designed to be self-binding contravenes the originally intended purpose. To what extent has the development of American society come into contradiction with the Second Amendment, which gives citizens the right to bear arms? Any self-binding mechanism responds conservatively to environmental contingencies. The concept of self-binding does not offer an intrinsic solution to this problem and thus it becomes a question of brute political luck or opportunity whether a rigid constitutional order will be in a position to cope with new challenges or whether an old rule may have consequences which could not have been foreseen by those who inaugurated these rules. It is a massive cost of self-binding that societies lose flexibility.

Ten years ago, Andrew Arato presented the outline for a constitutional reform in the US, proposing the constitutionalization of semi-presidentialism and cohabitation as well as a move toward a proportional electoral system (Arato 2000b). His suggestions can be read as a reaction to tremendous external changes of the American political system over the last two centuries. In order to judge these proposals in a fair way, the formula of constitutional self-binding turns out to be counterproductive. The formula systematically undermines the legitimacy of constitutional reform proposals in the name of rules from a normatively privileged past, and in its political consequences the conservative formula forces constitutional reformers to look for evolutionary ways instead.

3.3 The meaning of the binding formula

When the American framers of 1787 set the standard for impeachment in terms of "treason, bribery, and other high crimes and misdemeanors," they left the interpretation of these terms to posterity (Arato 1999: 145). The Republican attempt to impeach President Clinton brought the problem into full (camera) light: how is this standard to be interpreted?

In our private everyday life, binding formulas are usually unequivocal ("please don't give me cigarettes!"). But even the instruction not to hand over my car keys in case I have too much to drink leads to conflicts of interpretation in practice. For example, there may be differences of opinion about whether my blood alcohol level is already high enough for the case of self-binding to apply (although in this case we might follow the intuitive rule that the conflict itself is already an indicator of too much alcohol). In the realm of politics, the question of interpreting binding formulas arises in an incomparably more virulent way. For example, what does the statement in Article 1 of the Basic Law mean that human dignity shall be inviolable? The disagreement ranges from the question as to what qualifies as a human being, and from which point in time (abortion law, genetic engineering) to the various concepts of what constitutes dignity. This difficulty is resolved in practice in the American and German legal systems by the existence of a special institution that is to function as "*Hüter der Verfassung*" and interpret the formulas of self-binding in appropriate fashion. To what extent is this procedure legitimate if the majority of the democratic sovereign also explicitly invokes the content-related *telos* of the formula of self-binding, but gives it a competing interpretation, as has been the case several times in the Federal Constitutional Court's decisions regarding the unconstitutionality of abortion laws? Rulings handed down by the US Supreme Court during the Lochner era in the nineteenth century are an even more chilling example.

How high, one must ask, is the risk that the institution charged with safeguarding the formula of self-binding may distance itself from the original content of the formula? The accusation, among others, that the Federal Constitutional Court illegally constructs a higher system of values out of the constitutional provisions of the Basic Law follows this argument. No matter how you look at it: institutional decisionism (in favor of the Federal Constitutional Court or the majority of the population) is unavoidable; this decision, however, does not necessarily result from the theorem of self-binding, but is an additional obligation that modern political systems enter into.

3.4 Individual self-binding and collective self-binding

In the summer of 2010, the Turkish government conducted a referendum on a reform of the old constitution from the days of the military dictatorship. The governmental proposal won by a high margin. Andrew Arato, who originally was involved in the Turkish reform project, strongly criticized some components of the final proposal. According to him, the revised constitution gives majorities too much political power over minorities and over the constitutional court. The new constitution has the potential of majority imposition (Arato 2010). The constitutional organization of the relationship between majorities and minorities in a democracy has implications for the general relationship between individual persons and the political collective in a constitutional order. It also raises the question about the transferability of constitutional arguments from the individual level to the collective level.

The original starting point of Jon Elster's concept of self-binding in the late 1970s and 1980s had been the individual actor. Elster simply transferred the example of Ulysses as an individual person to the level of a collective of persons. And although he acknowledged that this transfer might be problematic (Elster 1979: 123; 1991: 130), he interpreted constitutions along the way of Ulysses' strategy to have himself bound to a mast. Only in his later writings – in particular in *Ulysses Unbound* (Elster 2000: 92–96) – did Elster "recant" (Elster 2007: 245) on his early interpretation of constitutions as precommitment devices, but at this time the formula had already become common usage among constitutional theorists.

At this point, we have reached the core of the problem of using the self-binding formula in modern constitutional thought. Is it convincing to make an analogy of individual strategies for outwitting the weakness of the will on the one hand to strategies for a collective entity on the other? In my view, this analogy is misleading. It has two main flaws. First, it is theoretically inconsistent and second, it normally does not fit with the intentions of those actors who make constitutions.

In order to make such an analogy, the theory must depart from its pure contractual starting points and must assume something akin to a separate "entity" of a collective actor as a full unit of will and action. Such a collective actor must be understood an intergenerational social entity, which Andrew Arato identified in the work of European advocates of undivided, sovereign constituent power such as Carl Schmitt (Arato 1994: 99). Arato places the idea of "post sovereign constitution making" (Arato 2006b: 93–97; 2009: 59–76) in contradistinction to this old-fashioned model, as he considers it more legitimate from the point of view of democratic theory because it takes into consideration the multiplicity of political actors in a modern society.

In contrast to Arato's preferred model of constitution-making, any discussion of a coherent "collective actor" in a strong sense must rely on naturalistic, ethnic, religious or other metaphysical assumptions about those who are included and those who are excluded from the collective in question. In addition, it involves a high degree of uniformity and a strong sense of collective identity. Individuals are seen as citizens who have to develop such a strong feeling of identity with the political collective that they emotionally experience the binding force of the constitution as part of their personal will. Such assumptions are in contradiction to the individualistic starting point of the self-binding formula.

Second, the framers of a constitution do not want to bind themselves; they mainly try to bind others. They want to bind those who are the minority during the process of constitution-making, and they try to make it difficult or even impossible for them to prevail with their political agenda. In addition, they want to bind future generations and make it impossible for them to do things which the constitution believes should be avoided in the future. This kind of shackles or bindings may be justified or not – but instead of being understood as "self"-binding, it is more accurate to call them "binding of others."

3.5 Multiple actors

The problematic analogy provokes another objection. In his article "Impeachment or Revision of the Constitution?" Andrew Arato discusses the formula "original intent of the framers" (Arato 1999: 145) and elaborates the role of this reference point for conservative theorists in the field of constitutional theory in the US. In contrast to them, liberals have grown accustomed to basing their methodology on interpretative activism in order to defend constitutional reform. This debate illuminates a question which must be raised regarding the self-binding formula, too, and points at the duty to obey collective instances of self-binding.

In order to describe the problem more clearly, it is helpful to differentiate not only the two conditions t_1 and t_2 in the process of a self-binding mechanism, but rather the three conditions past, present and future. For actors in the present, the question is: what obligations can arise from a case of self-binding that was put in place by an almost completely different population (for example the American Founding Fathers)? This leads not only to the fundamental question of what commitments we have vis-à-vis the past, but, even more, calls attention to an asymmetry. Strictly speaking, only the generation alive at the time of the constitutional convention has made use of both moments of the process of self-binding, that is, both t_1 and t_2.

This leads to serious questions about the legitimacy of such a binding mechanism: Is the concept of self-binding suitable, or is it not rather a case of being bound by others, if we are to give reasons why citizens of the Federal Republic of Germany in the year 2010 are to be guided by provisions that were given constitutional form in 1949, as the essence of their political experience, by politicians who are now long dead? If one is to represent this condition as self-binding and not as being bound by others, one cannot avoid the additional metaphysical assumption of a collective being with a single will, for example the nation, which has bound itself.

If we look into the future, we end up with different, but similarly precarious consequences: even if we acknowledge the binding effect of the past without reservation, that acknowledgment does not yield a right for us to make commitments for future generations. If we have the desire to bind them to our regulations nonetheless, the only way to legitimate our intentions is to give them all the good reasons we know of to encourage them to establish certain binding rules themselves.

3.6 The spirit may be willing, but the flesh is weak

In his ingenious commentary on Georg Lukács theory of reification, Andrew Arato pointed out the limits and paradoxes of historical materialism, which was to be applied to itself as well. According to Lukács, the industrial proletariat in developed capitalist societies is (nearly) completely integrated into the ideological framework of commodity fetishism (Arato 1972). In some of his writings in the 1980s about political sociology, about the cultural criticism of authors of the Frankfurt School and about "Eastern Marxism," Arato also dealt with the problem of "false consciousness" and authentic desires (Arato 1982, 1993: 84–104). I do not want to rehash this debate or come up with a theoretical solution on my own with regard to the Marxist quest for the "objectively correct consciousness." But the old Marxist suspicion that (at least) sometimes (at least) some people are not fully aware of their "objective" preferences poses the question of the status of the persons (or collectives) who try to bind themselves in certain situations.

According to the basic logic of the concept of self-binding, an actor gives an instruction at a point in time t_1 that declares in advance that another instruction given by him at t_2 will be null and void. It is important to note that this logic only offers an unproblematic solution to the problem of *akrasia*, if there is no doubt that the person who binds himself or herself really is aware of his or her own mind at t_1. After all, one could easily imagine the opposite situation: the meta-instruction may be given in a state of insanity, and the person acting, in control of his or her senses again, cannot liberate himself/herself from these strictures.

Normally, the mental condition of people binding themselves may be relatively simple to diagnose in straightforward cases in everyday life such as the declaration to quit smoking or "no car keys if I'm drunk!" But how could one ascertain the "sober" or "drunken" state of a collective? What about the framers of the American constitution and their (irrational) fear of the underclasses (Arato 1996a)? What about the political passions during the different processes of constitution-making in the East European transitions, some of them in "instances of full-fledged revolutionary breaks" (Arato 1994: 102) and others by slowly making amendments to the old constitutions (Arato 2000a: 167–197)? When were the French people most in possession of their senses, in 1789, 1793 or 1799? Were the fathers and mothers of the German Basic Law really in their right minds when they drafted Article 16 on asylum of the Basic Law, or was their mental state that of a post-fascist trauma – as critics contended when the right to asylum was scrapped, for all intents and purposes, by a change of the constitution in the early 1990s? The same argument could be advanced (quasi from the Left) regarding the anti-plebiscite thrust of the Basic Law; after all, we know today that the plebiscitary component of the Weimar Constitution was in no way responsible for the failure of the republic. To turn a long list of historical questions into one conceptual question, which cannot be answered by constitutional theory: How do we distinguish between "morally reflexive constitutionalism" and "morally regressive constitutionalism"? Andrew Arato in his historical work has pointed out a lot of historical evidence that constitutions are sometimes written in politically turbulent times. Constitution makers are sometimes themselves in a passionate mood.

3.7 Weakness of the system

Andrew Arato felt provoked by the politics of the George W. Bush Administration to spend a large amount of his time, energy and academic work on it. He focused his critique not only on the Iraq War and the American strategy to influence the making of a new constitution in Iraq but also on the "the Specter of Dictatorship" (Arato 2002b: 457) which he identified in the emergency government and the military tribunals by the Bush Administration against so-called terrorists. Contrary to the reigning myth, as Arato points out, the US had come close to dictatorship more than once in its long history (Arato 2002a, 2002b, 2006a). Civil liberties, which are guaranteed in a constitution, are the normative core of any modern democratic political system. But how secure are these civil liberties in times when the government successfully manipulates the public and when politicians use the language of *angst?* How binding is the self-binding of the political system when the government wants to get rid of some of the rules?

Any successful mechanism of self-binding must be able to rely on the fact that the person or institution charged with ascertaining the external causality is in fact able to carry out the task. I must be able to depend on my friend not handing me my car keys in case I am inebriated, even if I threaten him or her with violence. We citizens must be able to rely on the constitutional barriers actually having the effects for which we created them in the first place. We must have good reasons to assume that – for example – a constitutional court may successfully defend these barriers and not simply follow the intentions of the government. And we must have good reasons to assume that these institutions do not serve private interests, or, in contrast, even strengthen the feared destructive effects.

Regardless of how one might assess the accomplishments of the US Supreme Court or the German Constitutional Court in some individual cases: the assumption that institutional binding arrangements will always work as originally designed can only be considered heroic in light of the complexity and interdependency of modern political systems. The self-binding formula distracts our attention from the possibility that the institutions which are designed to bind and to secure may potentially fail to do so.

4 Conclusion: the notorious ABC of politics

To sum up the last section: All seven objections in the list strongly call the transfer of the concept of self-binding into constitutional theory into question. If one really wants to keep the concept of self-binding as a strong legitimizing argument for modern constitutional democracy alive, one has to be able to refute not just one or two, but all seven objections. If there is even only one objection that cannot be successfully refuted, the theoretical concept of self-binding will have to be given up as a way of justifying modern constitutionalism. In my view, the seven objections are strong enough to abandon the idea of self-binding as a theoretical way of justifying the normative validity of modern constitutions. Instead, constitutions should be understood as strong rules by which we intend to bind others (see Zintl 1994).

Jon Elster has recently also become more skeptical about the transfer of the concept of self-binding from the individual to the collective level. He acknowledges that this conceptual extension is at least "dubious" (Elster 2007: 244) with respect to constitutions: "societies are not individuals writ large" (Elster 2000: 167). Rather than a political community binding itself, minorities are bound by majorities and future generations by the present one. But he still insists that "the idea of constitutional precommitment is not meaningless" (Elster 2000: 96).

What remains today from the debate between rational-choice, liberal and deliberative variants of making use of the concept of self-binding? In my view, the debate indicates that we need to return to a more "realistic" theoretical approach of dealing with questions of constitutional theory. Political action takes place in three different dimensions: Arguing, Bargaining and Commitment – one may call it the basic ABC of politics. Any political order needs to establish a meaningful arrangement between these three modes. Constitutional patriotism cannot simply be purchased; it requires the identification attained by commitment. Bargaining entails the procedural risk that bargaining power will result in distortions in the input area of the political process; for this reason, it requires arguing as supervision. Arguing, finally, suffers from the fact that purely moral considerations lack concrete power to form motives; therefore, it needs accommodating forms of commitment. All three modes are vulnerable to self-destruction, too: Bargainers alone will be unable to deal successfully with questions of climate change and natural resources of future generations. The mode of strong commitment must be checked when it sabotages the exchange of arguments. And the moral-philosophical discourse of arguing has to be integrated and regulated in a manner that enables the production of decisions.

If we switch from Elster's concept of instrumental rationality to the concept of communicative rationality in Jürgen Habermas's theoretical work, arguing can be seen as the normatively privileged mode within the ABC. From this Habermasian starting point, any reflection upon the best arrangement between arguing, bargaining and commitment has to take place only in the mode of arguing. However, even such a normative switch does not avoid the following problem: of all three modes, arguing is not only the mode designated to define roles in the relationship between arguing, bargaining and commitment but at the same time it is the mode which is the most fragile among the ABC.

A promising meta-strategy to deal with the strategic vulnerability of arguing may be seen in a kind of negative approximation whose course takes an institutional detour: if we can make plausible that instances of self-binding were undertaken under procedural conditions that are favorable for the mode of arguing, then it may be plausible that we may identify cases of arguing. Such procedural standards include publicness, openness of the agenda and unrestricted participation, among others. Now, this assumption is hardly suited to find empirical evidence to support it, especially for the formulation of constitutions. The debate about the American constitution can be reconstructed as nothing less than a classical example of a complex bargaining process (see McGuire 1990). In addition, the circumstances of the formulation of the German Basic Law as well as the new constitutions in eastern Europe (see Lijphart 1992; Arato 2000a) or in Iraq after the US invasion (see Arato 2009) also give little reason to hope that the actors involved will modify Ferdinand Lassalle's famous 1862 statement that all constitutional issues finally will turn out to be issues of power.

Thus it seems to me that any attempt by modern theorists of deliberative democracy to apply the concept of self-binding as an instrument to strengthen the rationalizing power of arguing during processes of constitution-making leads to an infinite regress. Instead, it would be beneficial if the critical theory of democracy were enriched by the more realistic perspective of those members of the Frankfurt School in the tradition of Franz L. Neumann, Otto Kirchheimer and A.R.L. Gurland who paid close attention to the use of power in their analyses of political processes. Andrew Arato's academic work in the fields of democratic theory and constitutional theory is an example that this "realistic" tradition of Critical Theory is still very much alive today.

Notes

1 I would like to thank Sandra H. Lustig for translating an earlier version of the paper and Kerstin Pohl for discussions about the limits of self-binding-strategies.
2 Johann Wolfgang von Goethe, *Goetz von Berlichingen mit der eisernen Hand* (1773).
3 Quoted in Elster (2000: 89).
4 See Rorty (1980), Wolf (1988) and Walker (1989). For an overview of the debate see the contributions in Peter/Schmidt (2007).
5 See Dennis/Söderström (2006) and Neumann (2007).
6 In an entirely different meaning, Arato used the term "self-limiting" in order to characterize the revolutionary changes in Central and Eastern Europe. See Arato (1993).
7 See for example the use of the self-binding formula by the President of the German Constitutional Court Thomas Vosskuhle (2010) and the references to the concept in: Böckenförde (1994), Vorländer (1999), Kis (2003), Zurn (2007), Brodocz (2009), Schaal/Ritzi (2009) and Wheatley (2010).
8 See Elster 1983: 114–116; 1989a: 19–23; 1989b: 36–38; 1989c: 194–200; 2000: 88–174; 2003: 1751–1772; 2007: 119–127 and 237–243.
9 All following quotes are taken from Elster (1979).
10 See Wolf (1988) regarding this discussion, which goes back to Aristotle's critical responses to an argument by Socrates.
11 See Thomas Schelling: "The legal, ethical, and policy issues arise mainly when a second party is enlisted. And there are the cases that appear to call for a judgment about the ambivalent person's true interests" (1984: 2).
12 For a critical review of Elster's account on this topic see: Offe (2008), Sauerland (2008) and Stykow (2008).
13 For a critical exchange about some of the logical assumptions in Elster's concept of precommitment see: Beckmann (2008) and Holzinger (2008).
14 This and the following quotes can be found in Holmes (1988).
15 Robert E. Goodin, too, followed this line of argument in his by now classic defense of political paternalism, cf. Goodin (1991).

References

Arato, A. (1972) Georg Lukács' Theory of Reification. *Telos* 11 (Spring 1972): 25–66.

Arato, A. (1982) Esthetic Theory and Cultural Criticism. In: A. Arato/E. Gebhardt (eds.) *The Essential Frankfurt School Reader*. New York: Continuum, 185–224.

Arato, A. (1990) Revolution, Civil Society, and Democracy. *Praxis International* 10: 24–28.

Arato, A. (1993) *From Neo-Marxism to Democratic Theory: Essays on the Critical Theory of Soviet-Type Societies*. London: Sharpe.

Arato, A. (1994) Constitution and Continuity in the Transitions. *Constellations* 1: 92–112.

Arato, A. (1996a) Slouching Toward Philadelphia? *Constellations* 3: 225–247.

Arato, A. (1996b) Reflexive Law, Civil Society, and Negative Rights. *Cardozo Law Review* 17: 785–790.

Arato, A. (1999) Impeachment or Revision of the Constitution? *Constellations* 6: 145–156.

Arato, A. (2000a) *Civil Society, Constitution, and Legitimacy*. Oxford: Rowman & Littlefield.

Arato, A. (2000b) The New Democracies and American Constitutional Design. *Constellations* 7: 316–340.

Arato, A. (2002a) Minima Politica after September 11. *Constellations* 9: 46–53.

Arato, A. (2002b) The Bush Tribunals and the Spector of Dictatorship. *Constellations* 9: 457–476.

Arato, A. (2006a) Their Creative Thinking and Ours: Ackerman's "Emergency Constitution after Hamdan." *Constellations* 13: 546–572.

Arato, A. (2006b) Post Sovereign Constitution Making and Democratic Legitimacy. In: T. Stein, H. Buchstein and C. Offe (eds.) *Souveränität, Recht, Moral*. Frankfurt/M.: Campus, 92–105.

Arato, A. (2009) *Constitution Making under Occupation: The Politics of Imposed Revolution in Iraq*. New York: Columbia University Press.

Arato, A. (2010) The Constitutional Reform Proposal of the Turkish Government. *Constellations* 17: 345–350.

Arato, A. and J. Cohen (2009) Banishing the Sovereign? Internal and External Sovereignty in Arendt. *Constellations* 16: 307–330.

Barry, B. (1990) How Not to Defend Liberal Institutions. In: R.B. Douglass, G.M. Mara and H.S. Richardson (eds) *Liberalism and the Good*. New York/London: Routledge.

Beckmann, K. (2007) Thomas Schelling und die Militärstrategie. In: M. Leschke and I. Pies (eds) *Thomas Schellings strategische Ökonomik*, Tübingen: Mohr Siebeck.

Beckmann, K. (2008) Jon Elster und das Zeitinkonsistenz-Problem. In: M. Leschke and I. Pies (eds) *Jon Elsters Theorie rationaler Bindungen*. Tübingen: Mohr Siebeck.

Böckenförde, E.W. (1994) Die verfassunggebende Gewalt des Volkes. In: U.K. Preuss (ed.) *Zum Begriff der Verfassung*. Frankfurt/M.: Fischer, 58–81.

Brodozc, A. (2009) *Die Macht der Judikative*. Wiesbaden: VS-Verlag.

Buchstein, H. (2010) From Critical Theory to Political Science: A.R.L. Gurland's Project of a Critical Political Science. *Redescriptions* 14: 35–58.

Dennis, R.J. and U. Söderström (2006) How Important is Precommitment for Monetary Policy? *Journal of Money, Credit and Banking* 38: 847–872.

Elster, J. (1979) *Ulysses and the Sirens: Studies in Rationality and Irrationality*. Cambridge: Cambridge University Press.

Elster, J. (1983) *Sour Grapes: Studies in the Subversion of Rationality*. Cambridge: Cambridge University Press.

Elster, J. (1985) Weakness of the Will and the Free-Rider-Problem. *Economics and Philosophy* 1: 231–265.

Elster, J. (1989a) *The Cement of Society*. Cambridge: Cambridge University Press.

Elster, J. (1989b) *Nuts and Bolts for the Social Sciences*. Cambridge: Cambridge University Press.

Elster, J. (1989c) *Solomonic Judgements: Studies in the Limitations of Rationality*. Cambridge: Cambridge University Press.

Elster, J. (1991) The Possibility of Rational Politics. In: D. Held (ed.) *Political Theory Today*. London: Blackwell.

Elster, J. (2000) *Ulysses Unbound*. Cambridge: Cambridge University Press.

Elster, J. (2003) Don't Burn your Bridges Before You Come to it: Some Ambiguities and Complexities of Precommitment. *Texas Law Review* 81: 1751–1772.

Elster, J. (2007) *Explaining Social Behavior: More Nuts and Bolts for the Social Sciences*. Cambridge: Cambridge University Press.

Goodin, R.E. (1991) Permissable Paternalism. In Defense of the Nanny State. *The Responsible Community* 3: 42–51.

Hayek, F.A. (1960) *The Constitution of Liberty*. Chicago: Chicago University Press.

Holmes, S. (1988) Gag Rules and the Politics of Democracy. In J. Elster (ed.) *Constitutionalism and Democracy*. Cambridge: Cambridge University Press.

Holzinger, K. (2008) Kann man gegen sich selbst "spielen"? In: M. Leschke and I. Pies (eds.) *Jon Elsters Theorie rationaler Bindungen*. Tübingen: Mohr Siebeck.

Hume, D. (1739) *A Treatise of Human Nature*. Mineola, NY: Dower Publications, 2003.

Kis, J. (2003) *Constitutional Democracy*. Budapest: Central European University Press.

Levinson, S. (1996) A Constitutional Convention. Does the Left Fear Popular Sovereignty? *Dissent* (Winter 1996): 13–21.

Lijphart, A. (1992) Democratization and Constitutional Choices in Czechoslovakia, Hungary and Poland 1989–91. *Journal of Theoretical Politics* 4: 207–223.

McGuire, R.A. (1990) Constitutional Making: A Rational Choice Model of the Federal Convention of 1787. *American Journal of Political Science* 32: 483–522.

Neumann, M. (2007) Precommitment and Guidance: Lessons from the Bundesbank's History. In: European Central Bank (ed.) *Monetary Policy*. Frankfurt: European Central Bank, 8–16.

Offe, C. (1986) Die Utopie der Null-Option. In: P. Koslowski, R. Spaemann and R. Löw (eds.) *Moderne oder Postmoderne*. Weinheim: VCH.

Offe, C. (1989) Fessel und Bremse. Moralische und institutionelle Aspekte "intelligenter Selbstbeschränkung." In: A. Honneth, T. McCarthy, C. Offe and A. Wellmer (eds.) *Zwischenbetrachtungen: Im Prozess der Aufklärung. Jürgen Habermas zum 60. Geburtstag*. Frankfurt/M.: Suhrkamp.

Offe, C. (1992) Wider scheinradikale Gesten. Die Verfassungspolitik auf der Suche nach dem Volkswillen. In: G. Hofmann and W.A. Perger (eds.) *Die Kontroverse. Weizsäckers Parteienkritik in der Diskussion*. Frankfurt a.M.: Eichborn.

Offe, C. (2008) Die genetische Entschlüsselung der politischen Ordnung. Jon Elster über Selbstbindung und die Verfassungsprozesse in Osteuropa. In: M. Leschke and I. Pies (eds.) *Jon Elsters Theorie rationaler Bindungen*. Tübingen: Mohr Siebeck.

Peter, F. and H.B. Schmidt (eds.) (2007) *Rationality and Commitment*. Oxford: Oxford University Press.

Preuss, U.K. (1990) *Revolution, Fortschritt und Verfassung*. Berlin: Wagenbach.

Preuss, U.K. (1991) Die Chancen der Verfassungsgebung. *Aus Politik und Zeitgeschichte* 49: 12–19.

Rawls, J. (1992) *Politischer Liberalismus*. Frankfurt/M.: Suhrkamp.

Rorty, A.O. (1980) Self-Deception, Akrasia, and Rationality. *Social Science Information* 19: 905–922.

Rousseau, J.-J. (1762) *The Social Contract*. New York: Cosimo, 2008.

Sauerland, D. (2008) Was man aus den Arbeiten von Jon Elster über den Prozess der Verfassungsgebung in Mittel- und Osteuropa lernen kann. In: M. Leschke and I. Pies (eds.) *Jon Elsters Theorie rationaler Bindungen*. Tübingen: Mohr Siebeck.

Schaal, G. and C. Ritzi (2009) Rationale Selbstbindung und die Qualität politischer Entscheidungen. In: G. Schaal (ed.) *Techniken rationaler Selbstbindung*. Berlin: Lit-Verlag, 55–74.

Schelling, T.C. (1978) Egonomics, or the Art of Self-Management. *American Economic Review* 68 (Papers and Proceedings): 290–294.

Schelling, T.C. (1984) Self-Command in Practise, in Policy, and in a Theory of Rational Choice. *American Economic Review* 74 (Papers and Proceedings): 1–11.

Spinoza, B. (1677) *Tractatus politicus*. Lateinisch-deutsch. Hamburg: Meiner, 1994.

Stykow, P. (2008) Jon Elster und die Theorie der Verfassungsgesetzgebung. In: M. Leschke and I. Pies (eds.) *Jon Elsters Theorie rationaler Bindungen*. Tübingen: Mohr Siebeck.

Sunstein, C. (1991) Preferences and Politics. *Philosophy and Public Affairs* 20: 3–34.

Vorländer, H. (1999) *Die Verfassung. Idee und Geschichte*. München: Beck.

Vosskuhle, Th. (2010) Interview in: *Süddeutsche Zeitung*, October 18, 2010, page 5.

Walker, A.F. (1989) The Problem of the Weakness of the Will. Critical Survey. *NOUS* 23: 653–676.

Wheatley, S. (2010) *The Democratic Legitimacy of International Law*. Oxford: Hart.

Wolf, U. (1988) Zum Problem der Willensschwäche. *Zeitschrift für Philosophische Forschung* 39: 21–33.

Zintl, R. (1994) Skeptische Fiktionen, Selbstbindung und konsentierte Fremdbindung. In: J. Gebhardt and R. Schmalz-Bruns (eds.) *Demokratie, Verfassung und Nation*. Baden-Baden: Nomos-Verlag, 215–230.

Zurn, C. (2007) *Deliberative Democracy and the Institutions of Judicial Review*. Cambridge: Cambridge University Press.

4 Popular sovereignty

The classical doctrine and a revised account

János Kis

The classical doctrine of popular sovereignty (hence the Classical Doctrine) played a major role in justifying the tectonic changes of the seventeenth and eighteenth centuries from the Glorious Revolution in England to the Great Revolution in France. It continued its triumphant progression in the following two centuries by entering almost all democratic constitutions. Ironically, it fell into disrepute, during the same period, as a conception of political philosophy. Serious doubts of both normative and analytic character were raised about it. Some critics found it incompatible with liberal constitutionalism; others pointed out its internal inconsistencies.

One way to respond to such charges is to forget about the idea of popular sovereignty. This is the typical response of contemporary political philosophy. But the typical response is unhelpful. It drives a wedge between theoretical thinking and the constitutional realities of our times, and it leads to the judgment that a central principle of modern democratic constitutions is at best a harmless fiction and, at worst, a harmful myth. This is not a decisive reason, to be sure. It would not weigh much against the claim, would that claim be true, that political theory fares better without the idea of popular sovereignty.[1] But forgetting about popular sovereignty includes forgetting about the reasons that guided the rise of its idea in early modern political philosophy. Popular sovereignty was intimately linked to the fundamental idea that the asymmetry of the relationship between holders and subjects of political authority must be justified against the claim of symmetrical relationship between human persons as moral equals. If political theory declares popular sovereignty irredeemable, then it must reconcile the idea of political authority with the principle of moral equality on some other ground. And it is not obvious that such a venture is feasible. So the idea of popular sovereignty is worthy of an effort to rescue it from the charges of illiberalism and incoherence. This is the present chapter's aim.

My strategy is the following. I will start by isolating what I would call the core of the Classical Doctrine (or the Core Conception) from less central claims of that doctrine. Then, I will consider the main objections leveled at the Classical Doctrine. I will show, finally, that since these objections do not affect the Core Conception, the account of popular sovereignty can be restated in such a way that the core is combined with a set of revised claims. Finally, I will briefly discuss some normative implications of the revision.

1 The Core Conception

States are complex institutional systems. Their authority to make and enforce binding decisions is distributed over a large number of public offices. Those offices are united in a hierarchical order: it is true about any pair of offices, A and B, that either A is subordinated to B, or B is subordinated to A, or there is a third office, C, to which both A and B are subordinated. The relationship of subordination entails that the incumbent of a superior office appoints the incumbents of lower-level offices; gives orders, and delegates powers to them, and holds them accountable for their activities.

Hierarchy must start from somewhere. There must be an instance the incumbent of which gives but does not receive orders;[2] there must be an instance the incumbent of which has the power to authorize others to govern but does not obtain this power by way of authorization.[3] Call *supreme ruler* someone who gives but does not receive orders, and call *ultimate authorizer* someone who transfers powers but whose powers do not originate from transfer. Habitually, the term "sovereign" is used to refer both to the supreme ruler and the ultimate authorizer.

The powers of the supreme ruler are either held by the same person or body as those of the ultimate authorizer, or the two roles are assigned to different persons or bodies. The question is, then, whether the two sovereign powers can be legitimately united in the same agency. The answer of absolutist political ideology is "yes." The answer of popular sovereignty is "no."[4]

Its early advocates agreed that, in order to live in peace and justice, the people must be organized under a supreme ruler. They also agreed – with the exception of Rousseau – that the supreme ruler cannot be identical with the people. Rousseau insisted that by accepting a supreme law-giver other than the totality of the subjects of the law the people gives itself to servitude, and concluded that the only supreme ruler capable of legitimate authority is a legislative body the membership of which is coextensive with the totality of the law subjects. His contemporaries disagreed. They believed that direct democracy is neither feasible nor desirable: the supreme ruler must be an agency different from the people. Their conclusion was that the role of the supreme ruler and that of the ultimate authorizer must go apart. If the supreme ruler is a person or instance different from the people, then it cannot simultaneously possess the powers of the ultimate authorizer. In such a case, its authority to govern must take its origins from the people as ultimate authorizer.

Here is how the argument goes. State-governed societies are characterized by an asymmetrical relationship between those claiming a right to rule and the rest who are supposed to obey the former and to accept that they may be forced to obey if they do not do so voluntarily. Such an asymmetry needs justification, and two mutually exclusive strategies of justification are available. Political authority is either shown to be held in virtue of personal property of the individual in authority or it is shown to be bestowed on that individual by others.

The property in question may be some special status conferred on the ruler by God or it may be some special excellence such as outstanding practical wisdom or military virtue. Early modern political philosophy made a powerful case against both justificatory strategies. It argued that politics is a secular venture: the state has for its aim maintaining peace and order in this world rather than ensuring salvation in the afterlife. Thus, if a person has a special claim to rule, it must be due to his capabilities that make him uniquely fit for the sovereign's job. But capabilities cannot justify the claim to rule either.

This is because, as John Locke argued, human individuals are born free and equal, each having the right to lead their lives in their own ways.[5] I will call this *the principle of moral equality*.

Moral equality entails that none was born with a right to rule others nor was anyone born with an obligation to obey someone else.[6] That someone is a wise man or a man with unique military virtues may be a reason for others to act on his advice or to choose to follow him but it is not a reason to see him to be entitled to their obedience. In other words, political authority cannot be possessed intrinsically. But, then, it must originate from authorization. If there is such a thing as a right to rule, it must be possessed in virtue of an act of authorization performed by some other person. Call this *the authorization thesis*.

The authorization thesis leads to a puzzle. One cannot confer on someone else such authority that one does not possess in the first place. A supreme ruler may devolve authority to lower-level office-holders; but when he does so, he transfers to subordinates part of the authority he is already in possession of. But where does the authority of the supreme ruler himself come from? It cannot be received from another ruler superior to him, since having a superior entails not being a supreme ruler.

One way to resolve the puzzle would consist in abandoning the principle of moral equality. This option is unavailable, though. Modern political philosophers, be they of a liberal, conservative, socialist or libertarian stripe, disagree on how moral equality should be interpreted but they agree that it cannot be flouted altogether. They are also reticent to accept Rousseau's radical democratic solution of identifying the supreme law-giver with the totality of the law subjects. There is one possibility remaining, that of pursuing the strategy explored by Locke: sticking to the principle of moral equality, acknowledging the necessity of a supreme ruler different from the people, and revisiting the way the supreme ruler is authorized.

Authorization either proceeds from the top down or it proceeds from the bottom up. Top-down authorization consists in an act by way of which a superior transfers to a subordinate part of the authority he already has over a third person or group. Bottom-up authorization consists in placing oneself under the authority of a superior. Popular sovereignty argues that the authority of the supreme ruler cannot proceed from the top down; it must originate with those subjected to the supreme ruler's authority. Call this *the bottom-up authorization thesis*.

Authorization *by* the supreme ruler proceeds from the top down. However, authorization *of* the supreme ruler must proceed, as Locke famously suggested, from the bottom up. The first step towards reconciling political authority of a ruler over the governed with moral equality between the ruler and the governed consists in making the claim that the latter must be at the same time the ultimate authorizer of the former.

So bottom-up authorization is a necessary condition for mitigating the asymmetry of the relationship between someone in authority and the subjects of authority. But it is not a sufficient condition. To see why, let us consider a further distinction that was centrally important for the Classical Doctrine: that between *delegating* authority and *surrendering* it. Delegation of authority establishes a relationship between the authorizer and the recipient that we could call, using the terminology of contemporary economic and political science, a *principal-agent relationship*: the authorizer retains the right to define the aims to which the recipient can use the authority conferred on him and to hold the latter to accounts; he retains, furthermore, the right to withdraw the authority from the recipient and to keep it or re-delegate it to someone else, and in so doing the authorizer occupies the role of the principal and puts the recipient in the role of the agent. Abdication of authority is, on the other hand, total and irreversible; it does not define any principal-agent relationship between the giver of authority and its recipient. Compare the case of a king appointing a governor to a province of his realm with his surrendering the throne to the prince who is next in the line of royal succession.

Apparently, moral equality requires that the transfer of authority consists in delegation not abdication. This is because only in the first case is the asymmetrical relationship between the supreme ruler in authority and the subjects of his authority mitigated by a reverse asymmetry between the subjects of authority as principals and the supreme ruler as their agent. And only if the supreme ruler is an agent of the subjects as principals do the latter have the power to set the aims of his activities and to dismiss him if he departs from those aims in order to pursue his own purposes instead. But this conclusion raises a difficulty of which the advocates of the Classical Doctrine were keenly aware. While moral equality requires that the supreme authority is delegated, not surrendered, the political nature of the supreme authority requires that it is surrendered, not delegated. If individuals just delegate authority to the supreme ruler, then each individual remains free to withdraw that authority any time they believe the ruler does not use it in their best interest or in accordance with their best judgment of what is just and what serves the common good. But if this is so, and if the interests of the subjects may conflict, and if the subjects may disagree on what action do justice and the common good require, then none can have assurance that enough others will go along with the directives of the supreme ruler, and state-governed conflict resolution and cooperation collapse.

Popular sovereignty's solution to this difficulty consists in describing the act of authorization as delegating rather than surrendering authority but identifying the ultimate authorizer with the people acting as a collective entity. In other words, the decision to confer the authority of the supreme ruler on a person or an instance is not understood by the conception of popular sovereignty as derivable from separate choices taken by the individual subjects independently from each other: it is rather understood to consist in a collective act, each individual taking his personal choice with the understanding that he contributes his part to the collective act they together perform. The people as a whole can undo the collective act of authorization any time it so decides, but it can do this only by way of a collective decision: as long as the collective authorization decision stands unrevised, no particular individual can unilaterally rescind the authority relationship that ties them to the supreme ruler.

The people, thus, is a collective agency, capable of acting as a whole and of committing all its members. Call this *the collective authorization thesis*. The popular decisions commit all the individual members, even those who may have disagreed with them. Unanimous agreement is not necessary for signaling that the people has spoken. It is sufficient to show that a weaker requirement is satisfied – the early advocates of popular sovereignty typically proposed majority agreement.[7]

On the other hand, the people has not spoken if some of the subjects of the government are excluded from the collective authorization decision or, although not excluded, they have no equal part in it. Moral equality requires that the authority to make and enforce law should originate with the totality of those subjected to the law: the class of the authorizers of the supreme ruler must be coextensive with the class of all and only those individuals who are subjected to his authority. Moral equality requires, furthermore, that each participant of the authorization process should have equal part in it, and that all and only the members of the class of the law subjects are eligible to receive authorization to govern.

To take stock: the Core Conception insists that the ultimate authorizer in a realm is the people, i.e., a multitude of individuals with an equal moral status, coextensive with the multitude of the subjects of the law, and capable of acting as a collective entity. A government is legitimate if and only if its authority to make and enforce law is received from the totality of law subjects, acting as a body.[8] So understood, popular sovereignty is a principle mediating between the moral foundations of politics and political theory proper. It connects the requirements of moral equality to the specific – and specifically political – requirements that apply to state-coordinated political action.

The Core Conception is, however, incomplete in itself. It raises a number of important questions that need to be answered before one could claim to have established the truth of popular sovereignty. The Classical Doctrine is characterized as much by its answers to those questions as it is by the core conception it proposes for popular sovereignty.

First, if the sovereign authorizer is an ultimate authorizer, can his status and powers be legally defined? The classics believed that the answer must be "no": if an authorizer's status and powers are legally defined, then there must be a further authorizer lurking in the background, one from whom the legally defined status and powers take their origins, and so the legally empowered authorizer cannot be an ultimate authorizer. If this is true, and the classics believed it is true as of necessity, then the sovereign people is a supra-legal entity whose acts interrupt or terminate the ordinary workings of the law and give rise to a new legal system, free of the bounds of any positive law. I will call this *the legal vacuum thesis*. The legal vacuum thesis was believed by the classics to have an important substantive implication: if the people speaks unencumbered by pre-given legal rules, its pronouncement expresses its true will. Thus, in the legal vacuum created by its declaring the previous constitution void, the people gives itself a constitution that it really wants to have, and so it should have that constitution. Call this *the popular will thesis*.

Second, the collective authorization thesis and the popular will thesis raise parallel questions to which the Classical Doctrine suggests a common answer. The question from the collective authorization thesis goes like this. That the authorization is given by the people as a collective entity rather than by individual members severally matters precisely because the individuals may disagree with the decision that the people as a whole adopts and persists in. When the people has the capacity to adopt a collective decision, it has the capacity to adopt a decision that binds each member, even those who object to it. To put it differently, a group capable of adopting decisions as a whole is capable of committing, by the convergent choices of one part of its members, not just those members but the dissenting members as well. How can the act of the former commit the will of the latter? The question from the popular will thesis is very similar to this one. Any lasting constitution has force over generations whose members are different from those of the founding generation. How can the act of the latter commit the will of the former?

To anticipate, the answer of the Classical Doctrine was roughly this. Suppose it is true about more or less all members of any generation that they gave their personal consent to be bound by the law of their state. If so, then each member can be understood to have authorized the living generation of the people to adopt collective decisions in their name. Furthermore, if virtually all members of the living generation consent to be bound by the law of their state, then the living generation owns the constitution as if it had been due its authorship. Thus, the collective authorization and the popular will theses rest on what we could call *the consent thesis*.

The consent thesis does other work as well. Having the right to rule entails having the moral permission to make law and to enforce it coercively. The early advocates of popular sovereignty agreed, however, that coercing people to do something they have no moral obligation to do would be nothing but tyranny. They agreed, therefore, that the coercive enforcement of law is not morally permissible unless those governed have a moral obligation to obey the law. In other words, they believed that whenever the people confers the right to govern on the supreme ruler that right must entail a right to impose obligations on the governed. And they tended to interpret the act of authorization as an act of consenting that the ruler has a right to impose obligations by issuing laws.[9] The next sections will consider more closely these three theses: the legal vacuum thesis, the popular will thesis and the consent thesis.

2 The legal vacuum and the popular will theses

Can the status and powers of an ultimate authorizer be legally defined? The advocates of the Classical Doctrine believed that the answer must be "no." For suppose that the answer is "yes," and the ultimate authorizer's status and powers are indeed legally defined. Then, there must be a further authorizer in the background, one from whom the legally defined status and powers of the ultimate authorizer take their origins. In other words, the ultimate authorizer receives its authority from a further authorizer. This is a logical contradiction, though. So the advocates of the Classical Doctrine concluded that a legally empowered authorizer cannot be an ultimate authorizer and vice versa: an ultimate authorizer cannot have its status and powers legally defined. If this is true, and they believed it to be a conceptual truth, then the sovereign people is as of necessity a supra-legal entity, its acts interrupting or terminating the ordinary workings of the law and giving rise to a new legal system, not limited by any positive law.[10] This is what I called above the legal vacuum thesis.[11]

The legal vacuum thesis has momentous substantive implications. The activity of authorizing a supreme ruler can be broken down into acts of two distinct types: defining the role of the supreme ruler, the powers and disabilities attached to it on the one hand, and selecting the incumbent for that role on the other. Defining the role of the supreme ruler is an essential part of what we might call giving constitution to a political society. In other words, as an ultimate authorizer, the people is the final source of the constitution. Now the constitution it gives to itself may take up different forms depending on how the office of the supreme ruler, the powers and disabilities attached to that office, the distribution of the powers subordinate to it and their relationships to each other and to the supreme ruler as well as the rules of succession to the various different offices (that of the supreme ruler in particular) are determined. If the power of the people as ultimate authorizer is not limited by any positive law, then no legal regulation can restrict the choice of the constitution that the people may choose to give itself. The people should have whatever constitution it wants.

To put it more precisely, the people should have whatever constitution it wants once it declared the previous constitution null and void, and engages in constitution-making unencumbered by any pre-given legal rules and procedures. This specification is of enormous significance, since it relies on a distinction between two mutually incompatible political roles any individual may occupy over the course of their lives. As members of a state-governed political society, individuals are bearers of legal obligations and legal competences. As jointly constituting the sovereign people, they appear as not having any legal obligations, and their normative competences are understood to be fully independent from the law. The same person cannot conceivably play both roles simultaneously. Imagine someone bearing the obligation to obey the law as member of a state-governed society and, at the same time, being free to disregard the law as member of the sovereign people. The Classical Doctrine resolved the puzzle by assuming that the people enters the scene when it comes to declaring the constitution in force to discontinue and to adopting a new constitution in a legal vacuum. When the legal order is in good shape, and the law subjects tend to obey its rules, the people as a sovereign agency is dormant. When the people is awake and active there is no binding legal order.[12] The same individual who plays the role of a subject of the state in ordinary situations when the constitution is in force returns to his more basic role as member of the people in extraordinary situations of a constitutional void.[13]

The popular will, then, is identical with the collective will of the people as expressed by the acts of shaking off the chains of the constitution in force and of choosing a new constitution for itself. It is a will standing above not just the will of various different minorities but also the majority will formed in the course of the ordinary political process regulated by the rules of an existing constitution.[14] Popular sovereignty, as the Classical Doctrine understands it, is not about the sovereignty of the popular will formed within the framework of a democratic constitution. It is about the sovereignty of the popular will formed in an extraordinary process going on beyond the framework of any constitution, democratic or not. It does not insist that authoritarian governments must yield to democratic governments but that any government that the people as a collective entity refuses to accept as its own must go, and the people has the right to choose any kind of government it wants to have.

These claims found forceful expression in Sieyès' distinction between *constituent power* and *constituted power*, and in his claim that the constituent power is prior to any constitution and, therefore, free of legal limitations while the constituted powers have their source in foundational acts of the constituent power and must submit to the limits set by the latter. Constituent power is a higher source of law than any of the constituted powers – no matter how high the latter should be located in the hierarchy of a constituted government.[15] Call this view *constitutional populism*. We will turn to its characterization in Section Four, after considering the consent thesis.

3 The consent thesis

How can the people authorize others to impose obligations on them? Locke proposed the following answer. If humans are moral equals, then no human being has natural authority over any other human person. In other words, no human person has intrinsic capacity to change another human being's normative status by giving binding instructions to them. At the same time, each person has natural authority over themselves.[16] It is part of the moral status of a person that they have the capacity to change their own normative status by giving promises to others, engaging in contractual relationships with them, and so on. Call this *self-regarding authority*. The claim that self-regarding authority is an intrinsic moral property of the human person does not conflict with the principle of moral equality. Self-regarding authority is possessed by each human person equally: it is entailed by the status each of us possesses as free and equal persons.

At the same time, someone endowed with natural self-regarding authority has the normative capacity to transfer parts of this authority to others. He can *consent* to another person binding his conduct in ways he is able to bind his conduct himself. For example, A can undertake an obligation towards B to do x by giving B a promise to do x. By the same token, A can consent that B commands him to do x, with the understanding that B's command has binding force for him. Bottom-up authorization consists, thus, in transferring parts of the authority over one's own conduct to another person (or a group of persons). Since self-regarding authority is final, bottom-up authorization does not lead to the puzzle of the model of authorization from the top down.

It seems to lead to a different puzzle, though. Consent is required because individuals have an equal moral status. If this is true about each individual, then the government must have the consent of each individual, separately. However, authorization by the people is a collective act; it is given in the name of the totality of the members, including those who do not concur. We have seen that if the theory of political authority would interpret the authorization of the supreme ruler as a series of mutually independent individual acts, then it would run into a dilemma: it either would characterize authorization as an act of delegation, in which case it would not entail any right to enforce the law against defectors, since freely delegated power can be freely withdrawn, or it would entail the right to enforce the law at the cost of flouting moral equality, since it would require individuals to surrender their self-regarding authority altogether. Thus, authorization must be understood to consist in a collective act, performed by the people as a joint agency. But, then, we face another difficulty; the one that was mentioned towards the end of Section 2: How can the consent given collectively bind a particular individual who has not personally consented?

Locke's solution consists in distinguishing two steps in the process of authorization. Since he, faithful to the language of the Classical Doctrine, used the contract metaphor for describing the process of authorization, the two steps were presented by him as two contracts, the second being made possible by the first one. He described the first contract as creating political ties among a multitude of individuals, and transforming in this way the multitude into a civil society.[17] The people was, thus, taken to be a politically organized collective entity: the understanding was that by constituting a people, a multitude of individuals enables itself to performing collective acts – to making collective decisions, for example. Locke claimed that the first contract consists in a pact by way of which the parties surrender authority to the collective entity established by the pact: his view was that the authority conferred on civil society or the people must be understood to be completely and irrevocably transferred to it.[18] Unable legitimately to withdraw from the first contract, individuals cannot, according to this account, legitimately defect from the order established on their behalf by the second contract either. Thus, the supreme ruler has legitimate power to enforce that order against each individual who should refuse to comply. As a consequence, the political requirement obtains: the enforcement of the established order provides assurance to all that enough others will in fact comply, as long as the second contract remains in force.

The second contract, in its turn, is interpreted by Locke as a delegation pact rather than an abdication pact. As such, it is supposed to allow the people as a body – but not the individual members one by one – to declare the sovereign rule dissolved and all authority returning to civil society whenever the government degenerates into a tyranny or stops serving the common good. The underlying idea is that the delegation pact, while conferring on the supreme ruler political authority over everyone in the realm, defines his role at the same time as that of an agent of the people who is made the principal by the pact: the former must use its power to protect and promote the interests of the latter, and the latter is free to dismiss him any time he fails to do so. In other words, the asymmetry of the relationships of political authority is mitigated by a reverse asymmetry of the principal-agent relationship between the people and the supreme ruler.[19]

Thus, equality is preserved by the second contract by virtue of its being a delegation pact. The first contract is an abdication pact, to be sure, but it does not affect equality either. This is because it leaves the normative relationships among the parties unaffected: no individual resigns any right that the others would not give up as well, nor does any individual gain powers or privileges that the others would not come into possession of.[20]

In sum, the Classical Doctrine reconciles political authority with moral equality by suggesting that political authority is legitimate if and only if it carries the consent of those over whom it is claimed, and the subjects of authority can consent to political authority because they have the moral power to transfer (parts of) their self-regarding authority to others. To put it differently, legitimate political authority consists in self-regarding authority transferred to the supreme ruler by those who are subjected to his rule.

The Classical Doctrine suggests exactly the same answer to the question from the popular will. To recall, the question is this: Every political community ordered by a constitution has a founding generation whose members in their capacity as law subjects are bound to obey the constitution and, at the same time, in their capacity as the people are its collective authors. It also has later generations whose members are subjected to the constitution but it is unclear how they could claim collective authorship for that constitution. In order to show that they can, one has to point out that the people is not just a collective entity but it is a collective entity continuously existing over time so that, notwithstanding a complete change in its membership between time t_1 and time t_2, it is the same people that created the constitution in t_1 whose members are, in their capacity as citizens, subjected to the constitution in t_2. One way to do this could consist in making the assumption that the people as a collective entity exists independently of its membership: it has their own personhood and organic life extended beyond the lifetimes of particular generations. When nationalists of the age of Romanticism revisited the concept of the people, they gave it such an organicist twist. But organicism was alien to the Classical Doctrine. The classics rather tried to bridge the gap between the founding generation and the successive generations by taking recourse to the consent thesis. If each individual, should he belong to whichever generation, can be assumed to have given his consent to be a member of civil society, the consent thesis seemed to suggest, then each individual can be held to be part of the people – the collective entity claiming authorship for the constitution he is subjected to – no matter when he is born. In other words, the consent thesis was seen as solving two problems at the same time: it explained how an individual member of the founding generation who dissents from the constitution can nevertheless be considered as one of the constitutional authors, and it explained, too, how a generation of the people, different from that of the founders, can nevertheless be considered as belonging to the constitutional authors.

4 Constitutional populism

The Classical Doctrine is populist in the sense of its insisting that in any polity the basic institutional order must express the will of the people and, that, the people manifests its true will regarding the basic institutions of its polity when its action is not encumbered by any constraints, procedural or other, given prior to and independently from their spontaneous will formation.

The populism of the Classical Doctrine found expression in two different versions. In its anti-constitutionalist version, advocated by Rousseau, the doctrine insisted that no legislative powers can be legitimately delegated to any body which is not coextensive with the people itself. Only if each law subject directly participates in the process of legislation, only then can it be the case that each one obeys laws he gave to himself, and only if they obey laws they give to themselves can they be both subjected to the rule of laws and free at the same time. By authorizing a separate legislative body to make law for them, the people gives itself to servitude, Rousseau famously asserted. This means, however, that in a legitimate political order, the constitution does not stand above ordinary law: the people as legislature can change any constitutional provision any time, and so the constitution fails to constrain ordinary legislation.[21]

Unlike Rousseau's anti-constitutionalist populism, the version of populism professed by the mainstream classics from Locke to Sieyès was able to accommodate the hierarchy of constitutional and ordinary laws. It had room for constitutionalism in the procedural, *Rechtstaat* sense. Had it room for *liberal* constitutionalism as well?

Liberal constitutionalism insists that the constitution is more than a body of morally indifferent rules: it is first and foremost a body of moral principles that determine the way a political community should treat the individuals over whom its state has dominion. Was the Classical Doctrine's constitutional populism capable of accommodating constitutionalism in this more robust sense as well?

There is a reading of the Classical Doctrine that implies a negative answer to this question. This reading received paradigmatic expression in the work of Carl Schmitt, a belated and unorthodox follower of the classics. According to Schmitt, the act by way of which a people gives itself a constitution proceeds not just in a legal but in a general normative vacuum: it is not bound by any pre-existing normative principles, moral or other. For Schmitt, constitution-making essentially consists of an existential decision about the character of the community in which a people decide to live. The status of the members of the community, the principles fixing their rights and duties result from the foundational decision by way of which the people determines who it is, and who is their enemy: or so Schmitt argued.[22] To put it briefly, the basic constitutional principles as created *ex nihilo* by the decision of the people to give itself a constitutional identity of a particular type.[23]

Many of the contemporary advocates and critics agree that Schmitt's conception offers a correct interpretation of popular sovereignty as the classics understood it. For the advocates, this conception has much to recommend itself precisely because it entails that the people should literally have whatever constitution it wants, democratic or authoritarian, or other. The critics tend to reject the very idea of popular sovereignty for the same reason. As far as I am concerned, I rather tend to think that Schmitt is to be read not as a faithful interpreter of the Classical Doctrine but as a contrast to it.

To begin with, Schmitt's voluntarism is fatally flawed. A conception of normativity that takes the will of an individual or of a corporate body to be the ultimate source of norms must offer a ground for the claim that all norms are ultimately will-based. That claim, however, is itself of normative character. It entails that at least sometimes, the will of an individual or a corporate body formed and expressed under appropriate conditions has the force of a norm: if S wills that A does x, then A ought to do x. Suppose, with the voluntarist, that all norms are ultimately will-based. Then so is *this* norm. The voluntarist conception of normativity is laden by a vicious circle.

Furthermore, the basic principles recognized by liberal constitutionalism appeal, for their justification, to moral reasons, and moral reasons are prior to and independent of any decision-generated reasons, whether the decision in question is individual or collective. That treating a human person in certain ways (e.g., enslaving her) is wrong is a moral reason for not treating her in those ways. And if it is wrong, than it remains wrong even if someone in authority – or everybody, for that matter – approves of it. Or vice versa: if it is not wrong, then it cannot be made wrong by the disapproval of those in authority.

Consider the principle of human dignity, entailed in some form or other by all liberal constitutions. If human dignity does not matter independently of the founding will underlying a political community then the fact that the ultimate authorizer's will is that it should matter does not contribute a bit to the legitimacy of the constitution. And vice versa: suppose human dignity matters independently, and suppose that the ultimate authorizer's will is that it should *not* matter for the aims of the constitution. Then, the fact that human dignity does independently matter undermines the constitution's legitimacy, and the fact that the ultimate authorizer willed the constitution to be indifferent towards dignity does not clear a bit the taint on its legitimacy.

In sum, normative principles cannot be created *ex nihilo* by an act of will of an individual or a corporate body. Therefore, the legitimacy of constitutions cannot be based on the pure will of the founders.

What is more, Schmitt's existential decisionism was not shared by the classics. They did not take popular will to be unlimited let alone to be the ultimate source of norms. From Locke to Sieyès, they agreed that the founders of a constitutional order do not act in a normative vacuum. They believed that humans were born as free and equal and, that, as such they are bearers of inviolable natural rights. They believed that natural rights exist prior to and independently of any act of will and, that, their existence has momentous consequences for constitution-making. On the one hand, they endow their bearers with the status of an ultimate authorizer. It is because human individuals have natural authority over themselves that they are able, individually and collectively, to authorize others to govern them. So far, all the classics, including Rousseau, were in agreement. On the other hand, the classics tended to view natural rights as limiting the act of authorization, and limiting it from a standpoint that is not external but internal to it. As Locke famously put it, at least some of the natural rights are inalienable: the bearer of such a right has no normative power to transfer it to someone else.[24] None has a normative capacity to give authority to someone else to treat them as if they had no such rights. Of the major advocates of popular sovereignty, only Rousseau dissented from this idea, forcefully expressed by Locke.[25]

Given that, according to the Classical Doctrine, all political authority originates from transfer, the implication was that none can have legitimate political authority to cancel or infringe upon an inalienable right. Inalienable rights were, thus, seen to be imprescriptible and inviolable constraints on any legitimate political authority.

The mainstream Classical Doctrine can, thus, be interpreted as maintaining that the people is free to give itself any constitution it wants but only *within certain moral limits*: those set by inalienable natural rights. The Classical Doctrine provided a will-based account of what a legitimate constitution is. But it justified the claim that popular will has the force of creating constitutional norms by an appeal to underlying moral principles that it took to exist prior to and independently from the will formation of any particular individual or group of individuals, and it claimed that some natural rights being inalienable, they set internal limits to the people's constitution-making powers. Its view of constitutionalism was that constitutions, while being the highest embodiments of the will of the people, are constrained (and constrain action within their bounds) by moral principles that are objectively given. It regarded those constraints to consist in disabilities of the constitution-making will – in its disability to alienate inalienable rights – and, therefore, to limit the will internally rather than imposing limitations on it from the exterior.

To take stock: the Classical Doctrine's constitutional populism is not essentially hostile to liberal constitutionalism. The classics had an idea of how to reconcile the will-based view of constitutionalism with its principle-based view. Whether the reconciliation has a chance to succeed depends, ultimately, on whether the theses of consent, of the legal vacuum and of popular will – are defensible.

It is to this question that we now turn.

5 Objections

The objection to the consent thesis does not need any detailed discussion. It insists that, since consent cannot be understood to be given vicariously, the consent thesis relies on the assumption that each individual authorizes the people to enter into a pact creating the office of a supreme ruler having the authority to impose and enforce legal obligations. It, then, suggests that the individual acts of authorization are either actual or hypothetical. But they cannot be hypothetical since none is bound by an agreement they *would give* under counterfactual assumptions but have not in fact given. Therefore, the relevant act of authorization must be an actual one: only agreements *actually given* have binding force. Thus, in order to succeed, the theory must be able to show that each individual actually consents to be members of civil society. However, most individuals cannot be shown to have ever performed any act that counts as giving such consent. The consent account is a non-starter.[26] In order to rescue popular sovereignty, it must be shown to be separable from the consent thesis.

And if the consent account drops out, the collective authorization and the popular will theses drop out together with it. What remains is not popular sovereignty but tyranny of the majority over the minority and of the dead over the living.

Doubts are raised concerning the legal vacuum thesis as well. In one form, these doubts are related to the Classical Doctrine's commitment to the idea that the authority of the popular will rests on independent moral grounds and, that, those grounds set internal limits to it. Similar doubts would plague the legal vacuum thesis even if the Schmittian reading of the Classical Doctrine were correct, and the popular will would not submit to moral limits, internal or external. Let us consider the internal limits-related doubts first.

The claim that the normative capacity to transfer authority from the bottom up is internally limited rests, as we have seen in the previous section, on the assumption that at least some of the natural rights are inalienable. But, as Kant noted in his *Metaphysics of Morals*,[27] the questions of who has right to what against whom are subject to honest and deep disagreements. Even if these questions admit of a right answer, individuals tend to disagree on what the right answer is. Kant believed people need political authority precisely because unless they share a common legal system they have no public standards of justice that everybody is bound to accept. Only when united under a unique set of laws, are they able to subordinate their diverging subjective interpretations of the requirements of justice to a public interpretation binding for all, Kant insisted.

He failed to recognize, however, that if people disagree on the scope and content of natural rights, then they are likely to disagree on what powers they can and what powers they cannot validly confer on a supreme ruler; they are likely to disagree on how extensive the powers are that the supreme ruler can legitimately hold, and how deep his authority can be allowed to penetrate into the lives of the subjects. The authorization process must somehow deal with this difficulty. It must make sure that the collective authorization decision tracks the boundaries of inalienable rights correctly and, that, it does not award the supreme ruler with powers that his subjects have no normative power to transfer to him. In other words, the authorization decision is subject to epistemic requirements. In the absence of a prior agreement on the true boundaries of inalienable rights, the only way to make sure that the relevant epistemic requirements are met is to agree on a decision procedure that is at least as likely to enable the people correctly to track those boundaries (even as it disagrees on whether it does so) as any of its alternatives. Thus, the assumption that there is a right answer on matters of moral principle implies that the alternative decision procedures submit to a ranking in terms of their epistemic reliability. But if they do, then it is not the case that the people as a collective author of its constitution is free to give itself whatever rules and procedures it wants to have for regulating its constitution-making activities.

This idea was not beyond the horizons of the Classical Doctrine. Rousseau, who otherwise dissented from the mainstream, argued in great detail that the aim of popular decision is not revealing what the majority happens to want ("the will of all") but rather discovering what the common good requires ("the general will"). Rousseau went at great lengths to identify the procedure capable of tracking the true general will. But he, similarly to Kant, stopped short of recognizing that if the collective decisions can be ranked as more or less correct, and if the alternative rules and procedures for guiding the process of collective decision can be ranked as epistemically more or less reliable, then the people cannot be free to adopt whatever rules and procedures it wants for regulating its constitution-making activities.

If the popular will is indeed internally limited by the existence of inalienable rights, if the people disagree on its limits, and if therefore it needs decision procedures with a high degree of epistemic reliability so that they enable it to track the correct answer to the question of where those limits are, then the legal vacuum thesis must go.[28]

This conclusion may appear to be quick. It seems possible to agree, on the one hand, that the aims of constitution-making expect the people to settle on a decision procedure with a high degree of epistemic reliability and assume at the same time that that procedure is not legally fixed. The legal vacuum thesis needs to claim only as much that the formation of the constituent popular will is free of any pre-given *legal procedure*; it need not claim that it is free of pre-given procedures *altogether*. It may sit very conveniently with the assumption that the requisite rules and procedures come into existence as conventions, growing out of practices repeated over time spontaneously, without any conscious design or explicit agreement.[29] If so, then the people is nothing else but a particular group of individuals tied together by a web of pre-legal conventions that enable them to act and to take decisions collectively. Given such an assumption, the concept of the people remains that of a pre-legal or supra-legal agency, and it remains true that the people is capable of acting together in a legal vacuum.

If, however, popular sovereignty rests on prior and independent moral principles, then this escape route is unavailable. Given this assumption, what the requisite decision procedure is supposed to do is enable the people to adopt a constitutional order of the right kind. For popular sovereignty really to hold, the people must settle on a constitution that respects the moral principles underlying it, including the principle of inalienable rights. But its members are likely to be divided on what the relevant principles really are and what is it that they really require. Since they have to take and revise collective decisions under the circumstances of disagreement, mere conventions cannot provide them with an adequate procedural framework. They need rules and procedures that accommodate public argument on the controversial issues and allow them to change the existing rules and procedures as a conclusion to those arguments, consciously and deliberately.[30] It is an exclusive property of procedures that form a legal system that they include among them specific procedures for deliberately creating and amending rules in response to public argument. Whatever else the constitution-making procedures of high epistemic reliability should be, they must be procedures of a legal system.[31]

So the conclusion holds: if the popular will is subject to internal limits, the popular will thesis cannot be maintained simultaneously with the legal vacuum thesis. The legal vacuum thesis must go.

What if someone is ready to drop the idea of internal limits and adopt a Schmittian interpretation of the popular will? Even then, the legal vacuum thesis must go. Whatever the nature and status of the popular will should be, the people cannot be constituted as a collective entity capable of meeting common decisions unless it has pre-given rules and procedures. Popular sovereignty is a principle of very high abstraction. It insists that the authority to make law must originate with the totality of law subjects as a collective entity of equals, but it does not identify a particular set of individuals as one distinct people, nor does it decide what counts as an individual contribution to a popular decision, or how the individual contributions combine to yield a decision one can properly ascribe to the people as a whole. More specific rules are needed to settle these questions.

Let us address these claims one by one, beginning with the boundaries that separate one people from another. One may think that these boundaries coincide with those of the territory inhabited by a particular people: an individual who stays within the territory counting as member of the people, with individuals staying outside of its borders counting as non-members. Popular sovereignty requires, thus, that the people is taken to consist of all and only the individuals staying within the borders of the relevant territory. But the issue is not as simple as that. Suppose, for the sake of the argument, that the borders are fixed. Then, individuals can be roughly divided into four categories: those who were born inside the borders and never moved out; those who were born outside the borders and never moved in; those who were born inside the borders and moved out at some point; and those who were born outside the borders and moved in at some point. Individuals in the first category are non-ambiguously ranked with the people inhabiting the relevant territory; those in the second are non-ambiguously ranked with the outsiders to that people. The case of the third and the fourth categories is less clear-cut.

If someone moved out just today, he plainly counts as remaining an insider; if someone moved in just today she plainly counts as remaining an outsider. Consider now someone who moved out yesterday; then someone who moved out this week; or this month; or this year. We might add days, weeks, months and years, and yet agree that he is still an insider. Similarly, we will agree that she who moves in and stays for a couple of years is still an outsider. Suppose now that someone moved out (or in) many decades ago: we will naturally think of them as having changed their status. But the categories of clear insiders and clear outsiders are not separated by a sharp dividing line. A grey zone divides them, its boundaries being vague, and the status of the individuals within it being uncertain. If someone moved out six years ago, say, is he an insider or an outsider? If he moved out six years plus (minus) one month ago, is he an insider or an outsider? If he moved out six years plus (minus) one month and one week ago, what is he? The relevant moral principles do not determine a unique answer to such questions; they do not provide any criterion that would draw a sharp dividing line across the grey zone.[32]

If the people as a supra-legal entity is the source of all law in a state, then it is the people itself which has to sharpen the vague distinctions provided by the abstract moral principles underlying popular sovereignty; it has to agree upon the relevant criteria. But it can't do this, since it does not exist before the criterion is fixed. In order for the people as a collective entity to exist, some determinate rule identifying its members must already be available.[33]

Suppose now that the relevant criterion is fixed somehow. Then, popular sovereignty and the moral principles underlying it require that each individual has an equal part in the collective decisions of the people. They require, therefore, that the collective decision is aggregated from the contributions of each individual. It follows that each individual must have some act at hand that counts as his or her choice contributing to a collective decision. It also follows that the act must be understood by all to express his or her choice; it must be understood by all that the choice is expressed with the intention to contribute to the common decision; the act must be easy to perform, its meaning must be uncontroversial, and so on. But the relevant principles do not specify a unique act-type that alone would satisfy their requirements. People may express their will by raising their hand, stamping their foot, shouting "yeah" or "nay," and so on; they may perform one of these acts in the street (which one?), in the town hall, or at some other public place. There is no single salient way for an individual to contribute his or her part to a collective decision; for a people to be capable of meeting collective decisions, they need rules that identify a particular act-type as a public expression of the individual's will regarding an issue up for collective decision, and the particular circumstances in which an act of that type must be performed in order to count as contribution to the collective decision.

If the people as a supra-legal entity is the source of all law in a state, then it is the people itself which has to fix the relevant act-type and the relevant circumstances. But in order to do this, it must be able to identify the act-types that, if performed under certain circumstances, it must also be able to identify, count as individual contributions to the collective decision (about the relevant act-types and the relevant circumstances), and so it cannot be the original source of the rules specifying the relevant act-types and circumstances.

Finally, in order for the collective decision to be possible, aggregation rules are needed that combine the individual choices into a collective decision. Again, the principles underlying popular sovereignty determine the requirements any aggregation rule must satisfy to be eligible for its role, but they do not select a unique rule from among a number of rules that are eligible in this way. Consider the cases when the people chooses among more than two options. One may adopt a plurality rule for such cases: there is a one-off ballot, and the option receiving the largest number (although not necessarily the majority) of votes is the winner. Or one may adopt a majority rule, and repeat the ballot if no option receives majority, allowing only the two options with the largest number of votes to run again. Or one may proceed by comparing the options pair wise, the winner of each round competing with a new rival in the next one, until there is a final winner. Or one may allow each voter to rank the options according to their preferences, and attach a number to each option in descending order; then, the numbers attached by different voters to each option are added up, and the option obtaining the largest number is declared the winner, and so on. The case of binary choices seems to be simpler, but it involves a different kind of indeterminacy: the multitude of options may be reduced to two in many different ways…

This is a problem because different aggregation rules may combine the same set of individual choices into different and conflicting collective decisions. In other words, popular will varies not just in function of individual choices but also in function of the aggregation rule adopted, keeping the individual choices invariable. If the people as a supra-legal entity is the source of all law in a state, then it is the people itself who has to fix the relevant aggregation rule. But in order to do this, it must be able to aggregate the individual choices over the set of eligible aggregation rules, and it can't do this unless it is already in possession of an aggregation rule.[34]

The upshot is that the people cannot be a collective agency free to give itself rules and procedures. The moral principles that apply to its political self-constitution restrict the scope of the eligible rules and procedures, but they do not determine a unique set for them to be guided by. Because they do not determine a unique set of rules and procedures, such a set must be given as an institutional fact of a people's existence. But because they restrict the scope of the eligible rules and procedures, the institutional rules and procedures must satisfy certain normative requirements. The identity of those requirements, however, is subject to honest and deep disagreements. Hence the same conclusion we have drawn from an earlier argument: the disagreements on whether a particular set of rules and procedures is eligible must be resolved with the help of rules and procedures that constitute a legal system. The people as a collective author of a political constitution cannot be a pre-legal or supra-legal entity; it cannot act in a legal vacuum.

If this is true, the Classical Doctrine is doomed. Must we accept that the idea of popular sovereignty is itself doomed? We must if we find that it cannot be freed from the inconsistencies of the Classical Doctrine while preserving its normative appeal. I don't see any a priori reasons for believing that such a revision is impossible to carry out. And I see reasons for believing that it should not be easily given up.

For consider where the conclusion that the idea of popular sovereignty is incoherent or morally unattractive (or both) would leave us. It would leave us with a choice between abandoning the principle of moral equality and maintaining the Lockean claim that no group of individuals less inclusive than the one comprising all the law subjects can be justified by its intrinsic properties to occupy the positions of authority to make law. The principle of moral equality is not up for grabs, however: so we have no other option but to stick to the Lockean claim. Benjamin Constant seems to have wanted to reduce popular sovereignty to this negative claim.[35] But the Lockean claim is incomplete; it immediately raises the question: where does the authority to make law come from if not from the personal excellences of the legislators? Constant's position is unstable. We have to make our attempt to provide a suitably revised account of popular sovereignty.

6 Outlines of a Revised Account

The natural way to proceed is to return to the Core Conception and to see whether it can be rescued. To remind, the core of the idea of popular sovereignty consists in the following claims. No authority to make and enforce law is legitimate unless it originates from bottom-up authorization. The ultimate authorizer must be the people, the necessary and sufficient conditions for a multitude to form a people being as follows. First, it must comprise all and only those individuals who are subjected to the authority of a particular legal system. Second, all law subjects must have equal part in the authorization process. Equal part includes having an equal right to be one of those who, collectively, give authorization, and an equal right to be eligible for receiving authorization.[36] Finally, the multitude so identified must be able to act together as a collective entity.

Rescuing the Core Conception requires separating it from the theses responsible for the failure of the Classical Doctrine. The Core Conception proves to be viable if one succeeds in showing that the view so amended is consistent and attractive; that it makes sense and, that, it does significant work for political theory.

Is this a feasible venture? Is it worth trying? Not everybody agrees. Many think that popular sovereignty is an essentially confused and dangerous idea. The aim of the present section is to show that they are mistaken. Revising the Classical Doctrine is a worthy and promising venture.

The revision raises four distinct questions, and in what follows I will give some consideration to each of them. First, if we repudiate the theses responsible for the inconsistencies of the Classical Doctrine, how does the interpretation of popular sovereignty change? Second, is the Revised Account capable of dealing successfully with the difficulties that undermined the Classical Doctrine? Third, doesn't the Revised Account give rise to new difficulties, as intractable as those the Classical Doctrine runs into? And, finally, assuming that it is coherent: Does the Revised Account have any significant normative implications, on a par with those of the Classical Doctrine?

The first question directs our attention to the legal vacuum thesis. It is this thesis that contributes most to give the Classical Doctrine its characteristic shape beyond what is entailed by the Core Conception; it is the rejection of this thesis that implies the most significant changes in the understanding of popular sovereignty. As we have seen, the legal vacuum thesis holds that the people has the right and the capacity to shake off the constitution in force and to raise to a supra-constitutional platform where it gives itself a new constitution, not encumbered by any pre-given legal constraints. This claim has two aspects to it. On the one hand, it entails that popular sovereignty knows no legal limits. On the other hand, it entails that popular sovereignty comes into play in exceptional times. The legal vacuum thesis locates popular sovereignty in action at the rare moments when the people declares the continuity of the constitutional order interrupted or terminated. What citizens collectively do in normal times, within the framework of a constitution in full force, does not have the status of the sovereign acts of the people; it rather is constrained by the outcomes of sovereign popular action. The people as a sovereign body speaks in exceptional times only; in normal times, it is silent. So long as a citizenry does not go as far as to discontinue the constitutional order in force, its legal creations do not bear the mark of popular sovereignty.

Once the legal vacuum thesis is gone, the understanding of popular sovereignty must significantly change in both regards. Popular sovereignty cannot be understood to be a property of collective action *outside of* any legal system. Rather, the reference of its concept shifts to collective action *within* a particular legal system. It cannot describe exceptional acts of the people giving expression to its constitutional will free of any legal limitations. It rather will describe acts of the people as a joint agency defined by the law and enabled by it to take action with legal effect. With this shift, the understanding of popular sovereignty as a capacity to act in exceptional times gives way to seeing it as a property of the ongoing workings of constitutional regimes of a certain character.

The Revised Account does not take popular sovereignty to be the claim that the people has normative power to give itself the constitution it wants to have. It rather takes it to be a claim about the nature of the constitution the people should have. Once the legal vacuum thesis is dropped, the only meaningful way to understand popular sovereignty is to rank it with those normative standards that any legitimate constitution must satisfy. The mainstream Classical Doctrine agrees that the internal structure of a legitimate constitution must satisfy certain normative standards. It holds, for example, that legitimate constitutions limit the government's powers so as to protect the inalienable natural rights from invasion. But it doesn't rank popular sovereignty with those normative standards that the internal structure of a legitimate constitution is supposed to satisfy. For it, popular sovereignty is an external constraint on the legitimacy of constitutions:

it claims that an otherwise morally acceptable constitution is not a valid institutional creation unless it is accepted by the people free of the shackles of any legal institution. The Revised Account has no room for popular sovereignty having a separate status, distinct from that of the other conditions of legitimacy. It rather ranks popular sovereignty together with the normative standards that apply to the internal structure of constitutions. The Classical Doctrine was *externalist* in this sense, while the Revised Account is *internalist.*

To begin with, the Revised Account insists that a constitution is not legitimate unless it satisfies the requirements summed up by the thesis of political equality. It must provide that the role of the ultimate authorizer to make and enforce law is assigned to a class of individuals which is coextensive with the class of the law subjects; it must provide, furthermore, that the members of the class of authorizers have an equal part in the authorization process: an equal right to be one of those who, collectively, give authorization, and an equal right to be eligible for receiving authorization.

Clearly, political equality so understood is entailed by the principle of popular sovereignty but does *it* entail popular sovereignty? It does not, since popular sovereignty identifies a collective agent – the people – as the ultimate authorizer. Thus, the Revised Account is not an account of popular sovereignty unless it preserves this feature of the Classical Doctrine.

Just to recall: the Classical Doctrine argued for the collective authorization thesis in the following way. Political equality requires that the act of authorization consists in delegation, not abdication. But if individuals delegate authority one by one, independently from each other, then each individual remains free to withdraw the authorization any time they believe the government does not use it in their best interest or in accordance with their best judgment of what is just and what serves the common good. And if they are free to withdraw the authorization any time, then none can have assurance for enough others going along with the directives of the government, and state-governed conflict resolution and cooperation collapse. Hence the Classical Doctrine's suggestion that the authority to make and enforce law is delegated but that it is delegated by the people as a collective agency rather than by each individual independently from the others.

A move from an externalist to an internalist view of popular sovereignty does not affect this reasoning. If it was a valid reasoning in the framework of the Classical Doctrine, it remains a valid reasoning in the framework of the Revised Account as well. So popular sovereignty does not fall together with the legal vacuum thesis; it just changes its meaning and reference. In its internalist reading, it claims that if a constitution makes the possession of political authority conditional on delegation by the people, then to that extent it is legitimate; to the extent that a constitution fails to tie the possession of political authority to popular delegation, its legitimacy is diminished.

Let us address, now, the second question that asks whether the Revised Account survives the difficulties that brought down the Classical Doctrine. The difficulties raised by the legal vacuum thesis are gone, to be sure. What about the difficulties from the rejection of the consent thesis?

As we have seen, the consent thesis ties the theory of popular sovereignty to the theory of political obligation. It makes the act of popular authorization part of the process in which each law subject undertakes a moral obligation to obey the law. It is now generally considered to be a non-starter as a justificatory account of the claim that the law's addressees have indeed an obligation to obey the law. Clearly, the failure of the consent thesis does damage to the Classical Doctrine. Does it damage the Revised Account as well?

There is no reason for thinking that it does. Popular sovereignty asks and answers a question different and independent from that of political obligation. Its question is one of equality: that question is raised by the apparent conflict between the symmetrical nature of the relationship between individuals as moral persons and the asymmetrical nature of the relationship between an individual in authority on the one hand and an individual subjected to the former's authority, on the other. The criterion of success for an account of popular sovereignty is whether it does significantly contribute to reconciling political authority with moral equality, not whether it contributes to justifying the claim of political obligation. Furthermore, the consent thesis is just one among the rival theories of political obligation. Some of its rivals are similar to it in that they interpret political obligation as arising from a voluntary act performed by the law subject (see, e.g., the fair play account); others interpret political obligation as being incumbent on its bearers on grounds that need not include voluntary acts at all (see, e.g., the associative obligation and the natural duty of justice accounts). Popular sovereignty is neutral among these (and other) accounts. It is neutral even towards the claim that the government's monopoly and use of coercive force is not morally permissible unless the law subjects have a moral obligation to act as they are coerced to act. Popular sovereignty may hold even if this claim, so important for the Classical Doctrine, happens to be false. Actually, I believe it is true, but this is beside the point. What matters here is only that the theory of popular sovereignty is independent from the theory of political obligation. The consent account presupposes popular sovereignty but popular sovereignty does not presuppose the consent account or any other particular account of political obligation, for that matter. As a consequence, the difficulty related to the collective authorization thesis falls away. If authorization by a people satisfying certain egalitarian requirements does in fact mitigate the inequality built into the fact of authority, then it does its job without any residue whether or not the individual members consented to the people's authority to delegate authority. It is sufficient that each member has an equal part in the process.

What about the popular will thesis? The consent thesis suggested an answer to the difficulty the succession of generations seems to raise for that thesis. Its failure involved a failure of that answer and, with it, of the Classical Doctrine. Is the Revised Account similarly doomed to fail?

Not in my view. Once we move from the Classical Doctrine to the Revised Account, the very question from the popular will thesis goes away. The Classical Doctrine has to face this question because it interprets popular sovereignty as the right and the capacity of the people to give itself whatever constitution it should want. According to that doctrine, a constitution is not legitimate unless it is true that it is an extra-legal act of popular will. The Revised Account makes no such assumption, either explicitly or implicitly. It rather maintains that a constitution is illegitimate if its internal structure violates the principle of popular sovereignty.

Let us turn now to our third question: Perhaps the Revised Account gives rise to new difficulties, no less intractable than those the Classical Doctrine runs into. Here is the main candidate for such a difficulty. The externalist reading of popular sovereignty allows for a non-circular chain of authorization. The chain is non-circular because it begins with an agency that gives but does not receive authorization, and it ends with an agency that receives but does not give authorization. And this is so because all authority defined within a legal system takes its origins with the people, a collective agency standing outside of the legal system whose authority does not rely on authorization, legal or other. The internalist reading, in its turn, seems to give rise to a circular chain of authorization, the people giving authority to the legislator to make and enforce law, while the legislator giving authority to the people, by defining it as a particular collective agency and conferring legal powers on that agency. If the chain of authorization is circular in a system, then that system includes no ultimate authorizer: none, not even the people can occupy such a role in it. And if, in a system, the people cannot occupy a role of ultimate authorizer, then popular sovereignty cannot be made sense of in that system. So it seems that the revision comes at the cost of flouting popular sovereignty altogether. If this is true, then the Revised Account is not a new interpretation of popular sovereignty; it rather is a political theory excluding the possibility of popular sovereignty.

This objection has a bite, however, only as long as we accept that both what the people does and what the legislator does count as authorization. When the people elects a legislature, it surely authorizes the legislators. None has been born to be legislator, none can have the authority to make law for others without being authorized to do so, and popular sovereignty requires that the legislators derive their authority from the law subjects as a body. When the legislators, in their turn, define the people and its powers, do they perform an act of authorization as well? In my view, they do not. They do something else.

Compare what they do with the legal stipulation of basic constitutional rights. The basic constitutional rights are not created and conferred on their bearers by the legislature. They just give legal recognition to moral rights that their bearers possess prior to and independently of being subjects of the law. By incorporating those rights into the legal system the legislature does not *authorize* the rights bearers to exercise their moral rights; it just *enables* them to do so *with legal effects*. Similarly, the legislature does not authorize the people to authorize the legislature to make binding law; it just enables the people to exercise its right as ultimate authorizer with legal effect. True, there is a difference between the individual as a rights-bearer and a people as a rights-bearer. The individual's identity is fixed prior to any legal stipulation while the people needs legal demarcations for its identity to be fixed. Nevertheless, it is true about any legitimate constitution, that the totality of the law subjects are recognized by it to bear a basic right to collectively authorize the legislators, and to do so in a process in which they all have an equal part. Where this condition obtains, popular sovereignty obtains, and it obtains not in virtue of a legal decision but as a consequence of the moral equality of all individuals qua human persons.

7 Concluding remarks

Let me conclude this paper by addressing what I called the question of significance: Does the Revised Account have any important normative implications, on a par with those of the Classical Doctrine?

Towards the end of Section One, I stated that for the aims of the Classical Doctrine, popular sovereignty is a principle mediating between the moral foundations of politics and political theory proper: it connects the requirements of moral equality to the specific – and specifically political – requirements that apply to state-coordinated political action. This is clearly true about the Revised Account as well. For it, popular sovereignty sets the stage for a full-blown democratic theory.[37] So far the answer is obvious. But the question of significance asks something more. As it has been shown in Sections Two and Four, the Classical Doctrine has a more specific political implication. It claims that no true constitution can be made in any way other than through a process that begins by the people interrupting the continuity of the legal system in force and concludes by the people giving itself a new constitution unencumbered by any legal shackles. The question of significance asks whether the Revised Account has any specific implications of this order of magnitude.

Apparently, it does not. By making popular sovereignty an internal property of legitimate constitutions, the Revised Account seems to deprive itself of any theoretical tools for critically assessing constitution-making processes that start new democracies. I take Andrew Arato whose scholarship this tome is meant to celebrate to be claiming that this is a mistake. In his *Constitution-making Under Occupation* and elsewhere, Arato suggests a compelling theory of transitional constitution-making based on a robust implication of the Revised Account.[38] Transitional constitution-making is constitution-making that transforms a non-democratic regime into a democratic one. By the time when it comes to the transition, the old regime's political institutions (including its legislature) are revealed to be illegitimate: this is what makes the transition unavoidable. For the aims of the Classical Doctrine, such a transitional moment is one of interruption in the continuity of the legal system: the people does not accept the old regime any more. It follows, according to that doctrine, that the constitution adopted in the transitional moment has a chance to express the genuine will of the people and to gain the status of the true supreme law of the land. In my understanding, Arato argues against this from the platform of the Revised Account. He discusses the late twentieth and early twenty first century democratic transitions (of post-Soviet East Central Europe, South Africa and even Iraq) that he labels "post-sovereign constitution-makings." By post-sovereign, Arato means that the makers of the constitution have no sovereign power to act, as if in a legal vacuum, under any rules and procedures they should decide to give themselves. A very different and more complex process is going on: a constitutional transition carried out in two stages and by two different bodies.

Consider the so-called "velvet revolutions" in Eastern Europe, for example. With the only exception of Romania, the dismantling of the communist regime proceeded peacefully, involving at some point roundtable negotiations between delegates of the state party and those of the opposition-in-the-making. The negotiations sought an agreement on the ground rules of free (in the case of Poland, semi-free) elections, and insofar as the constitutions in force threatened to block the process leading up to the elections, the agreement included some constitutional amendments as well. Partial as these amendments have been in most cases, they had foundational significance. Rather than merely reforming the old regime, they put an end to it and laid down the bases for a new one.

The roundtables did not see themselves, however, as having a mandate for constitution-making. They invariably understood their task to be limited to facilitating the run-up to free, competitive elections, and were determined to leave it to an elected assembly to give constitution to the new regime.

They had no more formal authorization to make law for the old regime than they had popular authorization to make law for the new regime. In order for their decisions to come into legal effect, those decisions must have been sent for enactment to the old legislature – an institution whose legitimacy claim suffered a definitive blow from the very roundtable decisions. And so the agreements commanded no legitimate authority except insofar as they were meant to regulate the transition from the old regime to a new one and to provide assurance that both the holders of power and their opponents were to abide by those rules. This is true independently of how elaborate the constitutional material they produced.

The constitution-making profile of the "velvet revolutions" can, thus, be characterized as consisting of two stages. In the first stage, a roundtable agreement is struck on the ground rules of preparing and holding free elections. The second stage takes place when a body of freely elected representatives adopts, in the sovereign people's name, a new constitution.

Only when the second step is completed, is the constitution-making process complete and the resulting constitution fully legitimate. This is Arato's main thesis as I understand him, and this thesis articulates very forcefully the main consequence of the Revised Account. It insists that precisely because popular sovereignty is a normative property of legitimate constitutions, the transition cannot come to a completion without first laying down the ground rules for free and fair, competitive election based on universal, equal and secret ballot. A legislature issued from such an election, and only such a legislature, has genuine popular mandate in the possession of which it can give the political community a final and fully legitimate constitution.

In sum, what the Revised Account offers is not only a coherent alternative to the Classical Doctrine as a general interpretation of popular sovereignty; it also entails powerful implications that distinguish its position from its seventeenth-eighteenth century predecessor.

Notes

1 As Christopher Morris argues in his article, "The Very Idea of Popular Sovereignty: 'We the People' Reconsidered," in *Social Philosophy and Policy* 17 (2000) 1–26.

2 John Austin has put it in this way, following Jeremy Bentham; the genealogy of this definition going back to Hobbes. See J. Austin: *The Province of Jurisprudence Determined*, London: Weidenfeld and Nicholson (1832) 1954, 193 ff.

3 See T. Hobbes: "The Citizen," in Hobbes: *Man and Citizen*, Indianapolis, IN: Hackett 1991, Ch. IX, §§. 11–19; T. Hobbes: *Leviathan*, Cambridge: Cambridge University Press 1991, Part II, Ch. 19.

4 J. Locke: "An Essay Concerning the True Original, Extent, and End of Civil Government" (Second Treatise of Government), in Locke: *Two Treatises of Government*, Cambridge: Cambridge University Press 1988, Ch. XIII, §. 149.

5 Ibid., Ch. II, §. 4.

6 Ibid., Ch. VI, §§. 54, 70.

7 See ibid., Ch. VIII, §§. 96–99; J.-J. Rousseau: "On the Social Contract," in Rousseau: *Basic Political Writings*, Indianapolis, IN: Hackett 1987, Book IV, Ch. 2.

8 Actually, the classics understood the coextensiveness thesis with some qualifications. They believed, for example, that women are subject to the law but are not eligible to participate in the authorization process. They could think this because they understood the property of being born as free and equal persons as being born to become, through education and practice, free and equal persons. Given that the "natural role" of the women confines them to the household, or so the classics thought, women do not acquire the capacities of a fully free and equal person, and so they are not capable of nor do they have a legitimate claim for participating in the process in which the rulers are given authority to make law. For the way the general idea of moral equality and popular sovereignty exerted a pressure towards extending the suffrage see fn 36.

9 Locke: Second Treatise, Ch. VIII, §. 95.

10 For the classics' tendency to take the violation of ordinary legal procedures as evidence that the people enter the scene to form their sovereign will, see E. Moran: *Inventing the People*, New York; London: Norton 1988, 107ff.

11 For Madison's and Wilson's view that the Constitutional Convention as the embodiment of the popular will is free to disregard any pre-given legal dispositions see A.R. Amar and A. Hirsch: *For the People: What the Constitution Really Says About Your Rights*, New York: The Free Press 1998; see also B. Ackerman and N. Katyal: "Our Unconventional Founding," in *University of Chicago Law Review* 62 (1995) 475.

12 Locke: Second Treatise, Ch. XIII, §. 149.

13 See Locke's distinction between the people and a "constituted commonwealth": Second Treatise, Ch. XIII, §. 149.

14 Ibid., Ch. XIII, §. 157.

15 See E.-J. Sieyès: "What is the Third Estate?" in Sieyès: *Political Writings*, Indianapolis, IN: Hackett 2003.

16 Locke: Second Treatise, Ch. V, §. 27.

17 Early modern political philosophers used the terms "civil society" and "the people" as synonyms.

18 Locke: Second Treatise, Ch. VIII, §. 21.; cf. Rousseau: "Social Contract," Book I, Ch. 6; Book II, Ch. 4.

19 Second Treatise, Ch. XIX, §§. 214–217, 220. Cf. J.H. Franklin: *John Locke and the Theory of Sovereignty*, Cambridge: Cambridge University Press 1978, Ch. 4.

20 See Rousseau: "Social Contract," Book I, Ch. 6.

21 Ibid., Book I, Ch. 7.

22 C. Schmitt: *Verfassungslehre*, Munich; Leipzig: Duncker and Humblot 1928, §§. 7–8.

23 C. Schmitt: *Über die drei Arten des rechtswissenschaftlichen Denkens*, Berlin: Duncker und Humblot 1993, 21–24.

24 Locke: Second Treatise, Ch. II, §. 6.
25 Rousseau: "Social Contract," Book I, Ch. 6.
26 A.J. Simmons: *Moral Principles and Political Obligations*, Princeton: Princeton University Press 1979.
27 I. Kant: "Metaphysics of Morals," in Kant: *Practical Philosophy*, Cambridge: Cambridge University Press 1999, Part I, Sub-part i, Section 1, §. 44.
28 For the importance of the epistemic reliability of collective decisions, see J. Kis: "Constitutional Precommitment Revisited," in *Journal of Social Philosophy* 4 (2009) 570–594.
29 For the way conventions grow without conscious design, see D. Lewis: *Convention*, Cambridge, MA: Harvard University Press 1969, 5 ff.
30 For a multitude of individuals divided by pervasive and protracted disagreements but wanting to cooperate being in need of law, see J. Waldron: *Law and Disagreement*, Oxford: Oxford University Press 1999.
31 For the legal system as a unity of first-order rules applying to human conduct and second-order rules applying to making, amending and identifying first-order rules, see H.L.A. Hart: *The Concept of Law*, Oxford: Clarendon 1961.
32 For the dependence of the definition of a people on institutional rules, see A. Buchanan: "Political Legitimacy and Democracy," in *Ethics* 112 (2002) 689–719.
33 This argument was anticipated by David Hume in his essay "Of the Original Contract." In Hume: *Political Essays*, Cambridge: Cambridge University Press 1994.
34 For the dependence of a unique algorithm for aggregating individual votes into collective decisions, see W. Riker: *Liberalism Against Populism*, San Francisco, CA: W.H. Freeman and Company 1982. Cf. J. Coleman and J. Ferejohn: "Democracy and Social Choice," in *Ethics* 97 (1986) 6–25.
35 See B. Constant: "Principes de politique." In Constant: *De la liberté chez les modernes*, Paris: Hachette 1980, 271.
36 For the regulative role of this ideal of equality in the struggles for extending the suffrage, see P. Rosanvallon: *Le sacre du citoyen*. Paris: Gallimard 1993; A. Keyssar: *The Right to Vote: The Contested History of Democracy in the United States*, New York: Basic Books 2000.
37 To remind: the idea is that a constitution meeting the standard of popular sovereignty identifies the totality of the law subjects as equal citizens making decisions as a collective entity with the instance of the ultimate authorizer. This is a more austere view of popular sovereignty than that of Jürgen Habermas who, too, interprets popular sovereignty as part of the ordinary political process within a constitutional regime. For Habermas, popular sovereignty obtains if the formal political decisions emerge on the basis of informal deliberation going on in civil society. This account is hard to distinguish from a certain general conception of democracy. See J. Habermas: "Volkssouverenität als Verfahren," in Habermas: *Faktizität und Geltung*, Frankfurt/Main: Suhrkamp 1993.
38 A. Arato: "Post-Sovereign Constitution-making – The New Paradigm," in Arato: *Constitution-making Under Occupation: The Politics of Imposed Revolution in Iraq*, New York: Columbia University Press 2009.

5 Palestinians in Israel

The constitutional debates

Uri Ram

The state of Israel was designed by the Zionist movement as a Jewish state, and it was recognized as such by the United Nations in 1947. Yet being "Jewish" and being "Israeli" are not tantamount identities. About half of the world's Jewish population chooses to live outside of Israel; about one-fifth of the Israeli population consists of Palestinian Arabs, who are citizens of the state. Moreover, for many secular Israelis their assumed Jewishness does not mean much. If territory and language are major attributes of nationality then Jews outside Israel and Israeli Jews do not share the same nationality. Yet, peculiarly enough, the state of Israel is adamant to define its own identity as "Jewish" – rather than "Israeli" – and not to recognize an "Israeli nation," or "Israeli nationalism," which may be argued to be an outcome of its own history.[1]

Thus in Israeli identity cards, under the rubric "nationality" are marked religious categories. This adherence to quasi-primordial pre-political diverse identifications, and the disavowal of a common identity based on common citizenship, is the root cause of a constitutional strain and of inter-group rivalries in Israel, of a "demographic race" between the groups, and of the accusation that the Israeli regime turns towards an apartheid system. These features of Israel result from the quasi-ethnic characteristics of Zionist Jewish nationalism and they propel a protest among speakers of the Arab-Palestinian cause. Yet, unfortunately, as we see in this chapter, those speakers have also adopted the same ethno-national characteristics. The framing of the constitutional controversy in Israel in terms of two rival ethno-national groups, bars the development there of a discourse of universal citizenship.

The question of political democracy in ethnically divided states is one of the most important challenges of our time (cf. Peleg 2007). The centrality of a constitution which may serve as a lynchpin which links together peacefully the separate components of the polity, within a combined yet differentiated state structure, is becoming ever clearer. Andrew Arato, my mentor during my doctoral studies in the New School for Social Research between 1986 and 1992, is a leading scholar of democratic theory and constitutionalism (cf. Arato 2000, 2009; Cohen and Arato 1994; Fehér and Arato 1991; Rosenfeld and Arato 1998). My interest in these issues was inspired by Andrew, while I hope that I have in turn contributed to his interest in and understanding of the constitutional problems in Israel, as I continue to do, hopefully, in the present essay. This essay addresses the limitations of democracy in Israel, especially with regard to its Palestinian-Arab citizens, and the nature of several claims for a constitutional change, put forward by speakers of these citizens in 2007 in the form of "constitutional documents."

The chapter offers, first, a scrutiny of these constitutional documents and the claims made in them. It then proceeds to analyze and contextualize the documents, by reviewing three aspects of the political culture in Israel: the controversy about democracy in Israel; changes in the Israeli-Jewish political identity; and changes in the Palestinian-Arab political identity. Finally, the chapter offers a critique of these documents from a universalist perspective. It is argued that in their attempt to introduce the concept of a bi-national (or bi-ethno-national) state, rather than offering a transcendence of the ethnic principle of the Israeli polity, these documents in fact reproduce this principle. They thus leave unexplored the concept of Israel as a universal state of its citizens. Such a concept ought to include affirmative measures that will restore rights and compensate for lost property of the Palestinian-Arab citizens, but in which the situation of two "nations" will be considered the point of departure, rather than the point of destination, of the Israeli polity.

The constitutional documents

Motivated by the principle of ethnic nationalism and realizing that a Jewish state cannot be created and maintained without a solid Jewish majority, the Independence War of Israel served as an occasion for its armed forces to expel and to frighten out from its territories about 700,000 Palestinians and to demolish about 400 Palestinian villages (Morris 1989). Thus the Jewish state was formed in 1948 that accommodated in its inception about 600,000 Jews and 150,000 Arabs. This proportion has not changed much, and in 2011, within a population close to 7.6 millions, the Arab population amounted to 1.5 million.[2] While the state defines itself officially, since the 1990s, as "Jewish and democratic," it has become a common saying among the Palestinian-Arab citizens that the state is democratic for Jews and Jewish for Arabs. The constitutional documents were conceived in the spirit of this latter perception of the state.

The constitutional challenge posed by Palestinian-Arabs in Israel was formulated in several documents that were publicized in 2007 (sometimes called together "the visionary documents"), of which this chapter relates mostly to the following three:

- "The Future Vision of the Palestinian Arabs in Israel" (published by *The National Committee for the Heads of the Arab Local Authorities in Israel* [2007]).
- "The Democratic Constitution" document (published by *Adalah, The Legal Center for Arab Minority Rights in Israel* [February 2007]).
- "The Haifa Declaration" (published by *Mada al-Carmel – Arab Center for Applied Social Research* [May 15, 2007]).[3]

The documents touch upon issues of national identity, colonialist history, civil rights, equal citizenship and power sharing. They support the establishment of a Palestinian state in the occupied territories of 1967 but their main concern is the status of the Palestinian-Arab citizens within Israel in its 1948–1967 "green line" borders. The agenda advocated in these documents can be summarized in the following three major staples:

A. The definition of the situation: a "Homeland Minority" in an "Ethnocracy." The documents define the Palestinian-Arab citizens of Israel as an integral part of the Arab nation and the Palestinian nation and more specifically they define themselves in Israel as "homeland minority" or as "indigenous people." The regime in Israel is considered as colonialist and ethnocratic (the term will be explained shortly).

The "homeland" or "indigenous" categorization gains its significance in the face of the state's persistent refrain, throughout its sixty years, from conferring upon the Palestinian-Arab minority a statutory character of a collective national group. It is also important of course in terms of the ideological contest between Jews and Arabs on the (so-called) "right" over the land. The "homeland minority" claim emphasizes the prior rights of the Palestinians and sustains the view of the Jews as colonial invaders from abroad with the support of imperialist powers.

B. The rectification demand: restoration of rights, compensation of loss and equality in resource allocation. As a corollary of the above, the documents lay out a thorough indictment of the historical and contemporary wrongdoings and offenses that the state has perpetuated against the Palestinian-Arabs. These include, for instance:

> The policies and practices of Israeli governments have caused severe injustice to the Palestinian Arab minority since 1948, some of which continues today including this minority's physical detachment from its people and nation, the uprooting and destruction of villages, the demolition of homes, the imposition of military rule until 1966, the massacre of Kufr Quassem in 1956, the killing of young people in the first Land Day in 1976 and in mass protests of October 2000, the confiscation of properties from the Muslim Waqf, the expropriation of land, the non-recognition of Arab villages, the separation of families, policies of institutional discrimination in all fields of life, and the exclusion of the Arab minority based on the definition of the state as Jewish.
>
> (Adalah doc. p. 5)

The documents demand recognition by Israel of its responsibilities for all this, as well as compensation of property – especially land – and restitution of rights, and equality in allocation of resources.

C. The regime change demand: power sharing and veto rights. Finally, in order to reverse the situation described above of non-recognition of the Palestinian-Arabs collectively and to gain equality in distribution of power and of resources to them, the documents demand a radical transformation of the political constitution of Israel. They demand that Israel be transformed from a Jewish state into a bi-national Jewish and Arab state. In this state, first, the Palestinian-Arabs will become (equal) partners to power and decision making, and, second, they will get some form of autonomy (the Future Vision document refers to "institutional self rule in the field of education, culture and religion" and at another point to "national institutions relating to all living aspects"). To effect this, the demand (in some of the documents) is to create an autonomous representative body of the Palestinian-Arabs and/or to grant their parliamentary representative a veto power on Knesset decisions and enactments. The Adalah document proposes a veto power by the minority on Knesset bills.[4]

There is yet another set of demands that the documents present, and these relate to distributional inequalities both on the socio-economic level, and on the symbolic level. There are a great many issues here, but the distributional level is utterly subordinated in these documents to the level of recognition, and is thus in a secondary priority. The novelty of these documents is first and foremost in their reference to power politics and national recognition; the pragmatics of social justice are a much discussed issue, and will not be discussed here.

The "models of democracy" controversy

The first step taken here in order to decipher the claims made by the "visionary documents" is to anchor them in the controversy that has taken place in Israeli political sociology for more than two decades now, about the nature of democracy in Israel in general and the status of the Palestinian citizens in particular. One may discern *three main approaches* to the question of democracy in Israel: a *liberal approach*; an *ethno-centered* approach;[5] and a *socio-economic approach*. In each, in turn, one can discern two versions.

The *liberal approach* includes the following two versions:

First is the official and the hegemonic approach – the *liberal position*. According to it Israel is, as mentioned, a "Jewish and democratic state" simultaneously and this does not generate any problem. In this view Israel resembles almost any other standard democratic Western state, with universal rights and the one person one vote representative system, where there are majority and minority population groups (Yakobson and Rubinstein 2003).

The second liberal position is a moderate *critical version* of the first one. In this view, Israel is indeed a liberal democracy, but it nevertheless discriminates de facto its Arab citizens. The issue is thus grasped in terms of policies and the remedy that is prescribed is a more conscious and active policy of equalization and distribution.

Noticeably, the liberal position acknowledges explicitly the "Jewish-ness" of the state, but bases it on the nature of its majority group and its democratic prerogative. It acknowledges the damage that this inflicts on the minority group, but proposes to improve the individual situation of the members of this group, without any change in the regime structure, or the definition of the state that will recognize the minority in a statutory manner.

The *ethno-centered* approach to democracy in Israel, on the other hand, considers the presence of the two national groups in the state as the constitutive condition of it. The approach fully acknowledges the consequences of the struggle between these groups – though with two divergent conclusions drawn from this. These are the two ethno-centered positions:

The first ethno-centered position is labeled the "*ethnic democracy*" model (designated by Sammy Smooha; cf. 2002). While it excels in its realistic depiction of Israel, critics maintain that it falters in its normative acquiescence with this depiction. According to this model Israel is an exemplary case of a new type of democracy – an "*ethnic democracy*" – in which one ethnic group owns a kind of a "gold share" in the state. Members of other groups enjoy almost full individual citizenship but not equal collective rights. This is a democracy with a "low quality," but it is a price exacted in order to secure the Jewish people from a security disaster. It is argued that there are some other ethnic-democratic states and that this is a legitimate "model" of democracy.

The ethnic-democracy model is realistic and conservative. The realistic and radical response to it is delivered in the form of the "*ethnocracy model*" (designated by Oren Yiftachel; cf. 2006). Not incidentally the term "democracy" is absent from this model's label. According to it Israel is a state under the domination of only one "ethnos" – the Jewish ethnos – and the principled axis of the regime is the "Juadaization" of all material and symbolic resources of the country. Thus Israel does not simply "fail" to address fairly the concerns of its Arab citizens (as in the "soft" liberal version), but it is rather the constant rationale of the state to not only under-privilege non-Jews but to also render them to the status of second class citizens. Israel therefore is not democratic but rather ethnocratic, and its democratization must mean relinquish of the superiority and special status of the Jewish nation in the state. The Palestinian constitutional documents share unequivocally this view of the political regime in Israel.

The *social-economic approach* is historical and dynamic. The first version of it is the *"triadic citizenship model"* (designated by Shafir and Peled 2002). According to this model, there is in Israel a compound social regime of incorporation that includes three distinct discourses of citizenship: a republican Zionist discourse; an ethnic Jewish discourse; and a civic liberal discourse. The blend and relative weight of each component depends on changing circumstances and power relations among the groups in society. Making a long story short, the relative democratization that has taken place in Israel since the 1990s is related to the transition to capitalism.

The second version of this approach is the post-Marxist "bifurcation model" (designated by Uri Ram; 2007). This model focuses upon the recent transformation of Israel into a neo-liberal society under the impact of capitalist globalization. According to this model, in the wake of the nation-building and modernization stage underpinned by the collectivist orientation of the Labor movement, Israel has passed into a market-building and globalization stage underpinned by neo-liberal orientation. In this new post-Fordist reality Israel is bifurcating between a capitalist, liberal and de-colonization vector, on the one hand, and a neo-nationalist, communalist and pro-colonization vector, on the other hand (Ram 2007).

This has potential implications upon the relations between state and society, different state agencies and different groups. Israel's globalizing elites and wide middle classes have developed an interest in civil and market society, and have relegated nationalism to secondary preference. This results in a relative release of the ethnocentric nature of the state. On the other hand, it is exactly against this de-ethnicization that the lower classes are mobilized politically, utilizing Jewish religiosity and ethnicity as "cultural capital" in their response and struggle for social mobility (Filc 2007; Levy 2007; Peled 1998). Thus we witness in Israel a growing tension between liberalization, on the one hand, and ethnicization, on the other hand (or McWorld versus "Jihad"; Ram 2007).

Jewish-Israeli politics and identity

The next step towards deciphering the constitutional challenge of 2007 is to locate it in the context of some tensions and developments in Jewish-Israeli politics and identity.

In some sense, the Palestinian-Arab constitutional challenge of 2007 may be understood in the context of the "constitutional revolution" that took place in Israel in the 1990s, as well as of the accompanying post-Zionist critique on Israel, and also in the context of the limitations of these moments.

The "constitutional revolution" (henceforward CR) had been a judicial trend that was heralded by Supreme Judge Aharon Bark in 1992, on the basis of two "Basic Laws" that were enacted by the Knesset in this year – Basic Law: Freedom of Occupation and Basic Law: Human Dignity and Liberty. These laws anchored in Israel in an unprecedented manner the liberal principles of individual rights and of private property – thus accompanying, and also enabling, a transition from a collectivist society and centralized state into a competitive market society and civil society.[6]

Yet, the most ambiguous legacy of the first CR is exactly the manner in which it re-incorporated in the judicial arena the ethnic dimension of the state. In a famous axiom Israel was declared by the Supreme Court to be "a Jewish and democratic" state. This is a precarious and unstable coupling and it elicits lots of reactions: the Liberal center cherishes the radical transition to capitalism and the moderate version of nationalism implied; the nationalist and religious Right considers this formula to be "too democratic"; whereas lone critics from the Left consider it to be "too Jewish." The Arab constitutional challenge is one more voice directed at this concept and indicating the limits of the first CR.

The great achievement of the "first wave post-Zionism" was the ushering in of the counter-hegemonic concept "a state of all its citizens" into the public discourse, as against the dominant concept of "the Jewish and democratic state." "Second-wave post-Zionism" now further politicizes this concept and mobilizes the Arab citizens. One can say that the center of gravity of post-Zionism began to shift now from the intellectual "bubble" of Tel Aviv into the Arab cities and villages of the Galilee; from aloof university intellectuals to public activists; from the Jewish sector to the Arab sector; and from the judicial arena to the political arena. Post-Zionism thus came of age and passed its initial stage.

This constitutional challenge is indeed revolutionary in its potential. It is the first time in the history of Israel that actors among the Arab population not only protest against discrimination in various aspects of allocation of resources, but rather demand to transform the Jewish nature of Israel and to share power with its majority. In other words, it is the first time that the Arab sector does not speak the language of a marginal minority, but rather the language of a contender to hegemony. In the past, movements that tried to contest the Jewishness of the state were declared as a security threat and outlawed and disbanded.

"First-wave post-Zionism" was the radical liberal intellectual and political culture that accompanied this shift. Yet as the 1990s waned and the Jewish settlement in the Palestinian territories continued unimpeded and the "Peace Process" faltered, post-Zionism subsided. The decline of PZ was aggravated since 2000 by the Second Palestinian Intifada and since 2001 by the worldwide change in the political atmosphere in the wake of the Al Qaeda terrorist attacks on US cities.

But the implicit contradiction in the core of the Israeli polity that post-Zionism exposed did not disappear, quite the contrary. In 2001 Israeli security forces – under the premiership of Ehud Barak – shot to death twelve Palestinian citizens of Israel who participated in stormy demonstrations. This was a stepping-stone in the deterioration of the relations between the state and the Palestinian citizens. The result of the combined failure of "Oslo" and the continuous structural discrimination and systematic exclusion of the Palestinian citizens in Israel led to the surfacing of the "second wave of post-Zionism," this time in the shape of the public demand of the Arab citizens of Israel for a radical constitutional reform. But a fuller understanding of the constitutional challenge requires of course a consideration not only of the changes and tensions in Israeli society as a whole, but also a focus upon the dynamics of Palestinian-Arab identity and politics in Israel. To this we now turn.

Palestinian-Arab politics and identity

The final step – though of prime importance – to be taken here in order to analyze and contextualize the discussed constitutional challenge, is to consider it within the dynamic scene of Palestinian-Arab identity and politics in Israel, and especially of its "radicalization" in recent decades.

The Arab citizens of Israel are caught between the poles of universalism and particularism and also oscillate with the rest of the country – in their specific position – between them. In the brief moment of the Rabin government between 1993 and 1995 Israel recognized for the first time the Palestinian nation and the PLO as its representatives, and the Oslo accord seemed at the time to have led towards a Palestinian state. The spirit of peace generated a moment of unprecedented rapprochement between the Arabs in Israel and the state. Yet a shadow also loomed. To a great extent the move towards Israel's withdrawal from the occupied territories was motivated – as it still is – not by universalistic concerns but by the ethno-nationalist persistence upon the "Jewishness" of the state. Explicitly Israel seemed to say to the Palestinians that we "give up" your territories, you give us peace; implicitly it also transmitted to the Palestinians in Israel the message of: now there are going to be two states: one Jewish, one Palestinian; if you wish to stay here, you have to accept your secondary status as a minority in a majoritarian national state. So the potential consequences of a "two states solution" on the status of the Palestinian citizens in Israel were dubious.

But in any event, the consequences of the "peace" did not endure long enough to be tested. All hopes for a rapprochement were dashed after Rabin's assassination, and the cycle of violence was renewed with vengeance. In October 2000 the relations between Jews and Arabs in Israel came to their lowest ebb in recent times, when security forces killed thirteen demonstrators. Trust has not been re-established since (Or Commission Report 2003). Recent years had witnessed the continuous rising of ultra-nationalist Jewish politics (parties such as Shas and Israel Beitenu compete with the Likud on racist legislation) and the total demise of liberal politics in Israel (indicated by the constant shrinking of the Labor and Meretz parties in the Knesset). Arab politics retaliated in kind, and its center of gravity moved from the Communist Party to the ultra-nationalist party Balad.

The politics of the Palestinian-Arabs in Israel has radically transformed throughout time (Ghanem 2001; Reiter 2009). In 1949 they found themselves as a defeated and denigrated minority in a Jewish state, totally cut off from the rest of the Palestinian people and the Arab world outside of Israel. They received Israeli citizenship, but simultaneously were also subjected to a military regime and became totally dependent upon the government and the ruling party. An exception to this was the Communist Party, which under the protecting wings of Moscow became the major depositor of Arab-Palestinian nationalism in Israel. (In accord with Moscow the party became probably the first Arab political organ to recognize the existence of Israel and to support a "Jewish–Arab solidarity.") The Arab patriarchal social structure was exploited to maintain a clientelistic politics. The military regime was removed in 1966.

The consequences of the 1967 Six Day War changed the country overnight. The domination over the occupied territories brought together for the first time since 1948 the two separate communities of the Palestinian-Arabs: the community in Israel and the community in the West Bank and Gaza. If the long presence in Israel generated a degree of social and cultural "Israelization" of the Arabs in Israel, the meeting with the community in the West Bank and Gaza brought their "Palestinization" in terms of identity and ideology (Sammy Smooha 1989, 1992). In the mid 1980s the Communist Party reached the zenith of its popularity among Palestinian-Arabs, where it gained more than 50 percent of votes (in 1984). The decline and eventual fall of the Soviet Union (1989) and the general demise of the left were soon to hurt the party's status. In conjunction with this, the steep rise in the international exposure of the PLO and the consequences of the Islamist revolution in Iran (1979) invigorated the rise of

Palestinian-Arab nationalism in the Arab community in Israel (as well as the emergence for the first time in the 1990s of a significant movement of political Islamism in this community). As a result of all this, and together with the continuous and deepening estrangement of the state towards the Arab citizens, a further "radicalization" of Palestinian-Arab nationalist politics in Israel took place.

This radicalization was in turn facilitated by social processes that took place in the Arab sector in Israel, that are related to the general globalization of the country. I refer in particular to the emergence of wider strata of academicians, lawyers and other professionals. These strata have spawned a wide network of Arab civil society in Israel – which is relatively independent of the Israeli state. It is largely organized in the form of NGOs (non-governmental organizations) and its global reach furnishes Arab actors inside Israel with the financial means and – even more importantly – with an international political umbrella (on this see Payes 2005).

Thus we may summarize that Palestinian-Arab politics in Israel has gradually moved in the last half century from an initial parochial dependency towards a left-wing national-communism, and more recently towards an outright radical secular nationalism and simultaneously towards Muslim radicalism.

The constitutional challenge which we discuss here is a recent outcome of the political itinerary described above. The visionary documents thus represent Palestinian-Arab nationalism in Israel in the era of globalization, when politics evinces both bifurcation into "McWorld" versus "Jihad" and new combinations between them. It expresses the rise of radical secular nationalism in a context of a universal discourse of multi-culturalism and indigenous-peoples' rights. It is a product of the highly educated strata of the Palestinian-Arab population in Israel; a strata which is the vanguard of what was called "the stand-tall generation" of Arabs in Israel (Rabinowitz and Abu-Baker 2002), a generation which is both more explicitly Palestinian and more implicitly Israeli, which speaks now – like the rest of Israel – a language that blends and confuses cultural-nationalism with civic-libertarianism.

As this chapter goes to press, the Arab world is being shaken by mass revolts of "the peoples" against tyrants that have imposed autocratic regimes upon them for decades. The implications for the Palestinians in the occupied areas and within Israel are unclear as yet. But one may wonder whether the current impasse a) between Israel and Palestine (across the "green line") and b) between Israel and its own Palestinian citizens (inside the "green line") is a durable situation, or whether the "visionary documents" will turn into early indicators of a potential instability also in these cases.

Concluding comments and critique

The constitutional Palestinian-Arab challenge to the Israeli regime is of supreme importance on three counts.

First, it gives new and vigorous voice to the Palestinian-Arab citizens of Israel and makes true the promise of the "upright generation" to stand firmly by its rights.

Second, the documents place the discourse between the majority and the minority groups into a new stance, where it becomes clear that the issue is not that of "distribution," but rather that of "recognition," and thus of a change in the nature of the Israeli regime.

And third, this wave of demands will compel a "reality check" upon the state of Israel and the Jewish sector at large. Exposed to the new challenge, Israel will be pushed to drop the untenable gesture of being both Jewish and democratic, and to make an open and clear choice – either Jewish or democratic.

As a matter of fact, it seems that the initial reaction of Israel in the face of democratic challenges is to entrench the "Jewishness" of the state and to discard the democratic décor whenever and wherever it threatens to temper with this. And so, just as the post-Zionist challenge enters a new phase – an Arab phase – so also does the neo-Zionist nationalistic backlash enter a new phase of a risky move towards a hardening of the "Jewishness" of the state. Today it seems that there is an actual danger that the state is about to shed any guise of democracy and to turn into explicit apartheid policies of separation and repression (Navot and Peled 2009). The stalemate of the Israeli-Palestinian negotiations, and the sharp right-turn of the Israeli political center of gravity, indicate that direction.

Having said that, I argue in addition that the constitutional challenge as posed in the wave of documents discussed in this essay is limited, one sided, and short of offering a genuine promise of reconciliation and democracy; moreover, it may rather result in the escalation of the ethno-national conflict. The gravest problem with these documents is that they themselves are anchored fundamentally in an ethno-nationalist perspective, despite allusions to universalism and multiculturalism. Their underlying logic is that of ethno-national restitution, not of democratic resolution.

Ironically, the Palestinian-Arab constitutional documents present to the state of Israel a mirror-image of its own ethno-nationalist principles, rather than aiming to transcend these principles. And so, as far as the state is ethnonationalist – so do the documents define the Palestinian-Arabs on similar grounds; as far as the state does not recognize their national rights – neither do the documents recognize the national rights of Israel; as far as the state does not wish to integrate the Palestinian-Arab citizens in the tissue of its civic life – so do the visionary documents speak the language of separatism and aim to create separate and autonomous communities. And finally, as far as the state regards itself as single-national, so do the documents offer their own "double" single-national perspective called bi-nationalism. The universal vision of a non-national state, of a post-national state, of a democratic state of its citizens, remains, in these documents, unspoken and unexplored. Both the single-national Jewish vision (and actuality) and the bi-national vision suffer from nationalist blinders that prevent them from transcending beyond nationalism and imagine a democratic state of its citizens.

Notes

1 Whether this outcome is already actual or as yet potential is a disputed matter in Israel. See Ram 2011.
2 The data relates to Israel in the "green line" borders of 1949 and does not include the occupied territories from 1967.
3 Two other important documents in this "series" are: a judicial position document that was produced by the Moussawa Center (NGO) in conjunction with a United Nations agency; and an initiative by the Ibn Khaldun Center to create a separate elective representative body for the Palestinian citizens of Israel.
4 The veto power will be deposed in a special parliamentary committee, half of its members composed of Knesset Members from Arab parties; a special majority of the Knesset (two-thirds) will be able to overpower the committee. Alternatively any bill will have to be approved by 75 percent of Knesset members from Arab parties.
5 In the context of the current issue the term "ethno" refers to ethnos in the sense of defining a national category; so the relevant ethnos are Jews and Palestinian-Arabs. In a different context the term "ethnicity" is used in Israel to denote an inter-Jewish division between Ashkenazim (Westerners) and Mizrahim (Orientals); in this latter case the Hebrew word is "eda" (and in plural "edot"), to which the closest translation is community.
6 On another level these laws strengthened the status of the Judicial branch versus the two other governing branches, the Parliament and the Government, and established a Judicial check on the arbitrary power of the latter. In this regard the Supreme Court had become a champion of liberal citizenship rights, and thus became a target for attempts of curtailment by Jewish ethno-nationalist and religious groups, who argue that the court does nor represent the will of the majority. And on yet another level this revolution functioned to strengthen the position of the secular Ashkenazi middle class at a time that its political power was threatened in the representative political organs (Hirschl 2009). Overall, this constitutional revolution thus was part of what I termed the globalization of Israel and its post-Zioinization and of what Shafir and Peled termed the transition to a liberal regime of incorporation (Ram 2007; Shafir and Peled 2002).

References

The constitutional documents

The Haifa Declaration; Mada-al-Carmel; May 15th 2007 (Haifa). www.mada-research.org/archive/haifaenglish.pdf, visited August 1st 2007.

The Democratic Constitution; Adalah, The Legal Center for Aeab Minority Rights in Israel. February 2007. www.adalah.org/eng/democratic_constitution-e.pdf, visited August 1st 2007.

The Future Vision of the Palestinian Arabs in Israel. Published by The National Committee for the Heads of the Arab Local Authorities in Israel. www.mossawacenter.org/files/files/File/Reports/2006/Future%20Vision%20(English).pdf, visited August 1st 2007.

Other sources

Arato, Andrew. 2000. *Civil Society, Constitution, and Legitimacy*. Oxford: Rowman & Littlefield.

Arato, Andrew. 2009. *Constitution Making Under Occupation: The Politics of Imposed Revolution in Iraq*. New York: Columbia University Press.

Cohen, Jean and Andrew Arato. 1994. *Civil Society and Political Theory*. Cambridge, MA: MIT Press.

Fehér, Ferenc and Andrew Arato (eds.). 1991. *Crisis and Reform in Eastern Europe*. New Brunswick: Transaction Publishers.

Filc, Dani. 2007. *The Political Right in Israel: Different Faces of Jewish Populism*. London: Routledge.

Ghanem, Asad. 2001. *The Palestinian Arab Minority in Israel: A Political Study*. New York: SUNY University Press.

Hirschl, Ran. 2009. "The Socio-Political Origins of Israel's Juristocracy." *Constellations: An International Journal of Critical and Democratic Theory*. Special folio on Israeli Constitutionalism. Ed. Uri Ram. 16(3): 476–492.

Levy, Yagil. 2007. *Israel's Materialist Militarization*. Lanham, MD: Lexington Books.

Morris, Benny. 1989. *The Birth of the Palestinian Refugee Problem, 1947–1949*. Cambridge: Cambridge University Press.

Navot, Doron and Yoav Peled. 2009. "Towards a Constitutional Counter-Revolution in Israel?" *Constellations: An International Journal of Critical and Democratic Theory*. Special folio on Israeli Constitutionalism. Ed. Uri Ram. 16(3): 429–444.

Or Commission Report. "The Official Summation of the Or Commission Report." *Haaretz*, September 2nd 2003. www.haaretz.com//hasen/ShArt.jhtml?itemNo=335594, visited August 1st 2007.

Payes, Shany. 2005. *Palestinian NGOs in Israel: The Politics of Civil Society*. New York: Tauris.

Peled, Yoav. 1998. "Towards a Redefinition of Jewish Nationalism in Israel? The Enigma of Shas." *Ethnic and Racial Studies* 21(4): 703–724.

Peleg, Ilan. 2007. *Democratizing the Hegemonic State: Political Transformation in the Age of Identity*. Cambridge: Cambridge University Press.

Rabinowitz, Dan and Khaula Abu-Baker. 2002. *The Stand-Tall Generation*. Jerusalem: Keter.

Ram, Uri. 2007. *The Globalization of Israel: McWorld in Tel Aviv, Jihad in Jerusalem*. New York: Routledge.

Ram, Uri. 2011. *Israeli Nationalism: Social Conflicts and the Politics of Knowledge*. London: Routledge.

Reiter, Yitzhak. 2009. *National Minority, Regional Majority: Palestinian Arabs Versus Jews in Israel*. Syracuse, NY: Syracuse University Press.

Rosenfeld, Michel and Andrew Arato (eds,). 1998. *Habermas on Law and Democracy: Critical Exchanges*. Berkeley: University of California Press.

Shafir, Gershon and Yoav Peled. 2002. *Being Israeli: The Dynamics of Multiple Citizenship*. Cambridge: Cambridge University Press.

Smooha, Sammy. 1989 and 1992. *Arab and Jews in Israel, Vol. I & II*. Boulder and London: Westview Press.

Smooha, Sammy. 2002. "The Model of Ethnic Democracy: Israel as a Jewish and Democratic State." *Nations and Nationalism* 8(4): 475–503.

Yakobson, Alexander and Amnon Rubinstein. 2003. *Israel and the Family of Nations: Jewish Nations-State and Human Rights*. Tel Aviv: Schoken.

Yiftachel, Oren. 2006. *Ethnocracy: Land and Identity Politics in Israel/Palestine*. Philadelphia: University of Pennsylvania Press.

Part II

Civil society, populism, and the modern executive

Arato’s intellectual influence in the Americas

6 The concept of civil society and the Latin American debate on democratic innovation

Alberto J. Olvera

There are some books that become obligatory references in the sphere of international public debate because of their notable timing, political ambition and theoretical density. This is the case of Jean L. Cohen and Andrew Arato's 1992 book *Civil Society and Political Theory*. This book was timely because the international discourse regarding civil society emerged in the late twentieth century without a theory to explain its very existence. The clarification of the historical, political and intellectual conditions that opened the space for the rebirth of civil society, a task carried out by Cohen and Arato in the first section of their book, would have been, in itself, an important and appreciated contribution to knowledge. But our authors did something else as well. They developed a theory of civil society with an explicit political intention: to rethink democratic politics, going beyond liberal, republican and socialist thinking.

It is not surprising, then, that Cohen and Arato's seminal work had, almost immediately, worldwide impact. In Latin America, the book was widely read in English and even more once it was translated into Spanish in the year 2000.[1] Since then *Civil Society and Political Theory* has had several editions, citations of which count by thousands in books and articles published in the region in the past fifteen years. What was the reason for such a success?

Since the mid 1980s, most countries in Latin America have experienced processes of transition to democracy from authoritarian regimes. Civil society has been a very important symbolic instrument in this struggle. Well before Cohen and Arato's book was available, civil society was, as in Eastern Europe, an important element of identity building for the social movements of the period. Even in countries like Mexico where there was no transition at that time, the idea of civil society gained momentum because of processes of symbolic differentiation between the state and society.

In the beginning, the intellectual elaboration of the concept of civil society in the region was, as in Eastern Europe, based on the interpretation of social actors' intervention in the process of democratization. Later, during the period of consolidation and democratic normalization, it turned into a kind of programmatic instrument in the struggle between political projects, most of which turned to different versions of the idea of civil society to legitimate their strategic proposals. Political and intellectual confusion emerged and several new concepts, compatible, equivalent or similar to that of civil society (third sector, social capital, citizen participation, etc.) were introduced in the political and academic arenas by multilateral agencies, politicians and academics, fueling a situation that has been labeled a "perverse confluence" of opposite political projects using the same ideas and concepts (Dagnino, 2004).

In this historical context, Cohen and Arato's book was a timely instrument for the interpretation of the present and for the development of political projects oriented toward democratic deepening. The tripartite model (market, state, society) presented by those authors, as well as their model of the intermediate spheres of economic and political societies, helped to broaden the understanding of politics not only in transition periods, but also in the construction of democracy, by taking the politics of civil society beyond the limits of protest and the struggle for electoral democracy.

Civil Society and Political Theory helped to build a new field of knowledge in which, growing out of the concept of civil society, several new concepts were developed to improve and deepen the emerging field of radical democratic politics: public space, social movements, deliberative democracy, citizen participation, societal accountability. These concepts, closely interrelated, helped to differentiate the project of democratic, participative politics from that of a neoliberal and depoliticizing understanding of civil society.

The late 1990s and the first years of the new century were a time of conceptual confusion, but also of great democratic innovation in Latin America. It is relevant to analyze to what extent the concept of civil society contained the elements that allowed for such different readings and uses. By tracing the trajectory of the idea of civil society in Latin America, we can understand both its conceptual potentials and limits, and the ways in which the concept helped to envision the process of democratization in the region.

In this chapter I begin with a very brief discussion of Cohen and Arato's concept of civil society, concentrating on both its sociological and political contributions and deficits, as seen from the vantage point of Latin American societies. In the second section, I develop an analysis of the trajectory of the conceptual debate on civil society and related concepts in Latin America in recent years. In the last section some final remarks are offered.

I An internal (and friendly) critique

Jean L. Cohen and Andrew Arato developed their concept of civil society on the foundation laid by Jürgen Habermas's theoretical-historical claim regarding the primacy of *lifeworld* over *system*: "the institutional framework of a modern lifeworld stabilized by fundamental rights, which will include within their scope the spheres of public and private (from a lifeworld point of view)" (Cohen and Arato, 1992: 492). The "public" encompasses the public sphere, the set of arenas and sites where free (from systemic constraints) communicative interaction can be approximated in social praxis. The "private" is the terrain of familial and interpersonal relations.

In Cohen and Arato's perspective, civil society has two main components: on the one hand, the set of institutions that define and protect citizens' individual, political and social rights and facilitate their free association, creating the legal conditions for citizens to protect themselves from the strategic action of power and money. On the other hand, the set of social movements that posits new principles and values in the public sphere, while also watching over the effective application of already granted rights. In this sense, civil society consists of both an institutional element basically defined by the structure of rights in the contemporary welfare states and an active, transformative element constituted by new social movements (Arato, 1994).

The empowerment of civil society depends, in this perspective, on: (a) the development of the voluntary associations and social movements that constitute its social fabric and materialize new forms of solidarity; (b) the existence of a public sphere in which matters of collective interest can be discussed; and (c) the availability of institutional means to create bridges between civil society and the representative political entities. Cohen and Arato developed the concepts of "economic society" and "political society" to situate and analyze the intermediary institutions and actors that bridge civil society and both the economic and political systems.

The "institutional" definition of civil society helped to get past the "institutional deficit" encumbering new social movements theories (Cohen, 1985); that is, the fact that such theories could not explain how the symbolic and political successes of social movements are stabilized and eventually become a new political framework of action, out of which a new cycle of mobilization emerges. This centrality that Cohen and Arato give to law and rights shares with Habermas's theory a historically specific character. Only in the West have fundamental rights been effectively institutionalized and eventually extended in successive waves of "juridification" to the fields of political, social and economic freedoms and entitlements. In the rest of the world, Western institutions have often been formally adopted but in fact ignored or functionally utilized as instruments of domination.

A first critique of this definition of civil society thus comes from a counterfactual empirical argument: how is it possible that a civil society could exist at all in the almost complete absence of effective rights, as was the case in Eastern Europe before 1989 (socialist regimes) and in Latin America during the period of dictatorship (and in most of Asia and Africa and parts of Latin America even today)? How can civil society push forward the struggle for democracy when the material-legal-institutional conditions for its very existence are absent? Andrew Arato recognized this problem as early as 1994, concluding that the concept of civil society was in need of a sociological revision in order to explain the subsistence and reproduction of social networks in informal arenas in which resistance and solidarity can be practiced. Only if these arenas exist is it possible to imagine a more or less quick development of social movements once political conditions change (liberalization). To his merit, Arato, referring to social action in Eastern Europe before 1989, explained that

> the self-organizing movements, initiatives, associations and publics, putting the social in motion were also different than *either* the latent networks of societal autonomy *or* the institutionalized civil societies as we know them in the West. Thus, instead of using a single concept one faces the task to develop three and then link them together in a plausible historical manner.
>
> (Arato, 1994: 46, original emphasis)

This "sociological deficit" in Cohen and Arato's 1992 concept of civil society becomes even more serious if one considers that in several Latin American countries as well as in most of Asia and Africa, the very precondition of modernity (and of civil society), namely, the systemic differentiation between market, state and society, and the concomitant emergence of the modern, rights-holding individual, has not been completed or has been carried out in a highly deformed manner. Here the rule of law is still a pending political project, at least for the majority population. Broad areas of the economy are dominated, within the capitalist market, by informal networks, and as much as half the workforce is unemployed, or employed in the informal sector, without operative labor rights. Proportions that vary from 20 to 60 percent of the population live in illegal slums, without effective rights over their precarious homes and without access to decent services. Access to justice for the majority of the population is denied or conditioned by the government. Social action carried out by people living under these conditions is oriented most of the time toward drawing the government's attention to their basic needs, always in particular settings, without claiming universal rights. They want and need "to be governed," as the Indian political scientist Partha Chatarjee (2004) put it, for purposes of mere survival. Chatarjee, confusingly, designs as "political society" this vast aggregation of disperse social actors not linked by formal associations, who perform their actions in an almost total absence of public spaces, while clearly addressing specific government authorities by means of mobilizations. Their actions are "political," in the sense of creating direct forms of encounter between "populations" and state authorities in which power is the language of communication. Citizenship in the sense of exercise of rights is absent in this process, as well as civil society in the sense of institutions protecting rights. In most of the world, then, civil society lacks its fundamentals (for a vast proportion of the population), and the creation of these minimal preconditions is a fundamental task for the advancement of democracy.

We can point out a second deficit in Cohen and Arato's definition of civil society, this time of a political nature. Their concept of civil society inherits from Habermas the idea that it is possible to locate in the lifeworld an arena in which "communicative action" is more important than strategic action, be it organized by power or money.[2] Recognizing that in practice all actions are influenced by money and power and that strategic action needs communication to succeed, Habermas (1998) and Cohen and Arato locate in civil society a set of arenas in which communicative action still prevails. But given the difficulty in defining the limits of each type of action, it follows that it is also difficult to separate – except in ideal-type conceptualizations – the areas of action and the actors that intervene principally in either civil or political (or economic) society.

This consideration is important because the social actors who rescued the concept of civil society in Eastern Europe and Latin America established in practice two principles of action: self-limitation and autonomy, both studied by Cohen and Arato, whose generalization beyond certain historically specific situations can be misleading. "Self-limiting" social movements do not seek to occupy sites of power, but rather to control them (radical reformism). "Autonomy" refers to a classical liberal separation between state and society, a necessary symbolic and political move in situations of dictatorship and/or of authoritarian fusion, as in socialist and some populist regimes.

These principles were part of a democratic strategy in the historical period of transitions to democracy and the struggle against authoritarian socialism. At that time, the liberal separation between society and state was politically useful. But, as the analysis of transitions shows, this separation becomes less clear as soon as the authoritarian regime is forced to negotiate with the opposition and afterward to give up control of power. A critique of the hypothesis put forward by, for example, O'Donnell and Schmitter (1986), in which civil society activation was necessary in the launching of transition struggles but then, in the moment of negotiation, civil society should demobilize in order not to jeopardize the very negotiations, was presented by Arato (1996) (and by myself and Avritzer for Latin America [1992]). The critique pointed to the fact that civil society was the carrier of political innovations and the site of identity construction, thus its democratic potential extended beyond the establishment of electoral democracy. Civil society's role in the development of innovative democratic institutions was of paramount importance in and *after* the period of consolidation.

Such a critique implied not only a rejection of a limited understanding of civil society, but also a critique of the then-hegemonic concept of democracy as mere procedure to elect rulers (elite democracy theories). The politics of civil society, understood by Cohen and Arato as a "politics of influence" (following the systems-theory terminology), meant that civil society actors, by creating new meanings and values and criticizing power in the public sphere, were practicing "a dualistic politics of identity and influence, aimed at both civil society and the polity" (Cohen and Arato, 1992: 504). By criticizing the shortcomings of social-movements theories that concentrated only on social movements' capacity to achieve inclusion in the political system, our authors gave civil society a leading role in the political learning processes and offered an explanation of its "permanent" political functions in a modern democratic polity.

In doing this, however, a new problem emerged. The conceptual separation between civil society and political society turned opaque. How is it that civil society "influences" political society without being connected to it, at least in a symbolic, programmatic sense? Interestingly enough, Arato, analyzing the Hungarian experience, recognized that the differentiation between civil and political society was a tactical necessity of successful transitions, but that in practice, "elites and militants were pulled away from civil organizations and into fledgling parties, thereby promoting an implosion of many of the movements that previously occupied the center stage" (Arato, 1996: 2). It turned out that the same leaders who were originally civil society representatives became political leaders of emerging parties. There was, in the end, continuity between civil and political society through the personal trajectories of the only available opposition leaders, who acted as carriers of different political projects already – or at least potentially – present in society. The practical effect of this process was the sudden coming to the fore of the already existing political plurality contained in the very actors of civil society. The formal but artificial unity of civil society in the struggle against the authoritarian regime dissolved as soon as the need emerged to create political parties and organize the democratic struggle for power.

The way Cohen and Arato's concept of civil society was popularized and discussed during the period of transition to and consolidation of democracy, the period in which civil society performed a sort of heroic role, led analysts to emphasize the principles of autonomy and self-limitation, which implied a separation between civil and political societies.[3] But in fact, once the transition was over, in the sense of an electoral democratic breakthrough, maintaining that very separation as a conceptual strategy or as a political project turned into both an obstacle to the correct understanding of the role of civil society in the construction of operative democracies and a conceptual limitation in the practice of (democratic) politics.

At the same time, the neoliberal project of development pushed forward by the so-called "Washington Consensus" (Drache, 2001), promoted not only the privatization of extensive areas of government services, but also a new relationship between society and the state, in which "citizen participation," civil society-led accountability, civil society partnerships, and similar concepts were the axis of both a new liberal vision of the state and a new liberal-democratic role attributed to society. Indeed, multilateral agencies such as the World Bank, the Inter-American Development Bank, the United Nations, and many others, helped to make civil society a fashionable concept in the early 1990s.[4] This international process brought enormous popularity to a liberal concept of civil society, based again on the separation between state and society.

Cohen and Arato's concept of civil society contained elements that could support both a broader and more precise analytical framework and a democratic project with a potential to rethink democracy as an ongoing process of sociopolitical construction. But in order to do so, it needed further elaboration, a conceptual broadening and a correct historical contextualization. The recovery of these elements would take place in several arenas in the late 1990s and beyond. In Latin America this process has been carried out mostly through the study of citizen participation in public spaces (Avritzer, 2002), the struggles between political projects and the deployment of the "participatory project" (Dagnino *et al.*, 2006), "accountability politics" (Fox, 2007; Peruzzotti and Smulovitz, 2006) and, last but not least, the construction of effective citizenship (O'Donnell and Mariani, 2008; O'Donnell *et al.*, 2004).

II Some critiques and recent conceptual developments in Latin America

In a recent book, Evelina Dagnino, Aldo Panfichi and I (2006) argued that breaking free of the paradoxes that the analysis of civil society in the period of transition to and consolidation of democracy created is a fundamental task. We located three main problems, the first being the already mentioned homogenizing idea of civil society, which nurtured the image of civil society as a "pole of virtue" opposed to a state conceived of as the "embodiment of evil" (Dagnino, 2002). Against this reductionist interpretation, we propose the recognition of the heterogeneity of civil society in social, political and cultural terms (Dagnino *et al.*, 2006: 31–42).

Indeed, within civil society multiple and diverse social actors coexist, as do opposing political projects, cultural values and forms and practices of relationship with the state. Civil society actors adopt varied institutional formats (urban, professional, cultural or sports associations, unions, networks, coalitions, forums, clubs, etc.), defend different political projects, embrace multiple religions and develop distinctive cultural practices. Such heterogeneity is an expression of the political, social and cultural plurality of contemporary societies, and it is also the result of the structural complexity of society in most of the world.

As mentioned before, Andrew Arato (1994) recognized the need to develop specific concepts to differentiate the latent networks in society, the emerging movements in times of rapid political and economic change and the institutionalized civil society. We can add to this consideration the radical separation between an "integrated modern civil society," which can be internally differentiated according to the three above-mentioned categories, and the "disintegrated society" (or non-civil society) composed by the vast informal economy, illegal foreign immigrants, recent internal immigrants, victims of forced territorial expulsions (be it for racial, religious, political or delinquency-related reasons), structurally unemployed people, and the vast groups discriminated against due to race, gender, sexual orientation or religious factors. Moreover, there exists in Latin America and most of the world an "uncivil society" formed by all sorts of delinquent groups, mafias, "guerrillas," juvenile gangs, etc. This is the real complexity of society, with which we have to deal.

Notwithstanding the obviousness of these considerations, in the cultural imaginary of an entire generation of civil activists and in some of the current conceptualizations of civil society there still persists a vision of the "civil society sphere" as something homogeneous and characterized by some sort of shared civic virtue. Concomitantly, the idea of a homogeneous civil society goes hand in hand with that of a homogeneous state. This reductionism constitutes a conceptual limitation both in the analysis and in the construction of a democratic state.

Jeffrey Alexander, for example, argues that

> we need a new concept of civil society as a civil sphere, a world of values and institutions that generates the capacity for social criticism and

> democratic integration at the same time. Such a sphere relies on solidarity, feelings for others, whom we don't know but whom we respect out of principle, not experience, because of our putative commitment to a common secular faith.
>
> (Alexander, 2006: 4)

For Alexander, this commitment materializes in law and institutions, but also in a changing culture that finds ways of "repairing" its own authoritarian, intolerant flaws by means of social movements, cultural codes and a kind of circular return to the democratic fundamentals in times of distress.

Alexander has the merit of analyzing the structures of political representation and the institutions of the state not only as functional mediators between civil society and the state but as institutionalized expressions of values, norms and pacts that constitute the foundation of modern democracies. Yet despite all the historical and contemporary narrative displayed in Alexander's recent book, it nevertheless lacks a more complex vision of society as such, a sociology of law[5] and also what can be labeled an "anthropology of the state."[6] It is not enough to allude to the cultural contents of laws and institutions; their actual workings and practical effects on people's lives have to be studied in detail in their interaction with civil and political actors, markets and international institutions.

This version of pluralism assumes the integrative nature of a modern civic culture. Such a "culturalist version" of the civic sphere leads not only to a homogenizing version of civil society, but also of the state. Laws and institutions, abstracted from their actual contexts, would seem to represent the values that are "behind them." But actual states behave in very different ways depending on their particular histories and the specific correlations of forces in each historical period. I used the term "archeology of the state" to mean the accumulation of "tectonic layers" in the formation of state institutions, which, instead of being an incremental process, is full of breakthroughs, which do not always mean the destruction of old institutions and the development of new ones. Rather, such seemingly radical changes are, in practice, often a sort of superimposition of the new over the old. The preservation of old practices and cultures at the heart of new institutions is well known in Latin America.

The reductionist version of both civil society and state was linked to a second problem, the liberal separation between state and society, already analyzed in the previous section. This separation, a distinctive feature of democratic transition and consolidation of democracy theories, played an important role in both the dissemination of a limited concept of democracy and in the reproduction of the homogenizing ideas of civil society and of the democratic state. But, as mentioned, the success of democratic consolidations coincided historically with the emergence of neoliberalism in most of Latin America. Paradoxically, in the new period,

> all that was required was a switch from the interpretation of the state as an enemy with whom a relationship of confrontation was maintained to one of

> the state as an institution with which cooperation can and should be sustained – under the assumption that, given its democratic nature, it now legitimately responds to citizens' needs. Thus, the old confrontational notion [society against the state] could be turned around and a new imaginary of non-differentiation and de-politicization be constructed.
>
> (Dagnino *et al.*, 2006: 32)

In Latin America there was a surprisingly fast change from the concept of liberal differentiation (and opposition) between state and society to a liberal concept of integration and collaboration between "sectors." The "Third Sector" theory, developed in the early 1990s and popularized in Latin America through networks and generous financing of local and comparative research, emerged from a peculiar diagnosis of our time: in modern societies, the government is retreating from community life, the market cannot provide all of society's needs and, as a consequence, society is organizing itself to create the services and products it needs. The public sector, the private sector and the "third sector," that is, self-organized civil associations, complement each other (Salomon and Anheier, 1994).

The concept of a "Third Sector" concentrates on the "structural and operational" dimensions of civil associations: (a) their formal character, that is, their organizational permanence; (b) their private nature, combined with a non-profit character, which differentiate them from the market; (c) their capacity for self-government, which makes them independent from the state; and (d) their voluntary nature (Salomon and Anheier, 1994). Several problems arise from this concept. Voluntary action can be found in all forms of association, but permanence implies a high degree of institutionalization, which frequently leads to the displacement of voluntary action; moreover, the requisite of permanence can truly rule out the majority of social movements, which are nonetheless self-ruled. It is hard to establish the non-profit character of associations since regardless of their legal form, their actual insertion into the logic of the market can completely determine the real operation of each institution. To offer services to third parties cannot be considered a substantive criterion because services can be commercialized for personal or private purposes.

The notion of the Third Sector has helped to legitimize the transition from a concept of civil society organized around rights (that is, citizenship) and public spaces to another concept of civil society organized by private actions, in which the very practice of politics vanishes (Almeida, 2006).

The concept of Third Sector gained momentum in Latin America because it complemented another idea prevailing in the public discourse of the time: the reduction of civil society to the sphere of civil associationism. This interpretation was hegemonic in Mexico, where nongovernmental organizations (NGOs) and some social movements saw themselves as *the only* civil society. This reading was reinforced by some international NGO networks, such as CIVICUS (Oliveira and Tandon, 1994), as well as international development agencies. This vision was the result of another form of globalization: the growing internationalization of certain segments of civil society such as human rights groups and the environmental, pacifist and feminist movements, whose struggles created a previously non-existing front of civil pressure against some international agencies (Fox and Brown, 1998). From this dynamic emerged, since the end of the 1980s, a reconceptualization of civil society, which was narrowed down to mean the network of associations with the capacity to cooperate with governments in the implementation of public policies. The concept of civil society became a substantive element of the lexicon of the international development agencies, national governments and international foundations, but with the specific meaning of networks of NGOs (Tussie, 2000).

Meanwhile, in the international public arena a language of citizen participation was simultaneously emerging (Cunill, 1997). Participation was understood as a type of cooperation between citizens and governments in the implementation of public policies. Multiple governments around the world adopted the discourse of participation and even instituted some mechanisms that appeared to meet this claim (Hevia, 2006).

At the same time, the historic coincidence between the neoliberal implantation and the processes of re-democratization in most of Latin America also opened space to reconsider the themes of civil society and citizen participation in a distinct manner. The analysis of transitions to democracy included an evaluation of civil society as a promoter of the struggle for political rights and as a moral opponent to authoritarianisms of all types. The role of civil society in the transition indeed generated a liberal reading, grounded in the opposition between a virtuous civil society and an evil State, but also a republican reading that stressed the participative and co-generating dimension of a new democratic power that emanated from below. This discourse was articulated as an explicit political project in Brazil, where the idea of participation was the platform of a program oriented toward the "socialization of power," that is to say, a "sharing of power between society and the political system" (Alvarez *et al.*, 1998). Its moral and legal principles were built into the constitution of 1988, a legal framework that allowed the unfolding of innovative experiments such as the management councils (Dagnino, 2002); participative budgets (Avritzer, 2002) and other institutionalized public spaces.

This is precisely the third thematic area the concept of civil society helped to open up in the 1980s and 1990s: who were the actors who drove democratization in Latin America, and what was the real scope of processes of democratization? In one interpretation, civil society was the driving force, the synthesis of good causes and innovation. In another, civil society played only an instrumental role in a process in which political elites held command. If anything, "the debate on the role of civil society in the construction of democracy should be seen as a symbolic struggle over the place, actors and agenda of the dispute between distinct political projects" (Dagnino *et al.*, 2006: 26).

In this struggle, the concept of public space has been of paramount importance, and in one of its versions represented a result of the learning process propelled by the civil society debate. From the outset, the prevailing notion that "public" meant the State – in opposition to the private sector – had to be countered. At least in Mexico and Brazil, this was the dominant meaning sustained throughout the golden years of the developmental state (Cunill, 1997). The notion of "the public" as a social space is a relatively new concept, a usage that was first applied in Brazil. From this point of view, public spaces are those instances that allow for the recognition of, and give voice to, new actors and themes. These instances are not monopolized by any social or political sector or by the state, but are heterogeneous, reflecting social and political plurality. Public spaces therefore serve to make conflict visible, providing the conditions for conflicts to be dealt with in ways in which diverse opinions and interests can be recognized, and in which there is, ideally, a tendency toward the equality of resources among participants, in terms of information, knowledge and power (Rabotnikof, 2005).

Within the public arena, debate and argumentation are carried out, thus broadening the concept and the practice of politics, insofar as argumentation and debate allow for the recognition of new demands and the development of critique as a field of political action (Habermas, 1998). But, as Avritzer (2002) demonstrates, Habermas's analysis of the public space suffers from a fundamental limitation: the public space is understood as primarily defensive, a barrier to abuses of power, rather than an entity with offensive potential, capable of acting effectively over public power in ways other than the indirect mechanism of influence. In his view, public space does not effectively articulate reason and will, but leaves decision-making in the hands of politicians. One way of overcoming this limitation has been to move from discourse to deliberation, that is, those public forums (and associated accountability mechanisms) in which decisions are made jointly by citizens and public officials. These spaces are supposed to be connected to the state through a series of legal and institutional mechanisms that would give them the ability to implement public policies.[7]

The participative project is also present, to a lesser degree and with less ambition, in the Colombian constitution of 1991, and with much greater rigor and clarity in the Venezuelan constitution of 1999. The Peruvian constitution of 1993 also contains this class of precepts, as did the Bolivian constitution of 1994. The recent constitutions of Bolivia (2009) and Ecuador (2008) are directly predicated under the principle of participation, without this fact necessarily translating into operative institutions and truly democratic practices, although impressive democratic-participative experiences can be found in several countries, mainly in Bolivia. But only in Brazil has the participative project gone all the way from the constitution to operative institutions which now have more than twenty years of experience. As demonstrated by Hevia (2006), in other countries the necessary secondary laws have not been enacted and the few new "participative" institutions have no capacity to promote effective citizen participation. Those experiences are therefore more ambivalent than in Brazil. At least for the case of Venezuela, it is possible to venture the hypothesis of a combination of participative and authoritarian projects in which the authoritarian component has turned hegemonic in recent years (Olvera and Chaguaceda, 2009).

In most countries, the participative project coexists both at the constitutional level and in political practice with pluralistic and neocorporative mechanisms of representation of interests. This matrix has adopted the form of "representative" councils, more or less recognized publicly, in which specific public policies are discussed, but not decided. Generally speaking, the interests represented in these councils are those of the economically, socially and politically powerful social groups (Olvera, 2008).

There is yet another version of the liberal project: the citizen seen as a user of services, that is, as a client of public services. The World Bank in particular has encouraged this vision since the early 1990s. Thus, citizens come to be understood as "clients" and government as a "service provider." The rights of the citizenry are of no concern. There is no talk of rights and obligations, only a liberal-corporate vision of the functions of the state. Both liberal perspectives share a problem: neither is grounded in rights. Pluralist participation and client satisfaction are concepts that have no legal means of enforcement. The neoliberal project for the participation of citizens, in its various versions, lacks a suitable legal and institutional anchor and is based explicitly on the depoliticization of the relationships between governments and citizens.

Coherent with this approach is the use of the concept of social capital – also promoted by the World Bank – which supposedly explains the sociological infrastructure of social relations of cooperation between civil actors and government.[8] The merit of the concept of social capital is that it emphasizes the cultural factors of social action, transcending the narrow horizons of mere institutional design. Nevertheless, the main problem with this concept is that it is unable to clarify how ties of trust can be created in political contexts in which laws are not respected, social and cultural inequality among the actors is abysmal and the legitimacy of state institutions is fragile. Indeed, the theory of social capital cannot explain how interpersonal trust can turn into trust in institutions (Offe, 1999). Institutions are not people, and, consequently, the type of relationships that can be constructed in face-to-face interaction – something that occurs within associations and facilitates a relational sense of trust – cannot be projected onto them. Moreover, as Jean Cohen (1999) has pointed out, the concept of social capital is fragile since it does not explain life in society beyond local communities. Social life in complex societies demands generalized reciprocity and law abidance, among other cultural behaviors that do not spring spontaneously from interpersonal trust.

Within this framework emerged the new discourse of *accountability*. Understandably, disenchantment and frustration with limited concepts and practices of participation opened space for strong demands for real citizen control over governments. This discourse was adopted by international development agencies in order to attain the desired effectiveness of their own programs (Tussie, 2000).

But the discourse of accountability is also a reaction of civil society actors to both the continuity of widespread practices of corruption and the preservation of bureaucratic secretiveness, both of which are the basis of politicians and bureaucrats' discretionary power (Peruzzotti and Smulovitz, 2006). The struggle for accountability can also be understood as a social movement that defends the broadening of the concept of human rights in order to encompass the rights of information and participation (Olvera and Isunza, 2006).

The politics of accountability is another area of conceptual development related to the discourse of civil society. Certain civil society actors, and some intermediate institutions, such as the media, develop a capacity to oversee the performance of state institutions and to act as "sensors" of state failures and/or government disregard of social demands, working in a vibrant public sphere. However, as Arato (2006) and Peruzzotti and Smulovitz (2006) have convincingly argued, civil society actors working in the public sphere mainly perform the task of forcing the political system to activate its own internal mechanisms of control, ultimately helping classical political accountability to work. But this cannot happen without civil society and the public sphere acting as mediators between the people and the political system. This is precisely what accountability politics does.

This last consideration connects with another emerging field of debate in Latin America, albeit one that is not directly related to the civil society tradition (but which in fact complements it). Guillermo O'Donnell (2004 and 2008), one of the greatest Latin American political scientists, has recently pushed for a reconsideration of the role of the democratic state in the construction of an effective citizenship and more generally in the deepening of democracy in the region. By concentrating on the analysis of the "weak, anemic states" of Latin America, O'Donnell demonstrates that democracy (and civil society) needs a strong state (in terms of performance and respect for the law) to prosper. The homogenizing vision of the state, typical of both the period of transitions and consolidations and of most liberal understandings of democracy, is deconstructed in order to explain the correlation between weak states and weak citizenship. This problem is not only related to formal rights, laws and constitutions, but also has to do with institutional, cultural and representational deficits of actually existing states. A strong civil society and an empowered citizenship need a strong state, and vice versa. This mutual construction is, in this perspective, the real clue to democratic deepening.

Recent developments in democratic theory in Latin America, most of which have been inspired by the concept of civil society, are arriving at the same conclusion: democracy is always in construction, and its deepening depends on cooperation between civil and political actors. Democracy is a process of co-construction in which those actors collaborate in an institutional framework in which conflict over political projects is permanent. The mutual empowerment of a democratic state and of a democratic civil society is not a common result of actual political processes. It happens under certain historical conditions, and only if democratic actors are present at both levels.[9]

Final remarks

Jean L. Cohen and Andrew Arato's *Civil Society and Political Theory* has been a central reference in the ongoing debate over democratization in Latin America as the concept of civil society has been the cornerstone of both the most relevant political debates and opposed political projects. Civil society became such a fashionable category that many different institutions, from international development agencies to international and local NGOs, political parties and governments, have used it to promote their respective models of democracy.

The Habermas-inspired concept of civil society developed by Cohen and Arato helped to lay the foundations of a plausible theory for a new field of knowledge: radical democratic politics. By expanding the field of politics to social practices located in civil society, Cohen and Arato situated the sociological terrain of democratic innovation. The idea of the "politics of influence" recognized social movements' capacity not only to challenge hegemonic cultural codes, but also to openly intervene in the political field in the defense and promotion of rights, the control of government and the critique of power by means of all sorts of interventions in the public sphere.

However, this concept remained too close to Habermas's purely defensive understanding of the public sphere and his pessimistic opinion about the uncontrollable nature of systems. In fact, the politics of influence turned out to be limited to mostly defensive purposes, or in the best of cases, to "radical reformist politics" whose content and forms remained too abstract.

Recent developments in democratic theory in Latin America, inspired as they have been in the idea of an active civil society and a public space potentially open to innovation, have developed analytical strategies to locate the actors, arenas and processes of democratic deepening that go beyond the limits of "normal democratic politics." Such is the case of deliberative democracy, usually coupled with some version of the idea of citizen participation (Avritzer and Santos, 2002; Dagnino *et al.*, 2006), or with the concept of public space: "deliberative publics" (Avritzer, 2002). It is also the case of the recovery and revaluation of "accountability politics" (Fox, 2007; Peruzzotti and Smulovitz, 2006). Such conceptual developments have had to confront liberal versions of civil society (Third Sector, social capital, "NGOization" of civil society) which have been instrumental to the hegemonic neoliberal project. This battle thus far seems won for the cause of radical democracy in the intellectual arena, but not in the political field.

Notes

1 The book was published in Spanish in Mexico by the Fondo de Cultura Económica, the main academic publishing house in Latin America, in 2000. The first edition has been reprinted three times and a fourth is forthcoming. Previously, in 1999, I edited a book in Mexico introducing Cohen and Arato's ideas (Olvera, 1999).

2 Habermas explains this fact by means of the differentiation between systemic and social integration. The latter can only be produced through communicative action (Habermas, 1987).

3 See, for a perspective inspired by Cohen and Arato's ideas: Olvera, 1997, 1999; for liberal perspectives, Pérez Díaz, 1993 among many others.

4 For a vision of these ideas see: Tussie, 2000; World Bank, 1996, 1998.

5 Andrew Arato pointed out in 1994 that one of the shortcomings of his own theory was precisely the lack of a sociology of law and constitutionalism, a task he began to take on in the late 1990s.

6 I am thinking of Hevia, 2006, and Migdal, 2001, for example.
7 The bibliography on participation is enormous. For an overview and analysis of the Brazilian experience, see Avritzer, 2009.
8 For a review of the debate on social capital, see Edwards *et al.*, 2001; and Warren, 2001.
9 For a complete analysis of this process, see Dagnino *et al.*, 2006, introduction; and Avritzer, 2009.

References

Alexander, Jeffrey (2006). *The Civil Sphere*, Oxford University Press, New York.

Almeida, Carla (2006). "El marco discursivo de la 'participación solidaria' y la nueva agenda de formulación e implementación de las acciones sociales en Brasil," in: Evelina Dagnino, Alberto J. Olvera and Aldo Panfichi (eds.), *La Disputa por la Construcción Democrática en América Latina*, Fondo de Cultura Económica, Universidad Veracruzana, México.

Álvarez, S., E. Dagnino and A. Escobar (eds.) (1998). *Culture of Politics, Politics of Cultures*, Westview Press, Boulder.

Arato, Andrew (1994). "The rise, decline and reconstruction of the concept of civil society, and directions for future research," in: *The Public*, Vol. I, No. 1–2, Slovenia, pp. 45–53.

Arato, Andrew (1996). "Civil society, transition and consolidation of democracy," paper presented at: International Conference Democratic Transitions in Latin America and in Eastern Europe: Rupture and Continuity, 4–6 March 1996, Paris, France.

Arato, Andrew (2006). "Accountability and civil society," in: Enrique Peruzzotti and Catalina Smulovitz (eds.), *Enforcing the Rule of Law*, University of Pittsburgh Press, Pittsburgh.

Avritzer, Leonardo (2002). *Democracy and the Public Sphere in Latin America*, Princeton University Press, Princeton.

Avritzer, Leonardo (2009). *Participative Institutions in Democratic Brazil*, Woodrow Wilson Center, Washington DC.

Avritzer, Leonardo and Alberto Olvera (1992). "El concepto de sociedad civil en el estudio de la transición democrática," in: *Revista Mexicana de Sociología*, Vol. LV, No. 4–92, México City, pp. 227–248.

Avritzer, Leonardo and Boaventura de Souza Santos (2002). "Para ampliar el canon de la democracia," in: Boaventura de Souza Santos (ed.), *Democratizar a democracia: os caminos de la democracia participativa*, Civilizaçao Brasileira, Río de Janeiro, pp. 39–82.

Chatarjee, Partha (1999). "Os movimientos sociais e a construcao democrática: sociedade civil, esfera pública e gestao participative," in: Idéais, Instituto de Filosofía e Ciencias Humanas, Universidade de Campinas, No. 5, Campinas, pp. 96–127.

Chatarjee, Partha (2004). *The Politics of the Governed. Reflections on Popular Politics in Most of the World*, Columbia University Press, New York.

Cohen, Jean L. (1985). "Strategy or identity: new theoretical paradigms and contemporary social movements," in: *Social Research* Vol. 52, No. 4, pp. 663–715.

Cohen, Jean L. (1999). "Trust, voluntary association and workable democracy: the contemporary American discourse of civil society," in: Mark E. Warren (ed.), *Democracy and Trust*, Cambridge University Press, Cambridge, pp. 208–248.

Cohen, Jean L. and Andrew Arato (1992). *Civil Society and Political Theory*, MIT Press, Cambridge, MA.

Cohen, Jean L. and Andrew Arato (2000). *Sociedad civil y teoría política*, Fondo de Cultura Económica, Mexico City.

Cunill, Nuria (1997). *Repensando lo público a través de la sociedad. Nuevas formas de gestión pública y representación social*, Centro Latinoamericano de Administración para el Desarrollo (CLAD), Caracas.

Dagnino, Evelina (coord.) (2002). *Sociedade Civil e Espaços Públicos no Brasil*, Paz e Terra, Río de Janeiro.

Dagnino, Evelina (2004). "Sociedade civil, participaçao e cidadania: de que estamos falando?" in Daniel Mato (coord.), *Políticas de ciudadanía y sociedad civil en tiempos de globalización*, FACES-UCV, Caracas, pp. 95–110.

Dagnino, Evelina, Alberto J. Olvera and Aldo Panfichi (eds.) (2006). *La Disputa por la Construcción Democrática en América Latina*, Fondo de Cultura Económica, Universidad Veracruzana and CIESAS, Mexico.

Drache, Daniel (ed.) (2001). *The Market or the Public Domain: Global Governance and the Asymmetry of Power*, Routledge, London.

Edwards, Bob, Michel W. Foley and Mario Diani (eds.) (2001). *Beyond Tocqueville: Civil Society and the Social Capital Debate in Comparative Perspective*, New England University Press, Hanover.

Fox, Jonathan (2007). *Accountability Politics: Power and Voice in Rural Mexico*, Oxford University Press (Oxford Studies in Democratization), Oxford.

Fox, Jonathan and L. David Brown (eds.) (1998). *The Struggle for Accountability: The World Bank, NGOs and Grassroots Movements*. MIT Press, Cambridge, MA.

Habermas, Jürgen (1987). *The Theory of Communicative Action, Vol. II. Lifeworld and System: A Critique of Functionalist Reason*, Beacon Press, Boston.

Habermas, Jürgen (1998). *Between Facts and Norms: Contributions to a Discourse Theory of Law and Civil Society*, MIT Press, Cambridge.

Hevia, Felipe (2006). "Participación ciudadana institucionalizada: análisis de los marcos legales de la participación en América Latina," in: Evelina Dagnino, Alberto J. Olvera and Aldo Panfichi (eds.), La disputa por la construcción democrática en América Latina (México FCE).

Hevia, Felipe (2009). "Relaciones sociedad-Estado: análisis interactivo para una antropología del Estado," in: *Espiral, Estudios sobre Estado y Sociedad*, Vol. XV, No. 45 May/August 2009, pp. 46–70.

Mato, Daniel (coord.) (2004). *Políticas de Ciudadanía y Sociedad Civil en tiempos de globalización*, Facultad de Ciencias Económicas y Sociales, Universidad Central de Venezuela, Caracas.

Migdal, Joel S. (2001). *State in Society. Studying How States and Societies Transform and Constitute One Another*, Cambridge University Press, New York.

O'Donnell, Guillermo and Philippe C. Schmitter (1986). *Transitions from Authoritarian Rule. Tentative Conclusions about Uncertain Democracies*, The Johns Hopkins University Press, Baltimore.

O'Donnell, Guillermo and Rodolfo Mariani (coord.) (2008) *Hacia un Estado de y para la Democracia*, PNUD, Washington DC.

O'Donnell, Guillermo, Jorge Vargas, Gerardo Munck *et al.* (2004). *La Democracia en América Latina: Hacia una Democracia de Ciudadanos y Ciudadanas*, PNUD-Aguilar-Alfaguara, Buenos Aires.

Offe, Claus (1999). "How can we trust our fellow citizens?" in: Mark Warren (ed.), *Democracy and Trust*, Cambridge University Press, Cambridge. pp. 42–86.

Oliveira, Miguel Darcy and Rajesh Tandon (1994). *Citizens in Construction of Global Civil Society*, CIVICUS and McNaughton and Gunn, New York.

Olvera, Alberto J. (1997). "Civil society and political transition in Mexico," in: *Constellations, An International Journal of Critical and Democratic Theory*, Vol. 4, No. 1, April, pp. 105–123.

Olvera, Alberto J. (ed.) (1999). *La Sociedad Civil: de la Teoría a la Realidad*, El Colegio de México, México.

Olvera, Alberto J. (2004). "Civil society in Mexico at century's end," in: Kevin J. Middlebrook (ed.), *Dilemmas of Political Change in Mexico*, Institute of Latin American Studies, University of London, London, pp. 403–439.

Olvera, Alberto J. (2008). "Las relaciones entre democratización y participación em México: apuntes para su historia," in: *Controversia*, Tercera Etapa, No. 191, December, Bogotá.

Olvera, Alberto J. and Armando Chaguaceda (2010). "Is there participatory democracy in the ALBA countries?" in: *Envío*, No. 342, January, Managua, pp. 48–56, www.envio.org.ni/articulo/4145 (accessed 6 November 2010).

Olvera, Alberto J. and Ernesto Isunza (eds.) (2006). *Democratización, rendición de cuentas y sociedad civil: Participación ciudadana y control social*, Porrúa/Centro de Investigaciones y Estudios Superiores en Antropología Social/Universidad Veracruzana, Mexico City.

Pérez Díaz, Víctor (1993). *La Primacía de la Sociedad Civil*, Alianza Editorial, Madrid.

Peruzzotti, Enrique and Catalina Smulovitz (eds.) (2006). *Enforcing the Rule of Law: Social Accountability in the New Latin American Democracies*, University of Pittsburgh Press, Pittsburgh.

Rabotnikof, Nora (2005). *En Busca de un Lugar Común. El Espacio Público en la Teoría Política Contemporánea*, UNAM, México.

Salamon, Lester M. and Helmut Anheier (1994). *The Emerging Sector: An Overview*, The Johns Hopkins Institute for Policy Studies, Baltimore.

Tussie, Diana (comp.) (2000). *Luces y sombras de una nueva relación: El Banco Interamericano de Desarrollo, el Banco Mundial y la Sociedad Civil*, FLACSO-Temas Grupo Editorial, Buenos Aires.

Warren, Mark E. (2001). *Democracy and Association*, Princeton University Press, Princeton.

World Bank (1996). *The World Bank Participation Sourcebook*, The World Bank, Washington DC.

World Bank (1998). *Involving Nongovernmental Organizations in Bank Supported Activities*, The World Bank, Washington DC.

7 Civil society in Latin America

From the excluded other to democratic deepening

Leonardo Avritzer

Andrew Arato has been one of the most important theoreticians of democracy in the second half of the twentieth century. His academic career was constructed in the axis Budapest, Frankfurt, New York in which he became the key person in an important transformation of critical theory: the move from Marxism and neo-Marxism to a democratic theory centered on civil society (Arato and Gephard 1978; Cohen and Arato 1992). In the axis between New York and Frankfurt, Andrew Arato became the bridge between the criticisms on Marxist theory that emerged in Eastern Europe and the neo-Marxist tradition that thrived in New York academy around the journal *Telos*. The journal was the port of entrance of left wing European intellectuals in the United States, publishing articles of prominent figures like Jürgen Habermas, Claude Lefort, Alain Touraine and Cornelius Castoriadis. *Telos*' group, which had positioned itself very close to the original revolutionary utopia of Marxism, received an important grain of realistic political theory from Andrew Arato. He was the key figure in an important transition within critical theory from the utopia of egalitarian socialism in the East (Marcuse 1970) to a new drive for democracy in the West. In this process the concept of civil society was retrieved for a renewed democratic theory (Cohen and Arato 1992).

Civil society has been a marginal concept in the history of critical theory (Arato 1981; Wellmer 1971). In the tradition of critical theory, the concept of civil society had been shaped by Marx's criticism of the concept in Hegel's work (Marx 1975). For Marx, civil society was nothing more than an expression of the bourgeois world and should be conceptually placed within the market economy (Arato and Gebhardt 1982). Instead of a category of mediation between the market and the state as Hegel assumed, Marx understood civil society as an intrinsic part of the market society playing the role of being an expression of the abstract collective individual of bourgeois society. Hence, civil society could not be understood as part of the critical theory tradition defined by Marx as the "self-clarification of the struggles and wishes of the age." Civil society could not be seen at that point as fulfilling the struggles or wishes of a working class struggling for the franchise or social rights. In addition to that, if we consider the first generation of the Frankfurt School and its view, again we can see a complete disregard for civil society as a useful concept. In the discussion of the authoritarian state (Neumann 1957) or of the authoritarian personality, civil society was not considered relevant.

There is also a second element that should be taken into account: the hostility of the civil society concept to the non-Western cultures. The concept of civil society emerged in the history of thought intrinsically linked to the Western trajectory of establishing a demarcation between the West and the rest (Avritzer 2009). The idea of an intermediary sphere between the individual and the state emerges in Tocqueville, Hegel and Ferguson as a process of evolution within the European civilization process: Adam Ferguson is the author who best expresses this view in his work on civil society.

> The Southern hemisphere scarcely offers a subject of observation. The temperate zone is there still undiscovered. ... But the savage of South America notwithstanding the interposition of the nations of Peru and Mexico, is found to resemble his counterpart of the North. ... He is tenacious of freedom, has rudiments of policy and a national vigor...
>
> (Ferguson 1991: 117)

Thus, civil society theory in order to be reconstructed needed to be reclaimed both for a Marxian paradigm of social class centered on labor and from a European-centered civil society theory that considered the Southern population barbarian and non-democratic. Andrew Arato was the introducer of a concept in the critical theory tradition that opened the theory in both directions. In these brief remarks, I will first make an evaluation of the state of the art of civil society and democratic theory in the early 1980s and later move to Arato's contribution to both.

Civil society and democratic theory: the state of theory in the 1980s

Critical theory and democratic theory were in a big stalemate in the early 1980s. Critical theory was at this point abandoning what may be called "the production paradigm" (Habermas 1976), due to its inability to generate a normative foundation for politics. The debate inaugurated by Habermas acquired a huge impact in the United States' critical circles in which the practical orientation of critical theory has always been an important issue. This debate both in its European and its North American versions lacked political orientation. Some authors, among them Habermas himself, identified the new drive of critical theory with social movements (Habermas 1984). However, social movements could not become the foundation of critical theory's new orientation. They lacked key characteristics such as an institutional dimension able to tackle politics. At the same key movements in the East and the South emerged struggling for democracy. Solidarnosk (Touraine 1980), Argentine human rights movements (Jelin and Hershberg 1996), Brazilian urban reform and health movements all pointed in the direction of a new paradigm for politics (Avritzer 2002). This is the origin of the new drive for democracy within critical theory. Andrew Arato played a key role in this movement.

Arato's articles on Poland "Civil Society vs. the State" and "Empire vs. Civil Society" were written in 1981 and 1982 and summarized a new perspective on democracy and civil society. For him, the most important characteristic of the revival of the concept of civil society was a shift from the aim of democratizing the whole social system to the democratization of society properly speaking (Arato 1981). This shift introduced a necessity of further theorization on the new characteristics of democracy and civil society. This is the road that led to two breakthroughs in social and political theory: the overcoming of the dualistic views on civil society and the emergence of the concept of self-limitation.

Civil society theory was throughout the nineteenth century a dualistic theory connected with the liberal tradition. Initially the concept expressed several artificial distinctions: the distinction between economy and politics which avoided important politicization of the economic sphere (Santos 1995); the distinction between private and public with all artificial attributions given to the private sphere as the domain of liberty (Bobbio 1987); the distinction between the family and the state which precluded a theory of gender domination at the private level (Fraser 1989). Civil society played the role of establishing mediations among these different dimensions and the state (Edwards 2004: 7). However, these mediations were incomplete and did not theorize enough the problems of domination and politicization of the private, the family and the economy and made sense only within a liberal tradition of politics. Andrew Arato's work retrieved civil society from a conservative liberal tradition by proposing a tripartite framework within which both the civil and the political could be seen critically. At the same time, the differentiation between the civil and the political opened the space for the democratic deepening of the polity:

> From an analytical point of view the distinction between civil and political society helps to avoid the sort of reductionism that assumes that political activities with a strategic dimension are easily generated by societal associations and movements are somehow unnecessary.... From a normative point, treating political society as mediation within a many-leveled civil society has the possible advantage of establishing the priority of the non-strategic domains of solidarity, association and communication. ... The viability of a democratic political society may depend on the depth of its roots in independent pre-political associations and publics.
>
> (Cohen and Arato 1992: 79–80)

Arato with his view on the differentiation of civil and political as well as civil and economic society launched the foundation for an alternative concept of civil society that played two major roles: it could be extended beyond Western Europe and North America and it could become a realm of social differentiation and democracy. The latter aspect is the most important one: civil society in its nineteenth century version could not be more than a concept within the liberal tradition. Arato and Cohen gave it the possibility of going beyond such a dimension by playing an effective role in societal democratization, the role of effectively establishing an associative and collective dimension within political life. This dimension would play a key role in re-establishing equilibrium between the societal dimension and the political system within contemporary democracy as well as in process of transition from authoritarianism to democracy. This is the road that reconnected civil society with political processes taking place in Southern countries.

In addition to that Arato established a key concept for the understanding of democracy in the twentieth century, the idea of self-limited politics. The concept of fusion between state and society was part of a maximalist vision of politics inherited from the Marxian tradition (Kolakowski 2008). It assumed that the separation between civil society and the state was an artificial separation introduced by bourgeois society and that real politics or politics beyond the super-structure should preclude the separation between civil and political societies. The problem faced by a critical theory of civil society was how to retrieve the concept from the Marxian tradition and to create a concept that may have appeal for social movements. Arato's idea of self-limitation fulfilled both roles at the same time by showing the possibility of a self-limiting left politics and by clearly establishing an aim for democratic politics: the containment of the state, be it democratic or authoritarian. In this way, civil society theory has been able to move beyond the European tradition in two ways: by overcoming the tradition of fusion between state and society in real politics and by opening itself to political traditions that were just overcoming authoritarian experiences. This is what has led to the encounter between the concept of civil society and the Latin American tradition.

Civil society in Latin America: from the excluded other to political inclusion

Civil society in Latin America during the nineteenth century was an analytical and empirical impossibility. Civil society in its nineteenth century employment was part of a process of demarcation between Western and non-Western societies. The countries and the people of the South were seen as not belonging to such a tradition and as not being civilized. Clime, temper and social processes (Ferguson, Rousseau and Montesquieu) were the main explanation for the exclusion of the other which the concept of civil society incorporated through the demarcation between civil and uncivil.

The emergence of civil society in Latin America implied two processes: the first one, already mentioned above, was the broadening of its understating in which Arato's work has been the great breakthrough. The second process was a consequence of the anti-societal form assumed by authoritarianism in Latin America which deeply affected the social condition of the poor population (Oxhorn 1994). Brazil and Mexico passed through one of the fastest processes of urbanization in history with their populations being forcedly moved from the countryside to the city. This interference with the form of living of the poor stripped them of all rights. The organization of the Latin American poor to claim for social services is one of the origins of civil society. It took place in Brazil throughout the process of democratization (Avritzer 2002), in Chile after the authoritarian coup (Oxhorn 1994), in Mexico after the earthquake of 1995 (Ramirez 1990) and is still taking place in Argentina after the collapse of the system of social protection existent in the country. In all these cases, we see a new form of social organization that was not present in the region and which became a permanent feature of social organization.

A second reason that led to the re-organization of Latin American civil society was the opposition of liberal and middle class sectors to the lack of rules and accountability in the political and civil processes. The most important reaction to the lack of rules took place in Argentina with the formation of the human rights movement (Cheresky 2010; Jelin and Hershberg 1996). In the case of Brazil, the struggle for human rights led to the transformation of the Brazilian Bar Association (OAB) into one of the main oppositional groups to authoritarianism. Although these characteristics have been present throughout the whole democratization period, they continued to manifest themselves after democratization in struggles for accountability (Peruzzotti and Smulovitz 2006). It is from the result of this interaction between civil society and the state after democratization that different patterns of state–civil society relations emerged in Latin America.

Latin American civil society emerged or re-emerged during the so called process of "liberalization" of Brazil that started during the mid 1970s (O'Donnell Schmitter 1986). Liberalization was a moment in which the Latin American authoritarian regime released control over some prohibitions on voluntary associations' public meetings but not on the rules of political competition. Thus, students could reconstitute their movement, many professional categories such as architects, engineers and lawyers started to meet again and to re-organize their associations, many trade unions started to be run by the opposition and the ministry of labor did not dare to intervene. It was as a result of this process that many forms of civil society organization emerged in the region: (1) the organization of popular movements of the urban poor at the local level; (2) the organization of the *Sanitarista* movement for a Unified Health System in Brazil; (3) the movement for a National Urban Reform in Brazil; (4) the Human Rights movement in Argentina; (5) the development of many forms of organization in the Brazilian countryside including the emergence of the MST, the Landless Peasant Movement; (6) the development of monitoring organizations. These are not all the movements that emerged throughout this period. Feminist movements and black movements also emerged though initially they did not have as much influence as the movements singled out above. However, the political and the analytical problem faced by Latin American political actors was how to transform civil society organization into a permanent feature of the region's political field.

Andrew Arato's work supports an analytical framework to understand the processes mentioned above. For him, there is a double institutionality in modern societies, one that belongs to the administrative sub-system of the state with its specific forms of organization which are hierarchical and top to bottom. The other form of administrative organization belongs to the voluntary sectors of civil associations and is voluntary and horizontal. This is what allows a reflexive continuation of a project of social solidarity through the means of social innovation (Cohen and Arato 1992: 470). Civil society in Latin America expresses this project of continuation and reconstruction of the state and civil society relations in terms of its democratic practices (Peruzzotti and Smulovitz 2006). The main theoretical issue is how innovation relates to the state. This debate leads us to discuss the autonomy of civil society and how to theorize the different possibilities of state–civil society interaction.

The main characteristic of Latin American civil society during the period of democratization was the claim for autonomy from the state and political parties. This claim was very strong in Brazil. Brazil's history from the 1930s to the 1980s was a period of strong state intervention in the societal organization. During Brazil's democratization the claim for autonomy had three major meanings: first, organizational autonomy from the state. Labor unions as well as all other forms of organization of the poor claimed autonomy by social actors in the period from 1977 to 1985. Autonomy was understood as acting without asking authorization from the state and, at the same time, as ignoring the limits the state placed against voluntary associations (Avritzer 2009). This has meant that new voluntary associations would emerge and new forms of presenting claims in public to the state would become common practices. It was in this period that common practices that we may call a democratic repertoire of collective action by Brazilian voluntary associations developed. Practices such as petitioning state authorities, demonstrating in front of public buildings and organizing grassroots assemblies emerged in this period.

Second, autonomy also meant trying to propose forms of administration of policies without the participation of the state. Thus, the health movement of São Paulo during the first half of the 1980s proposed a form of organization of health policies independently from the state. Still during the VIII National Health Conference there were groups proposing the organization of health care independently from the state (Avritzer 2009). The movement for urban reform, in a similar fashion, proposed forms of local democracy independently from the state that would be able to veto state action related to urban policies (Avritzer 2009). In Porto Alegre during the late 1980s neighborhood associations also proposed civic decision-making on budget issues based on a council of neighborhood associations. These are a few examples among a large number of cases. We can also think about similar cases in other parts of Latin America. In the aftermath of the 1985 earthquake in Mexico City poor dwellers organized relocation and re-establishment of social services without the participation of the state (Ramirez 1990). Another good example is the organization of the population in Alianza Cívica to make a parallel counting of votes (Olvera 2003). Thus, during the first phase of civil society organization in Latin America we can note two phenomena: the first is quantitative growth in the number of voluntary associations dealing with the organization of the poor and the participation of civil society actors in the implementation of public policies. The second phenomenon is the idea that civil society may deal with public policies independently from the state. However, there is a watershed between the claim for state autonomy in this first phase (1983–1990) and the claim for autonomy during the second phase (1985 to today). This difference can be theorized in terms of the conflict between autonomy and self-limitation.

Andrew Arato's work assumed that autonomy and self-limitation completely overlap. The reason why they overlap is that in his analysis of civil society the issue of self-limitation acquires one major meaning, namely, not challenging state power in Eastern Europe in order to not provoke the Empire (Arato 1982). This has been the main concern of the author's work due to the intrinsic association between its theoretical elements and its political concerns. However, the forms of articulation between civil society and the state in Latin America went beyond that concern. As Latin American societies democratized civil society claimed participation in the implementation of social policies (Dagnino 2002; Olvera 2003). This was the movement that led to a new articulation between civil society and the state as I will show below.

Civil society in Latin America: from political inclusion to democratic deepening

Democratization in Latin America took place between 1983 when Argentina democratized and 1990 when Chile democratized. Between 1983 and 1990, Brazil, Uruguay and Peru democratized. The oldest authoritarian regime in the world, Mexico, lost elections in the year 2000, also leading to full re-democratization without constitutional reform. Throughout these processes the relationship between civil society and the state changed in most countries in the region.

In the case of Brazil, the period between 1985 and 1988 marks a watershed in Brazilian politics. In 1985, President Jose Sarney called for a National Constituent Assembly. The Brazilian NCA allowed popular amendments and triggered a popular campaign to get signatures to many proposals linked to public policies. Some of the most important civil society movements, such as the health and the urban reform movements and the MST, also joined the campaign for popular amendments (Whitaker 1994). This was a first important moment of a process of democratic deepening that created participatory institutions in the areas of health, urban planning, environment and social assistance (Avritzer 2009). A popular amendment in the area of health was presented with a little less than 60,000 signatures (Rodriguez Neto 2003). Its main elements were obliging the state to be the main health provider in Brazil; creating a unified national health care system without preconditions for access; decentralizing the provision of health care; and fostering broad popular participation in the elaboration and implementation of health services. In spite of the late insertion of subcontracting to the private sector, the health care movement was very successful within the

Constituent Assembly. The Constitution's Article 198 described health as an integrated system organized according to the following principles: (1) decentralization; (2) unified care with a focus on prevention; and (3) civil society participation in policy deliberation. The elaboration of the Health Care Statute (Lei Orgânica da Saúde, LOS) took almost two years after the completion of the 1988 Constitution. In the aftermath of the approval of law 8.142 many Brazilian cities enacted local laws. They all forecasted the organization of health councils based on the parity between civil society and the state. Today there are in Brazil more than 5,000 health councils.

In a similar fashion, the MNRU (the National Movement for Urban Reform) also made a proposal of a popular amendment in the area of urban politics. The popular amendment on urban reform was presented to the National Constituent Assembly with 131,000 signatures and unleashed a lobbying battle with conservative real estate interests. The thematic committee on Urban Issues and Transportation did not initially attract many powerful Constituents since conservative sectors had more pressing short-term issues. Real estate interests inside the Constituent Assembly sought to transfer the final decision on urban issues to another arena outside the constitution-making process in order to avoid the automatic application of any new legislation (Saule 1995: 28). Most of the subcommittee's proposals on urban issues remained intact, but they were integrated with a requirement that cities should have "Master Plans,"[1] a proposal made by "Centrão," the informal organization that gathered conservative interests during the Constituent Assembly. Thus, Paragraph 1 of Article 182 of the 1988 Constitution required both the participation of civil society organizations in the decision-making on urban issues and a city master plan approved by the City Council as mandatory to all cities with more than 20,000 inhabitants. All urban reform proposals were made dependent on fulfilling this clause. The consequence of the subordination of the urban reform agenda to master plans was what the Brazilian legal tradition calls a statute or an infra-constitutional process of specifying constitutional law. Thus, a 13-year battle followed the proposal of the regulating legislation by Senator Pompeu de Sousa and its approval by the Brazilian Congress in December 2001. After the 13-year legal battle in Congress the so called "Statute of the City" was approved in 2001. The Statute of the City requires mandatory city master plans with public audiences in every Brazilian city with more than 20,000 inhabitants.[2] In these audiences the presence of civil society associations is required. Hundreds of Brazilian cities today have city master plans in which civil society and state actors interact closely.

At the same that participation in the areas of health and city master plans unleashed a very intense form of participation based on civil society associations, participatory budgeting was also on the rise. Olívio Dutra was elected Mayor of Porto Alegre in 1988, and introduced participatory budgeting in the city. Participatory budgeting (PB) is a local participatory policy which responds to the plight of the poor in major Brazilian cities. It includes social actors, neighborhood association members and common citizens in a process of negotiation and deliberation which takes place in two stages: a participatory stage, in which participation is direct, and a representative stage, in which participation takes place through the election of delegates and/or councilors. The PB in Porto Alegre from 1990 to 2004 involved two rounds of regional assemblies, one round of intermediary meetings and the operation of a councilors' body called the PB council year-round. In these meetings, the population attends an assembly in each of the regions. In each of these assemblies the floor is open for about an hour, during which citizens express themselves about what has been taking place, about possible disagreement with the administration, and about what should be done in the region in the coming year. Participation in these meetings is crucial because they constitute the basis for participating in the remaining parts of the process. Participation is individual but individuals throughout the registration process are required to demonstrate membership in voluntary associations. In addition to that, the regions in Porto Alegre that have showed more willingness to participate through the process of implementation of participatory budgeting (1990–1992) were the ones with the highest number of neighborhood associations (Wampler and Avritzer 2004). Again, we can see a strong interaction between membership in civil society organizations and the operation of a participatory process by the state. With the consolidation of participatory budgeting in Porto Alegre many leaders of neighborhood associations would participate in PB councils and later in the state institutions in charge of PB such as CRC (Coordination of Relations with the Community) and Gaplan (Planning Cabinet).

Thus, we can note a strong change in the focus of civil society participation from the mid 1980s to the mid 1990s. During the mid 1980s Brazilian civil society was concerned with autonomy, democratization of public policies and the establishment of forms of public control over the state. From the mid 1990s on, Brazilian civil society became concerned with the establishment of a very broad form of public participation in most areas of public policy and with joining the state in the implementation of participatory forms of public deliberation. This has led to a change in the way in which autonomy vis-à-vis the state was conceived.

The key issue to be understood in the process of organizational transformation of Brazilian civil society[3] is that civil society growth and political influence in Brazil, seen in the long run, did not follow an autonomous or a dependent logic but rather a mix between autonomy and dependency. The implementation of participation in areas such as health and urban planning showed a different feature of Brazilian civil society, namely, its interrelation with the state in the deliberation on public policies. This is a characteristic that is not exclusive from Brazil. Rather, it also takes place in many South American countries such as Uruguay in the Tabarez Vasques administration and in the experiences in Rosario and Buenos Aires in Argentina (Chavez 2004; Goldfrank 2001). These new experiences in South America pose new issues for a civil society theory, namely how to understand self-limitation and autonomy in different political contexts.

Civil society, self-limitation and democracy in Latin America: a few concluding remarks

Andrew Arato's work is based on two main concerns that came from two different traditions: the concern for self-limitation that came from the Eastern European experience with the struggle against totalitarianism and the concern for democratic deepening that came from the Western tradition. In his work, self-limitation and autonomy expressed the two concerns that the author wished could be placed together. Andrew Arato's civil society theory made a huge contribution to several important political traditions: the Eastern European tradition of societal democratization from below and the Western tradition of state limitation and civil society control. However, it would not be an exaggeration to point out that the author's most important contribution was an unanticipated one, namely his contribution to the Latin American tradition of democratic deepening.

Democratic deepening is a specific Latin American tradition created from the engagement of civil society actors with the state. Though broadly unanticipated, it may be derived from long term concerns of Arato's work, in particular his remarks about the double institutionality of civil society and its capacity to advance a new form of public administration. This analysis called attention to the fact that the bureaucratic top down mechanisms introduced by the modern state to rule are not the only alternative and may be offset by more democratic mechanisms. The latter have emerged in Brazil and Latin America as a whole and have generated a possibility of a more democratic bottom up form of ruling (Avritzer 2009). New participatory institutions such as policy councils and participatory budgeting have their origin in this analytical possibility which has generated practical problem solving mechanisms in politics through participatory processes.

This horizontal form of ruling allows us to conceive in a different way the relationship between civil society and the state. Arato's seminal work on civil society opened new venues in this process of conceiving the administrative organization of the modern state. It has generated many new productive ways to deepen democracy, some of them broadly practiced in Latin America today. It is up to the new generations of social scientists to advance in the huge theoretical avenues created by this amazingly creative democratic theorist.

Notes

1 City Master Plans or *planos diretores* are not per se conservative devices though they have been considered conservative by the urban reform movement due to the way they emerged during the Constituent Assembly. Some Brazilian cities such as Porto Alegre have had city master plans since the late 1970s. The novelty introduced by the Constituent Assembly was the link between having a city master plan and being able to introduce the other participatory devices approved by the Constitution in its urban chapter. See Avritzer 2009.

2 There is a very interesting case of cancellation of the city master plan of Salvador, Bahia due to the violation of the public audience requirement during the Imbassay

mayorship. The city of Salvador called just one public audience during the preparation of its city master plan. The public audience was not broadly publicized and Ministerio Publico (the Public Prosecutor) asked for its cancellation which was granted by a Salvador court (Avritzer 2009).

3 Gurza Lavalle, Houtzager and Acharya misunderstand the most important characteristics of this change in perspective by civil society actors. According to the authors,

> the dichotomous reading of state–society relations, born in the struggles against various types of authoritarian rule in the second half of the 1970s and 1980s, has been central to the literature on civil society and has unfortunately been reinforced recently. ... Although discussions of civil society have abandoned early oppositional interpretations of state and society in order to address a series of emerging themes – citizenship, new participatory spaces, local development, governance and accountability – the dichotomous interpretation of state-society relations has largely been reproduced, albeit in more subtle forms.
>
> (Gurza Lavalle *et al.* 2003)

The metaphor suggests autonomous agents who cross paths, discover certain overlapping interests and choose to engage with each other through various institutional mechanisms. In contrast to the authors' argument all the recent literature on civil society emphasizes the interconnections between civil society and the state. The reason is very simple: the full autonomy model was linked to social actors' conceptions and not to a pre-conceived normative conception as the authors claim. See Dagnino 2002; Avritzer 2004.

References

Arato, A. (1981). "Civil Society vs. the State: Poland 1980–81." *Telos* 47, pp. 23–47.

Arato, A. (1982). "Empire vs. Civil Society: Poland 1981–82." *Telos* 50, pp. 19–48.

Arato, A. and E. Gebhardt (eds.) (1982). *The Essential Frankfurt School Reader*. New York: Continuum.

Avritzer, L. (1995). "Transition to Democracy and Political Culture: An Analysis of the Conflict Between Civil and Political Society in Post-authoritarian Brazil." *Constellations. An International Journal of Critical and Democratic Theory* 2:2.

Avritzer, L. (2002). *Democracy and the Public Space in Latin America*. Princeton: Princeton University Press.

Avritzer, L. (ed.) (2004). *A participação em São Paulo*. São Paulo: Editora UNESP.

Avritzer, L. (2009). *Participatory Institutions in Democratic Brazil*. Washington and Baltimore: Woodrow Wilson Center Press and The Johns Hopkins University Press.

Bobbio, N. (1987). *The Future of Democracy*. Minneapolis: University of Minnesota Press.

Chavez, D. (2004). "From Frente Amplio to Nueva Mayoria: the Uruguayan left faces the prospect of government." Paper presented at the XXV International LASA Meeting, Las Vegas, Nevada.

Cheresky, I. (2010). *Ciudadanos y Política en los Albores del Siglo XXI*. Buenos Aires: Manantial.

Cohen, J. L. and A. Arato (1992). *Civil Society and Political Theory*. Cambridge, MA: MIT Press.

Dagnino, E. (2002). *Sociedade civil e espaços públicos no Brasil*. São Paulo: Paz e Terra.

Edwards, M. (2004). *Civil Society*. Cambridge: Polity Press.

Ferguson, A. (1991). *An Essay on the History of Civil Society*. New Brunswick: Transaction Books.

Fraser, N. (1989). *Unruly Practices: power, discourse and gender in contemporary social theory*. Minneapolis: University of Minnesota Press.

Goldfrank, B. (2001). "The Fragile Flower of Local Democracy: a case study of decentralization/participation in Montevideo." *Politics and Society* 30, pp. 51–83.

Gurza Lavalle, A., P. Houtzager and A. Acharya (2003). "Beyond Comparative Anecdolatism: Lessons from Civil Society's Participation in Sao Paulo, Brazil." *World Development* 33:6, pp. 951–964.

Habermas, J. (1976). "Towards a Reconstruction of Historical Materialism." In: J. Habermas, *Communication and the Evolution of Society*. Boston, MA: Beacon Press.

Habermas, J. (1984). *The Theory of Communicative Action*. Boston, MA: Beacon Press.

Jelin, E. and E. Hershberg (1996). *Constructing Democracy: human rights, citizenship, and society in Latin America*. Boulder, CO: Westview Press.

Kolakowski, L. (2008). *Main Currents of Marxism: the breakdown*. London: W.W. Norton.

Marcuse, H. (1970). *One Dimensional Man: studies in the ideology of advanced industrial society*. Boston: Beacon Press.

Marx, K. (1975). *Early Writings*. New York: Vintage Books.

Neumann, F. (1957). *The Democratic and the Authoritarian State*. New York: The Free Press.

O'Donnell, G., P. Schmitter and L. Whitehead (1986). *Transitions from Authoritarian Rule: Latin America, Vol. II*. Baltimore: The Johns Hopkins University Press.

Olvera, A. (2003). *Sociedad Civil, Esfera Pública y Democratización en América Latina: México*. México: Fondo de Cultura Económica.

Oxhorn, P. (1994). *Organizing Civil Society*. State College: Penn State University Press.

Peruzzotti, E. and C. Smulovitz (eds.) (2006). *Enforcing the Rule of Law: social accountability in the new Latin American democracies*. Pittsburgh: Pittsburgh University Press.

Ramirez, J. M. (1990). "Urban Struggles and Their Political Consequences," in: J. Foweraker and A. Craig (eds.) *Popular Movements and Political Change in Mexico*. Boulder, CO: Lynne Rienner.

Rodrigues Neto, E. (2003). *Saúde: Promessas e Limites da Constituição*. Rio de Janeiro: FIOCRUZ.

Santos, B. de S. (1995). *Pela Mão de Alice*. São Paulo: Cortez.

Saule, Jnr, N. (1995). *O Direito à cidade na Constituição de 1988. Legitimidade e eficácia do Plano Diretor*. São Paulo: Dissertação de Mestrado em Direito PUC-SP.

Touraine, A. (1980). *Solidarity*. Cambridge: Cambridge University Press.

Wampler, B. and L. Avritzer (2004). "Participatory Publics: civil society and new institutions." *Comparative Politics* 36: 291–312.

Wellmer, A. (1971). *Critical Theory of Society*. New York: Seabury.

Whitaker, F. (1994). *A saga das emendas populares*. Sao Paulo: Brasiliense.

8 Between authoritarianism and democracy in Latin America's re-founding revolutions

Carlos de la Torre[1]

Using "ballots not bullets" Hugo Chávez, Evo Morales, and Rafael Correa have embarked on revolutionary projects to "refound" their nations. New constitutions that expanded individual and collective rights have been drafted under their leadership. Their governments reversed neoliberal economic policies with a postneoliberal commitment to social justice, a stronger role for the state in the economy, and nationalism. Their regimes are creating institutions to complement liberal institutions with direct and unmediated forms of democracy, in order to perhaps in the future replace these institutions.

These self-described revolutionary projects took place in nations that experienced drastic crises of democratic representation. Despite efforts of political reform, decentralization, and the inclusion of previously excluded groups such as indigenous people, women, and Afro-descendants, real existing democracies in Bolivia, Ecuador, and Venezuela continued to be exclusionary, and were based on clientelism, corruption, and on politicians' instrumental use of laws (Buxton 2005; García Linera 2005; Pachano 2007). In these contexts of profound political instability and distrust in models of liberal democracy, intellectuals and activists advocated for projects of substantive democratization.

Are these regimes creating institutions that could improve the quality of democratic representation and participation in their nations? Or, on the contrary, are substantive models, in which these regimes draw inspiration, dangerous to liberal freedoms and pluralism? These questions are of theoretical and normative importance. Whereas academics close to these regimes are trying to improve democracy by implementing substantive models of democratization, Andrew Arato, building on Hanna Arendt, warned that "the radical pursuit of substantive values of democracy – popular sovereignty, genuine representation, community or their combination – at the cost of democratic procedures" could lead to authoritarianism or even to "revolutionary dictatorships that will use substantive democratic claims of legitimacy to justify their creation of entirely new political regimes" (Arato 2000: 942).

This article analyzes different examples of the tensions between models of substantive and procedural democratization. The chapter starts with a review of models of indigenous communal democracy, and on how these ideals have been put in practice in Evo Morales' government to decolonize Bolivia. The second section of this chapter analyzes the participatory institutions created by Chávez's Bolivarian Revolution. To what extent do these institutions correct the deficits of participation of "formal" democracies? A third section studies Rafael Correa's citizens' revolution. After four years in power Correa's regime has yet to create equivalents to the Bolivarian Circles, or the Communal Councils of Venezuela. Moreover, this leftist president is in a conflict with almost all organized groups of civil society such as teachers, workers, state employees, students, and the indigenous movement.

Indigenous communal democracy: decolonization and authoritarianism in Bolivia

Scholars contend that the values of communal solidarity, equality, and consensus that are at the root of indigenous democracy differ fundamentally from the individualistic ethos on which liberal-representative democracy is built. Communal indigenous democracy is presented as a form of rule that may prove effective in democratizing previously racist and colonial forms of domination, including liberal democracy characterized by critics as a neocolonial imposition (Patzi Paco 2004; Rivera 1990). Aymara leaders have referred to Bolivia's representative democracy as 'q'aracracia, a term that "combines 'q'ara' ('plucked', 'bare' or 'hairless' in Aymara and Quechua, meaning 'white person') with 'democracia'" (Albro 2005: 434).

In communal indigenous democracy participation is an obligation linked to the economic, political, and ritual duties of the members of the community. Community assemblies are undifferentiated institutional spaces where participants make decisions, administer justice, and construct authority. All participants deliberate until they reach a consensus and a decision is made. Leadership is considered a duty and rotates among community members. Representatives named at the local level that serve in higher committees are held accountable to their constituents and have to implement what has been decided by their collectivities. "In indigenous communities democratic rules do not apply, but a form of authoritarianism based on consensus" (Patzi Paco 2004: 117). Those who dissent and do not follow collective decisions are considered traitors, a crime punishable by measures such as monetary fines, ostracism, and occasionally by means of physical penalties, such as whipping.

Some scholars contend that indigenous communities have retained the same economic, political, ritual, and insurrectionist practices that they had in pre-Hispanic times (García Linera 2009: 43–44; Rivera 1990: 100). This usage of the past is not a reflection of poor or sloppy scholarship by academics that are well versed in Marxist's debates of articulation. Their strategic use of a homogenous precapitalist past is explained by their intention to question capitalist neocolonial models of modernity. They romanticize peasant communitarian practices to criticize capitalism. However, because of their idyllic view of indigenous communities as egalitarian institutions based on the principles of reciprocity, deliberation, consensus, and direct democracy academics have failed to properly analyze the extent of class, educational, and gender differentiations in these communities.

If power differentials exist, it is logical to assume that some members of the indigenous community might have discursive expertise that will allow them to present their cases using a technical or "educated" language in the deliberation process. Managing the "correct" discursive expertise that allows one to "speak well" is highly valued in Bolivia's assembly democracy (Lazar 2008: 244). Indigenous people who do not have the same levels of education will have difficulties finding the right words to articulate their positions. For example, "women often talk of themselves as lacking the knowledge necessary to speak publicly" (ibid., 244). When they address assemblies their voices often do not carry the same authority as that of their male counterparts. If these academics want to paint communities as spaces where debates among equals flourish, they will have to acknowledge the disruptive influence of gender and class inequalities on the processes of deliberation.

Following constructs of pristine precapitalist indigenous communities conceived of by intellectuals, Evo Morales frequently idealizes community life, and he presents "nostalgic images of 'true democracy' built on pure, egalitarian indigenous ancestral ways" (Lindholm and Zuquete 2010: 43). He has reiterated: "In my community [the indigenous] lived in solidarity. In my community of origin there was no private property. In my community of origin there was no individualism. ... In my community we did not know about money, but we lived well" (quoted in Albro 2005: 444). This romantic portrait of communal life contrasts with Morales' autobiographical descriptions of growing up in his rural community in abject poverty and with his accounts of how as a child he dreamed of the luxury of perhaps one day riding on a bus, and even eating oranges and bananas (Stefanoni and do Alto 2006: 54).

Following the lead of Marxist-Indianist scholars such as Álvaro García Linera (Bolivia's vice-president), Raul Prada (former assemblyman and Minister of State Strategic Planning), Luis Tapia, and others, Bolivia's 2009 Constitution redefined the Bolivian state as "plurinational and communitarian." The Constitution of 2009 grants indigenous rights such as autonomy, self-governance, and the right to culture. It recognized

> 36 indigenous languages as official languages of the state (Article 5), describing the "moral ethical" basis of Bolivia's plural society as resting on indigenous cosmological principles such as "to live well" (Article 8), and formally embracing a "democratic participatory, representative and communitarian" mode of government inspired by indigenous communities.
>
> (Albro 2010: 79)

President Morales follows the practices of communal democracy when he consults policies with social movement organizations. For instance he gave a parallel state of the union address of his first year in government to peasant organizations and unions (F. Mayorga 2009: 158–159). He discussed fundamental governmental policies such as the law on education, coca leaf, and social security after consulting with peasant, indigenous, and other popular organizations (García Linera 2009: 90). Scholars contest the extent to which these long meetings – which sometimes last for about 20 hours – are based on the participation of all, or on the imposition of Morales' criteria. For some this is a democracy of the social movements (García Linera 2009). For others, the regime uses followers to intimidate the opposition through mass rallies and other forms of collective action (R.A. Mayorga 2009; Van Cott 2009).

Morales and his party Movement to Socialism (MAS) share majoritarian views of democracy and, as the opposition claims, their disregard for liberal democratic rights could lead to authoritarianism. Morales has not respected the rule of law or the independence of the judiciary (Barrios 2008; Gamarra 2008). Power is concentrated in the president who is also the head of the MAS party and of Chapare coca growers. Yet an exclusive focus on liberal norms and values tells only part of the story of what is happening to Bolivian democracy. As García Linera argues perhaps the most important process going on in Bolivia is the process of decolonization. "We have put indigenous people in the government in record numbers and appointed them to positions they never held before ... Now an indigenous person can be anything from president to a construction worker" (in Farthing 2010: 31). The symbolisms of power attest to the hopes and promises of overhauling the legacies of colonialism. Nancy Postero writes,

> On January 21 [2006] Morales participated in a popular ceremony at Tiwanaku, a pre-Inca site near La Paz, where, after walking barefoot over coca leaves, he was blessed by Andean religious leaders and recognized as the Apamallku, the highest indigenous authority. To the thousands of admirers shivering in the freezing altiplano morning, he declared, "A new millennium has arrived for the original peoples of the world."
>
> (Postero 2010: 18).

The themes of the ending of neocolonial oppression, racism, and the exclusion of indigenous people were also central motifs in his official inauguration address (Morales 2006). The empowerment of indigenous people has been evidenced in the symbolic changes in the Bolivian political landscape. Indigenous rituals are performed in the presidential palace, previously a center of white power. The MAS "congressional bloc after the 2006 election consisted of 72 representatives of whom 43 were indigenous; 12 senators of whom three were indigenous (and one female). Its first cabinet included 4 indigenous people (two of whom were women)" (Hylton and Thomson 2007: 27–28).

The cultural and symbolic inclusion of indigenous people is carried with populist understandings of rivals as enemies. The authoritarian specter is present in small communities and at the national level. For example, after learning the results of the 2005 presidential election in the small village of Quilacollo an indigenous leader affirmed: "in our community there was one vote for Tuto Quiroga [Morales' rival in the election], we are going to investigate who this is because we cannot tolerate betrayals by our own comrades" (Stefanoni and do Alto 2006: 20). This undemocratic view of opponents as enemies characterizes the president and vice-president's worldviews and speeches. Nancy Postero quotes Jorge Komadina Rimassa who argues that Morales has defined enemies at different levels.

> At the external level, the foreign, specially the United States, the drug Enforcement Administration, and the transnationals, are the enemies of the nation and the sovereign. At the domestic level, the oligarchy, whites, and Western culture are the enemy, as opposed to the people, the indigenous, and specially the Andean. Finally, at the level of the economy, neoliberalism and the traditional parties are the enemies, opposed to socialism, social movements, and peasant economic strategies.
>
> (Postero 2010: 29)

Participatory democracy under Chávez's Bolivarian Revolution

The Venezuelan Bolivarian Revolution provides an interesting case to study the conditions under which participatory democracy can fulfill its promises. Since the 1980s organizations based in the middle and popular classes demanded participatory democracy without the mediation of political parties. The left, especially La Causa R, advocated for a Constituent Assembly understood as the ultimate expression of popular sovereignty for the refoundation of the republic on an entirely new basis (Raby 2006: 155). Building on the prevailing antiparty feelings, and popular sectors' view of democracy as social justice and equality Hugo Chávez promised an alternative model to representative party democracy. Participatory democracy became enshrined in the 1999 Constitution. Article 62 mandates "all citizens have the right to participate in public affairs." Chávez' government has created a series of institutions such as Technical Water Roundtables, Bolivarian Circles, Urban Land Committees, and more recently Communal Councils to advance participatory and protagonist democracy.

Following Marxist models of pyramidal democracy, communal councils are seen as the first step towards the socialist transformation of the state. Communal councils are organized when

> communities of between 200 and 400 families in urban areas, or 20 plus in rural areas, would meet in an open citizen's assembly and elect a communal council. … The citizen's assembly is the sovereign body, discussing and taking all decisions on what projects, development plans or other activities the community wanted to pursue.
>
> (Bruce 2008: 140)

An association of councils will constitute a commune that in turn will form socialist cities.

Based on a study based on a survey of 1,200 councils Machado (2008) shows that most of their projects focused on infrastructure, services, and urban renewal. Studies of communal councils differ in their evaluation of how many people in the community participate. Using the America's Barometer 2006–7 nationwide survey of 1,500 respondents, Kirk Hawkins (2010: 41) concludes that 35.5 percent participate in Communal Councils, an exceptionally high figure of about 8 million participants. Results based on ethnographic research show lower levels of participation. Margarita López Maya reports, "out of the 350 or 400 hundred families that made a communal council in Caracas no more than fifteen people actively participate" (2010: 37). Most of these are women who had previous experiences of participation.

Some studies contend that community councils are departing from paternalist and clientelist traditions towards "popular responsibility in the construction of collective responses to attain a better life" (Machado 2008: 50). However, not all studies agree with this positive evaluation. Communal councils, in their views, are not autonomous, as they were created and regulated by a charismatic president that neutralizes or prevents autonomous grassroot inputs (Ellner 2010: 79–80; López Maya 2010). They depend on the unilateral and centralized decisions of President Chávez on the amount of money to be distributed and on how to spend it.

Those actively involved in communal councils feel included, and empowered. An activist explains:

> Now they say, "We are useful." Before we felt worthless because they didn't take us into account. They covered our mouths with a little handout. … For me participatory democracy is giving power to the people … for the people to administer their own resources.
>
> (Martínez *et al.* 2010: 293)

Participants of communal councils often talk about feeling positive because they have contributed to improve their lives by building "a nice neighborhood with all the services" or of the "satisfaction to see that your neighborhood is doing well" (interviews by Lopéz Maya 2010).

As these testimonies illustrate it is important to move beyond the homogeneous "Chavista" label in order to explain Chávez's appeal to different poor people's constituencies. Clientelism and material distribution in exchange for loyalty is an important explanation of why poor people participate in communal councils and support Chávez. Other activists purposely differentiate community activism from politics. An activist explains that she is not interested in politics or the colors of ideologies: "If the PSUV tells me, listen we are going to improve the appearance of 30 houses, I say cool, great!" As many poor studied in other Latin American nations it appears that women community activists are using the resources and opportunities given by the government without necessarily buying its ideology or goals of "socialist transformation." "We are not a capitalist enterprise, nor socialist, nor anything. We are a community organization."

As in other Latin American countries it is mostly women who participate in community activism. Patriarchal gender roles, their exclusion from traditional male spheres, and their centrality in the life of their barrio explain their participation and empowerment (Fernandes 2007: 111). It seems that these women are using whatever the government offers to improve their lives and communities and in the process feel that they belong, are important, and are taken into account.

Activists who became involved in leftist politics well before Chávez are using the openings of the political system in order to advance their agendas, and in the process some are entering into conflicts with the government. For example, Wayúu indigenous people of the state of Zulia, with the support of ecologists and the Asociación Nacional de Medios Comunitarios, Libres y Alternativos (ANMCLA) are resisting open coal mining operation (Fernandes 2010: 237–255, Martínez *et al*. 2010: 205–217). The goal of the state is to increase coal production in Zulia from 8,000 to 30,000 tons. The Wayúu have entered into conflict with the Ministry of Popular Power for Indigenous People and with the National Indigenous Council of Venezuela. The leadership of the Wayúu charged these government institutions with trying to coopt and silence them by denouncing them as anti-Chavista counter-revolutionaries. They strategically use Chávez's words to say that the president has said no to coal. In demonstrations in Caracas the Wayúu and their allies, "took the language and symbols of the Chávez government itself, to challenge its plan for coal mining" (Fernandes 2010: 244). Their manifestos quote the constitution articles that protect the environment, and give self-determination to indigenous groups. This confrontation illustrates that for some activists participation is not reduced to acclaiming Chávez in plebiscites and in the plazas.

The Venezuelan experience demonstrates that experiments in participatory democracy have different meanings for the actors involved. It seems that despite the revolutionary goals of the government these experiences are similar to other forms of community organizing where a small number of women use state resources to improve the lives of their communities within the constraints of limited resources and clientelism. For those who actively participate in the different Bolivarian institutions, it has meant a new sense of dignity and inclusion. Yet Chávez's charismatic leadership has set the limits for popular autonomy, as the "revolutionary process" is centered on his figure, his wishes, and his dreams. It remains an open question if common people will be successful when – as in the struggles over coal exploitation in Zulia – they articulate demands that go beyond the wishes of their charismatic leader, or of state bureaucracies.

The Chávez phenomenon runs much deeper than clientelist material exchanges based on oil rent distribution. Chavismo is a political movement of almost biblical proportions.

> Chávez often appeals to a highly religious population with his rhetoric of an evangelical preacher, involving love and redemption; his millenarian notion of a new start after the evils of the past; and his campaign posters featuring portraits similar to evangelical depictions of Christ.
>
> (Fernandes 2010: 106)

A former Maryknoll Catholic missionary from the United States told journalist Bart Jones (2007: 158) "for years many Venezuelans had been waiting for someone to come to their rescue, a modern day Bolívar who would avenge the crooked politicians and set the country on a path to prosperity." Chávez is perceived as a redemptive figure, "the current incarnation of the liberator" (Arenas and Gómez Calcaño 2006: 97). Chávez is also perceived as Christ. An interviewee of Ian Bruce (2008: 139) asserted, "Chávez is like Christ, and we are going to be his apostles."

Chávez's rhetoric has politicized relations of inequality between different classes and ethnic groups. He has reclaimed Venezuela's indigenous and black heritages that were downplayed by the *punto fijo* white elites (Buxton 2009: 161). He has tapped into the "deep reservoir of daily humiliation and anger felt by people of the lower classes" (Fernandes 2010: 85). As a result of his Manichaean discourse he is able to constantly mobilize his followers to win elections, and defeat "the oligarchy" in the streets by bringing larger numbers. Chávez's populist mobilization has on the one hand activated and incorporated previously excluded people. But, on the other, he has coopted or reduced the autonomy of organizations of civil society. This is why as in other populist experiences there are collusions between attempts of top down mobilization and responses and demands from the grassroots that go beyond the intentions of their leaders. His personal authority is unquestionable. In a speech on January 23, 2010 Chávez asserted, "I demand absolute loyalty to my leadership. I am not an individual, I am the people" (quoted by Lander 2010: 17).

Rafael Correa: between a citizens' revolution and the cooptation of social movements

In contrast to the "explosion of popular power" in Venezuela, Rafael Correa's government has not yet created institutions of popular participation similar to the Bolivarian Circles or the Community Councils. This is strange because participatory democracy was one of the mottos of the movement that took Correa to power in 2006. Ecuadorians had been demanding participatory democracy, and invented short term institutions of radical participatory assembly democracy such as the "people's assemblies" created after the overthrow of President Abdala Bucaram in 1997, the "people's parliament" that was formed around the time of the uprising that ended with Jamil Mahuad's presidency in 2000, and "neighborhood assemblies" established after President Lucio Gutiérrez was removed from power in 2005. The height of citizens' participation in Correa's administration took place during the drafting of the constitution of 2008 when the National Assembly opened its doors to citizens' organizations to present their demands and proposals on how to create a new inclusive and democratic constitution.

Rafael Correa won the 2006 elections on a platform that strongly criticized neoliberalism and promised to organize a new constituent assembly to institute a new social pact. He was the self-proclaimed leader of a citizens' revolution against the "partyarchy" that had appropriated the will of the people. His platform was for the creation of "an active, radical, and deliberative democracy." It aimed to establish a "participatory model that will allow citizens to exercise power, take part in public decisions, and control the actions of their representatives." The new Constitution was going to be drafted with the participation of all mobilized citizens so that all could appropriate it as their own.

These democratizing proposals went hand-in-hand with an anti-institutional stand. Correa ran as an outsider without presenting candidates for the Congress, promising to close it and replace it with a constituent assembly. After winning the election, Correa's government used laws instrumentally to get rid of 57 opposition congress members. Later, the National Assembly assumed all legislative powers after declaring that Congress was in a "recess." Because Correa ran as an anti-party outsider, he did not build a political party but rather a movement. Alianza PAÍS (AP) combined a self-conception as a citizens' movement (where Correa was just another citizen) with a charismatic construction of Correa as the embodiment of the citizens' revolution.

The tensions between activation and autonomy were evident in the constituent process. In contrast to previous processes perceived as closed, the drafting and the discussion of the new constitution were transparent and open. When Alberto Acosta, one of the founding members of AP, was president of the Assembly, the goal was to engage in pluralist deliberations. It was an experiment in deliberative democracy that finally could not be fully realized under Correa's charismatic leadership. Correa became impatient with debates in the assembly that might have cost votes in the ratifying referendum. Correa disapproved of Indianist proposals to make Kichwua an official language; ecological protectionist plans to forbid open-pit mining operations, and feminist discussions about abortion and gay rights. He accused his own assembly-people of delusion through "left wing-infantilism." He also worried that the assembly would not have a Constitution ready by a previously promised date. In the end, Correa asked the political bureau of his party to request Acosta's resignation from the presidency of the Assembly. After naming a new president more in tune with Correa's wishes, the assembly expedited its job and fulfilled its timetable. The new constitution was approved in a referendum with 64 percent of the vote, but at the cost of limiting deliberation on its content and of not following its own internal institutional procedures.

Correa understands democracy in substantive terms as social justice. In a conference at Oxford he differentiated formal democracy understood as "the right to vote" from real democracy, based on "equity, justice, and dignity," and the "rights for education, health, and housing" (Correa 2009c). In order to fulfill his vision of democratization his administration increased social spending from 4.8 percent of the GDP in 2006 to 8.1 percent in 2009 (Ponce and Acosta 2010: 10). Correa's social programs such as the human dignity bonus that gives 35 dollars a month to the very poor, housing projects, the distribution of food, and bonus to protect the high altitude páramo are well received by indigenous people, and the poor. An indigenous woman from Tixan in the Province of Chimborazo said:

"Today I am grateful to God and to president Correa. I have the bono and buy food, pay for electricity, and can buy a little something for my kids" (Tuaza 2010). Another woman corroborated, "Thanks to the President I get 35 dollars."

In order to benefit from these programs individuals in rural areas have to belong to a community organization and because the main autonomous indigenous organization the Confederation of Indigenous Nationalities of Ecuador (CONAIE) is in a conflict with the government parallel organizations have been created (Dosh and Kligerman 2009; Martínez Novo 2009; Ospina 2009; Tuaza 2010). Social distribution then becomes a tool to bypass autonomous indigenous organizations, and beneficiaries feel obliged to the president. As one respondent said: "The government takes care of us, we have to be grateful" (Tuaza 2010). In December 2009 many communities did not join CONAIE's protest because they were afraid of exclusion from the government's housing program.

Correa has gradually become a master in using a Manichaean populist rhetoric. "We have to defeat the oligarchy, the partyarchy, and the wigs who want to go back to the past" (Correa 2008). Politicians, journalists, and anybody who opposes or challenges him have been labeled as a *pelucón* (wig). Social movements have also been the targets of his belligerent rhetoric. In July 2008 he called ecologists "*aniñaditos*" (well to do infantile and not fully masculine pampered kids) "with full bellies who oppose everything all the time." He contended that "infantile radical" ecologists are "the main danger to our project" (ibid.). A few months later he corroborated: "We always said that the main danger to our political project, after defeating the right in elections, are the infantile left, ecologist, and indianists" (Correa 2009a). In October 2009 in the midst of a conflict over the use of water he called the leadership of the indigenous organization CONAIE, "golden ponchos" and "Indian wigs" out of touch with their social base.

The term "citizens' revolution" allows Correa to legitimize his regime with notions of the need for a total rupture with the existing order to bring meaningful and long lasting change. In front of an audience of policemen he said: "Nobody takes a step backwards. This revolution will not be sold nor will it surrender" (Correa 2009b). The notion of a total rupture with the immediate past helps to paint the series of elections carried under his regime as Manichaean struggles between historical projects (Conaghan and de la Torre 2008). Because the goal is to construct an entirely new regime, the tools used to implement change are not necessarily required to respect procedures or the rule of law. The argument that the county is undergoing a revolutionary process justified the illegal closing of the Congress, the war against the media, the defamation of former allies, and the attacks on "corporatist" social movement organizations.

Correa argues that existing social movement organizations are corporatist and defend their narrow private interest. His regime is in conflict with all organized groups of civil society such as teachers, students, state employees, and the indigenous movement (Martínez Novo 2009; Ospina 2009). Correa might be governing for the people but without their autonomous input and participation. Correa's regime did not have the urge to organize supporters beyond clientelist networks during elections. After conflict with organized groups climaxed in a police uprising in September 2010 that ended in a shootout between policemen and the military, the government might increase its efforts to organize supporters. As Roberts (2006) argued, perceived or real conflict over elite privileges encourages populists to build long lasting organizations. Correa's regime might move from delegitimizing the leadership of social movements to directly organizing supporters from the top down.

Conclusions

The three regimes analyzed in this chapter share the use of a populist discourse that divides the people from the oligarchy as antagonistic poles. Their discourses moreover polarize these societies and transform politics into struggles for higher moral and ultimate values. Politics "ceases to be seen as an instrument for the incremental adjustment of conflictual interests and becomes instead a politics of 'ultimacy', where ultimate issues are at stake in a once-and-for-all confrontation" (Michael Barkun cited by Zúquete 2007: 203).

The continuous activation of common people in elections and plebiscites, and the attacks on elites in the name of the people are allowing supporters of these regimes to claim that they are living under revolutionary moments. In Venezuela a "Bolivarian revolution" is taking place, in Bolivia a "cultural and democratic revolution," and in Ecuador a "citizens' revolution." Revolutions signify the active participation of common people, their politicization, and their presence in the streets. Polarization in permanent elections helps to create a revolutionary atmosphere in which people feel they have embarked on an extraordinary project. Revolutionary times have the particular quality of making people feel part of a project and a moment where a new chapter in history is being written. It forces people to take sides, and does not allow for skeptical bystanders. Society becomes polarized and simplified into two antagonistic blocks: the camps of history and anti-history.

Revolutions are ruptures of legitimacy and legality (Arato 2004: 170). These Andean revolutions were created as liberations from illegitimate neoliberal regimes headed by well entrenched decaying political parties. The revolutionary construction of a new order was carried through constitutional assemblies. Between liberation and revolutionary construction (Arato 2004: 173) during the political and legal vacuum of drafting new constitutions these regimes followed alternative paths. In Venezuela and Ecuador the constituent assemblies dissolved congress and assumed legislative powers. In Bolivia the constituent assembly, where Morales had a majority, coexisted with a senate in the hands of the opposition. The concentration of power in the executive allowed Correa and Chávez to boldly and rapidly restructure institutions. In Bolivia there were conflicts, a stalemate over procedures, and a danger of regional secession. What at first appeared as a propitious condition for change in Venezuela and Ecuador led to regimes where authoritarian traits are overtaking democratic freedoms, rules, and institutional arrangements. The danger of authoritarianism in Bolivia, although present, could be avoided because the MAS had to negotiate with the opposition. If the origins of the new Venezuelan and Ecuadorean regimes lay in the instrumental use of laws that led to the illegal appropriation by assemblies of legislative powers, in Bolivia the MAS had to negotiate with the opposition over the rules of the game (Gray Molina 2010).

Venezuela and Ecuador confirm Andrew Arato's assessment that substantive projects of democratization that bypass procedures might end in authoritarian experiences. The constituent assemblies in these two nations exercised arbitrary authority without the constraints of the rule of law or the separation of powers and following Schmitt could be called "sovereign dictatorships" (Arato 2004: 173). Chávez and Correa concentrated power in the executive and there is little independence between the different branches of government. These regimes are in war with the privately owned media, adversaries are transformed into enemies of their revolutions, and the electoral playing field is eschewed as incumbents use state resources and intimidate the opposition. These governments do not value pluralism, and do not always respect individual rights. Chávez's government is no longer a democracy but a competitive authoritarian regime (Corrales 2010), and Correa might be rapidly following this path. In competitive authoritarian regimes "elections are regularly held and are generally free of massive fraud, yet incumbents routinely abuse state resources, deny the opposition adequate media coverage, harass opposition candidates and their supporters, and in some cases manipulate electoral results" (Levitsky and Way 2002: 53).

An exclusive focus on the authoritarian traits of these regimes presents an incomplete picture. These regimes are certainly anti-liberal but not fully undemocratic. At the same time that these populist leaders close spaces for pluralism the state has returned to distribute mineral resource wealth, and to protect the poor and the disadvantaged. In Venezuela social spending increased at 314 percent between 1998 and 2006 (Corrales 2010: 45). Poverty declined from 48.6 percent in 2002 to 28.5 percent in 2007 (Madrid *et al.* 2010: 166). Correa's administration also increased spending in social programs. The results of the increase in social spending under Correa's administration are not impressive. Before Correa took power poverty declined from 49.1 percent in 2003 to 37.4 percent in 2006. Under his regime it was reduced to 35.8 per cent in 2009. Poverty was reduced in urban not in rural areas. Extreme poverty actually increased for indigenous people from 36.8 percent in 2006 to 45.8 percent in 2009.

Chávez and Correa differ in the efforts that they have put into creating institutions for participation. Chávez created a variety of institutions to make participatory democracy work. These institutions have empowered common people who feel that they are in charge and can bring change to their communities. Yet their empowerment is constrained by Chávez's charismatic leadership as he sets the boundaries of participatory democracy. Like poor people in other Latin American nations some get involved in order to benefit from clientelist distribution. Previously organized leftist groups use the opening of the system to press claims and demands that sometimes transcend the directions of their leader. Nonetheless, in order to not be branded enemies of the revolution they have to accommodate their autonomous demands to the rhetoric, goals, and directions set by Chávez.

Correa is the clearest case of top down mobilization and cooptation of social movements. There are not institutional innovations to make participatory and deliberative democracy work. Participation is reduced to voting and to cheering for Correa in different political campaigns. Correa's administration deemphasized democratic deliberations while giving priority to technocratic top down policies. The process of electing the members of the Citizens' Participation and Social Control Council illustrates Correa's technocratic approach. The seven members of this council tasked to encourage participation and in charge of naming the authorities in charge of accountability such as the General Prosecutor and the national Ombudsman were chosen based on how well they performed in a standardized multiple choice test, and by their merits as illustrated by their resumes (Pachano 2010: 24). Correa prioritizes technocratic criteria for governing on behalf of the poor but without involving the citizenry or their organizations. His regime so far has not needed to organize supporters in permanent organizations. Ephemeral clientelist networks have sufficed to win elections and plebiscites. As the level of polarization and conflict increases his regime might need to organize supporters in a more hierarchical and permanent basis.

Chávez and Correa follow top down approaches to organization. They have little patience with autonomous social movements, and have actively tried to directly supervise grassroots organizations. Correa and Chávez have resorted to a leadership style based on unity and command from above where the leader appears to be the condensation of diverse demands made from below (French 2009: 367). Morales follows a leadership style based on convergence and persuasion allowing for more autonomy to his grassroots constituency (French 2009: 367). In addition of bargaining with regional elites his government negotiates with autonomous and powerful social movement organizations. Bolivia is undergoing a process of decolonization and empowerment of indigenous people. Models of indigenous democracy based on consensus and the direct participation of all are advocated as cures for liberal individualism, and to the problems of representation and participation of liberal democracy. These proposals of decolonization are plagued with problems that might contradict their democratizing goals. Indigenous democracy is built on images of indigeneity that do not allow for the discussion of how power relations work inside indigenous communities. These idealized constructs do not address how status, educational, and gender differences interfere with processes of deliberation as they give more authority to the voices of males who master "technical" or "educated" discursive competences. When idealized images of community travel from the local to national levels these projects might become authoritarian as communitarian values have predominance over individual values. Communitarian models do not provide spaces for dissent, pluralism, and make participation a duty and not a right that can be exercised or not.

These regimes claim their legitimacy in a populist glorification of the common man. In Bolivia the strength of social movements, the inclusion of marginalized native peoples, and the need to negotiate with regionally powerful elites will perhaps allow for the emergence of multicultural autonomous citizenships. The Venezuelan and Ecuadorean regimes are undermining the conditions that might allow for autonomous model citizenships to thrive. The state is colonizing autonomous organizations of civil society, and attempting against civil rights and the institutional foundation that allows a strong civil society to emerge. Without strong institutional bases civil society and citizenship are weak and are prone to interference and manipulation from the state. As in previous populist experiences in Latin America "the limited and selective provision of social rights of citizenship served to legitimate and consolidate hierarchical patterns of state-society relations. Social actors were deprived of autonomy through policies of state corporatism, clientelism, and populist appeals" (Oxhorn 2009: 229).

As Cohen and Arato argued, institutionalized rights are the foundation of civil societies.

> Focusing on the institutional spheres of civil society, we can isolate three complexes of rights: those concerning cultural reproduction (freedoms of thought, speech, and communication); those ensuring social integration (freedom of association and assembly); and those securing socialization (protection of privacy, intimacy, and the inviolability of the person). Two other complexes of rights mediate between civil society and either the market economy or the modern bureaucratic state (political rights of citizenship and welfare of clients.
>
> (Cohen and Arato 1992: 441)

Even though the new constitutions of these three nations expand rights, as in previous populist experiences rights are selectively enforced. Political rights are understood as free and open elections but not as an even electoral field. In addition, limited social rights such as the missions in Venezuela, the bonus of human dignity in Ecuador, and Morales' bonus for school children are given as favors to the poor but in exchange these leaders demand loyalty. Civil societies are further weakened as states are strengthened, and as the rights that guarantee cultural reproduction and ensure social integration are limited.

These regimes claim their legitimacy with notions of revolution. The call for revolutionary transformation, at the same time that it increases the level of participation, presents politics as zero sum struggles between antagonistic camps. The search for a total rupture with the past, in line with populist traditions, has the virtue of involving people in politics and the danger of bypassing institutions and the law leading to personalism and authoritarian plebiscitary acclamation of self-described saviors. These populist ruptures also led to the creation of a new order. The state returned to protect common people from the excesses of the market economy, to increase social spending, and to reclaim a central role in development. These "citizens' revolutions" also meant the replacement of old politicians by new elites. New Constitutions have expanded and deepened social, political, and individual rights. Unfortunately these rights that look great on paper are selectively implemented. Life under a constant "revolution" has come at the cost of many of the freedoms and practices of liberalism. It seems that the baby of liberal democracy has been thrown into the dirty water of neoliberalism, patrimonial, and clientelist political systems. Without values of pluralism, civil rights, and the construction of political opponents as rivals who share the same discursive and institutional spaces, the authoritarian, messianic, and Jacobin temptations could in the end prevail in these experiments.

Note

1 Thanks to the Woodrow Wilson Center for International Studies, to the Center for International Studies at Grinnell College, and to FLACSO-Ecuador for the time and support to work on this project.

References

Albro, R. (2005) "The Indigenous in the Plural in Bolivian Oppositional Politics," *Bulletin of Latin American Research* 24 (4): 433–453.

Albro, R. (2010) "Confounding Cultural Citizenship and Constitutional Reform in Bolivia," *Latin American Perspectives* 37 (3): 71–90.

Arato, A. (2000) "Good-bye to Dictatorships?" *Social Research* 67 (4): 925–955.

Arato, A. (2004) "The Occupation of Iraq and the Difficult Transition from Dictatorship," in Ronald Dworkin, ed., *From Liberal Values to Democratic Transitions. Essays in Honor of János Kis*, Budapest and New York: Central European University Press.

Arenas, N. and Gómez Calcaño, L. (2006) *Populismo Autoritario: Venezuela 1999–2005*, Caracas: CENDES.

Barrios, F.X. (2008) "The Weakness of Excess. The Bolivian State in an Unbounded Democracy," in John Crabtree and Laurence Whitehead, eds., *Unresolved Tensions. Bolivia Past and Present*, Pittsburgh: University of Pittsburgh Press.

Buxton, J. (2005) "Venezuela's Contemporary Political Crisis in Historical Context," *Bulletin of Latin American Research* 24 (3): 328–347.

Buxton, J. (2009) "The Bolivarian Revolution as Venezuela's Post-crisis Alternative," in Jean Grugel and Pía Riggirirozzi, eds., *Governance After Neoliberalism in Latin America*, New York: Palgrave.

Bruce, I. (2008). *The Real Venezuela. Making Socialism in the Twenty-first Century*, London: Pluto Press.

Cohen J. and Arato, A. (1992) *Civil Society and Political Theory*, Cambridge, MA: MIT Press.

Conaghan, C. and de la Torre, C. (2008) "The Permanent Campaign of Rafael Correa: Making Ecuador's Plebiscitary Presidency," *International Journal of Press/Politics* 13: 267–284.

Corrales, J. (2010) "The Repeating Revolution: Chávez's New Politics and Old Economics," in Kurt Weyland, Raúl Madrid, and Wendy Hunter, eds., *Leftist Governments in Latin America. Successes and Shortcomings*, Cambridge: Cambridge University Press.

Correa, R. (2008) "Intervención Presidencial en el Aromo," Manabí, July 15, 2008.

Correa, R. (2009a) "Informe a la Nación en el Inicio del Tercer Año de Revolución Ciudadana," Quito, January 19, 2009.

Correa, R. (2009b) "Intervención Presidencial en el Acto de Entrega de Armas en el Comando Provincial de Manabí," Portoviejo, March 12, 2009.

Correa, R. (2009c) "Experiencia de un Cristiano de Izquierda en un Mundo secular," Oxford Union Society, October 26, 2009.

de la Torre, C. (2010) *Populist Seduction in Latin America*, Athens: Ohio University Press.

Dosh, P. and Kligerman, N. (2009) "Correa vs. Social Movements: Showdown in Ecuador," *NACLA* (September–October): 21–24.

Ellner, S. (2010) "Hugo Chávez's First Decade in Office: Breakthroughs and Shortcomings," *Latin American Perspectives* 37(1): 77–97.

Farthing, L. (2010) "Controlling State Power. An Interview with Vice President Álvaro García Linera," *Latin American Perpectives* 37 (4): 30–33.

Fernandes, S. (2007) "Barrio Women and Popular Politics in Chavez's Venezuela," *Latin American Politics and Society* 49 (3): 97–127.

Fernandes, S. (2010) *Who Can Stop the Drums? Urban Social Movements in Chávez's Venezuela*, Durham and London: Duke University Press.

French, J. (2009) "Understanding the Politics of Latin America's Plural Lefts (Chavez/Lula): Social Democracy, Populism and Convergence on the Path to a Post-neoliberal World," *Third World Quarterly* 30: 349–370.

Gamarra, E. (2008) "Bolivia: Evo Morales and Democracy," in Jorge Domínguez and Michael Shifter, eds., *Constructing Democratic Governance in Latin America*, Baltimore: The Johns Hopkins University Press, pp. 124–151.

García Linera, A. (2005) *Democracia en Bolivia: cinco análisis temáticos del segundo Estudio Nacional sobre Democracia y Valores Democráticos*. La Paz, Bolivia: Corte Nacional Electoral, República de Bolivia.

García Linera, A. (2009) *Biografía Política e Intelectual. Conversaciones con Pablo Stefanoni, Franklin Ramírez y Maritsella Svampa*. La Paz: Le Monde Diplomatique.

Gray Molina, G. (2010) "The Challenge of Progressive Change under Evo Morales," in Kurt Weyland, Raúl Madrid, and Wendy Hunter, eds., *Leftist Governments in Latin America. Successes and Shortcomings*, Cambridge: Cambridge University Press.

Hawkins, K. (2008) "La Organización Populista. Los Cículos Bolivarianos en Venezuela," in Carlos de la Torre and Enrique Peruzzotti, eds., *El retorno del pueblo. El populismo y nuevas democracias en América Latina*, Quito: FLACSO, pp. 125–160.

Hawkins, K. (2010) "Who Mobilizes? Participatory Democracy in Chávez's Bolivarian Revolution," *Latin American Politics and Society* 52 (3): 31–66.

Hylton, F. and Thompson, S. (2007) *Revolutionary Horizons. Past and Present in Bolivian Politics*, London and New York: Verso.

Jones, B. (2007) *¡Hugo!* Hanover: Steerforth Press.

Lander, E. (2010) "¿Quien Ganó las Elecciones Parlamentarias en Venezuela? ¿Esamos ante la última oportunidad de debatir sobre el rumbo del proceso de cambio?" unpublished manuscript.

Lazar, S. (2008) *El Alto, Rebel City. Self and Citizenship in Andean Bolivia*, Durham and London: Duke University Press.

Levitsky, S. and Way, L. (2002) "The Rise of Competitive Authoritarianism," *Journal of Democracy* 13 (2): 51–66.

Lindholm, C. and Zúquete, P.J. (2010) *The Struggle for the World. Liberation Movements for the 21st Century*. Stanford: Stanford University Press.

Lopez Maya, M. (2005) *Del viernes negro al referendo revocatorio*, Caracas, Venezuela: Alfadil.

López Maya, M. (2010) "Los Consejos Comunales en caracas Vistos por sus participantes: una exploración," unpublished manuscript.

Machado, J. (2008) *Estudio de los Consejos Comunales en Venezuela*. Caracas: Fundación Centro Guamilla.

Madrid, R., Hunter, W., and Weyland, K. (2010) "The Policies and Performances of the Contestatory and Moderate Lefts," in Kurt Weyland, Raúl Madrid, and Wendy Hunter, eds., *Leftist Governments in Latin America. Successes and Shortcomings*, Cambridge: Cambridge University Press.

Martínez, C., Fox, M., and Farrell, J. (2010) *Venezuela Speaks! Voices from the Grassroots*, Oakland: PM Press.

Martinez Novo, C. (2009) "The Indigenous Movement and the Citizens' Revolution in Ecuador: Advances, Ambiguities, and Turn Backs," unpublished paper delivered for the Conference *Outlook for Indigenous Politics in the Andean Region*, Center for Strategic International Studies, Washington DC.

Mayorga, F. (2009) *Antinomias. El azaroso camino de las reformas políticas*, Cochabamba: Universidad Mayor de San Simón.

Mayorga, R.A. (2009) "Sociedad civil y estado bajo un populismo plebiscitario y autoritario," in Cynthia Arnson, ed., *La Nueva Izquierda en América Latina: Derechos Humanos, Particpación Política y Sociedad Civil*, Washington: Woodrow Wilson International Center for Scholars, pp. 109–119.

Morales, E. (2006) Discurso de posesión del Presidente Constitucional de la República Evo Morales Aima.

Ospina, P. (2009) "Corporativismo, Estado y Revolución Ciudadana. El Ecuador de Rafael Correa," unpublished document.

Oxhorn, P. (2009) "Beyond Neoliberalism? Latin America's New Crossroads," in John Burdick, Kenneth Roberts, and Philip Oxhorn, eds., *Beyond Neoliberalism in Latin America. Societies and Politics at a Crossroads*. New York: Palgrave Macmillan, pp. 217–233.

Pachano, S. (2007) *La trama de Penélope. Procesos Políticos e Instituciones en el Ecuador*, Quito: FLACSO.

Pachano, S. (2010) "Democracia representativa y mecanismos de democracia directa y participativa," unpublished document.

Panizza, F. (2008) "Fisuras entre populismo y democracia en América Latina," in Carlos de la Torre and Enrique Peruzzotti, eds., *El retorno del pueblo. El populismo y nuevas democracias en América Latina*. Quito: FLACSO, pp. 77–97.

Patzi Paco, F. (2004) *Sistema comunal: una propuesta alternativa al sistema liberal: una discusión rica para salir de la colonialidad y del liberalismo*, La Paz, Bolivia: Comunidad de Estudios Alternativos (CEA).

Ponce, J. and Acosta, A. (2010) "La pobreza en la revolución ciudadana o ¿pobreza de revolución?" *Ecuador Debate* 81 (December): 7–20.

Postero, N. (2010) "Morales's MAS Government. Building Indigenous Popular Hegemony in Bolivia," *Latin American Perpectives* 37 (3): 18–34.

Raby, D.L. (2006) *Democracy and Revolution. Latin America and Socialism Today*, London: Pluto Press.

Rivera, S. (1990) "Liberal Democracy and Ayllu Democracy in Bolivia: The Case of Northern Potosi," *The Journal of Developmental Studies* 26 (4): 97–121.

Roberts, K. (2006) "Populism, Political Conflict, and Grass-Roots Organziation in Latin America," *Comparative Politics* 38 (2): 127–148.

Roberts K. (2008) "El resurgimiento del populismo latinoamericano," in Carlos de la

Torre and Enrique Peruzzotti, eds., *El retorno del pueblo. El populismo y nuevas democracias en América Latina*, Quito: FLACSO, pp. 55–77.

Stefanoni, P. and do Alto, H. (2006) *La revolución de Evo Morales: de la coca al palacio*, Buenos Aires: Capital Intelectual.

Tapia, L. (2006) *La invención del núcleo común. Ciudadanía y gobierno multisocietal*, La Paz: Muela del Diablo.

Tuaza, L.A. (2010) "La relación del gobierno de Rafael Correa y las bases indígenas: políticas públicas en el medio rural," unpublished manuscript.

Van Cott, D.L. (2009) "Indigenous Movements Lose Momentum," *Current History* 108 (715): 83–89.

Zúquete, J.P. (2007) *Missionary Politics in Contemporary Europe*, Syracuse: Syracuse University Press.

9 The bad uses of the concept of populism in Latin America

Nicolás Lynch

I discovered the critical theory of democracy in the classes of Andrew Arato, 25 years ago, in the Graduate Faculty of the New School for Social Research of New York. It was not just the texts, many of them previously unknown to me, to whom Andrew exposed us, that left their mark. It was also the intellectual curiosity that he awakened in us for the authors, and for the life experience that he and each of the academic friends that he invited to the seminars to debate with us brought. Their works on the political theory of civil society were a formidable inspiration for me and for an entire generation of social scientists in Latin America, in the redoubled effort to deepen the critique of power from a post-Marxist perspective and renew the foci on democracy in Latin America. Andrew has not just established a formal academic relationship with those who approached him to receive his teachings, but also an emotional commitment with what we do and with the different countries from which we come. The constant exercise of critique in our work has thus been nourished by a master who is also an example of rigor, tolerance and friendship.

Introduction

Criticism tends to be against power. It is in this process that spaces of exchange and currents of thought arise (Eagleton 1984). What better exercise of criticism then than to unravel the meanings of the concept of *populism* in a region of the world such as Latin America, with its deep contrasts and bitter debates about power.

In Latin America populism as a movement and subsequently as a concept was born against power: first against oligarchical power and now against neoliberal power, but always challenging the establishment and in contrast to the uses of democracy. Certain populism has been the *bête noire* for a certain concept of democracy and vice versa. Seeing the debate today, we want to affirm, along with Enrique Dussel (2010), that in the region there has been an authentic and historic populism as well as a pejorative populism, the former as a demand of the people, beyond whether it may have been a manufactured phenomenon or a real subject, and the latter as a fear of the former. A similar thing has occurred with democracy. This has oscillated between the imported concept that was sold to us first by the oligarchs and subsequently by the ideologues of the transitions, and which has been elaborated in the region as resistance to the dictatorships and also as an alternative political construction. For all this, the academic use of the relationship between populism and democracy has been inseparable from the immediate political debate about the same and, on this path, the powerful media use of these concepts.

It is time, then, to decipher the lights and shadows of these uses in a reality historically marked out by its imports and autochthonous creations. I think that what has happened with the use of populism, at least since the middle of the 1990s, has been a replacement and not a critique. What should have been an analysis of the crisis of Latin American democratization has been replaced with a word of supposed multiple significations. Therefore, I propose to explain in the next few lines the possible, and non-exclusive, relationship between populism and democracy in the Latin American region.

1 What is the use of populism in Latin America today?

The word *populism* has once again invaded political analyses in Latin America. This familiar old concept, or unfamiliar for some, is offered to explain everything. Yesterday, it was historical populism, the movements and/or popular-national governments, which came to be called Latin American populism, which we thought were delimited in their historical structural conception and location. But then, in the 1990s, neoliberal populism, or neo-populism, was used to explain the treason of the old, mass parties and the clientelism of this decade, and afterwards the radical populism of certain countries whose governments have turned to the left in recent years; all this, to address nothing less than the academic organization of these uses, without taking into account the profuse media reiteration of populism that has served to discredit any politician who does not like the neoliberal order.

Are we dealing with the same phenomenon whose interpretation serves the same concept or with distinct phenomena that need different conceptualizations? I have argued for the second analysis on various occasions and think that what the invasion of recent years seeks is to avoid an analysis of the crisis of liberal, specifically elitist, democracy in the region rather than deepening the study of new phenomena. For this, it is necessary to destroy the original signification of historical populism in Latin America in such a way that leaves the idea that populism is simply a behavior that can be repeated at any moment and that today is expressed in those governments that seek to build new political orders in the region.

For this, I believe that populism, in its historical and interpretative sense, must be understood as a first moment of Latin American democratization, a first moment that opens possibilities for democratic development, both liberal and participatory. This perspective of populism as democratic possibility is certainly distinct from populism as an authoritarian threat and promoter of disorder, which is what has usually been presented.

2 On what evaluation is it based?

Most of those who believe that populism as a category remains useful maintain that with the turn to the left of Latin America, we have been living an authoritarian regression in the region. This regression is endangering the 30 or more years of almost uninterrupted democracy that we have experienced in this zone of the world. This conception assumes that Latin America would have joined, since approximately 1978, what Samuel Huntington (1991) calls the "the third wave" of democratization on the planet. This evaluation supposes a comparison between democracies, liberal in this case, and populism, in which progress is part of the former and backwardness part of the latter.

This evaluation contrasts with another that does not consider what has happened a regression or authoritarian threat but a deepening of democracy in the region, for the characterization of which it is insufficient to resuscitate a category that requires an emphasis on the elements of the democratic crisis, questioning and project. In this evaluation what is happening is the deepening of the contradiction between democracy in its liberal, Huntington-type version, restricted to individual and political rights, and the neoliberal economic restructuring, through the policies of shock, that seeks to eliminate rights in general. This contradiction has developed in the region through the social movements of resistance that then expressed themselves as electoral triumphs and eventually in governments that have sought to develop democracy incorporating the demands of society.

What has happened is that the new change from the centrality of the market to the centrality of politics[1] has caused a profound commotion in the groups of power in the region because it displaces interests, above all economic interests that have been established – firmly, it was believed – into the shadow of neoliberal hegemony, and eventually property rights are threatened, by the return of the State and economic regulation. Likewise, this democratization has tended to enter into a tension with a liberal understanding of individual property, of political pluralism (Macpherson 1970); in which freedoms are confused with properties, as has been the case with the debate about the laws to regulate private media oligopolies in Argentina and Ecuador.

3 A concept of democracy that allows us to understand populism

For this reason, to understand the relationship between populism and democracy it is fundamental to begin with a definition of the latter that effectively allows for an accounting of the process of democratization of Latin America and, within this process, of the populist phenomenon.[2] This definition cannot be restricted to that of elitist democracy that the transitions of the 1970s and 1980s sold to us, a minimalist concept that understands this political regime as a collection of procedures of basically electoral character, which guarantee certain individual and political rights, but exclude social rights; a regime whose objective is the defense of the lives and property of individual citizens and their electoral channeling, concerned that the elections be free but not that fair. From this point of view, what is happening today in Latin America is effectively an authoritarian regression because to broaden the existing democracy, the taming of individuals must be affected; in this case large asset owners who tend to capture the State and place it in the service of their interests. For this reason, I want to test a distinct concept of democracy that may be articulated by actors, institutions and structures with a historical vision of the problem.

I propose an approach that understands democracy as a form of social life and institutional organization, a product of the relationship between the State and the population of a determined territory throughout the historical process (Weber 1979; Tilly 2007). In this regime, through mechanisms agreed with the populace, who become citizens, the corresponding decisions are taken. Democracy is thus a product of the conflict and cooperation between social and state interests in dispute for the resources of society. This democracy also supposes a State and a nation, or at least a reference of national identity, in the process of construction (Linz and Stepan 1996); likewise, the State with the sovereign capacity to take decisions necessary for its development and not to fall hostage to external powers. Without the State and a reference of national identity, the construction of democracy is impossible. In the same way, the democratic regime cannot be an empty republic, as were many nominal democracies in Latin America until well into the twentieth century. Democracy needs citizens who develop themselves and may not be cut off as the subjects of rights. Finally, democracy must count with mechanisms of mediation, beyond even the traditional political parties, who aggregate and articulate the social interests in order that these be adequately represented by organizations that develop a process of plural competition within the frameworks of the rule of law, with thoughts of assuming the respective government.

This definition of democracy that responds to the dynamic of the social forces in each place allows a better focus on the process of democratization in the region, which has three periods: The populist or popular national, between 1930 and 1978; that of the transitions and neoliberalism, from 1978 to 1998; and that of the turn to the left from 1998 to the present. Democratization means the broadening of democracy not just as a multiplication of electors who vote but also as individuals who access rights and become citizens. The order of these three classic types – individual, political and social – in the definition of Marshall (1996) can vary, but the idea is the formation of a subject with rights. Thus, from the first period I take up the politics of inclusion of all, via the path of mobilization against oligarchic exclusion; from the second of these human rights, electoral participation, rule of law in the face of the horrors of the military dictatorships; and from the third, social justice, the new role of the State and national independence in contrast to the logic of the market and neoliberal exclusion. From this perspective, I place populism as a first stage in the process of democratization of Latin America. A stage in which, for the first time, all inhabitants of a country are considered as political subjects of reference, as a first step in the recognition, still only partial, of their status as citizens. This recognition of the other has extraordinary social repercussions and will be the base for the building of a representative regime.

4 Populism as political behavior

Those who use the category indiscriminately, for yesterday, today and tomorrow, tend to understand it as a political behavior, by the leader in relationship to his followers – understood as the masses – with a discourse of popular and national recognition and the favoring of supposedly irresponsible policies;[3] a behavior whose rhetoric develops a "false confrontation" between the people and the oligarchy (de la Torre 2008) as the axis of its actions. In this process, the leader, with varying levels of charisma, develops a network of clients in which favors are exchanged for votes and which provides a base for his political support. Understood this way, populism can disappear and reappear thus setting the scene for similar behavior in different eras. Defined in this way, the concept has passed from the academy to the media and is used as a catchall to describe any alternative to elitist democracy that attracts popular recognition.

Perhaps the more interesting variant of this conceptual use is that of Enrique Peruzzotti (2008) who describes populism as a form of direct democracy, criticizing representative democracy as an elitist form, whose inspiration is Carl Schmitt (1982). The problem, from the Schmittian perspective, is the mediations, institutional in this case, that impede identification between the people and their governors in order to achieve the objective of political unity. Peruzzotti explains, and this raises our interest, this type of recovery of democracy by populism as a reaction against elitist or minimalist Latin American democracies in general and, more recently, against the so-called delegative democracy proposed by O'Donnell (1992). However, and the very appeal to Schmitt presages this, Peruzzotti does not find a democratic pathway out of this populist democracy and ends up insisting on a political field of mediations that promote horizontal accountability in a society organized to control political power. This is a valid concern regarding the problem of institutional crisis. Nevertheless, it may also be a way of saying that populism, for the alternatives that it attempts to present is, at the end of the day, an authoritarian option.

Other tributaries of the behavioral definition of populism were those that in the 1990s coined the term neo-populism; these were Kenneth Roberts (1995) and Kurt Weyland (1997). As I have argued on another occasion (Lynch 1999) what happened with those who proposed this conceptual journey was a case of epistemological stretching that, as Sartori (1970) explains, consists of ridding the original concept of its substantive attribute to convert it into a vague term with which almost any use can be made. This use of populism as "neo" privileged the actions of the leader over the social democratizing content and its eventual political consequences. Its examples, however, refuted them on their own. In this, were mixed Collor, Menem and Fujimori, offering a combination of neoliberalism and populism in which they sought to draw parallels between the terrible expropriation that we Latin Americans suffered in the 1990s with the redistribution promoted by classic populism, based solely on the fact that this was the result of actions from above and via a clientelistic network.

Nonetheless, the uses of populism as a behavior did not stop with the attempt to explain neoliberal governments. They have been projected into the present decade to also explain what is today referred to as radical populism (de la Torre and Peruzzotti 2008). In this case, the spotlight has focused on Hugo Chávez of Venezuela, Rafael Correa of Ecuador and Evo Morales of Bolivia. For them, the qualifier has been related to the themes of institutionality and social movements, in Venezuela, to the destruction by the traditional parties that existed before Chávez, which has allowed him to fill the space with mobilizations and institutional arrangements managed from above and in the second and third cases by an ancestral institutional weakness. In the theme of social movements, Evo Morales' Bolivia does not qualify as populist either in the behavioral version due to the tradition of autonomy of the social movements from the State, including the current government. That leaves just the cases of Chávez's Venezuela and Correa's Ecuador. The former may be an attempt at populist resurrection, condemned to failure by being out of step with the country. The institutionality destroyed by the partydocracy which Chávez defeated is now reappearing in a democratic opposition that offers what the *caudillo* lacks, that is to say pluralism. The case of Correa is more complex and may possibly be the most similar to the saga of classic populism that did indeed emerge from the "time tunnel." This is a leadership that seeks to constitute a people clearly defined by its opposition to the partydocracy, a precarious institutionality that gives space to the movement and the leader, and a program that appeals to national recognition. However, it appears more respectful of its opponents and more pragmatic in the international arena, which distances it from a strictly ideological script and makes it appear more plural. Thus, this radical populism is the reality of a group of governments of the left with some populist heritage, for good or ill, in line with national history.

5 Populism as program and movement

In any case, those of us who locate it historically understand that populism, or, as Gino Germani (1965) preferred, *lo nacional popular*, is a social and political movement that at times transforms into government and that has as an objective of the nationalization of the State and the integration "from above" of the popular sectors into modern society, via participation as mobilization. In this movement the leader plays a central role, with the followers identifying with him, forming an emotional or charismatic community in relationship with him. These followers are reconstructed as a "people," a subject which finds its dynamic and finally its identity in the populist imagination, in the confrontation with the exclusive oligarchy.

In this last definition of Latin American populism lays a phenomenon delimited in time, which belongs, in general terms, to the moment of transition between a traditional society and a modern society, as signaled by Germani

(1965). A transition that, of course, can take different periods of time in each society, but which tends to be associated with the moment, of varying lengths, of rupture with the oligarchic regime and the start of the national state institutionalization, in which political democracy is formed in a republic of citizens and economic autonomy is sought in the process of integrating the habitants of a determined country into a national market.

Out of this conceptual contrast arises the issue of democracy. For those who understand populism as a behavior, the authoritarian temptation is the dominant tendency and perhaps the only one within populism. The role of the leader in the vertical relationship with his followers clouds all else and the masses become a malleable reference of the former. This vision is helped by the perspective that places the whole above the parts, of which a good example is the position of the "Anti-imperialist State" of Haya de la Torre (1972), which distances populism from pluralism and takes it to the denial of political competition.

This vision, nonetheless, due to its limited focus on the present, leaves to one side the process of Latin American populism in four ways: First, in taking into account participation as social and political mobilization, which supposes a door of access to the citizenry, in many cases the first for popular majorities. Participation as mobilization achieves its meaning in contrast with the exclusion of society and the oligarchic political regime, in some realities even in contrast with the institutions of oligarchic democracy, which were political regimes of restricted competition. In this mobilization, the subjects of politics stop being the elites and instead become all people who belong to the territory of the country in question. The citizenry and finally society are drastically broadened. This type of participation is the start of modern politics in Latin America.

Second, we must look within the possibility that this process opens up for representative democratic integration, where the most important effect of the populist stamp lies in the broadening of suffrage and in some cases political competition. What is more, in this way many political parties convert themselves into democratic parties, submitting themselves to the rules of electoral democracy.

Third, there are the opportunities for self-constitution of the popular subjects which are expressed in the greater protagonism of social organizations, perhaps in a first moment when part of the movement is bound with a party or *caudillo* or is a support of a government, but always as a form of organization of the major social interests. Finally, as indicated by Carlos de la Torre (1992), this can be found in the terrain of subjectivity for access to a symbolic dignity in racist and exclusive societies.

However, both Germani (1965, 1973) and Vilas (1995) believe that the greatest democratic effect of populism is in its social democratization. For them, this is about the rupture with the subordination of a servile character and the end of the exclusion of the social majority by the dominant institutions, achieving a freedom previously unknown in daily life, which multiplies the number of individuals available for representation. This will mean access to participation for the population via its own social organizations, access to rights guaranteed by the State and the consequent development of the citizenry, as well as the strengthening of civil society.

The inclusive nature and the social democratization perhaps are the most important characteristics of populism because both give power to the popular majorities which previously lacked them, a power that, otherwise, tends to transcend the populist phenomenon. This power arises from and in many cases promotes a socially distinct citizenry from that restricted to a few of the individual and political rights of elitist democracy. It is from there that the notion arises of populism's promotion of social rights as comparable with an irresponsible behavior that damages rather than benefits the community, because it is giving power to those who did not have it in detriment of the traditional elites.

The populist process opens up the possibility of democratization, nothing more nor less. This is a possibility that is not an unavoidable necessity, depending as it does on the actors and history of each country. Populism may evolve very well within an authoritarian regime rather than a democratic one, as happened with the hegemonic party in Mexico for more than 60 years. The same happens with social organizations. These can continue, associated with privilege and selling themselves to the highest bidder, becoming mercenaries or breaking with the populist tutelage, that is to say, to constitute themselves as organizations independent of the State and/or political movements in order to define themselves as free subjects that defend the interests of their members.

All this makes populism the first great democratizing wave in Latin America, prior to the oligarchic regimes, which we can broadly place between 1930 and 1978. It is important to emphasize this because during the era of transitions to democracy the subject presented itself in such a way that it was publicly assumed that these transitions were the beginning of the only Latin American democratization. In reality, the transitions began the second wave of democratization in the region, which took place approximately between 1978 and 1998, which finally led to, as we will see later, the current moment of the turn to the left that comprises the third great democratizing wave in Latin America.

Nevertheless, populism corresponds to a stage of development in Latin America and does not constitute a form of carrying out politics that can reappear at any point in time. Considering populism as historically determined takes us to the realization that it is an exhausted phenomenon, which completed its role in the development of the State, society and economy in the region, but that once they have developed, reaches the end of the road. Of course, the populist time is not the same in all countries and we have too belated attempts that, for this reason, are condemned to failure. One early example of this exhaustion was the military dictatorship of General Juan Velasco in Peru in the 1970s. A later example is the government of Hugo Chávez in Venezuela, which regressed from a democratic origin to authoritarian forms. This does not mean that there are no populist characteristics, such as the charismatic *caudillo* or the clientelistic networks, which are reproduced in Latin American politics, but these are, within the current context, a legacy rather than characteristics of a present model.

A singular position in this debate, which insists on the ahistorical use but with a positive appreciation of populism, is that of Ernesto Laclau (1979, 2005). For Laclau, populism is a discursive construction from a hegemonic leadership, subject and *caudillo*, which constitutes the subject people in opposition to its enemies, the block in power or oligarchy in the Latin American case, an interpolation where the leader and the effective connection that he establishes with the people plays a central role. This populism then, more than a behavior, becomes a specific form of building the political in a space of precarious institutionality. Although I disagree with this ahistorical use, I find interesting the process of constructing a populist identity from a hegemonic center characterized by a leader and the construction of the subject people in opposition to his enemies as Laclau notes. This also allows a better understanding of the populist phenomenon from the mentioned historical perspective.

Here, I want to highlight the aspect that tends to generate the deepest controversy. I am referring to the opposition between people and oligarchy, typical of populism, which Carlos de la Torre considers Manichean and without which this political phenomenon cannot be understood. !s it populism exclusively that constitutes subjects from an opposition? I think not. Populism as much as diverse types of political platforms, including leftist ones, constitute subjects and draw a political field around opposites. The problem is, rather, if this is inherently authoritarian or not. I do not believe so either. Oppositions are indispensable when there is a need to establish a new hegemony. In order to finish with the oligarchy it was necessary to confront it; to finish with military dictatorships of the 1970s and also the 1980s, and to finish with the odd couple of neoliberalism and transitions in equal manner. The problem is not oppositions but rather that the new hegemony has a democratic orientation.

Oppositions, irreducible ones in this case, and hegemonies, tend to be alien concepts to liberal pluralism, which understands the actors in a non-antagonistic competition for power, translated through this process only as a government. The problem with this liberal pluralism is that it comes from realities such as the existent hegemony, which is, at least apparently, unquestionable, so unquestionable that it tends to disappear from the eyes of everyone. This does not mean that a certain hegemony that has constituted the given political order and regime does not exist. From there arises, it appears to me, the fear of opposition and of course also of the new hegemonies that belong not just to populism but also of the profound democratic renovation through which the region has been advancing in recent years.

6 Transitions and the fallacy of consolidation

What those who want to settle for an analysis of current Latin American reality that qualifies the region's new governments as populist do not see is the process of democratic transformation that has occurred. This analysis assumes (Levine and Molina 2007), following Huntington, that we have lived an uninterrupted democratic course, at least since 1978, that has thrown up problems in recent years due to the supposed populisms.

The so-called transitions to democracy that began in the second wave of democratization in Latin America, from 1978 to 1998, with the passing from dictatorships to elected governments, were a political phenomenon of extraordinary importance accompanied by the return of the rule of law, with the rules, at least formally, that go with it. Among the questions that this democracy brought, or in some cases raised for the first time, were those of human rights, especially the right to life, which was so important following the political and military repressions. These rules are the great contribution of the transitions and the liberal regimes that they constituted because their lack of enforcement had been common currency in the history of the region, and after their almost complete disappearance during the dictatorships an awareness of a negative example was created that today is difficult to reverse.

The rules, nonetheless, which I recognize as a virtue, are also the great limitation of this democracy inaugurated with the transitions. This is because the existing poverty and inequality in the region make the rules not sufficient as a political promise, and that there must be guarantees of rights and of the provision of public goods that allow for the well-being of the population. These democracies were constituted, however, as regimes of a liberal representative type that guarantee a minimum level of civil and political rights but leave to one side social rights. These regimes, in addition, were completed around the era – in some cases before and in others after its foundation – of the economic model of neoliberal adjustment of the so-called Washington Consensus. The conservative vision thus beat the progressive one during the process of transitions, successfully selling the idea, in many cases initially true, that the "agreed rupture" (*ruptura pactada*) and political moderation was the best recipe for successful transitions. In terms of the State, the triumph of the conservative vision also meant the triumph of an exclusive State, in contrast to the populist State that had tended to be the State of all, or at least the majority. This exclusive State is the one that was due to enter into crisis years later when it showed itself incapable of satisfying the demands of those excluded by the neoliberal model.

For this reason, I hold that democracies that are the product of transitions will become overburdened in the phase of consolidation. What will happen is what I call the "fallacy of consolidation." Juan Linz and Alfred Stepan (1996) indicated how democracies can be considered consolidated when democracy is the "only game possible" in a given country, that is to say, when the distinct social and political actors believe that they can only achieve their objectives by democratic means. Nonetheless, this is in contradiction to the neoliberal model, which is based on mass expropriation of the rights of popular majorities, especially workers, as well as on a massive expropriation of public assets in favor of certain minorities who, supposedly, should begin or re-begin the economic movement. This expropriation of rights and public goods also signifies the transfer of political power away from the hands of unions, popular organizations, parties and the State itself, in order to hand these to others, big business, technocrats aligned with the model and security agencies.

In these conditions, in which politics cannot fulfill its role of relieving social inequality but rather deepens it, democracy in a liberal representative sense may not be the only game possible. In terms of the strategic calculation, it is logical that those who see their power diminished attempt to recover it by mobilizing the masses. This has been the case with several of the crises that initially have given rise in Latin America to the movements of anti-neoliberal resistance and eventually to governments of the left and center-left. For this reason, I argue that adopting the logic of verifying the fulfillment of certain rules is in fact mistaken when it comes to analyzing the problem of democratic consolidation. It is indispensable, for this purpose, to advance another concept of democracy.

7 How neoliberalism brought an end to the transitions

How then has the crisis of elitist democracy been a product of the transitions in the conflict between electoral participation and economic and social exclusion?

In the process of Latin American democratization, the odd couple of transitions and neoliberalism mark a regression in the face of the first wave of democratization characterized by historical populism. The inclusion that characterizes the latter in the face of the exclusion of the former would lead to the couple breaking up and the transitions to the failure of a political project. Neoliberalism means, as we have noted, an enormous expropriation of social and public goods through the restriction of rights and privatizations, but also the imposition of a mercantile logic on social development, as well as an indiscriminate economic opening up, along with the consequent mass unemployment and the restriction of informality, thus abandoning the goal of economic inclusion and full employment to which the popular national project aspired.

Neoliberalism is possible in Latin America due to a combination of two factors: the economic and political exhaustion of populism and the hegemony staked out by a new economic model that assumes itself to be the only way out of the capitalist crisis caused by the rise in the price of oil in 1973. What is more, it is implemented via shock therapy (Klein 2007), that is to say as a package of economic measures elaborated by a group of technocrats isolated from the population and launched by a political elite in a moment of vacuum and social confusion that creates the very conditions for its acceptance.

There were three objectives: to immediately apply a new model, cause fear in the population – and in the process, wipe out the collective memory of the prior social rights and services – and finally, waving the flag of a supposed efficiency in a moment of confusion, discredit opponents.

This has been completed with a dynamic of treason-repression of parties and governments both democratic and authoritarian, and likewise the initial resistance of distinct social movements. The dynamic began with the repression of the military dictatorships in the Southern Cone of Latin America, which tested out the first forms of neoliberalism in the 1970s. It was continued with the open and frontal treachery against their own electoral promises by Carlos Menem in Argentina and Alberto Fujimori in Peru. And there were significant milestones in the defeat of social movements in Bolivia in the 1980s and in the formidable popular resistance against the adjustment in the Venezuelan *Caracazo* of 1989. This dynamic of treason-repression and resistance incubated a contradiction that finally was expressed in the turn to the left in Latin America over the last decade.

8 The turn to the left

The election of a dozen different governments, and the reelection of some of them, from 1998 marked the beginning of a third period in the democratization of Latin America and it is unquestionable that this has represented a break from the period immediately prior to the transitions and neoliberalism. This is the nucleus of our debate, rupture or continuity in the democratization of the region. Due to its content, I have called change that this produced the "turn to the left" (Lynch 2009); I believe that this is about a movement of social and democratic reform that seeks to recover social justice in the distribution of resources, promote the participation of the population in decision-making, affirm the State as the principal actor, and achieve a greater autonomy from the United States. First of all, this marks a very important change with the previous period because governments will be elected that will do what they say, in contrast with those that developed their campaigns with a specific platform but subsequently did whatever they liked.

In most of the cases it is movements that convert into governments via social mobilizations which carry them to the electoral triumph of their political expressions, as well as successive ratifications via the ballot box. All of this corroborates a tendency that forms part of the process of democratization. Likewise, in ideological terms, this marks the return of politics and the public as organizers of social life, against the technocratic discourse of the dominance of the market and the micro-economic logic of cost-benefit, which has become the media's common sense of reference.

Why is this of the left? For many observers, who start out from a principally Marxist point of view, the leftist nature of this turn is in doubt, due to the fact that it is not an anti-capitalist movement. Nevertheless, I think that the phenomenon expresses what has been a fight for social justice and democracy in the world that is, as Bobbio (1996) notes, a struggle against social inequality and not exclusively an anti-capitalist battle. In this sense, it is nourished by a rich Latin American tradition that includes, in the view of Emir Sader (2008, 2009), the populist movements and governments, the Marxist left and social anti-neoliberal movements of recent years.

This change also marks a hegemonic displacement in Latin America, from neoliberal domination to the current turn to the left. This new hegemony is still in the process of consolidating its leadership but it already clearly views its objective as achieving a place for Latin America in the current multi-polar world, at a prudent distance from the previous hegemony that had as its axis the United States.

However, this movement is not exempt from authoritarian temptations, in some cases resulting from the resistance to change manifested by the social and political actors that enjoyed the previous situation, as well as the personal approach of some of these leaders who collide with plural competition among the distinct political options. For this reason, I argue that this third phase in Latin American democratization has three possible paths of development: The greatest democratization, which appears to be the dominant current scene; revolutionization, which combines demagoguery with polarization against the empire of the North; and neoliberal regression, which is the opposite of what is happening currently and is promoted by the United States, rightwing governments and their internal allies in each country.

In the last decade or so, I believe the democratizing tendency has been consolidated, both in the processes that have followed the constitutional path, such as in Bolivia and Ecuador, as well as in those that have inserted themselves into democratic regimes that were already established, such as in Brazil, Uruguay and Argentina. Perhaps the exception is Venezuela which, having been the country that began this third stage of democratization, has taken a more authoritarian turn which has led it to a sharp conflict with the opposition without any solution in sight. The rightist axis, in any case, has maintained itself as with the victory in Chile of the conservative candidate and its continued success in Colombia, even though it confronts important challenges from leftwing oppositions in both Mexico and Peru. A simple regression and return to the previous neoliberal hegemony, as expected by some observers, has not happened and, rather, albeit without the initial momentum, the new democratizing process has settled in.

The touchstone in this new situation in the region is respect for political pluralism, in other words respect by the opposition for governments of the left and center-left. This has presented problems in all the Latin American democracies, but above all in those that seek to construct an order with a new political hegemony. In the prior phase, the ideological strength achieved by the coupling of the transitions and neoliberalism was sufficiently great as to present itself as democracy "for everyone," until it was defeated by the social movements and antineoliberal political options. In this new moment, when efforts were made to include social rights as an indispensable part of the democratic order, those who defended the notion of a regime restricted to procedures have claimed that they are being excluded from the political system. The challenge of the moment is, therefore, to find a way to include all the actors in a wider democracy, whose definition goes beyond individual and political rights, with a social citizenry that takes up the existing claims for justice and national independence.

Conclusion

What have developed in Latin America in the last decade and more are not populist regimes that threaten democracy but rather movements and governments of the left and center-left that drive programs of social and democratic reform. These movements and governments promote a new political hegemony that proposes greater citizen participation both in the processes of decision-making and in the redistribution of economic surpluses, by which they distance themselves from the democratic regime exclusively in the interest of the economic elite. The qualification of these governments as populist seeks to avoid an analysis of the crisis of elitist democracies in the region and block this bankruptcy with a concept, which the media have given a pejorative meaning, while equally promoting the wiping out of historical populism from the collective memory of the region.

The interesting thing, nonetheless, is that this situation allows the development of new democratic foci that seek to interpret what is currently happening in Latin America. These new foci recover democracy as a regime that arises from the connection between citizens and the national State and from the conflict between different social interests. Likewise, they indicate the necessity of the Nation State for democratic development and the importance of mechanisms of mediation between the citizen and political power so that pluralism can exist.

Finally, it also arises that the regimes resulting from the last stage of political development constitute the third wave of democratization in the region. In contrast to the image that is presented of the transitions 30 years earlier, democracy in the region has been a process that has in recent years once again placed on the table inclusion of the people, the rules from the transitions, social rights and national independence.

Notes

1 Norbert Lechner (1996) uses these terms, in the decade of the 1990s, to describe the opposite transition from the centrality of politics and more specifically of the State to the centrality of the market.
2 For a broader discussion of this point, consult Lynch (2009), where I examine the construction of another democratic approach.
3 An exception to this ahistorical use, but with a distinct, positive connotation, is that developed by Ernesto Laclau, as we shall see below.

References

Bobbio, N. (1996) *Left and Right: The Significance of a Political Distinction*. Chicago: University of Chicago Press.

de la Torre, C. (1992) The ambiguous meanings of Latin American populisms. *Social Research* 59(2) (Summer).

de la Torre, C. (2008) Populismo, ciudadanía y Estado de Derecho. In C. de la Torre and E. Peruzzotti (eds.) *El retorno del pueblo. Populismo y nuevas democracias en América Latina*. Quito: Flacso. Sede Ecuador.

de la Torre, C. and E. Peruzzotti (eds.) (2008) Introducción. El regreso del populismo. *El retorno del pueblo. Populismo y nuevas democracias en América Latina*. Quito: Flacso. Sede Ecuador.

Dussel, E. (2010) El pueblo, lo popular y el populismo. *Pensando el mundo desde Bolivia. I Ciclo de Seminarios Internacionales*. La Paz: Vicepresidencia del Estado Plurinacional de Bolivia.

Eagleton, T. (1984) *The Function of Criticism*. London: Verso.

Germani, G. (1965) *Política y Sociedad en una época de transición: De la sociedad tradicional a la sociedad de masas*. Buenos Aires: Paidós.

Germani, G. (1973) *Democracia representativa y clases populares*. México: Serie Popular Era.

Haya de la Torre, V. R. (1972) *El antimperialismo y el APRA*. 4th edn. Lima: Amauta.

Huntington, S. P. (1991) *The Third Wave: Democratization in the Late Twentieth Century*. Norman: University of Oklahoma Press.

Klein, N. (2007) *The Shock Doctrine: The Rise of Disaster Capitalism*. New York: Metropolitan Books.

Laclau, E. (1979) *Política e ideología en la teoría marxista*. México: Siglo XXI editores.

Laclau, E. (2005) *On Populist Reason*. London: Verso.

Lechner, N. (1996) Las transformaciones de la política. *Revista Mexicana de Sociología* 58(1) (January–March).

Levine, D. H. and J. E. Molina (2007) La calidad de la democracia en América Latina: una visión comparada. *América Latina Hoy* 45.

Linz, J. J. and A. Stepan (1996) *Problems of Democratic Transition and Consolidation: Southern Europe, South America, and Post–Communist Europe*. Baltimore: Johns Hopkins University Press.

Lynch, N. (1999) Neopopulismo: un concepto vacío. *Socialismo y Participación* 86 (December) Lima, Perú.

Lynch, N. (2009) *El argumento democrático sobre América Latina*. Lima: Universidad Nacional Mayor de San Marcos. Fondo Editorial de la Facultad de Ciencias Sociales.

Macpherson, C. B. (1970) *La teoría política del individualismo posesivo*. Barcelona: Fontanella.

Marshall, T. H. (1996) Citizenship and social class. In T. H. Marshall and T. Bottomore (eds.) *Citizenship and Social Class*. London: Pluto.

O'Donnell, G. (1992) ¿Democracia delegativa?. *Cuadernos del CLAEH* 61.

Peruzzotti, E. (2008) Populismo y representación democrática. In C. de la Torre and E. Peruzzotti (eds.) *El retorno del pueblo. Populismo y nuevas democracias en América Latina*. Quito: Flacso. Sede Ecuador.

Roberts, K. (1995) Neoliberalism and the transformation of populism in Latin America: the Peruvian case. *World Politics* 48 (October).

Sader, E. (2008) The weakest link? *New Left Review* 52 (July–August).

Sader, E. (2009) *El nuevo topo. Los caminos de la izquierda latinoamericana*. Buenos Aires: Siglo XXI editores.

Sartori, G. (1970) Concept misformation in comparative politics. *The American Political Science Review* 64(4) (December).

Schmitt, C. (1982) *Teoría de la Constitución*. Madrid: Alianza Editorial.

Tilly, C. (2007) *Democracy*. Cambridge: Cambridge University Press.

Vilas, C. (1995) Estudio Preliminar. El populismo o la democratización fundamental de América Latina. In Carlos Vilas (compilador). *La democratización fundamental*. México: Consejo Nacional para la Cultura y las Artes.

Weber, M. (1979) *Economía y Sociedad*. México: Fondo de Cultura Económica.

Weyland, K. (1997) Neopopulismo y neoliberalismo en América Latina: afinidades inesperadas. *Pretextos* 10 (September).

10 A trickling fountain or a devastating torrent

Andrew Arato's theory of the modern republican executive

Maria Victoria Crespo

> All have noted with dismay the paradox of an executive having a superabundance of power coupled with extreme weakness. The executive has been unable to repel foreign invasion or suppress seditious plots except by resorting to dictatorship. The Constitution itself as if to correct its fault, goes to extremes in order to provide in profusion those powers which it jealously guards. Thus, the government of Colombia is either a trickling fountain or a devastating torrent.
>
> Simón Bolívar (1951), Message to the Congress of Ocaña, May 1, 1828

One of Andrew Arato's main theoretical and political concerns in the 2000s focused on the modern republican executive, specifically its purely presidential form. Arato's research on the presidency was motivated by a variety of historical events including the last wave of transitions to democracy and subsequent constitution making processes that took place in Eastern European and Latin American countries in the 1980s and 1990s; the strengthening of the American presidency after 9/11, the peculiarities of George W. Bush's administration and the American occupation of Iraq; the use and abuse of (legal and extra-legal) emergency powers around the world from Russia to Colombia, and even in the US; and the reemergence of populist forms of leadership in Latin America such as Hugo Chávez's presidency in Venezuela. Hence, Arato's work on the modern presidency is another demonstration of his intellectual commitment to political theory, comparative analysis and contemporary political issues.

Arato's theory of the presidency developed in three moments, of course, with a significant overlapping from one phase to the other. First, he focused on the relationships between the presidency and transitions to democracy (1990s-2000). Second, he studied the structural and political linkages between presidentialism, emergency regimes and dictatorship (2001–2006). Finally, he offered his more comprehensive reflections on the interactions between the presidency and sovereignty (2006–2010). Even though his work during the 1990s is mostly known for his inquiries on civil society, he also rigorously introduced institutional concerns to democratic studies, in relation to both the *processes* and the *outcomes* of these transitions (Arato 1994, 1995–1996, 2000a, 2000b, 2002c, 2005b). Arato's writings during this period were part of the turn towards bringing the classical debate on presidentialism "back in" the fields of political science, political sociology and comparative constitutionalism. This trend took place during the "third wave of democratization" of the 1980s and 1990s when dozens of countries went through transitions from authoritarian to democratic regimes (Huntington 1991). Most of these transitions entailed different types of constitution making processes. The different political groups involved in constitutional politics faced fundamental choices on the form of government, among them, the pivotal option between presidentialism, parliamentarism or (the sometimes overlooked) hybrid forms such as semi-presidentialism. Therefore, transitions to democracy constituted the political context that led towards the reemergence of institutional concerns in the social sciences and revived the classical discussion on presidential government (O'Donnell *et al.* 1986; Linz 1990, 1994; Mainwaring 1990, 1993; Lijphart 1992; Linz and Valenzuela 1994; Linz and Stepan 1996; Mainwaring and Shugart 1997; Stepan 2000). In fact, in Arato's (2005b: 10) view, this debate represented "the main political science contribution to substantive problems faced by constitution makers." (See, Arato 1994, 1995–1996, 2000b, 2002c, 2005b.) During this phase Arato already considered the effects that presidents may have on transitional political and constitutional developments and outcomes (Arato 2000a: 239, 2002c: 225–227), anticipating what in his most recent book he calls "revolutionary-populist sovereign constitution-making" (Arato 2009: viii).

While the 1990s were characterized by a fair political optimism brought by transitions to democracy, the *pax americana* and the Bill Clinton era, the 2000s were disrupted by 9/11, Bush's questioned administration, the war on Iraq, and the shadows of American interventionism and imperialism internationally, and even of dictatorship within the US. In this context, Arato engaged in a provocative discussion on the materialization of an emergency regime in the US and its relationship with presidential politics and (lack of) legitimacy (Arato 2002a, 2002b, 2006). He boldly proposed a full codification of emergency powers in the US. The purpose of this legislation was to avoid the greater danger of relying solely on the executive's powers or the extra-legal prerogative in times of crisis (Arato 2002b, 2006). During this period of authoritarian tendencies and crisis government in the US, he reflected on the paradoxical constitutional structure of presidential government. Originally, the presidency had been designed to block sovereignty claims raised by the legislative branch, but under strict constitutional checks itself to avoid similar usurpations on its own behalf. Arato (2000b, 2001, 2002b) sharply pointed out that the resulting presidential design was characterized by an oscillation between political strength and constitutional weakness, which historically had led to a circle of impotence and authoritarianism in the US and elsewhere. In other words, presidential government tends to be dangerous to constitutional democracies not only because of its *extra-constitutional political strength* – exacerbated by its democratic legitimacy – but also due to its *constitutional weakness*. In his view, this institutional structure in the US has historically led to war to gain legitimacy and political power. During this intellectual stage, Arato discussed "American exceptionalism," and the possible reasons why the US flawed presidential system nevertheless avoided stepping across the legal threshold to dictatorship, and whether such reasons – imperial expansion, the American Constitution, common law flexibility, liberal ethos of the elite, etc. – continued to apply in the Bush days.

Arato's latest works focus on the relationships between the presidency and the question of sovereignty. The enigmatic concept of sovereignty has captured Arato's theoretical interest in the past years. In my view, he has connected his insights on the presidency to concepts and historical processes that in one way or another are related to the problem of sovereignty: revolutions, state formation, emergency regimes, dictatorship, constitution making and war. Therefore, *sovereignty* will serve here as the interweaving concept that will bring together the different dimensions of Arato's theory of presidential government. For this purpose, I rely on Arato's published works, but also collect his thoughts on the presidency expressed in the context of several seminars and lectures imparted at The New School for Social Research in the period that spans from 2002 to 2006.[1]

In this chapter, first, I intend to offer a systematic approach to Arato's conception of the presidency by focusing on a theoretical and historical problem: "that of the embodiment of sovereign power (popular *and* state sovereignty) in the republican executive" (Arato, 2006, "Adventures of Popular Sovereignty," Seminar, The New School for Social Research). I look at the "double origin" of the presidency, which according to Arato needs to be traced in "kingship and republican fears." The chapter then examines the problem of incarnation of popular sovereignty by the executive, which frequently has resulted in explosive manifestations of plebiscitary democracy and/or dictatorship. Thus it considers the political dilemma of "embodiment" and representation of sovereignty by a single person. Second, by establishing an analytical link between Arato's conception of the presidency and his theory of dictatorship, I analyze the relationship between the presidency and emergencies, *coups d'état* and constitution making. Finally, I consider the specificities of the American presidency, including the issue of war and empire. The three sections of the chapter are analytically connected to the concepts of popular sovereignty, as well as *internal* and *external* state sovereignty.

Origins and embodiments of the modern republican executive power

In his *Constitutional Theory*, Schmitt (2008: 316) interprets presidential government as the outcome of a revolutionary historical development that goes from king to president. In a brief passage that he dedicates to the presidency – interestingly within the chapter on monarchical doctrine – Schmitt identifies a triple origin of the presidency: monarchical, republican and revolutionary. According to Schmitt, countries that have experienced *revolutionary processes* which have made monarchies "unconceivable" required "an autonomous chief of the executive branch, which should have a representative character." The president is thus "the republican version of the monarch of the parliamentary monarchy" (Schmitt 2008: 316). Likewise, Arato has focused on the "double origin of presidential government, monarchical and republican," in revolutionary contexts. Relying on a wide array of modern and contemporary authors (Kelsen 1945; McIlwain 1947; Bendix 1978; Kantorowicz 1997; Vile 1998; Schmitt 2008) and the classical works of Aristotle, Machiavelli, Locke, Montesquieu and Blackstone, he has theorized on the genealogy of the presidency. Arato links presidential origins to monarchy, specifically, the political structure of kinship and the monarchical prerogative, but also the doctrine of separation of powers, which was primarily developed for monarchical government. However, he has also underlined the republican and revolutionary foundations of presidential government. The puzzle of presidential government is that in order to secure the principle of separation of powers, and avoid tyrannical government, a monarchical type of executive is needed. To illustrate this, in relation to the birth of the American presidency, Vile (1998: 171) has pointed out:

> ... the fear of legislative tyranny was so strong and the need for executive independence loomed so large in the minds of the delegates that they were prepared to move towards the partial restoration of some of the former prerogatives of the Crown, which the early State constitutions had ruthlessly stripped away.

Since its very origins, presidential government already contained the paradox of being at the same time a single person executive and the constitutional creation of a republican political thought and project that categorically rejected concentration of power in a single individual:

> Both classical republican thought and the modern doctrine of popular/national sovereignty have been historically hostile to the incarnation of all power in a single person or institution, and doctrines of mixed government and the separation of powers expressed this strong reservation. The modern republican executive was consciously designed to block sovereign pretensions of legislatures, without however the possibility of similar "usurpation" on its own behalf.
>
> (Arato, 2006, "Adventures of Popular Sovereignty")

Therefore, presidential republics have a contradictory structure: the presidency is the monarchical element in the notion of mixed government that defines republics. It is conceived as a single person executive office endowed with powers that resemble the prerogatives of the monarch. However, presidential government is also a revolutionary constitutional creation meant to *replace* the monarchical executive power, and as such is founded on the principle of popular sovereignty. Thus, in theory, the president can never become sovereign – if there is a sovereign, it is the people. To secure that, the president is institutionally checked by the legislature. Following Arato's argumentation, this paradoxical origin resulted in an institutional design that includes strong powers that resemble monarchical prerogatives: the president typically is the Commander in Chief of the Army, Navy and Militias; conducts war, executes law and has legislative veto; is in charge of the general administration of the state and its internal and external security; appoints ambassadors, consuls and army officials; signs international treaties and grants pardons. However, these powers also have strict constitutional limits since most of them require congressional or the Senate's approval, sometimes even with qualified majorities. This is what Arato (2002b: 465) calls the "weak-strong" constitutional structure of presidential government: "The separation of powers of the American type has, as elsewhere, promoted a pattern of oscillation between a weak executive and a presidency assuming a type of leadership that breaks through constitutional limitations." According to Arato, the presidency moves from weak periods – usually during normalcy – to strong phases, particularly in times of crises or national emergencies. It is important to underline that both moments can be pernicious to constitutionalism – while the strong presidency may culminate in outright dictatorship, its weakness might lead to desperate leadership, dictatorial tendencies or constitutional interruptions such as *coups d'état*: "the step from fatal weakness to a dangerous assertion of arbitrary authority can be a very small one" (Arato 2001: 289–290).

Presidential leadership that either "steps across the legal threshold" or "comes close" to dictatorship became more common with the expansion of suffrage and the rise of plebiscitary democracy, mainly during the twentieth century. This process provided the presidency with an alternative and autonomous source of legitimacy. In the context of Arato's genealogical analysis, the fact that the modern republican executive emerged in revolutionary contexts leads to the question of *popular sovereignty* and how historically it has turned into the main vehicle for unaccountable and uncontrollable executive power not only in France and Latin America, but also, occasionally, in the United States. During revolutions, the question of the locus of sovereignty typically arises since there is a vacuum of power and legitimacy that must be filled. Claude Lefort refers to this process as the "pathology" of modern democratic revolutions, namely the urge to fill a political and symbolic space that would otherwise be left empty, which in turn leads to "embodied" and "absolutist" models of sovereignty.[2] The empty space of sovereignty is filled by a new, absolute, superior political body, the people themselves – the People in the Shoes of the King formula – or by a new authoritarian personification, be it a Caesar, Robespierre, Napoleon or Bolívar. Pathological or not, revolutions do require an answer to the question of sovereignty: Once the king is nullified as the sovereign, the question of *who the sovereign is* inexorably comes to the surface. The answer from modern revolutions is, naturally, "the people." However, the people, either as an abstract political entity or as a sociological category cannot exercise such sovereignty; the people must be represented (Schmitt 2008: 240).[3] The sovereignty of the people thus acquires two dimensions: the electorate and its representatives (Morgan 1989; Baker 1990; Kantorowicz 1997; Wood 1998).[4] In this context, Arato points out, an institution or a person that represents, exercises and sometimes even usurps popular sovereignty emerges as an assembly, a Congress or some sort of personified power previously exercised by the king. This personified form may adopt different names and institutional forms such as president, consul, director, dictator, protector, etc. (Arato, 2006, "Adventures of Popular Sovereignty").

Thus, in spite of being an institution conceived to avoid legislative usurpations of popular sovereignty, the fact that the president is a "natural body" (Kantorowicz 1997) facilitates a sort of identification (Schmitt 1994: 26–29) between the people and the executive leader. This leader historically and politically develops into the embodiment of such popular sovereignty. In *The Crisis of Parliamentary Democracy*, Schmitt introduces this notion of identification, which captures the relationship of the presidency with the two Schmittian formal political principles of representation and identity (Schmitt 1994, 2008: 239–252). The simultaneous proximity of the president to the representative figure of the king on the one hand, and to the people on the other – actually the two sovereigns or subjects of the constituent power – elevates the presidency to a particularly privileged position in terms of political legitimacy. Since immediate identity with the people is impossible, Arato observes that Schmitt solves this problem by "doubling the principle of representation" through the concept of identification (Arato, 2006, "Adventures of Popular Sovereignty"). Arato notes the plebiscitary legitimacy superiority of the single person executive, which facilitates identification, over a plural assembly of numerous representatives (also see Marx 1963: 32–33). Like the monarch, the president as head of state represents *the unity of the state* (state sovereignty). However, the democratically elected president also may represent *the people as a whole* (popular sovereignty). Thus the president is at the heart, and the head, of a government constructed on plebiscitary foundations.

Therefore, one of the main aspects of Arato's theory of the modern republican executive is the problem of the incarnation of popular sovereignty by the executive, which historically has resulted in different forms of plebiscitary democracy and dictatorship. One of the main traits of presidential government is that it carries an internal tension between constitutionalism and democracy. This tension is intensified in extraordinary political moments such as crises, transitions, wars and constitution making processes. This conflict between constitutionalism and democracy, inherent to presidential government, also has to be interpreted along the lines of its "weak-strong" structure. It is a common assumption that presidential government is dangerous to constitutional democracy because the president might be too strong, namely what in Latin American contexts has been called "hyper-presidentialism" (which includes broad emergency powers, executive decree powers, legislative veto, congressional delegations, etc.). Additionally, presidents may also convert their plebiscitary legitimacy into political strength. Their democratic origin might enable strong presidencies to violate the principles of constitutionalism based on their plebiscitary legitimacy and majoritarian claims. Yet, presidential government can threaten constitutional democracy not only because of its *strength* but mainly its *weakness*, the "two possibilities within the same structure" (Arato 2005b). Rigid constitutional constraints may result in a presidency with tied hands (caused by rigidity of the term of office, checks from the legislative branch, limited powers, impeachment, political removal, restricted reelection, etc.) and thus to frantic authoritarian leadership. Moreover, doubtful or tied democratic majorities or congressional opposition and deadlocks resulting from intermediate elections may also undermine presidential democratic legitimacy. These structural constitutional and political weaknesses can also be conducive to democratic breakdown and dictatorship, the topic of the following section of this chapter.

Presidentialism and dictatorship

One of Arato's most important contributions to political sociology and political theory is his *reconceptualization* of Carl Schmitt's theory of dictatorship. Asserting that the most promising approach to such constitutional ruptures remains the legal one, Arato (2000c: 934) defines dictatorship in relation to legality, that is,

> the complete, unambiguous, but in its legal form exceptional primacy of prerogative and discretionary power (uniting executive, legislative, and judicial powers) in a society that has a rationalized legal order, justified by reference to that legal order or a new (constitutional) order of polity and society.

Arato conceptualizes dictatorship in relation to the prerogative and the suspension of law, but, as several authors have acknowledged (see Marx 1963, 1978: 538; Schmitt 1999), it might also have democratic legitimacy claims. Within his revision of Schmitt's theory of dictatorship, Arato (2000c: 928) has pointed out that "the crucial difference between commissarial and sovereign dictatorship is the reliance on legality in the one case, and on legitimacy without legality in the other."[5] He however observes that Schmitt's theory is incomplete since there are "unresolved problems of origins and temporality." Therefore there is a multiplicity of dictatorships that cannot be explained by using the Schmittian ideal types of dictatorship. For example, many modern dictatorships begin with *coups d'état* without any legal authorization. To the extent that they are extra-legal, these coups are not commissioned. They are not sovereign either, since their rulers often seek to make the crisis situation indefinite in duration and do not attempt to return to the old order or institutionalize a new regime (Arato 2000c: 931–932). In the case of sovereign dictatorship, the problem arises when these dictatorships become permanent, namely when the exception becomes the normal institutional functioning of government. Another problem pointed out by Arato is that the two Schmittian types of dictatorship are actually sovereign, since the commissioned dictator also holds sovereign powers.

In his reformulation of the legal approach to dictatorship, following the categories of János Kis' (1995) typology of regime change, Arato keeps legality and legitimacy as models of justification of dictatorship, but the term "revolutionary dictatorship" is used instead of sovereign dictatorship. Since many modern dictatorships are not necessarily commissioned, he replaces the Schmittian commissarial dictatorship by the concept of "protective dictatorship" to refer to "all cases that are oriented to the defense of a given legal order, whether or not the introduction of exceptional rule was legal or illegal, through coup or *autogolpe* (self-coup)" (Arato 2000c: 934). He thus expands the meaning of the concept of dictatorship by including a new type that refers to regimes which emerge from illegal coups. Yet his redefinition also allows to take into account what Linz (1978: 76–77) has called "legal revolution," meaning negotiated transitions towards democracy that follow a path of legal continuity which avoids dictatorship (see Table 10.1). Arato's (2000c: 945) redefinition also includes the tendencies of certain dictatorships to permanence, a fact that can be explained by the combinations of protective-revolutionary and revolutionary-protective types, which "are in service of self-preservation or self-perpetuation" (see Table 10.1). This synchronic and legal conceptualization of the presidency should be complemented with Arato's (2003) diachronic conceptual history of dictatorship. In a remarkable manuscript (included in this volume) Arato (2003) historicizes the concept of dictatorship by showing how it shifted from its "classical meaning," a virtuous Roman institution conceived to save an endangered republic, to a political form that involves concentration of absolute power by a single political entity, that is, the "modern meaning" of the term.

In my view, Arato's theory of dictatorship is analytically linked to his conception of the presidency. Arato's intellectual concerns regarding modern republican executives are related to the four instances of dictatorship: emergency regimes (legal and extra-legal); *coups d'état* and constitution making processes, which include the role that the executive may play during legal revolutions and negotiated transitions (i.e., "round tables" "post-sovereign constitution making" etc.); or in revolutionary contexts (i.e., "executive constitution making" [Arato 2000a] and "revolutionary-populist sovereign constitution making" [Arato 2009]). In Arato's works, this relationship between the executive and dictatorship is also analytically connected to his insight on the oscillation between strength and weakness of presidential government.

Table 10.1 Types of dictatorship according to Arato's redefinition of the Schmittian concept of dictatorship and relationships to presidential government

Oriented to legality	*Oriented to democracy*
Legally established	
I. Protective – Commissarial Presidential emergency powers	II. Rupture Negotiated or coordinated transition Role of pre-existent or future presidents in round tables or constitutional negotiation. [This category escapes dictatorship]
Illegally established	
II. Protective – Extralegal Presidential *autogolpe* or *coup d'état*	IV. Revolutionary "Executive" or "revolutionary-populist sovereign" constitution making

In the post 9/11 context, one of Arato's main intellectual and political concerns was the evolving emergency regime in the United States. In the 2000s, he consistently pointed out the "significant diminution of civil liberties" in the US and analyzed how this country had come close to dictatorship during the so-called War on Terror. During this period he focused on the problem of constitutional dictatorship, emergency regimes, the line between exceptional ruptures *within* and *of* legality and (dictatorial) normalcy, and the bounds of legality of this type of measures (Arato 2002a, 2002b, 2006). He worked on the history of the jurisprudence on emergencies in the US. He was also very involved in the debate on emergencies that took place in American academic and political circles in the aftermath of 9/11 (Schlesinger 1973; Fisher 2004; Yoo 2005; Tushnet 2005; Ackerman 2006; Cole 2006; Scheuerman 2006). However, in Arato's view most of the problem during the Bush years' crisis was specifically related to the lack of codification of an emergency regime and, more generally speaking, to the historical development by which:

> the US Constitution in Hals Kelsen's *material* sense has gradually come to provide for an emergency regime that puts the fate of our liberties squarely into the hands of an executive that in moments of crisis tends to escape the control of other branches. Finally, to make the unpleasant picture complete, given the structural weakness of the executive's position in normal, internal affairs – even when (unlike today!) [i.e., Bush] he has genuine electoral majority – there is now good reason to assume that the American president has developed a material (though not ideal) interest in external conflict, and even internal crisis. And it was always during severe external and internal crisis that the specter of dictatorship reared its ugly head in this country.
>
> (2002b: 457–458, original emphasis)

Therefore, his argument was not only related to emergency regulations but the whole US presidential design (Arato 2002b: 465). Arato correlates the "structural" weakness of the presidency to a historical tendency to exploit crises to enhance presidential authority and legitimacy in the US. This remark is also valid for other presidential regimes. For example, in Latin America, the use of emergency powers has historically been more common among weakened presidencies in unstable or critical moments. In contrast, strong and legitimate popular presidencies do not *need* to rely on their emergency powers, since they have been able to seize political control and institutions.

The second analytical and historical moment in which the presidency and dictatorship meet is "extra-legal protective" dictatorship, best exemplified by *coups d'état* and *autogolpes*. Even though in this context he refers to extra-legal ruptures, I should mention that Arato also foresees the possibility of constitutional coups, as shown in his interpretation of the Bill Clinton impeachment crisis (Arato 1999: 148–152). The fact is that presidential government is particularly unstable and propitious to constitutional disruptions. The expected rivalry between the executive and legislative branches of government due to the principle of separation of powers is enhanced by their autonomous *democratic legitimacy*. On this topic, Arato (2000b: 322, 2002c: 225, 2005b: 10–11) has a conversation with Juan Linz (Linz and Valenzuela 1994). On the basis of Latin American experience, in a seminal essay Linz observes that presidential systems represent an open door to dictatorship and authoritarian rule. The idea that presidentialism "is a system of dual democratic legitimacy" is at the heart of Linz's argument: in presidential systems *both* the president, who is elected directly or indirectly by the people, and an elected legislature (unicameral or federal) enjoy democratic legitimacy. The dangerous corollary of this feature is that mainly in times of crisis or political wearing out, it tends to create dysfunctional presidencies through tensions or "deadlocks" between the executive and the legislative branches, since there is no method to resolve *who* "is better legitimated to speak in the name of the people: the president, or the congressional majority that opposes his policies?" (Linz 1994: 7). The conflict between both political branches is intensified by the *constitutional rigidity* of the system since both, president and Congress, are elected for a fixed term. As Linz (1994: 7) observes, impeachment, generally the provision established to "solve" this type of scenario, is highly complex, legalistic and slow. Thus, it is not surprising that the most plausible outcome is a military intervention as a "moderating power" (in the cases of weakened presidencies) or a self-coup (*autogolpe*) (in strong presidencies) orchestrated by the president against the legislature (the classical example being Louis Bonaparte).

Last but not least, considering Arato's most recent works, there is the relationship between presidentialism and constitution making. Arato identifies several methods by which the presidency may influence constitution making processes. However, unlike Bruce Ackerman (1992: 52–57) who argues that the president should have a leading part in mobilizing for a constitution, he is critical of the role that a preexisting president may play. According to Arato, presidents usually distort constitutional negotiations or facilitate authoritarian outcomes. In the context of his works on transitions to democracy and political change, he has observed that in revolutionary constitution making episodes the president may carry out a *coup d'état* from above (*autogolpe*) against established institutional authorities, but the subsequent constitution making will be informally influenced by the authoritarian president. This is for example Arato's analysis of Boris Yeltsin's coup and the resulting Constitution of the Russian Federation of 1993 (Arato 2002c: 225–227). A second pathological possibility is populist constitution making. In theory, the president cannot be the subject of the constituent power of the people, but he can certainly claim to represent or embody it. This is the method that Arato (2000a, 2009) calls "constitution making through a popular executive power," or more recently "populist constitution making." In *Civil Society, Constitution, and Legitimacy*, Arato explicitly considers this situation as a type of democratic constitution making, which combines an executive proposal approved by a general popular plebiscite. Another possibility is a president carrying a popular majority and a strong democratic legitimacy that might push for a constitution making process to *constitutionalize* (following or infringing the existing amendment rule) an authoritarian political project, usually involving presidential unrestricted reelection and perpetuation in power. There are many Latin American examples of this: the classical populist episode of Juan Domingo Peron's regime and the resulting "Peronist" Constitution of 1949. A more moderate manifestation of this were the constitution making processes that took place in the context of "delegative democracies" (O'Donnell 1991) in the 1990s such as the constitutional reform led by Carlos Menem in Argentina in 1994. More recently, there is the populist revival and the constitutional reform by Hugo Chávez's Bolivarian Revolution in Venezuela. Finally, I should mention that according to Arato the involvement of the executive power in a constitution making process is not necessarily pathological by definition: "Admittedly, the link between the role of a presidential figure in constitution making, and a presidentialist outcome may not be absolute" (Arato 2005b: 12). However, this is usually due to the leader's "self-restraint," a very frail quality to rely on. Nonetheless, Arato's categories admit the possibility of a president playing a "virtuous" role in "legal revolutions" or "negotiated transitions," namely the third box in Arato's model, which actually evades dictatorship. As a member of the previous regime or as a leader of the opposition and "future" executive, the executive may hypothetically smooth negotiations and/or round tables with all the existing political groups or parties for the creation of a constitutional draft within legality, namely, while the preexistent legal framework and institutions are (really or fictionally) in place. However, normatively and politically speaking this certainly does not represent the most promising scenario:

> While each historical period, however, may have a Washington, a San Martín, a Havel or a Mandela – capable of great self-limitation in constitutional politics or state-making, there always seem to be many more Bonapartes, Bolivars, De Gaulles, Walesas, Yeltsins, Illiescus, Menems, Fujimoris and Berishas whose ideas of democracy are equivalent to the expansion of their own plebiscitary power.
>
> (Arato 2005b: 12)

Presidency, war and empire

One of the questions that cuts across Arato's political thought on the modern presidency is related to the supposed American *exceptionalism*. In fact, one of Arato's (2000b, 2002b, 2005b) more provocative academic proposals in the past decade was to push for rigorous comparative analyses between the US and other presidential systems, a frequently neglected intellectual enterprise in the field of comparative politics.[6] With respect to the presidency, Arato's inquiries were related to the possible reasons why the US historically avoided stepping across the legal threshold to dictatorship and whether those reasons continued to apply during the Bush administration.

Relying on several commentators, Arato's analysis of the American presidency begins from the assumption that rather than being a univocal and unambiguous institution, its history falls into distinctive periods, regimes or stages (Wilson 1917, 1956; Neustadt 1960; Schlesinger 1973; Lowy 1985; Ackerman 1991, 1998; Skowronek 2000).[7] In Arato's view a historical movement between strong and weak presidencies has disrupted these stages. Nevertheless, following Steven Skowronek's (2000) analysis, he acknowledges that in the twentieth century the presidency has also shown a linear development by which it has become more plebiscitary and increasingly central in foreign affairs through congressional delegations (Schlesinger 1973; Fisher 2004).

In order to present Arato's views on the American presidency, I should make an additional analytical point. Conceptually, Arato identifies two perilous models of the presidency, which correlate to the question of political embodiments of sovereignty that I have addressed in the first section of this chapter: (1) the presidency was originally conceived to represent *state sovereignty* and the unity of such state, and in its most extreme form this notion of the presidency would correspond to what Schlesinger (1973) calls "the imperial presidency"; (2) historically, the presidency also became the embodiment of *popular sovereignty* through a symbolical identification between the presidency and the people. According to Arato, Caesarism would be the pure type of this political form. Of course, these are ideal types, and historical manifestations of these forms are less extreme. According to Arato, presidentialism reaches its most dangerous potential when imperial and plebiscitary forms come together. Historically, one may predominate over the other (for example, Abraham Lincoln was at critical moments the embodiment of the American state but not a plebiscitary president) or may fuse (Franklin D. Roosevelt being the paradigmatic case), although the US has escaped the more extreme pure forms of Caesarism (Arato, 2006, "Adventures of Popular Sovereignty"). Even though Arato acknowledges that there were some *exceptional* plebiscitary and imperial episodes in the US during the nineteenth century, he observes that the *normalization* of the plebiscitary and imperial presidency (in different degrees and forms) in the US took place after the 1940s during Franklin D. Roosevelt's third presidential term.[8] However, he observes how the *strong* presidencies of the period between Roosevelt and Richard Nixon, and once again with Ronald Reagan, were followed by phases of presidential *weakness*.

This correlation between two distinctive forms of sovereignty and the presidency, in the US is also historically related with the entanglement between internal and international affairs. In this respect, Arato's views on the peculiarities of the American presidency have been particularly influenced by Theodore Lowy's (1985) work. Lowy (1985: 4–7) notes that since Roosevelt's administration, the personal, plebiscitary presidency has become the centerpiece of American government. Structurally, the rise of the *personal presidency* has been enabled by the growth of the executive branch's administrative capacity. There has been a large number of additions to presidential power in the areas of defense and military policy, as well as economic affairs. Presidential power has also been enhanced by "emergency powers" granted to the president by Congress through explicit statutory authorizations. Another new element since

Roosevelt has been the cult of personality. Once in power, the personal president has to "keep the initiative" and the appearance of leadership from the White House. The president must keep receiving messages from "the public." In other words, the president extends democratization by appearing to make himself more accessible to the people. The strengthening of the American presidency, however, has also made it more vulnerable. Thus the rise of the plebiscitary presidency has also exacerbated the paradox between the strength and weakness of presidential government: unrealistic campaign promises create a set of expectations almost impossible to fulfill. Lowy's (1985: 161) analysis of foreign policy issues is particularly penetrating since he points out the "intermingling of institutions of domestic and foreign politics." According to Lowy (1985: 161, 162), Americans never developed "a distinction between domestic and foreign affairs, either in theory or in practice." Moreover, "American political leaders could use the world outside as a garbage dump for domestic conflicts." Lowy (1985: 165) argues that the amateur, anti-diplomacy and unilateral (thus imperial) American foreign policy tradition has contributed in enhancing the plebiscitary presidency: "Lack of institutional unification has had to be compensated for by emotional or charismatic unification." This insight, Arato observes, discloses the mutual reinforcement between the plebiscitary and imperial dimensions of American presidentialism.

Now, the question is why despite its undeniable and actually quite frequent episodes of "constitutional dictatorship," the US has avoided the Latin American more "disruptive cycle" between weak presidencies and "extra-legal" and "permanent" dictatorship. In this line of interpretation, Arato observes that the "distinctiveness" of the American presidency is related to such interrelation between domestic and international affairs, in which the American executive has objectively (and perhaps subjectively) used the American privileged position in international relations as a "safety valve" for internal conflict and presidential legitimacy deficits. According to Andrew Arato, the US escaped the "Latin American Path" not because of the personality, virtue, liberal ethos or the "creative statesmanship" (Ackerman 2005) of the American elite, and certainly not because of the American written constitution and institutions, but due to the president's historical and political capacity to channel domestic discontent through military and political adventures abroad.

Notes

1 Mainly the following seminars: "Theory and Practice of Dictatorship" (2003); "Theories of Presidential Government" (2003); "Concept, Theory and Practice of Dictatorship" (2005); "Adventures of Popular Sovereignty: The Presidency and the People" (2006); "Sovereignty: An Interdisciplinary Seminar and Lecture Series" (Jean Cohen and Andrew Arato, The New School for Social Research, Columbia University, 2006). I was his student and assistant in these seminars. Of course, the usual caveats for responsibility for errors apply here.

2 For Claude Lefort, this resurgence of the "Theologico-Political" is a pathological manifestation of democratic revolutions, since in his view the peculiarity of modern

democracy is that power becomes "an empty space," "power belongs to no one and those who exercise power do not possess it; that they do not, indeed, embody it." See Lefort (1988: 225). The absolutist theory of sovereignty emphasizes its absolute, perpetual, irrevocable and indivisible features. The sovereign is an "uncommanded commander." Jean Bodin's theory of sovereignty is of course the most representative example. See Bodin (2007, chapter 8). "Embodied" or "personified" models of sovereignty look for a natural person – the king, the emperor, the pope, etc. to be the incarnation of sovereignty. In the context of modern revolutions this person *represents* and *exercises* sovereignty in the name of the people. This opposes the notion of sovereignty as an abstract power vested in the commonwealth, which cannot be the property of a natural person. Bodin's Theory of Sovereignty is the classical example for the "personified" model, although he does mention sovereignty as an abstract and collective power of the commonwealth at the beginning of his famous chapter. In theory and history we have seen that popular sovereignty is compatible with both the absolutist and the personified models of sovereignty.

3 As Schmitt (2008: 240) observes, even in the most direct democracy, there is political representation. In such extreme case: "only all adult members of the people act and then only in the moment when they are assembled as the community or as the army."

4 This is the "King's two bodies" doctrine applied to the sovereign people. This doctrine, as formulated in the Middle Ages, was based on the notion of the two bodies of Christ. Later in sixteenth century England it emerged as the juridical fiction of the king's two bodies: a "body natural," which is a body mortal, subject to nature, accidents, defects, imbecility, etc. and a "body politic," which cannot be seen, but is supernatural, infallible, immortal and omnipresent (Kantorowicz 1997: 9). For the people's two bodies doctrine in the context of modern revolutions, see: Morgan 1989; Baker 1990; Wood 1998.

5 In *Die Diktatur* Schmitt ([1921]1999) distinguishes two types of dictatorship: commissarial dictatorship, based on the Roman model of dictatorship, and sovereign dictatorship, which refers to modern revolutionary dictatorship. Both types of dictatorship are commissioned by a higher authority, for a temporary period and a particular purpose, the former by constituted and the latter by constituent powers, theoretically the sovereign people. While commissarial dictatorship is instituted to protect an *established* legal system, sovereign dictatorship is meant to *establish* a new constitution. In the case of commissarial dictatorship, Arato (2000c: 927–928) observes that there is a legal source for the commission, an already existing authority or *pouvoir constitué*, and thus there is legal continuity during the suspension of the constitution. While in sovereign dictatorship there is a shift from legality to legitimacy as the sovereign dictator is the commissioner of the *pouvoir constituant*.

6 I should mention the seminar "Democracy in the Americas" imparted along with David Plotke and Martín Plot in Spring 2002, and for a second time with David Plotke in Spring 2004.

7 For example, Woodrow Wilson (1917, 1956) identifies two stages in post-civil war government. The first one, centered on Congress, is described in his book *Congressional Government in the United States*, and a second stage is characterized by the rise of the presidency, depicted in his *Constitutional Government in the United States*. Richard Neustadt (1960) introduced the distinction between pre-modern and modern political/institutional contexts regarding the exercise of power and types of political leadership. In the modern era, the "presidential power to persuade" has become increasingly central. Theodore Lowy (1985) also distinguishes between a congress-centered First Republic, and, since the 1930s, a president-centered Second Republic that "can best be described as a plebiscitary republic with a personal presidency." Bruce Ackerman has also identified at least three different constitutional regimes in the United States: the Founding, Reconstruction and The New Deal. However, for Ackerman (1991, 1998) these regimes do not correspond to a mere periodization of American

constitutional history, but each of them involves a constitutional break with the previous one. The presidency, Ackerman claims, has been a crucial actor in leading constitutional change from one regime to another. Steven Skowronek (2000) identifies a cyclical movement between four patterns of presidential leadership: reconstruction presidents, articulation presidents, disjunctive presidents and preemptive presidents. These patterns are defined by the "politics presidents make" in three orders of action: constitutional, organizational and political.

Accounts of the American presidency have also been characterized by the idea of a pendular movement between Congress and president. For example, Arthur M. Schlesinger (1973: viii) in *The Imperial Presidency*, analyzes "the appropriation by the Presidency, (…) of the powers reserved by the Constitution and by long historical practice to Congress." Nevertheless, in his account Congress always makes a comeback, and his history of the imperial presidency involves a chain of presidential actions and congressional reactions regarding foreign affairs and emergencies. Louis Fisher (1997) has also studied the relations between president and congress in historical perspective.

8 In the context of the literature on the presidency there is no agreement on the date of emergence of the plebiscitarian presidency. In Arato's view this is related to different existing definitions of the plebiscitarian presidency and the inadequate distinction between exceptional plebiscitarian presidencies and the normalization of this type of presidency (Arato, 2006, "Adventures of Popular Sovereignty"). Bruce Ackerman (2005) has provocatively argued that actually Thomas Jefferson was the first plebiscitary president of the United States, since he was the "the first leader to claim a mandate from the people." In "Politics as a Vocation" Max Weber (in Gerth and Wright Mills 1958: 107–108) identifies the plebiscitarian aspects of Andrew Jackson's presidency. Theodore Lowy (1985) offers a different account of the rise of the plebiscitary presidency, which in his view was born in 1936. For Skowronek (2000) it emerged in the 1970s with the apogee of mass media.

References

Ackerman, Bruce (1991, 1998) *We The People*. Vol. I, II. Cambridge: Harvard University Press.

Ackerman, Bruce (1992) *The Future of Liberal Revolution*. New Haven and London: Yale University Press.

Ackerman, Bruce (2005) *The Failure of the Founding Fathers*. Cambridge: Harvard University Press.

Ackerman, Bruce (2006) *Before the Next Attack*. New Haven: Yale University Press.

Arato, A. (1990) "Thinking the Present: Revolution in Eastern Europe, Revolution, Civil Society and Democracy," *Praxis International*, Issue. No. 1+2.

Arato, A. (1994) "Constitution and Continuity in the Eastern European Transitions, Part I: Continuity and its Crisis," *Constellations, An International Journal of Critical and Democratic Theory*, Vol. 1, Issue 1, December.

Arato, A. (1995–1996) "Forms of Constitution-Making and Theories of Democracy," *Cardozo Law Review*, Vol. 17.

Arato, A. (1999) "Impeachment or Revision of the Constitution," *Constellations, An International Journal of Critical and Democratic Theory*, Vol. 6, Issue 2, June.

Arato, A. (2000a) *Civil Society, Constitution, and Legitimacy*. Lanham, MD: Rowman & Littlefield Publishers.

Arato, A. (2000b) "The New Democracies and American Constitutional Design," *Constellations, An International Journal of Critical and Democratic Theory*, Vol. 7, Issue 3, September.

Arato, A. (2000c) "Good-bye to Dictatorships?" *Social Research*, Vol. 67, No. 4, Winter.

Arato, A. (2001) "Congressional or (Weak) Presidential Government: The Results of the Election Crisis of 2000," *Constellations, An International Journal of Critical and Democratic Theory*, Vol. 8, Issue 3, September.

Arato, A. (2002a) "*Minima Politica* after September 11," *Constellations, An International Journal of Critical and Democratic Theory*, Vol. 9, Issue 1, March.

Arato, A. (2002b) "The Bush Tribunals and the Specter of Dictatorship," *Constellations, An International Journal of Critical and Democratic Theory*, Vol. 9, Issue 4, December.

Arato, A. (2002c) "The Roundtables, Democratic Institutions and the Problem of Justice," in Bozóki, András, *The Roundtable Talks of 1989. The Genesis of Hungarian Democracy: Analysis and Documents*. Budapest: CEU Press.

Arato, A. (2003) "Conceptual History of Dictatorship (and its Rivals)." Manuscript.

Arato, A. (2005a) "Post-Election Maxims," *Constellations, An International Journal of Critical and Democratic Theory*, Vol. 12, Issue 2, June.

Arato, A. (2005b) "Constitutional Learning," *Theoria*, Vol. 44, Issue 106.

Arato, A. (2006) "Ackerman's Constitution after Hamdan," *Constellations, An International Journal of Critical and Democratic Theory*, Vol. 13, Issue 4, December.

Arato, A. (2009) *Constitution Making Under Occupation: The Politics of Imposed Revolution in Iraq*. New York: Columbia University Press.

Baker, K. (1990) *Inventing the French Revolution. Essays on French Political Culture in the Eighteenth Century*. Stanford: Stanford University Press.

Bendix, R. (1978) *Kings or People: Power and the Mandate to Rule*. Berkeley and Los Angeles: University of California Press.

Bodin, J. (2007) *On Sovereignty*. Cambridge: Cambridge University Press.

Bolívar, Simón (1951) *Selected Writings of Bolivar*. New York: The Colonial Press.

Cole, D. (2006) "In Case of Emergency," *New York Review of Books*, July 13.

Fisher, L. (1997) *Constitutional Conflicts between President and Congress*. Kansas: University Press of Kansas.

Fisher, L. (2004) *Presidential War Power*. Kansas: University Press of Kansas.

Gerth, H.H. and Wright Mills, C. (eds.) (1958) *From Max Weber, Essays in Sociology*. New York: Oxford University Press.

Huntington, S. (1991) *The Third Wave, Democratization in the Late Twentieth Century*. Norman: University of Oklahoma Press.

Kelsen, H. (1945) *General Theory of Law and State*. Cambridge: Harvard University Press.

Kantorowicz, E.H. (1997) *The King's Two Bodies, A Study in Medieval Political Theology*. Princeton: Princeton University Press.

Kis, J. (1995) "Between Reform and Revolution: Three Hypotheses about the Nature of Regime Change," *Constellations, An International Journal of Critical and Democratic Theory*, Vol. 1, Issue 3, January.

Lefort, C. (1988) *Democracy and Political Theory*. Minneapolis: University of Minnesota Press.

Lijphart, A. (1992) *Parliamentary versus Presidential Government*. New York: Oxford University Press.

Linz, J. (1978) *The Breakdown of Democratic Regimes, Crisis, Breakdown & Reequilibration*, Baltimore and London: The Johns Hopkins University Press.

Linz, J. (1990) "The Perils of Presidentialism," *Journal of Democracy*, Winter.

Linz, J. (1994) "Presidential or Parliamentary Democracy: Does It Make a Difference?"

in J. Linz and A. Valenzuela (eds.) *The Failure of Presidential Democracy: The Case of Latin America*. Baltimore: The Johns Hopkins University Press.

Linz, J. and Stepan, A. (eds.) (1996) *Problems of Democratic Transition and Consolidation: Southern Europe, South America and Post-Communist Europe*. Baltimore: The Johns Hopkins University Press.

Linz, J. and Valenzuela, A. (eds.) (1994) *The Failure of Presidential Democracy: The Case of Latin America*. Baltimore: The Johns Hopkins University Press.

Lowy, T.J. (1985) *The Personal President: Power Invested, Promise Unfulfilled*. Ithaca; London: Cornell University Press.

McIlwain, C.H. (1947) *Constitutionalism Ancient and Modern*. Ithaca: Cornell University Press.

Mainwaring, Scott (1990) "Presidentialism in Latin America," *Latin American Research Review*, Vol. 25.

Mainwaring, Scott (1993) "Presidentialism, Multipartism and Democracy: The Difficult Combination," *Comparative Political Studies*, Vol. 26, No. 2, July.

Mainwaring, S. and Soberg Shugart, M. (eds.) (1997) *Presidentialism and Democracy in Latin America*. Cambridge: Cambridge University Press.

Marx, K. ([1852] 1963) *The Eighteenth Brumaire of Louis Bonaparte*. New York: International.

Marx, K. ([1975, 1891] 1978) "Critique of the Gotha Program," in Robert C. Tucker (1978) *The Marx–Engels Reader*. New York, London: W.W. Norton & Company.

Morgan, E.S. (1989) *Inventing the People: The Rise of Popular Sovereignty in England and America*. New York; London: Norton & Company.

Neustadt, Richard (1960) *Presidential Power: The Politics of Leadership from FDR to Carter*. Cambridge: Harvard University Press.

O'Donnell, Guillermo (1991) *Counterpoints: Selected Essays on Authoritarianism and Democratization*, Indiana: University of Notre Dame Press.

O'Donnell, G., Schmitter P. and Whitehead, L. (eds.) (1986) *Transitions from Authoritarian Rule: Southern Europe*. Baltimore: The Johns Hopkins University Press.

Scheuerman, W.E. (2006) "Emergency Powers," *Annual Review of Law and Social Science*, Vol. 2.

Schlesinger, Jr. Arthur (1973) *The Imperial Presidency*. New York: Houghton Mifflin Company.

Schmitt, Carl (1994) *The Crisis of Parliamentary Democracy*. Translated by Ellen Kennedy. Cambridge: MIT Press.

Schmitt, Carl (1999) *La Dictadura* [*Die Diktatur*]. Translated by José Díaz García. Madrid: Allianza Editorial.

Schmitt, Carl (2008) *Constitutional Theory*. Durham and London: Duke University Press.

Skowronek, S. (2000) *The Politics Presidents Make: Leadership from John Adams to Bill Clinton*. Cambridge: Harvard University Press.

Stepan, A. (2000) *Arguing Comparative Politics*. New York: Oxford University Press.

Tushnet, M. (2005) *The Constitution in Wartime: Beyond Alarmism and Complacency*. Durham: Duke University Press.

Vile, M.J.C. (1998) *Constitutionalism and the Separation of Powers*. Indianapolis: Liberty Fund.

Weber, Max (1978) *Economy and Society*. 2 vols. Edited by Guenther Roth and Claus Wittich. Berkeley and Los Angeles: University of California Press.

Wilson, W. (1917) *Constitutional Government in the United States*. Columbia: New York University Press.

Wilson, W. (1956) *Congressional Government: A Study in American Politics*. New York: Meridian.

Wood, G.S. (1998) *The Creation of the American Republic, 1776–1787*. Chapel Hill and London: The University of North Carolina Press.

Yoo, J. (2005) *The Powers of War and Peace: The Constitution and Foreign Affairs after 9/11*. Chicago: University of Chicago Press.

Part III

Arato's theory of modern dictatorship

Editors' introduction

Enrique Peruzzotti and Martín Plot

As we have already pointed out in the Introduction to the volume, at the time of the consecutive constitutional crises of Clinton's impeachment and the contested presidential election of 2000 in the United States, Arato was working on questions of the modern executive, legality, and legitimacy, and their historical and theoretical articulations in the field of constitutional design. This research found renewed urgency in the immediate aftermath of 9/11 and its triggering of the Bush Administration's "war on terror." The earliest results of these investigations were published in *Social Research* and *Constellations* during the first half of the past decade, offering theoretical, comparative, and interpretive approaches to the question of dictatorship. The longest, most comprehensive manuscript, however, remained unpublished until now.

The text – "Conceptual History of Dictatorship (and its Rivals)" – is a comprehensive historical study of the classic, early modern, and modern theorizing of different forms of the undivided exercise of political authority. The text is not, in fact, a semantic history of the *notion* of "dictatorship." It is, rather, the diachronic analysis of political philosophy's reflection on a set of conditions and circumstances that sometimes included and sometimes excluded the dimensions of exceptionality, institutionalization, legality, legitimacy, and monocracy. The pre-modern and early modern competing notions had been tyranny and despotism. These two concepts dominated both concerned literature and political discourse until the nineteenth century. The actual notion of dictatorship – of Roman origin, of course – mostly retained its institutional, un-polemical, even virtuous nature until its early twentieth century association with the European Fascist and Nazi regimes. The reemergence of the concept of dictatorship, however, precedes the negative connotation it acquired in the past century. It is probably the advent of the republican era with the French Revolution that reactivated the concept, still positively valued as a specific institution, more at the service of, than a threat to, the Republic. Since – as Arato says in dialogue with Koselleck – concepts have *meaningful histories*, however, this transition from the prevalence of the notions of tyranny and despotism to that of dictatorship revealed a fascinating ray on conflicting understandings of legality and legitimacy in the exercise of political power.

From Robespierre to Marx, "dictatorship" was used ambivalently, sometimes as problematic, sometimes as necessary instances in the advent of an increasingly democratic understanding of collective life. Tyranny and despotism, however, retained their negative connotation during the entire nineteenth century – until they became archaic in the twentieth, decidedly associated with pre-modern, pre-democratic times. Arato reminds us, in his reading of the main theorists of the French Revolution and its social and political aftermath – Tocqueville and Marx – of both authors' inconsistent use of the terms. Tocqueville first persuaded us of the inappropriateness of the notions of tyranny and despotism to describe freedom's fundamental threat in a democratic, egalitarian age; only to offer the concepts of "tyranny of the majority" and "new despotism of our times" immediately afterwards. Marx, for his part, accused all states of just being oppressors' dictatorships over the oppressed. At the same time, however, the "dictatorship of the proletariat" was put forward as the most democratic of all regimes yet known, being moreover the final, definitive moment in the exercise of a power that would subsequently abolish itself.

It was in this nineteenth century context of conceptual ambiguity and inconsistencies that the modern and contemporary rival notions of Bonapartism, autocracy, and totalitarianism made their appearance in both theoretical and political discourse. The first two of them dominate Arato's analysis – with the latter having an indirect presence in the investigation, since the ideas of "totalitarian dictatorship" and totalitarianism did indeed rival that of "simple" dictatorship for the description of both the Nazi and Stalinist regimes and he had already discussed them elsewhere (Arato 2002). Bonapartism was, however, the one notion that found its context of application in the immediate aftermath of having written the manuscript. To put it simply: "An occupation regime is inevitably a foreign dictatorship," (Arato 2009: 15) and a foreign dictatorship is the most succinct available definition for Bonapartism. On 19 March 2003, the United States invaded and occupied Iraq, and, in Arato's own words:

> Indeed, the category of Bonapartist dictatorship is applicable to [the US' rule in Iraq] in two ways, as the depiction of a foreign-imposed transformational regime and of a dictatorship that uses democratic public relations and a façade of participation, representation, and consultation to hide its authoritarian practices.
>
> (Arato 2009: 18)

As we have just said, however, concepts have meaningful histories, and the context inaugurated by the American invasion, occupation, and – fundamentally for Arato – destruction of the Iraqi state allowed for a description that came also very close to that of the sovereign, revolutionary dictatorships theorized by Carl Schmitt. In a way, Arato's entire book on the "politics of imposed revolution in Iraq" (Arato 2009) is a theoretical and interpretive study of the tension and intertwining between three models of constitution making, all of them showing their "elective affinity" with the political regimes that might be instituted in their wake. The American occupiers alternatively adopted both the position of a revolutionary, sovereign dictatorship and that of an old regime's implementation of a barely disguised imposed constitutional design – and neither of both alternatives has an elective affinity with democracy. As the book argues though, the clash between the occupiers' attempt at revolutionary imposition and their main opponent, al-Sistani's preference for sovereign constituent assemblies, forced the implementation of the third model: Arato's favored postsovereign constitution making. Sadly, however, in the end the model was hopelessly deformed by the Americans' persistence at imposition.

In short, the manuscript we are publishing here should be seen as one of the fundamental pieces of Arato's preparatory studies for the analysis of constitutional politics, emergency regimes, and modern forms of dictatorship. The potential contexts of application for those preparatory studies, as could be clearly noticed in reading the text, were first closely related to the elective affinity between war and dictatorship – and between war and tyranny, despotism, or Bonapartism – given the fact that the US had just declared a "war" with no end in sight, thus creating the conditions for a permanent "emergency" regime. The invasion and occupation of Iraq added to the picture the question of "regime change," or of transition from authoritarian rule, a situation that could benefit from the comparative and theoretical knowledge acquired during the experiences in Latin America and Eastern Europe during the 1980s and 1990s. Arato, a scholar of those transitions and a democratic and constitutional theorist, alerts us here of the urgent need of further theorizing the question of dictatorship in our times.

Conceptual history of dictatorship (and its rivals)[1]

Andrew Arato

Concepts have meaningful histories (Koselleck).[2] Because they have *histories*, any essentialist understanding of concepts is untenable. There is no essential meaning that would be unalterable with the passage of time and the shift of context. But because the histories of concepts are *meaningful*, the purely conventionalist understanding of their semantics is also misleading, at least with regard to those concepts that are embedded and involved in social and political life and conflict. Orwell's *1984* rightly denounces the propagandistic view that political concepts are malleable without limit. Indeed, the point of referring to "war" as "peace" is parasitic on the presumed and socially shared meaning of peace and it is highly doubtful within the terms of the novel that all of the people of Oceania are likely to accept the new usage without important mental reservations. While there are often political or social scientific redefinitions of concepts, these shifts of meaning are generally successful either when the new meaning is built on a dimension of an earlier one or when a new social and political reality requires conceptualization in terms of something already familiar and yet in some important way related to the new.

The history of the concept of dictatorship represents a powerful confirmation of the idea of the meaningful history of concepts. There is indeed an immense gulf between the traditional (ancient to early modern) and modern meanings. The modern revival was powered by the need to conceptualize new social and political realities. There were however many terms available in principle to deal with historically unprecedented forms of authoritarian rule. It is highly significant that the term "dictatorship" clearly triumphed by the twentieth century over adversaries that now have a distinctly archaic or anachronistic ring (tyranny, despotism, and autocracy) as well as new competitors that seem to be historically too specific (Caesarism, Bonapartism, and, again, autocracy).[3] Having absorbed some features of the rival categories, dictatorship was established because of implicit meanings that plausibly, even if ideologically, link the very different contexts of two fundamentally different "dictatorships," Republican Rome's and the contemporary world's. In my view, these linkages have to do with the problems of emergency or extraordinary government, that cannot be avoided as long as we face the issues of maintaining the rule of law and popular government as well as establishing and preserving republican forms of rule over large territories. Understanding why dictatorship was chosen thus requires an analysis not only of the concepts, but also of the contexts. But, the fact that it was dictatorship that was chosen rather than its competitors is an important clue to the meaning of the new, specifically modern forms of authoritarian rule, to their problems, their desperate need of legitimacy, the formulas of legitimation, and to the general relevance of these forms to modern politics everywhere.

Tyranny

Dictatorship's main competitors in the history of political thought, *tyranny* and *despotism*, were not only significant alternatives, but were in fact predominant until relatively recently. Much of classical and early modern political theory considers these concepts, but not dictatorship, to indicate fundamental forms of government.[4] It is astonishing how deeply and continually involved classical political theories have been with tyranny and despotism – and, with their negation, political freedom. But it is not difficult to surmise the main reason. Ancient political theorists, and to a lesser extent their early modern successors, lived and wrote in republics or under dualistic political arrangements like the *Ständestaat* (the estate system, or its remnants under the absolute monarchy) that represented islands in a world of kingdoms and empires, most of them various forms of authoritarian and, potentially or actually, arbitrary forms of rule (Montesquieu 1994). Living in republics that have already experienced authoritarian forms of rule and were almost always threatened, internally and externally, by their restoration, thinkers were forced continually to reflect on the differences of their own political arrangements and the ones they were threatened by. Given the pervasiveness but also the variety of monarchy both in their environment and in the past *ages of presumed glory* of their own polities, it was rarely convincing to denounce all forms of non-republican rule as equally illegitimate or unjust. Distinctions had to be and were made among various forms of monarchy. Finally, well before Hobbes, having experienced or learned about the history of disorder and instability of most known republics, political theorists were obsessively concerned with the problem of order and stability. But, unlike in the case of Hobbes, there was equal concern that solutions to the problem of order can threaten the very republican (or "constitutional") identities that they sought to protect. The Roman dictatorship was indeed an institutional attempt to solve the problem of republican order within republican identity, but the political theorists who first focused on this institution had to admit that even this solution arguably ran the risk of its degeneration in the "tyrannies" of Sulla and Caesar. Since solutions of the problem of order (Hobbes) often tended to entail outcomes (e.g., in most readings Hobbes' own) that reintroduced disorder on a higher, "secondary" level in the form of authoritarian unpredictability, violence, and arbitrariness,[5] the problem of arbitrary, lawless non-republican forms of government appeared as a potentially permanent and intractable problem at least before the end of the eighteenth century. The concepts of tyranny and despotism gave important, well-developed, and sophisticated tools to all thinkers concerned with this problem in ages of kings, when republics were vulnerable to transformation into the wrong type of monarchy.[6]

Very likely, among the Greeks the term tyrant (*tyrannis*) originally referred to just one form of monarchy among warriors, who lived under forms of one-person rule achieved through inheritance, election, and conquest.[7] Since all of these ultimately rested on military and warrior qualities there was no need to consider any of these forms entirely arbitrary in origin, and the modalities of rule (intelligent/stupid; orderly/capricious; consultative/autocratic) that are well known from the *Odyssey* and *Iliad* were not logically linked to any of these possible origins. It was sociological insight into what was later understood as the problem of legitimacy, as well as historical experience, that led to an understanding of tyranny (monarchy by conquest) as conducive, whatever the initial intentions of the tyrants, to irrationality, arbitrariness, and excessive violence. Herodotus is probably transitional in this context: the critic of monarchy, Otanes, in his dialogue about forms of government (admittedly polemically) uses *tyrannos* and *monarchos* interchangeably, while the defender of monarchy, Darius, insists on the distinction, and wishes to speak of his recommended form only at its best. Later in *The Histories* however Herodotus in his own voice denounces tyranny as the most unjust and bloody system of all.[8] The distinction between right and wrong, legal and illegal forms, is a staple of the theory of the Socratic philosophers (Xenophon[9], Plato, Aristotle, and their heir Polybius) of the six (or seven) types of government. While there are differences among the main texts, three fundamental and internally related differences of monarchy and tyranny (and between all right and wrong forms) were solidly established by these thinkers:

1 The king rules legally, the tyrant illegally. (This idea hides in reality two pairs of distinctions: coming to power legally/illegally; when in power ruling legally/illegally.)
2 The king rules over the willing (with “consent”), the tyrant over the unwilling.
3 The king rules in the common interest, the tyrant in his own interest.

As Plato and Aristotle both realized to various extents, the problem of combinations across the three or four distinctions was hardly eliminated in this complex many-part definition. There are in fact sixteen ($2\times2\times2\times2$) possible combinations in the most elaborate scheme of types. Thus if *pure* tyranny means coming to power *and* ruling in the ruler’s private interest over the unwilling, and its *pure* contrary (whatever we are to call it) means coming to power *and* ruling in the public interest over the willing, there are logically at least fourteen other possibilities of mixed types.[10] Aristotle has to admit for example that someone who came to power illegally (the popular and traditional mark of the tyrant) could try to rule like a king and probably should do so in the interest of his self-preservation[11] thereby obliterating the sharp difference not only between lawful (rise to power) and lawless (manner of rule), but also particular and general interest (now tendentially identical) within the operation of this form of rule. Rereading Aristotle one could thus come to the conclusion, as did Rousseau[12] that tyranny (unlike despotism) entailed by definition illegal acquisition of power but could involve legal rule. However, for Aristotle, a type of tyranny itself could be legally and constitutionally mandated, and thus be "legal" also in terms of its origin.[13]

There seems to be little problem with evaluating *pure tyranny*. Whatever the picture of individual tyrants like Pisistratus, for the Socratic philosophers, as for Herodotus before them, this type at least was consistently viewed as the worst of the forms of government. Even Plato, who deemed monarchy as the best of the "second best," i.e., of the lawful three types, saw tyranny as the worst of the three wrong types. If he seems to represent an exception in the evaluation of tyranny (as opposed to kingship) in the history of political thought it is because he tacitly introduces what is in effect a mixed type. The ground is prepared by his contrast between the "best" and the six other forms that included the three "second best," based on the criterion of the guidance of the ruler(s) by either rational knowledge (the best) or by law (the second best three types), that leads to a distinction between justice and law. In the *Statesman* it is claimed, admittedly by the Eleatic Stranger and not Socrates, that if a ruler (one, more, or even in the less likely case of many) possessed genuine knowledge (on his own or because of his reliance on a philosopher), being lawful or lawless, ruling the willing or the unwilling could make no difference as to the quality of the rule.[14] Thus such a ruler would be tyrannical by two criteria, but not by the third, because being just he could not rule in his own interest alone or primarily. This view is consistent with the more famous doctrine of *The Republic* concerning the best rule by philosopher kings or kingly philosophers. It is however also consistent with the even more strong argument of *The Laws*, this time presented by the Athenian Stranger, according to which a new and better form could be best introduced by a young tyrant who could rely on the services of a philosophical legislator. Here the illegality that is stressed seems to refer to the origin of the given rule.

While probably attempting to answer Plato's apparent praise of tyranny, Aristotle's drawing out the distinction between the interest of all (corresponding to justice) and self-interest does not solve the problem raised by his master, since legality and the common interest could also conceivably diverge. There is thus a marked divergence between the polemical treatment of tyranny in the Socratic philosophers and the various mixed possibilities their own definitions give rise to that are in fact treated with more sympathy and understanding. It is the polemical thrust that will be objected to by Hobbes who was to famously argue that tyranny is monarchy to its enemies.[15] But even before him, Machiavelli was to ostentatiously disregard the distinction in *The Prince*,[16] and Bodin was to de-emphasize the distinction between right and corrupt forms by presenting monarchy as a form of sovereignty along with three alternative principles of government, i.e., the medieval *royal*, *lordly* (*seigneuriale*) and *tyrannical* monarchies, that subtly subsumed the despotic (i.e., patrinomial) under the feudal sounding term *seigneuriale*.[17]

The change occurred more gradually than some readers of modern political theory may think. Machiavelli was deeply influenced, and possibly Bodin was as well, by the massive reappearance and re-evaluation of the problem of tyranny in the Italian city states of the late medieval period and the early Renaissance.[18] Whether established by victorious *condottieri* or aristocratic factions or popular pressure, the *signori* of Italian cities were "illegitimate," i.e., were neither dynastic nor, in the strict sense, feudal rulers, who came to power either lawlessly or through popular support or, more likely – as the Duke of Athens in Florence – extra-legal pressure, and who governed according to their inclination or *raison d'état*, but not by established law or custom.[19] Occasionally, Renaissance writers distinguished between two meanings of tyrant, one defined by the arbitrary practice of the rule, and the other by lack of legitimate title to rule.[20] While enemies of the new signori either chose to make no such distinction or focused on the first meaning, namely arbitrary and unjust rule, their apologists obviously preferred the second meaning, mere illegitimacy of origins. Among the latter, Burckhardt rightly notes that a new principle of justification for occupying the place of the king seemed to emerge; personal merit or ability that was often coupled with support for a brilliant intellectual life linked to the court and its patronage.[21] Thus unusually in the history of the concept of tyranny, the Renaissance signore had important intellectual defenders or propagandists among the *humanists*, generally but not exclusively those who were supported by individual tyrants. Signori were variously defended for overcoming republican factional strife that came to threaten the independence of city states, for supporting the arts and the humanities, and, anticipating a strain of argument in Machiavelli, for succesfully resisting "barbarian" incursions into the peninsula. Even the Florentine chancellor Salutati in his *De Tyranno* chose to defend tyranny, the right sort linked to Caesar's example, at a time when the independence of his city was under the deadly threat from the bad sort, the Milanese signore, Giangaleazzo Visconti.[22]

Nevertheless, the most important civic humanists in Florence not only rejected tyranny, but helped to establish the mission of republican Florence in the defense of liberty in the face of authoritarians ruling in the whole region.[23] Thus civic humanists defended Brutus against even Dante's condemnation, and the idea of tyrannicide was formulated as a morally legitimate mission.[24] As the argument progressed, increasingly little distinction was made between kingship and tyranny on both sides. Thus not only tyranny was condemned, but all precocious anticipations or imitations of absolutist state making on the Italian peninsula.[25] In other words, defenders of republics anticipated the later critics of monarchical despotism, but still using the traditional, city state-centered concept of tyranny. A similar polemical position (resembling Otanes' argument in Herodotus) returns in the North, and is openly formulated by the uncompromisingly anti-monarchist Etienne de La Boetie who posited the identity of king and tyrant.[26] The anti-absolutist Monarchmachs, taking their stance around the inherited estate constituions of medieval Europe, and France in particular, refused to go so far. Hobbes on the other hand was to accept this very identification but with reverse evaluation, and had little trouble representing the anti-tyrannical mode of thinking as a form of opposition to the modern sovereign state, one moreover incompatible with the scientific, i.e., dispassionate and non-polemical understanding of politics.[27]

Despotism

Yet even in the context of succesful European statebuilding the battle between partisans of limited or constitutional or aristocratic monarchy and the advocates of absolutism was not to be supressed on the political as well as intellectual levels. Polemical, value-laden concepts could not (or not yet) be banished by social scientific fiat. The traditional conception of forms of government could gain a new lease on life by a theoretical turn that pointed both beyond typological confusion and the limitations of concepts tailored to the problems of unstable city republics. Both the modernizing theory of state sovereignty and the platonizing doctrine of the apologists of absolutism could best be battled by reviving the originally Aristotelian theory of despotism. This revival was so successful that for some the term *despotism* nearly totally displaced *tyranny* (Montesquieu, Kant), while for others became its interchangable synonym (republican thought from Cicero[28] to Machiavelli and even to the Americans and Tocqueville) or a deeper and more sophisticated framework within which the concept of tyranny could be interpreted (Rousseau).

Aristotle's original achievement lies less in the six forms of government and the doctrine of tyranny that he merely reinterpreted, than in applying the non-political or economic categories of despot, despotic, and despotism to politics. It was this move that allowed him to present himself as the defender of the *polis* versus Plato whom he subtly portrayed as its enemy. The very beginning of the *Politics* gives us a clue as to the importance of the matter: Plato, according to Aristotle, confuses *political* and *despotic* forms of rule, statesman or politician (*politicos*) and despot (*despotes*), as well as the very different sciences that are to deal with each, those of politics and household management (*oikonomia*).[29] It should not concern us here that Aristotle means to make this point a clue to Plato's pan-theoretical view of politics, including his justification of philosophically enlightened arbitrary forms of rule as the highest or best.[30] More to the point is Aristotle's move from despotic household (adjectival form: *despotike*) to Asian despotisms (substantive form: *despoteia*, despotism), and from there back to the *polis* with a new and deeper theory of corrupt forms (that are potentially despotic, but are not identical to despotism). It is this movement that was to later allow the relocation of the problem of authoritarianism from the *personally* arbitrary, lawless, and egotistic rule of tyrants, to the *structural* forms of suppression of freedom in large-scale territorial states.

Despotic rule is identified by Aristotle as one of the three forms relevant to the household, the one of the despot or master over slaves. The other two, monarchical over children (and the household as a whole) and political over women are thus not despotic. But wherever un-free, quasi-slave populations are ruled by a monocratic ruler sanctified by a traditional, usually inherited right to rule, as in most of the neighbors of the Hellenes, we encounter according to his view despotic rule.[31] To Aristotle political, including monarchical forms of household rule are, as in the theory of the right political forms, law governed and in the interest of all. Despotic rule, however, like tyranny, is arbitrary, in the interest of the ruler only, and potentially violent. Unlike tyranny, however, both in the household and in (non-Greek) states, despotism is a legitimate form of rule, sanctified by custom and tradition, in the Asian monarchies at least, over the willing.[32]

So far Aristotle was merely systematizing the meaning of terms and distinctions as used by the Greeks of his time, and certainly even earlier. The decisive move comes when, reinterpreting the corrupt forms, he notes the despotic tendency in each: "Those constitutions which consider only the personal interest of the rulers are all *wrong* constitutions, or *perversions* of the right forms. Such perverted forms are *despotic*; whereas the *polis* is an association of freemen" (my emphases: III. vi 1279a). The point is then repeated emphatically in the case of tyranny: "single person government of the political association [*polis*] on the lines of despotism" (III. vii 1279b), still decisively though more analogically in the case of democracy (IV. iv 1292a) and less clearly in the case of oligarchy (V. vi 1306b).[33]

For Aristotle the (tendential) destruction of the *polis* (in translations: of the *res publica*) by despotic trends had several meanings beyond the decline of the three differentiating principles of the right forms (again: lawfulness, voluntariness or consent, rule in the common interest). First, as even his terminology reveals, citizens tend to lose their very status, being turned into mere subjects or inhabitants, in effect little more than slaves (Mandt 1973: 657). Thus one could speak of the decline of the famous definition of the *polis* as *isonomia* in a double sense: not only law but also political equality of members is sacrificed. Of course since each citizen is himself an *oikos despotes*, a natural limit of the process would have been the household with its non-metaphorical form of slavery. But, second, the state is tendentially turned into an immense household with the patrimonial implication, one that Aristotle does not draw, that the property including the slaves of the citizens comes under the control of the despotic ruler or rulers. Third, the sharp distinction between public and private realms is obliterated as the non-political principle of the latter (rule over the un-free) is extended to the former as well.[34] Finally, the social bond itself, symbolized by the idea of friendship in Aristotle's work, is in danger of being decisively threatened. The tyrant will aim at creation of mutual distrust and will thereby break the spirit of his subjects, and make them incapable of action (Montesquieu 1994: IV. xi 1295b; V. xi 1314a; Mandt 1973: 657).

Without a doubt then, the theory of despotism yields not only a contrast of Greek and Asian political forms, but also a deeper understanding of the problem of the corruption, i.e., authoritarian transformation of the Hellenic institutions themselves. At the same time, with the reinterpretation of tyranny as despotic a contradiction seems to be built into its very definition: tyranny is single-person government of the *polis* that is tendentially at least identical to the form of government of something other (household, extended Asian territorial state) than a *polis*. There are two ways of reading this line, both justified by other texts, and both highly influential in the history of thought.

1 Tyranny and despotism, i.e., household rule extended to the state, remain different in spite of being internally related (just as Greek household and Asian monarchy are different). This is so not only because of the legitimacy of the origins of despotism that is never doubted by Aristotle, but also because in a *polis* it is almost impossible to fully realize the despotic principle. A democracy would turn anarchic and tyranny too would be plagued by instability. Thus Aristotle in a famous passage that foresees the routinization and monarchization of some tyrannies recommends that lawful and publicly interested conduct could lend stability to tyrannies (V. xi). While it is then a question whether tyranny is being transformed into a mixed type, nevertheless the option itself distinguishes this particular rule over a *polis* from true despotisms where there is no traditional law (*nomos* vs. *lex*) (Barker 1969) to follow, nor a public association to serve. Aristotle of course was well aware of the difference between a system in which the word of the ruler was the only meaning of law, and one in which a *nomos* defining citizen or human obligation in a *polis* could be and was repeatedly violated by a ruler. Thus Creon in *Antigone* was a tyrant and not a despot. The real danger in republics is thus tyranny, and despotism often becomes a polemical charge made against tyrants, who were thereby said to be behaving like "barbarian" rulers.

   This line of interpretation was characteristic of republican thought as long as the distinction was made between tyranny and despotism. But even when the concept of despotism was de-emphasized, as from Cicero to Machiavelli, the focus on the category of tyranny could have meant that despotism was kept in reserve, to describe the large territorial states that were not traditionally the concern of republican thinkers, until encountering the reality of the modern state that made traditional republicanism increasingly irrelevant.

2 With the definitive end of city states as politically significant formations, modern, especially American republicanism built on the second possible interpretation of Aristotle that tended to treat despotism (increasingly central to liberal thought) as more or less a synonym for tyranny. Originally, the point was applied to all three wrong forms, and this too was later revived even if the stress remained on one-person rule.[35] In this interpretation, the perverted, wrong forms imply the destruction of the *polis* by imposing a principle entirely incompatible with it, namely despotic rule. Thus fully realized tyranny – and likely democracy, and possibly oligarchy too – are despotisms. Historically more important, one could interpret the absorption of the *polis* in Hellenistic kingdoms, or the Roman republic in the empire, as the transformation of what began as tyranny (e.g., Caesar's) into full-fledged

despotism that destroys the public space. In this interpretation, the more radical one characteristic of early liberal anti-absolutist trends, despotism rather than tyranny is the fundamental problem, even if tyranny remains an issue to the extent of being the process of establishing a despotic logic. When this happens, however, as Hobbes suspected, legitimate monarchs can be said to be hardly preferable to (or different than) tyrants and despots to the extent that they too turn society into a household, destroy traditional legality, the public space, and the social bond.

Despotism or tyranny?

Thus, Aristotle's early modern successors were not only given a rich storehouse of categories for the analysis of authoritarian despotic trends but also several choices concerning their relative importance and relationship. Subsequent thought could accordingly neglect either the category of despotism or tyranny, absorb them in one another, or use them both either as distinct or as internally related. The more traditional republican interpretation focusing on tyranny is still very much present in the Machiavelli of the *Discourses* who, unlike the author of *The Prince*, is still fundamentally concerned with the stability and corruption of primarily city state republics.[36] While *The Prince* uses neither term it implicitly treats the objects that the terms despotism and tyranny traditionally described as quite distinct forms of kingship. The object of despotism is introduced under the heading of the old, traditional Asiatic monarchies (distinct from the European feudal kingdom) whose rulers reduce their subjects to servants or slaves (ch. IV). The problem of tyranny, constituting the main theme of the work, is presented as that of new monarchies established through violence and occasionally plebiscitary consent. The success of the latter and its stability are treated primarily as technical matters, with the traditional category of virtue having been transformed into the necessary leadership qualities in peace and especially war needed to make new princes triumph. *The Prince* makes little distinction between new rulers who rule in the public interest and lawfully and those who do not, though the appearances of doing so are deemed quite important.

It is quite otherwise with the *Discourses*, which revive both the doctrine of the six forms of government, and the traditional condemnation of tyranny as the worst (I: ii and x).[37] This work, no longer concerned with kingship, uses the category of despotism only occasionally, and then as a synonym for tyranny. Caesar and Appius (the leading Decemvir) are said to be both tyrants and, occasionally, despots (I: xxxiv; xxxvii, and xl). Machiavelli clearly misses the opportunity of accusing Caesar for having prepared the ground for an Asian form of imperial rule in Rome, and the much earlier reference to the Decemvirs indicates that the category of despotism was not used in the Aristotelian sense vaguely present in the discussion of the Persians and Turks in *The Prince*.

The strength of Machiavelli's position lies certainly not in his de-differentiation of tyranny and despotism that mirrors earlier and anticipates later republican thought, but in his convincing analysis of the different origins of tyranny (sometimes called despotism) in monarchies, republics, and under mixed governments. While Plato and Aristotle were aware of this potential of republics, they have primarily focused on tyranny as a monarchical form and treated the difference between a tyrant that emerges through democratic discontent and the "tyranny" of an extreme democracy in a confusing way. Machiavelli however clearly distinguishes between one-person usurpers who grab power violently under monarchies, and create new institutions in their interests, and tyrants who come to power during disorders in republics, due to the strife of factions or classes. Because tyrannical rule is inevitably suffered by the many, he makes clear that it is not the people who are tyrannical even in the most "licentious" republic (licentiousness is his term for the corrupt popular form [I: ii]) though their disorder or their pressure may lead to the assumption of power by future tyrants. At the same time, tyranny is (inconsistently) no longer restricted to one-person rule. He speaks for example of the degenerate form of aristocracy as oligarchic tyranny (I: ii), possibly using tyranny in the sense of Aristotle's despotism indicating the inner logic rather than the personnel of authoritarian rule. Thus, in the brilliant analysis of the Decemvirs, bitter class war between plebeians and patricians is presented as the context of the emergence of a form of *group* tyranny that would have been irresistible if it consistently adhered to a populist (today we would say plebiscitary) character (I: xxxv and xl). The interpretation of tyranny as a monarchical form survives, however, and even the rule of the Decemvirs is presented as culminating in the dominance of one of them, the leader Appius.

Paradoxically, at the same time, the Decemvirs help Machiavelli argue that foundation of new laws should be the work of a one-person lawgiver, resembling Plato's idea that enlightened tyranny may be the best source of change toward the best, but with a significant difference: Machiavelli's sagacious legislator, using extraordinary, authoritarian, and violent means must act on behalf of the public good if he is to establish a good constitution, thus cannot be a tyrant by the classical definition. Tyrannical, i.e., self-interested legislators, if successful, will give birth only to tyranny, and deserve only "execration" (I: ix, x). Whether or not a lawgiver or legislator is to be treated as a tyrant or the practitioner of a highly praiseworthy "mixed" form is not to be judged merely in terms of psychology or intentions: "When the act accuses him, the result should excuse him." The intention to act on behalf of the public must accordingly be realized in institutions that block the way to "pure" tyranny, like the establishment of a Senate by Romulus with which to share power (I: ix, x). What is central in other words is that the extraordinary power required for original legislation be abandoned, once the new law is in place, in favor of power-sharing institutions, something the Decemvirs tried to avoid, unsuccessfully, when they sought to make their extraordinary authority permanent.

With all his brilliant criticisms of tyranny, Machiavelli never takes up the Aristotelian idea of its despotic logic penetrating more deeply than a mere form of government; indeed despotism does not appear as a problem for him for European states. As readers of the last chapter of *The Prince* often argue, he was an advocate of state formation in Italy on the Western European pattern that in the early sixteenth century meant a rationalized version of the Feudal state or *Ständestaat*. Though he sees the state-forming expansion of the French monarchy and conceptualizes it under the heading of a mixed monarchy, in terms of their institutional structure and mores Asia and France are seen only in terms of an absolute contrast (chs. III and IV). It was to be otherwise for thinkers from Bodin to Tocqueville who understood the formation of the modern state in terms of the neutralization or elimination of the traditional estates and corporations. For these authors despotism became a problem they had to deal with either in their defense or their condemnation of absolutism. Since analogies between the great Asian monarchies and the new types of state administration in Europe seemed unavoidable, the defenders of the modern state makers who were still steeped in the republican literary tradition at least did their best to keep despotism free from the taint of tyranny.

One approach relied on the option of the continued differentiation of despotism and tyranny in Aristotle. William of Ockham (Richter 1968) and Jean Bodin (Mandt 1973) heavily influenced by the Aristotelian text but each facing entirely different problems proceeded to list royal, lordly (despotic) and tyrannical forms of monarchy as entirely independent types, in effect de-dramatizing the polemical concepts, and producing (deliberately it is assumed in the case of Bodin) a positive re-evaluation of despotism. The negative evaluation of tyranny, central to republican thought, remains but the definition of tyranny implies usurpation or illegitimate origins that were not characteristic of the absolute monarchs. Hobbes revises this view in a way that makes the doctrine of absolutism more consistent. Origins do not matter: both legitimate origins and violent ones based on force are rooted ultimately in fear; contracts based on fear are illegitimate only once a state is instituted (Hobbes 1998: II. 20, 138–145). Tyranny is a mere polemic term, another name for monarchy used by its enemies (Hobbes 1998: II. 19, 129–138). Despotism is sovereignty achieved by conquest or victory in war; its subject population consents to its servitude to preserve its life. Thus despotic monarchy is fully legitimate on the bases of an argument first made for slavery as a kind of contract between conquerors and conquered (Hobbes 1998: II. 20, 138–145). Aristotle's admonition that the state is not a family is accepted, but only because of the relative size and strength of the two formations. Unlike in Bodin there is no possibility in Hobbes of a wrong monarchy, i.e., a tyrannical one that comes to power by usurpation – i.e., illegally. But the use of despotism as a legitimating category for dynastic even if arbitrary rulers is common to both positions.

A neglect of the theory of the despotic logic of tyranny also characterizes the position of John Locke. From an anti-absolutist perspective that retains some of the traditional republican cast, Locke discusses and condemns despotism, tyranny, and usurpation in separate but successive chapters of *The Second Treatise* (Locke 1988). His discussion of despotism takes a clear step back from Hobbes to Aristotle, in that the contrast here is not only with paternal but also with *political* forms of power (Locke 1988: 380–383). But he does not treat despotism in a purely Aristotelian manner since only paternal power is assigned to the household, and despotic power is understood as that attained by conquest and, contrary to Hobbes, has no contract or covenant of any kind at its bases. It is merely "the state of war continued." To be sure the idea that under despotic rule people have no property retains something of the idea of an *oikos* writ large, where the master is the sole owner. Despotism can be lawful according to Locke *only* as regards captives taken in a just war, but it is not said for how long. While Locke's ambiguities regarding the legitimacy of slavery recall Aristotle's vacillation, as a political form of the state despotism in any case can never be legitimate, whatever its origins. He grants the right of despotic rule over defeated enemies that engaged in an unjust war. But he is careful (in the chapter *Of Conquest*) to deny the same right of the conqueror over the parts of the defeated population that did not engage in war, as well as his own companions. Even the absolute right over the property and family of the defeated combatants are denied. Thus no political system of legitimate despotic rule can emerge from what was seen by Hobbes too as its only source, military conquest.

The conquest/despotism relationship is parallel to the usurpation/tyranny link, though the latter pair, apparently little more than merely the domestic version of the former, can never according to Locke imply even partial legitimacy. The category of usurpation helps to solve an ambiguity in Aristotle, still there in Bodin, concerning the category of lawful that can mean either origins or manner of rule. Thus an important distinction, never clearly made by the ancients, is made, but at the cost of diminishing the importance of the other one between illegality and abolition of the rule of law that is implied by the Aristotelian distinction between tyranny and despotism. To Locke, neither illegal assumption of rule nor violating inherited legality when ruling can be justified, and he does not say which of these two mixed types is preferable. Nevertheless, he admits that subsequent consent can legitimate a usurper's rule (Locke 1988: 397–398), while there is nothing that can make right substituting "private will and appetite" for the laws as the bounds of power, and for the good of the public (Locke 1988: 398–405).

Evidently the distinction between external and domestic conquest is more successful in distinguishing between conquest and usurpation as origins, than despotism and tyranny as forms of rule. In at least one place, in the section on conquest (Locke 1988: 394–397) despotism and tyranny are even used interchangeably. The target in the case of both categories is in fact the Stuart effort in England to justify and institute absolutist monarchy. Despotism is denounced by refuting supposed rights stemming from conquest, because, as he indicates, defenders of absolutism used (absurdly enough if true) the Norman Conquest as their ultimate source of justification (Locke 1988: 386–387). And in the case of tyranny, it is hardly an accident that the words of James I who after all came closest of all English monarchs to absolutism, are used to establish its character and definition. This very possibility shows however that in the case of England a polemical use of either category to denounce monarchical centralization and prerogative had only a limited application; indeed, as we will see, Locke himself turns out to be a defender of a relatively strong and formally unrestricted version of the royal prerogative.

Continental critics of absolutism, encountering highly bureaucratic models of state formation, would be far less tolerant of the prerogative (see Tocqueville's recollections on the link of strong executive and administrative centralization), and found in the Aristotelian category of despotism an important tool in denouncing absolutism. These anti-absolutist authors who unearthed the more critical strata of the concept of despotism initially represented the interests of the aristocratic estates. Nevertheless, they became the progenitors of early liberalism that came into being in aristocratic colors. Given the fact however that they were not directly concerned with threats to republics, here the category of despotism either absorbed the concept of tyranny, or at least dwarfed it in importance. Defending very different institutions than Aristotle, and facing a very different threat, this tradition, relying on new categories, developed the classical category of despotism.

Undoubtedly, the massive reintroduction of the category of despotism was heavily influenced by Montesquieu's *The Spirit of the Laws* (1748), that makes this type one of the three (counting aristocracy and democracy as one, the republic) fundamental forms of government.[38] The category of tyranny indeed has no independent existence in this work, which was clearly intended as a critique of the absolutist state in formation. It was otherwise in the earlier work *Considerations on the Causes of the Greatness of the Romans and their Decline* (1734),[39] where there is only one mention of despotism, consigning the type to Asia, and defining it merely as a non-moderate type without dissension (94). That the topic is not yet the critique of absolutism is indicated by the fact that European monarchies are treated like in *The Prince*, as moderate, but here because submitting to a version of the separation of powers (147). The history of the Roman republic however is treated as a continual and eventually losing battle against tyranny: of Tarquin (25), of the Decemvirs (29), of the first and second triumvirates (104), of Sulla (123), of Caesar (108), of Augustus (123), and of the emperors in general (146–147). The Romans of the traditional republic are depicted as united by "a single hatred of tyranny" (92–93). Initially, the defining key to the category seems to be usurpation; Tarquin's rule, e.g., is presented as in relatively favorable terms. Gradually however the term is redefined in terms of absolute and arbitrary monarchical rule, with or without constitutional cover. Yet, we should probably not be misled by the fact that Montesquieu repeatedly misses the opportunity of describing the new servitude and atomized depolitization of the Roman citizenry under the emperors as the triumph of Asiatic despotic forms (115, 121–123, 129–130). The key sociological turn of the later Montesquieu is already anticipated when he points out that something unprecedented occurred in Rome, with the death of Caesar: "the tyrant was no more, but there was no liberty either" (113). Nevertheless, even this insight does not lead him to describe the transformation that so corrupted the people as to successively submit to tyrants, and only to tyrants, as a road to despotism with a different principle of government than the virtue of republics.

Undoubtedly, the fact that the topic of *Considerations* is the decline of republics rather than the maintenance of monarchies, as in *The Spirit of the Laws*, is responsible for the huge terminological difference between the two works, as well as with the terminology of the classical orators and polemicists relied on. Because of the peculiar status of a territorially expanding Rome as first an imperial republic and then an empire with republican residues, Montesquieu is capable of making some astonishing observations concerning authoritarian forms peculiar to republican contexts, the relationship of prior popular sovereignty to the enhancement of absolutism (138), or the republican rather than monarchical nature of military government (152), ideas that will reappear in modern understandings of dictatorship, first in the work of Benjamin Constant.[40] More immediately fruitful for his own work, and his epoch, was *Considerations*' redefinition of tyranny, under at least the emperors of Rome, as the unification of all political magistracies into one and thus the abrogation of the separation of powers and thus of all checks on arbitrary power (147). This idea will be the bases of his specific contribution to the Aristotelian theory of despotism in books II to VIII of *The Spirit of the Laws* (Montesquieu 1994: 10–130) and will influence not only Rousseau and Kant, but the theorists of the American Revolution as well.

A clue to the radical displacement of the category of tyranny in *The Spirit of the Laws*, and its absorption in or interchangeable use with the concept of despotism, is given right in the beginning, on the level of definitions. Whereas *monarchy* is one-person rule under "fixed and established laws," *despotic government* is one "where a single person directs everything by his own will and caprice" (Montesquieu 1994: II. 1, 10). At first appearance, it seems as if tyranny has been merely renamed despotism, something that occasionally happens in republican thought from Machiavelli to Madison. But this appearance is wrong, as Montesquieu follows Aristotle's discussions of despotism, with its orientalist paradigm. The stress on single-person rule will disappear as the deformations called variously tyrannical and despotic are discussed. The people, under conditions of extreme equality, can submit to a tyrant or a despotic power or can "[act] the tyrant themselves" (110–111); and an arbitrary aristocracy "is a despotic state swayed by a great many despotic princes" (112). The deformations have to do with the proper nature of each form of government, but the definitions somewhat haphazardly[41] derived from the ancient theory of the three types of government do not sufficiently describe these. Montesquieu goes beyond them by adding his famous social psychological principles (virtue for republics – types –, honor for monarchies, and fear for despotism) as well as features of institutional design internally linked to these. These design elements include, in a democracy, choosing magistrates and judges by a combination of lot and election; in an aristocracy (unclearly 11; 112) the principle of electing the members of the aristocratic body and its senate if there is one; and in a monarchy the existence of intermediate bodies of (hereditary) nobles (15, 156). Consistently with the idea of the rule of law, the judicial power at least must be independent of the other powers in all the right forms (76–80). Even in the case of aristocracy the ruling body is said to unite only executive and legislative powers (13), and aristocratic republics like Venice where this is not provided for are said to be deficient in liberty with at least some despotic institutions (152–154). By implication then, the road to despotism is marked by the attack on the rule of law, and of agencies capable of enforcing this. The case is however put entirely generally in terms of the separation of powers. Indeed, in terms of the issues of his own time, it is the reduction and atomization of estates, corporations, free cities, and the political role of societal orders in general that he chalks up to the despotic tendencies of Richelieu, Louis XIV, and John Law (17, 55–56, 113). In France where the parliaments represented the highest judicial instances of the state this accusation subsumes part of the idea of despotism as encroachment on the separation of powers. After his famous discussion of the separation powers that represented a misunderstanding of the English government of his time, the issue is put relatively clearly (Montesquieu 1994: XI. vi 156–156). Only a regime of the full separation of the three powers is a regime of political liberty. Only monarchy qualifies completely, and most republics only partially. The kingdoms of his own time separate powers differently than the English, and then only partially. These monarchies, he says, border on political liberty, "and if they did not border upon it, monarchy would degenerate into despotic government" (Montesquieu 1994: XI. vii 166–167). Thus despotism is here understood, confusingly, as (being produced by) the absence of a separation of powers of either (what he chose to understand as) the English type, or some relevant substitute, such as perhaps the ancient city republics and the European kingdoms capable of saving a sufficient number of intermediary powers from the *Ständestaat*.[42]

Thus Montesquieu followed Aristotle in explicitly arguing that despotic trends within non-despotic governments were always a matter of degree and extent (Montesquieu 1994: VIII. viii 115–116). The obvious and vulnerable "orientalism" of his conception too resembled that of Aristotle, now in a polemical function directed against an enemy that was far less likely to follow an Asian imperial route than some Greek tyrants, and of course the kings of Macedon. On the bases of rather patchy and superficial understanding of Asian monarchies, and following Locke, perhaps also of Aristotle's considerations of patrimonial rule, Montesquieu maintained that despotism represented a threat to private property. Eventually, this notion will be turned by others to radically denounce the mainstay of the modern state, namely taxation. Montesquieu on his part merely works it into the study of some of the corrupt forms, focusing more on actual confiscation and particularly oppressive forms of taxation. His poor knowledge of China and other Asian monarchies and in particular his rather unique idea that the normal succession in Asian monarchies involved usurpation, was to invite Voltaire's condemnation (Montesquieu 1994: V. xi and xiv 57–58, 59–63).

An Asian model plays little role for Rousseau and Kant, who make the link of the separation of powers and authoritarian forms much clearer in two-track conceptions even more faithful to the spirit if not the letter of Aristotle than Montesquieu. To Aristotle despotism represented a different form of life than the *polis*, thus the destruction of the latter, while, in the more plausible interpretation, tyranny was only the worst form of government of the *polis* with strong despotic tendencies. Despotism accordingly is a life without *nomos* while tyranny is a political condition where the *nomos* is known but violated. (Again: Creon is a tyrant, not a despot. The law Antigone relies on is still *nomos*, whatever the word of the king.) The difficulty was that the term *polis* signified both a political structure of a state of free men and, incorporating the household, a form of social life as well. Focusing on the political dimension alone could lead to putting despotism and tyranny on the same level, overlooking the double character of Aristotle's conception and, very likely, the differences between tyranny and despotism, as in the case of Montesquieu. Quite innovatively, Rousseau and Kant recover this duality, but on the purely political level. The distinction is between sovereignty and form of government in the former, more precisely put as form of domination as against a form of regime in the latter.[43] In each case despotism concerns the more fundamental level where each author sees a threat to the separation of powers.[44] Of course more than the separation of powers is at stake for Rousseau. His sovereign is the supreme legislature and, in a legitimate political system, a popular republic, the sovereign legislature is the citizen body as a whole. Despotism concerns the confiscation of popular sovereignty by a government, by the executive that assumes legislative powers. In this conception monarchical, aristocratic, and democratic government become tyrannical and oligarchic, and ochlocratic when they act in a lawless manner, though it is difficult for Rousseau to actually conceive a lawless democracy, a purely ideal system in his view, which by implication however would have no separation of powers (Rousseau 1996: 92–95).

According to Rousseau tyranny has two meanings, the "ordinary" one depicting a king who governs with violence, in a lawless and unjust manner, and the "strict sense" of a private individual who usurps royal authority, a usurper. He does not seem to make up his mind whether a tyrant in the strict sense seeks to govern according to the laws, or it is an open question whether or not he will do so. The famous line, according to which "the tyrant need not be a despot, but the despot is always a tyrant" means that a despot is always a usurper and a lawless ruler, while the tyrant (by definition) only is a usurper. Of course, this would mean that a tyrant who does govern in a lawless manner would also be a despot. But the identification seems hard to reconcile with the sharp opposition according to which the tyrant usurps royal (governmental) authority, while the despot is a usurper of sovereignty itself. Thus a lawless tyrant could still coexist with a legislative power that makes legitimate law, while a despot could not, since he would destroy the very possibility of legitimate law making by his usurpation. Obviously Rousseau did not consistently think through his two-level conception, and he does not therefore rediscover the Aristotelian idea of the degrees of despotic transformation as the difference between tyrannical *governments* that violate the law (and popular sovereignty), and *despotic* regimes that abolish the rule of law (and popular sovereignty) altogether.

Rousseau, always an opponent of absolutism – that he depicted as universal despotism in the Second Discourse – was (uniquely in his time) still involved in the problems of small-scale civic republics. As he tried to produce an original synthesis of liberal and republican doctrines, both the concepts of despotism and tyranny remained important for him and he made an attempt to distinguish between them, perhaps more sharply than Aristotle himself and, without a sociological conception of the roots of despotism, perhaps less successfully. Kant too was interested in opposing monarchical absolutism in the name of both liberal and republican principles, but in a period when suddenly the latter were reformulated in the two democratic revolutions as pertinent to large-scale territorial states. Unlike Rousseau, however, but like the tradition including Montesquieu and the American framers, Kant was critical of the extreme democratic position as well. Thus he does not follow the two-part conception of Rousseau ultimately resting on the idea of popular sovereignty as the bases of genuine republics. Instead he revives the more traditional dualism of Bodin of the holders of ultimate power (*forma imperii*) and the form of regime or government (*forma regiminis*) (Kant 1963). The former are the three traditional types based on numbers (one, some, and all) without being initially presented in pairs of right-wrong, moderate-corrupt. But a polemical turn is indeed taken by Kant when he asserts that the regime form is *republican* when there is a genuine separation of powers and the rulers are representative of their subjects. The only alternative on this level is despotism.

Unlike his forerunner Rousseau, Kant does not go on to apply concepts of tyranny or usurpation to forms of government or regime. Here too the issue remains despotism and the logical connections of forms of ultimate power and forms of government. Accordingly, reversing all traditional usage, monarchy and aristocracy can be either republican or despotic because both can realize representation and separation of powers. The system however that Rousseau considered possible only for gods or angels, namely "democracy," *must be despotic* according to Kant who thought (similarly to Madison) that governments should be designed rather for a race of rational devils. This view of democracy to be sure is what the tradition focused on, namely direct, non-representative, and extreme egalitarian popular rule where the magistrates had no independence vis-à-vis the popular assembly. Montesquieu too has used the classical views of tyranny to conceptualize democratic corruption in a way that anticipates, again in the path of Aristotle (*Politics* IV. iv 1292a) the idea of the tyranny of the majority (VIII. 2). Similarly, for Kant too violation or absence of separation of powers or mixed government nevertheless remains the main key to the understanding of despotism. The new element, discussed by Montesquieu only under the heading of the English system, but not in relation to the general forms of government, is representation. To Kant, as to Madison, a republic is by definition a representative system, while non-representative ones are perforce despotisms. Only a representative system is capable of a full separation of powers, and democracy by definition excludes representation as well as the principle of election.

Despotism and tyranny in America

In terms of a much too crude schema of liberal, anti-absolutist, and traditional republican thought we might say that the category of despotism became dominant for anti-absolutist liberals, while those still attached to traditional republican politics held on to the category of tyranny whether or not they clearly distinguished it from despotism. Only where anti-absolutism and traditional republicanism came together as in the case of Rousseau was there an attempt to develop and use both clearly differentiated categories in an original way. In Kant's more modern republicanism based on representation the traditional category of tyranny with its primary relevance to city states loses its importance. On the other hand, the growth of the modern state, both in its absolutist and revolutionary forms, kept the despotism problem on his agenda. If Kant represented one possible republican road from Rousseau, the thinkers of the American Enlightenment developed another, contrary one, at least up to the Revolutionary War when large standing armies appeared on the scene. Initially, it was not the survival of city republics, but the absence of a central territorial state or even credible attempts to build one that made the despotism problem less relevant, while threats to their communal self-governments helped keep alive the issue of tyranny. The Machiavellian influence is real, but its importance was also the function of a political world where rather than absolutist statebuilding, an arbitrary act of the traditional authorities (king, parliament, and royal governors) was the source of grievances.[45] Even the mercantilist policies of the Crown and Parliament were regarded this way: as attacks on traditional rights that remained valid and binding. If the importance of the category of despotism on the European continent and especially in the works of the much-revered Montesquieu led to some use in America as well, the meaning was at first absorbed in that of tyranny. Here an Asiatic transformation of the polity seemed a very remote possibility at best, in spite of Montesquieu's depiction of the Spanish American Colonial world in these terms (*The Spirit of the Laws* VIII. 18) Only the problem of militarism raised the issue of central government, resembling in some ways European states, but the return to locally based militias after the Revolutionary War seemed to put this issue to rest. It was the inter-related questions of states' rights and slavery that were to raise the problem of despotism in really serious, independent, and competing ways, paradoxically on both sides of the great divide.

In general, despotism was less of an intellectual problem not only in the American colonies of Great Britain, but in the mother country as well, in contradistinction to the European continent where the absolutist process of statebuilding was dominant. Locke's treatment of despotism was admittedly exceptional, but he was writing at a time, on behalf of the anti-Stuart cause, when the issue of English absolutism was not yet fully decided. In the eighteenth century, even the likely relevant issues of royal "corruption" and standing armies did not raise the specter of absolutism as the Court and Country factions were united in Parliament, and by other symbiotic relationships.[46] By the late eighteenth century, for Paine, the author of *The Declaration of Independence*, and for Madison despotism and tyranny were the same, though given the great influence of Montesquieu the traditional concept of tyranny that supplied their common meaning, did absorb some of the newer connotations of the term despotism. Paine does make an important distinction between government and regime, more similar to Kant's than to Rousseau's dualism, that in any case could have given him the opportunity to make the Aristotelian distinction in a new and forceful way, but he too applies categories of tyranny and despotism indifferently to either (Paine 1984: 47). The same indifference is present in *The Declaration of Independence* that speaks of both absolute Despotism and absolute Tyranny, with a few sentences apart, as if they were the same. Jefferson still has the same ambiguity with him much later in life when he speaks of Bonaparte's "maniac tyranny" in one place, and his "chains of despotism" in another (Jefferson 1984, "Letter to Lafayette" 655; "Letter to George Ticknor" 683). This fluctuation is also there in the *Federalist Papers* with Madison in #47, 48, 53 preferring to use the concept of tyranny (Hamilton *et al.* 1970: 245–255, 272–275), Hamilton the Lockean usurpation in #28 and 29 (Hamilton *et al.* 1970: 133–141); but alternating between tyranny and despotism in quite similar contexts in #1 and 9 (Hamilton *et al.* 1970: 1–4, 48–53), and where these concepts are generally understood in terms of the abrogation or elimination of the separation of powers that signified the essence of despotism to Montesquieu and Kant: "The accumulation of all powers, legislative, executive or judiciary, in the same hands, whether one, few or many, and whether hereditary, self-appointed or elective, may justly be pronounced the very definition of tyranny" in #47, 48 (Hamilton *et al.* 1970: 245–255). Here Madison relied explicitly on Jefferson's *Notes on Virginia* where the latter famously noted that "One hundred and seventy-three despots would be surely as oppressive as one. … An *elective despotism* is not the government we fought for" (Jefferson, *Notes on Virginia* 237). The indifference to the legality of origins and to the three numerical parameters of holding power (thus the classical doctrine of the three forms) indicates the influence of the originally Aristotelian theory of despotism. The fact however that Madison simply substitutes tyranny for despotism in Jefferson's "definition" indicates their common distance not only from Aristotle, but also Rousseau whose relevant distinctions did not apparently impress these Americans. The attempt moreover to provide the definition of tyranny/despotism in terms of the absence of the separation of powers does not make clear enough whether the absence of the separation of powers is (as Kant thought) already tyranny/despotism, or that it only leads to it more or less inevitably. Yet the stress on the separation of powers in either case is important, because, in spite of the words of the *Declaration*, Americans of the Revolutionary period did not seriously maintain, unlike Montesquieu and his French heirs, that the dangers they faced were the adoption of the methods of despotic-patrimonial governments absent in England itself.

The authors of the *Federalist* feared another possibility more, one also known to the ancients, namely that direct democracy or its embodiment in the system of majoritarian representation may have directly or indirectly tyrannical consequences, either suppressing the rights of minorities or through the anarchical struggle of factions, inviting intervention by a strong hand. In this argument it is unclear whether these tendencies were supposed to be cured by the separation of powers, which they in any case threaten. Fearing the legislative expression of what was not yet called "the tyranny of the majority," Madison thus applauds the further division of the law-making body into two chambers, one of them supposedly free of popular passions (Hamilton *et al.* 1970: 314–326).

Madison however does not restrict himself to dangers to the separation of powers; like Kant he defines republic as representative and elected government, and tyranny becomes also the abrogation of regular elections (#48 and 53) (Hamilton *et al.* 1970: 251–255, 272–276). "Where annual elections end, tyranny begins" was the original revolutionary position, according to Jefferson as well. (Jefferson, 1984, "Letter to Samuel Adams" 557). Of course, the American version of the modern separation of powers rests on separate elections. Therefore the abrogation of elections would tend to imply, in a modern society at least, the concentration of all powers in the hands capable of interfering with the electoral process. That is likely to be the executive that ordinarily has the military command, in spite of the precedents of the Long Parliament and the Septennial Law. Thus republican thought in America, in the beginning, tirelessly stressed the danger of monarchical restoration latent in our presidency.[47] In the *Federalist Papers* it falls to Hamilton to defend the new Constitution against that charge, as well as the more serious related one concerning the dangers of standing armies in peace time, perhaps because he was known to be an advocate of monarchy or a monarchical presidency.[48] His discussion deals with the charge of monarchy only in terms of a broad caricature (*Federalist* #67 and 69), somewhat disingenuously given his views at the Federal Convention where he called in effect for a lifetime presidency explicitly because this would be an elected monarchy. Thus it is surprising that he returns to the anti-absolutist concept of despotism when he takes up the specific charge of the anti-Federalists that a national standing army, however small, can become the foundation for a "military despotism" (*Federalist* #16). It was a favorite claim of Hamilton that it was the weakness of government rather than its strength that tended to lead to tyranny (*Federalist* #9, 20). Accordingly, he tried to turn the tables on the opponents of the Constitution by arguing that it would be a national government without some (i.e., judicial!) powers over individuals that would because of its weakness need to rely on a standing army, and thus involve the danger of military despotism (Federalist #16). This round however was probably won by the anti-Federalists, in particular Patrick Henry and "Brutus." The former pointed out the dictatorial powers given to Washington ("an American Dictator") and proceeded to ask whether any future presidents could be trusted with such powers without the danger of tyranny (Storing 1985). Washington, whom others called the American Cincinnatus, was of course not president in 1781, and was only expected to assume such office when the debate took place. Yet Henry had foresight enough when he deliberately mixed together the three figures of general, dictator, and president, sensing perhaps the dangerous potential of mixing the powers of the Roman dictator with the prerogative powers of a *regular* chief executive. Similarly though more accurately "Brutus" raised the identical question with respect to the dangers of a standing army that won the Revolutionary War. Here too the figures and histories of Caesar and Cromwell play the role of warning the possible transformation of military dictators (understood in the Roman sense) into tyrants or despots. In fact Brutus goes further even than this last claim (and the Roman concept of dictatorship!), and maintains that a commander-in-chief of a standing army like Washington, but without his republican patriotism, would be able "to dictate" a constitution and laws "at the point of a bayonet" (Storing 1985: 158–159).

The same argument was already expounded by Jefferson in *Notes on Virginia* in 1782. He discusses (failed) proposals in the Virginia House of Delegates in 1776 and 1781, in the face of British invasion, to appoint a dictator invested with all powers on the Roman model. He interprets this model as that of a temporary tyrant or omnipotent despot, that according to him at least even in Rome proved fatal when "after a few examples" the office was made "perpetual." His somewhat doubtful reading of history thus makes him one of the first republican or liberal authors who interprets the concept of dictatorship in mostly negative terms, through the lenses of Caesar's usurpation, as a form of potential tyranny (244–247). (Consistently enough: he was opposed to the possibility of suspension of habeas corpus in emergencies, in the US Constitution. "To James Madison" 1788: 450–451). The argument was strongly reinforced almost twenty years later by the then recent experience of Bonaparte's *coup d'état*. In a letter he writes:

> My confidence has been placed in the head, not the heart of Bonaparte. I hoped he would calculate truly the difference between the fame of a Washington and a Cromwell. Whatever his views may be, he has at least transferred the destinies of the republic from the civil to the military arm. Some will use this as a lesson against the practicability of republican government. I read it as a lesson against standing armies.[49]

Critics of the new constitution feared yet another road to tyranny in the United States, other than the threats of the legislature or the executive to the *separation* of powers.

Indeed, the main anti-Federalist, and later Republican fear concerned the exposure of another republican institutional arrangement to tyrannical or despotic usurpation: the *division* of powers, or federalism in the later sense of that term. Pamphlet writer after pamphlet writer, speaker after speaker at ratifying conventions raises this issue, linked to the supposed impossibility according to Montesquieu of a continental republic or of republics within a large territorial state with or without a standing army ([*Maryland*] *Farmer* 263–264; *The Impartial Examiner* 281–282 in Storing 1985). If federalism was the solution to the dilemma, this solution was supposedly under constant threat by the explicit and implied powers given to the "federal" government by the constitution. If however, the argument went, the powers of the states were much diminished, the United States could not preserve its republican form. This issue remained on the order of the day in the struggle between Federalists and Republicans, in the various nullification debates, and of course in the struggle over slavery and secession.[50]

No author is more involved in all of these debates than John C. Calhoun, the most important political theorist of the South. As if recapitulating the European pattern of development a century earlier, his preferred term of art (as Lincoln's) is despotism rather than tyranny. As earlier, at issue is large-scale, territorial state formation. To Calhoun the question is no longer whether free republics could be linked together at all in a large-scale territorial entity (in his view this was done successfully though vulnerably in the United States Constitution), but whether and how their freedom could be preserved. In considering this question, he understands the enemy to be majoritarian, or numerical democracy or what he called "king numbers." Thus like Madison he fears the despotism of the majority, but rather than on sociological grounds as did Tocqueville roughly at the same time, on the bases of a constitutional-political argument to which he gives a new twist. The most radical version is presented in the *Disquisition on Government* (1850) (Calhoun 1992). Despotism is still understood in terms of the negation of constitutional government, but the latter is defined not in terms of the separation of powers, but Calhoun's own doctrine of "concurrent majorities" which would give any large constellation of minority interests (in his arbitrary reading: the states) a veto over decisions of the majority. Admittedly, the opposite of constitutional government is said to be absolute government, e.g., absolute democracy; each of the three traditional forms has an absolute deformation. It is only however a causal argument that connects absolute government to tyranny. An absolute democracy is according to him inevitably forced to use force against minority interests, and then it is almost unavoidably driven into the hands of the one most efficient in the use of force, a master or a military despot (Calhoun 1992: 24, 28–29, 34–35).

The argument is applied to America in *A Discourse on the Government and Constitution of the United States* (1851) (Calhoun 1992: 120–124, 449, 496ff.). The theory of constitutionalism in terms of the concept of concurrent majorities is central for this work too, though Calhoun never raises the possibility that interests could be other than territorial, and that states as territories have internally a plurality of interests. Thus the question of the concurrence of non-slaveholding interests or of the slaves themselves does not ever arise. Calhoun seeks to defend only the veto power of sovereign units in a system that he interprets as a confederation, at least in terms of its constitutional norms. Thus, like most eighteenth century anti-federalists, his initial focus is on the national legislative power, and, unlike them, in the American context he is less interested in military despotism. While in Congress the question of the territories did threaten the constitutional limits to the rule of mere numbers (and thus the bulwarks set up against the abolition of slavery through legislation or amendment), in the long run, the standing army (where the South was particularly well represented) did not turn out to be a dynamic force on its own or in the hands of a general. Where he is most insistent, given the Marshall Court, was in noticing the strengthening of national state sovereignty (to him confiscation of sovereignty!) through the institutions of the Federal courts,[51] and, more germane to the topic here, the Federal presidency whose plebiscitary potential Calhoun was probably first to fully register (Calhoun 1992: 158–159), not surprisingly, given his run-ins with Andrew Jackson during the nullification and force bill controversies! Writing during Louis Bonaparte's presidency, but just before his "Eighteenth Brumaire" in 1851, Calhoun projects a presidential *coup d'état* by which the American presidency would lose its elective character and become absolute. Even before that final stage, the judiciary is likely to come under his control through the power of appointment (160) and "the election of the President would become the all-important question" (215). Of course, it was the election of a president that triggered, after his death (but as Calhoun foresaw and instigated) the rebellion against what the deep South at least understood as tyranny or despotism coupled with confiscation.

Surprisingly perhaps, on the other side, the side of abolitionism, concepts of despotism and tyranny assumed a somewhat muted function. Very likely the fact that these concepts were inherited from the republican vocabulary of slave-holding republics played a role. Tyranny was difficult to use, since its critique would not have touched the *oikos*, that Southern ideology never tired of stressing was the presupposition of also the free *polis*. (This point was already made at the Federal Convention by C. Pinkney [Koch 1985: 505].) Tyranny was a form of rule over the free, and the abolitionists were concerned with the unfree. Despotism in principle would have been more appropriate to describe the oppression of slavery, since the *despot* was a master over the un-free. Yet *despotism* strictly speaking would have meant the extension of the arrangements of the household to the *polis*, something that was at most a tendency in the slaveholding South (Freehling 1991) which on the whole retained its republican institutions among the free, however corrupted and deformed in many cases. If interchangeable references to tyranny and despotism, but with general preference for the concept of tyranny, nevertheless made their appearance among the abolitionists, this probably had to do with the enormous influence of the text of *The Declaration of Independence* among them, often favorably juxtaposed to the Constitution and its compromises with bondage. Abolitionist author after author refers to the hypocrisy of having rebelled against absolute tyranny or despotism in the name of principles of equality and universal rights, and maintaining at the same time conditions of fundamental inequality and rightlessness.[52] The latter is sometimes called tyranny, or tyrannical, but without any attempt to define or justify the use of these terms. The implication is that to maintain some people in a rightless condition without justification is itself tyranny, whatever the character of the political system. A system of majority rule based on the rule of law, a constitutional republic can thus be a tyranny (Garrison in Lowance 2001). As in the case of Tocqueville, this extension threatens to rob the concept of tyranny of its political focus.

The foundation for a different approach was available at the time of the Founding. The strongest criticism of slavery in Jefferson's writings starts out from the fundamental relationship of the slaveholding household: "The whole commerce between the master and the slave is a perpetual exercise of … the most unremitting despotism. … The parent storms, the child looks on … thus nursed, educated, and daily exercised in tyranny ..." (Jefferson 1984: *Notes on Virginia* 278). Note that Jefferson is still using despotism and tyranny more or less interchangeably, as was his practice. Here however while he does not characterize the polity itself as despotic or tyrannical, his argument, unknown in the ancient world and disregarded by Calhoun, focuses on the negative socialization, corruption of masters, and warns about the danger of slavery to republican forms. There was an echo of this reference to a mere "domestic" institution in Madison's remarks at the Constitutional Convention, avoiding however the political terms tyranny or despotism. He referred to slavery as the "most oppressive dominion ever exercised by man over man," based on "the mere distinction of color" (77). As often, it was another Virginian, George Mason, who came closest to Jefferson's views at the Convention: "Every master of slaves is a petty tyrant. They bring the judgment of heaven on a Country."[53]

The theoretical option of moving from domestic despotism to political tyranny was generally not followed by the abolitionists, who, less schooled in classical thought, preferred the term tyranny and did not distinguish between the levels of social relations and the political system, or even try to explain how republics can be or become tyrannies. Here Jefferson's influence was probably counterproductive, since contrary to the *Declaration*, *Notes on Virginia* was generally despised in abolitionist circles because of its absurd racist ravings (256ff.). Relying on other framers, William Lloyd Garrison gets closest to a viable alternative when he adopts something like the notion of the tyranny of the majority so liked by Southern ideologists, which leads him to frankly admit that his was in effect an aristocratic position – to be sure in a quite different sense than that of Calhoun. But like most abolitionists, Garrison's use of the term tyranny remained most of the time on a reduced, polemical level, as at the famous moment in 1853 when he burned a copy of the US Constitution with the (hardly unjust if imprecise) words "So perish all compromises with tyranny" (Lowance 2001: xxviii).

It was Abraham Lincoln, with pre-Civil War perspectives on emancipation and race not so far removed from *Notes on Virginia*, who was to return to aspects of Jefferson's more sophisticated usage. In the denunciations of Lincoln (and more occasionally of Jefferson Davis) that inevitably followed the outbreak of the War, the terms tyranny, despotism, and dictatorship all played a somewhat interchangeable role. (John Wilkes Booth saw himself as tyrannicide: his famous words were "Sic semper tyrannis.") Lincoln himself, like Jefferson, used despotism and tyranny interchangeably, sometimes in sequential sentences. But he seemed to prefer "despotism" possibly because of its value in describing the system of social domination of the slave-owners. His usage moves between the political and social levels, but without identifying the two. He repeatedly speaks of "returning despotism" or "resumption of tyranny" as the Republic's political future if a new "Dred Scott decision" were to reimpose property in slaves in the North, and not only in the territories, or if the Confederacy were victorious. In the first case what he means is that given strong anti-slavery sentiment, re-imposition could not be enforced democratically and resistance would have to be violently crushed. Thus tyranny as a political form would become a serious threat. The specter of Confederate victory has a related but also different meaning. On the one hand he does accuse Southern leaders of harboring dreams of quashing popular government, which even in the slave-holding states could come to threaten the slave-holding minority. At the same time he identifies the slave system as despotic because it is *already* a caste society, and accuses its leaders of wishing to further extend the principle by turning free labor into a rigid caste. Here the allusion was perhaps to Asian forms, linking despotism and caste. Undoubtedly propagandistic in its intent (Lincoln 1998: "First Annual Message to Congress," December 1861, p. 325), this conception, rather than identifying slavery and tyranny, only locates the potential cause of the latter in the former. Or: it points to the foundations of political despotism in the despotic "domestic" relationship of slavery.

Lincoln's reference to the "crowned heads" rooting for the South, has to do not so much with the specific nature of the slave system, than with the replacement of a free republic and its principle of "all men are created equal" with "a returning despotism," that is "classification, caste and legitimacy" (Lincoln 1998: "Letter to Pierce" 216). The same fears acquired new urgency during the beginning of the Civil War. Astonishingly, Lincoln was not sensitive to the possibility that the term despotism and the reference to European monarchs would be used to denounce wartime political centralization, large standing armies, and wholesale denial of traditional rights for which he (and in the South: Jefferson Davis!) was the main person responsible.[54]

For himself, he mobilized the traditional Roman concept of dictatorship once used for Washington, meaning a constitutional interruption of constitutional government for the sake of the constitution (Lincoln 1998: 4 July 1861 message; Letter to Corning on the suspension of habeas: Carl Schmitt in *Die Diktatur* [1922, 2012] called him commissarial; Rossiter 1948 in *Constitutional Dictatorship* "constitutional dictator" par excellence). To be sure he had already some difficulty using the actual term of dictatorship in its classical sense. In a letter (Congressman or Senator Browning) he uses "dictatorship" (his quotes) to describe an absolute authority of a general (Fremont) to "do anything he pleases" in a theater of war, leading to illegal, i.e., permanent confiscation, through granting letters of manumission to slaves. Dictatorship in this construct means usurping the rights of the legislature, since even in a military necessity a general or a president can only use men and goods for the duration of the emergency, and cannot change their original legal conditions. Even a president cannot use the justification of "saving the government" for making "permanent rules of property by proclamation." This was said just two years before the Emancipation Proclamation that did exactly that, though not based on the concept of "dictatorship" but that of war powers authority, ultimately derived from the Lockean prerogative. He still tried to do this within the conception of military necessity, but now at times defining the latter as the need to appeal to Blacks who could thus be induced to join the union army (Lincoln 1998: Emancipation Proclamation 368; "Letter to Conkling" 393). Yet he still tried to draw a line between military policy and legislation by refusing to extend the proclamation to previously exempted (i.e., already under Union rule) territories in Virginia and Louisiana ("Letter to Chase" 394). Without military necessity, presidential confiscation would enter "the boundless field of absolutism." This was a new term for what was previously described as "dictatorship," that even without the quotes retained its newly negative meaning even after the proclamation. On 26 January he wrote to General Hooker:

> I have heard ... your recently saying that both the Army and the Government needed a Dictator. Of course it was not *for* this but in spite of it, that I have given you the command. Only those generals who gain successes, can set up dictators. What I now ask you is military success, and I will risk the dictatorship ... [And after accusing Hooker of damaging the sprit of the army by criticizing the president:] Neither you, nor Napoleon, if he were alive again, could get any good out of an army, while such a spirit prevails in it.
>
> (Lincoln 1998: 372)

Here the concept of dictatorship, modeled on Caesar and Napoleon, occupies the boundless field of absolutism. To the charge that his own emergency measures suppressing a host of fundamental rights may open up the field for just such a dictatorship, permanent rather than temporary, he replied in terms of a facile and poor analogy of a healthy man who would not take the emetics prescribed previously during a temporary illness ("Letter to Corning"). Unsurprisingly, he did not convince his enemies (nor probably some allies as well) who now also at times understood dictatorship (his own) in the sense that came close to a synonym, or a modern replacement, of tyranny or despotism. Americans were thus involved in a transformation of concepts that already had occurred in Europe in two stages, during the French Revolution and during the revolutions of 1848, one that involved the beginning of the emergence of the *modern* concept of dictatorship.

Decline of tyranny and despotism as polemical concepts

The understanding of despotism propagated by the discontents of modern state formation in Europe and America by proponents of the anti-absolutist position was of course strongly rejected by the defenders of the "enlightened' absolutist monarchy like Voltaire and the Physiocrats as well as by advocates of the centralized, national republic such as Alexander Hamilton. The best among them pointed both to the irrelevant "orientalism" of the implied projection, as well as the misrepresentation of the "orient" itself inevitably entailed. Although the absolutist state builders and their defenders, monarchical, reformist, or revolutionary could not have found comfortable the description of their projects as despotic or as despotisms, eventually they came to live with the terms. While the term "enlightened despotism" may not have been an authentic eighteenth century one, other concepts like (absolute) state sovereignty, absolutism, absolute monarchy, divine right of kings, enlightened absolutism, legal despotism and, finally, despotism of liberty were all attempts to escape or justify the odious label that the defenders of the society of orders and estates, *Ständestaat* as well as civic and corporate independence and religious dissent managed to pin on the state-makers (op. cit. Richter 1968). These efforts recall, in the face of an Aristotelian onslaught, Plato's arguments on behalf of rational or scientific but not necessarily legal or popular rulers, as well as his vision (partially revived by Machiavelli) of the role of tyrannical legislators in dramatic change. Some of them in fact incorporated the idea of reformist or revolutionary transformation of the absolutist regime. What is nevertheless surprising is that while state making was a dramatic success on the European continent, its intellectual defense in conservative, reformist, or revolutionary forms was feeble from the outset – because of the association with "despotism." Enlightened and legal despotism were almost immediately regarded as mere rationalizations of despotism, in other words the unreformed absolutist monarchies. Similarly, the despotism of liberty or virtue was easily unmasked as mere legitimation attempts for a terror regime without freedom or virtue.

The attempt of the radical revolutionaries in France to utilize the labels of despotism, tyranny (and: dictatorship, but positively only by Marat) with the old trope of Montesquieu fear reappearing as a positive affirmation of terror (Richter) was the most dramatic failure.[55] The reality could not be simply named, it had to be made legitimate, and this could not be easily done in a world that newly produced liberal constitutions linked to declarations of rights. The new *state* could be made legitimate in other words, but only under a constitutionalist rather than despotic *regime*. This was misunderstood by both the opponents and defenders of absolutism and terror. Few understood outside of Great Britain (until authors like Constant, Hegel, and Tocqueville) the compatibility of a liberal regime (if well designed) with a strong state. (Even in America these were seen as contraries on both the Federalist and Republican side, by both Hamilton and Jefferson.) With the success of state formation all over the continent, and in post-Civil War America too (see Bensel 1991 and Skowronek 1982 on the American state for two outstanding but different views), the charge of despotism, that made the differentiation of state and regime so difficult, became increasingly as obsolete as did tyranny before, with the decline of traditional republicanism.

With Napoleon, the last great French state-maker and perhaps the first modern dictator, despotism and tyranny made a full return for the last important time as polemical concepts denouncing arbitrary rule (Nolte 1973). But in this period or soon afterwards, serious interpreters like Benjamin Constant and Alexis de Tocqueville recognized that they and their fellow critics were trying to subsume something radically new under old and supposedly anachronistic concepts. Both efforts, still deeply rooted in old usage, were ambivalent, but each understood something of the new even if they came up with no definitively new concepts.

In Constant's important work on Napoleonic rule, *The Spirit of Conquest and Usurpation*, the terminology at least is traditional, most closely resembling that of John Locke's categories (Constant 1988). The conception behind the terms however is new and innovative. As was increasingly the case in the late eighteenth and early nineteenth centuries for those who preserved both terms, Constant used despotism and tyranny almost interchangeably (Constant 1988: 74, 88, 114). Including Napoleon, but carefully sparing the monarchies of his own day, he defines only despotism:

> I mean by despotism a government in which the will of the master is the only law, where political bodies if they exist are only his instruments; where the master regards himself as the only owner of his empire ... where courts are subjected to the whims of power, where their sentences are annulled; where those acquitted are dragged in front of new judges ... instructed that they are there only to condemn.
>
> (Constant 1988: 114)

It is possible that he would have adopted the same definition for tyranny. But it is however the case that few examples of despotism could be said to involve all of its elements. Napoleon for example not only did not consider himself the sole owner of his empire, but was instead sponsor of a civil code affirming a staunchly bourgeois property order. There seems to be moreover a tendency in Constant's thinking to use despotism for a type of monarchy and tyranny for republican terror (Constant 1988: 101ff., 104ff.) but we are told that the principle of the two forms, "arbitrary power," is in any case the same (Constant 1988: 115).

There is nothing particularly unique or surprising in Constant's understanding of despotism/tyranny. He himself seems quite aware of speaking of something traditional when he maintains that in the modern age characterized by the monetarization and commercialization of relationships, the transnational nature of human ties, and the importance of the private sphere despotism is almost impossible to maintain for a long period (ch. 18). Of course the question is how long is long? Perhaps the lifetime of a single despotic leader is meant to define the external limits. That claim is somewhat at odds with several aspects of Constant's argument, his treatment of the dictatorship problem, and his discovery of modern militarism.

There are times when Constant seems to expand the concept of despotism, and the adjectival form *despotic*, as to be the genus of all authoritarian forms. It is under the heading of regular governments resorting to "illegal and despotic measures" that he discusses emergency or crisis government, without distinguishing between the Roman dictatorship as well as the Lockean prerogative. He speaks of "despotism" that regular governments establish at intervals, in times of crisis (101). Indeed, his definition of despotism does allow him to conceive of particularly harsh and consistent emergency government as a species of temporary despotism or "temporary tyranny" as Jefferson called it. The terminology nevertheless indicates a very negative attitude toward classical understandings of dictatorship as well as the prerogative. Unusually for his time, but similarly to Jefferson already before Napoleon's coup, Constant condemns all arbitrary, oppressive, and "illegal" measures even on behalf of the maintenance of free institutions in a republic or a constitutional monarchy. The reason is that oppressive and arbitrary measures to ward off oppressive and arbitrary government are not only logically self-contradictory, but because they will very likely accustom the holders of power to use more and more frequently, and the subjects to accept, supposedly efficient, time-saving authoritarian instruments. Thus the exception will become the norm (134–137). A similar logic is at work when despotic measures are used to establish a new republican or constitutional regime. Reflecting on the experience of the reign of terror, Constant staunchly maintains that liberty can be no more established than preserved by despotic or tyrannical means (110ff.).

While in the case of the revolutionary establishment of a free government, legal means that would guide change, rooted in the legality of an arbitrary system, are not available,[56] the same is not true in the case of the preservation of such a government. While Constant does not distinguish between legal provisions for the adoption of normally extra-legal measures, and their illegal utilization, the argument seems to be directed at both versions.[57] He concedes the existence of fundamental threats and emergencies to political orders that cannot be conjured away. Yet he recommends as always less risky responding in terms of "adhering, more scrupulously than ever, to the established laws, to tutelary procedures, to preserving safeguards." He is above all concerned with the problem of using emergency as *pretext* of any party ready to identify "the interests of state with the destruction of its [the party's] enemies" (136).

He could have also said, and certainly meant to say, that the pretext of emergency allows the identification of the interest of state with the rule of the holder of emergency power. Since however one never runs out of enemies especially after having taken despotic measures, the two points amount to the same thing: the interest and proclivity of the holder of *temporary* emergency powers to make his rule *permanent*. While Constant does not make the connection explicit, given the carrier of Napoleon all his readers had to immediately see the link between his critique of emergency government and what he called *usurpation*.[58] Thus while his denunciation of the *classical* dictatorship was not unique for liberal thought at least, it was the category of usurpation that represents his specific contribution to the emergence of the *modern concept* of dictatorship, and it is under this heading that he stumbles into new forms of authoritarianism appropriate for the modern age.

Usurpation is still seemingly a traditional category. In Locke for example it implied coming to power illegally, a traditional attribute of tyranny that he defined rather by ruling in an illegal way once in power. Constant's definition includes both of these ideas, one generally a consequence of the other, but either sufficient to define a usurper. As he puts it "[A] usurper is one who, without the sanction of the national will, seizes power, or who, having been invested with limited power, exceeds the limits prescribed" (Constant 1988: 158). Thus a usurper by definition comes to power *or* transgresses his legal powers in ways that are both illegal and illegitimate.[59] In the case of Bonaparte both parts apply: he came to power in a *coup d'état*, and continually violated or abrogated his own legal order. Constant thus asserts that "[Y]ou see no usurper who has not twenty times repealed his own laws and suppressed the forms he has just instituted..." (Constant 1988: 91). Legal arbitrariness is indeed an important element of the distinction between monarchy and usurpation (for a full list of differences: Constant 1988: 87–91), but it seems to amount to what was said to be the common principle of despotism and tyranny. There are moments of rhetorical excess *when Constant brings these three* terms very close together (Constant 1988: 88), but his more serious point is that despotism and usurpation are different. There is indeed a difference between transgressing law and having no formal laws to transgress, a point Constant does not clearly make. But he makes a similar and more inclusive argument when he actually contrasts usurpation and what he calls consolidated (i.e., traditional, monarchical) despotism. "Despotism banishes all forms of liberty; usurpation needs these in order to justify what it replaces; but in appropriating them it profanes them" (Constant 1988: 95). Despotism in other words suppresses (or does without) elections, public trials, free speech and press, while usurpation uses mock or caricatured and manipulated forms of these institutions.

The same could have been said regarding the transgression of a variety of other modern institutions including rule of law and separation of powers. Constant's first important innovation is clearly thematizing in other words a form of authoritarian rule that operates with at least a facade of modern institutions inherited from republics and constitutional states and in the face of modern public opinion. Thus usurpation cannot be satisfied as despotism in ruling "by means of silence," it establishes rather a plebiscitary public sphere (Habermas) that condemns the subjects to speak (Constant 1988: 95–97). That they say the right thing is guaranteed not only by coercion, but also by the control of information, and the production of events that build support. Constant summons as his witness Napoleon, who supposedly maintained that "one must give the French something new every three months" (Constant 1988: 89).

Napoleon is of course the paradigmatic usurper of the nineteenth century – the term was commonly used for him in European courts and in *émigré* circles, but in Constant's text the point seems contradictory since here the Corsican was also called a despot, the only one in Europe in 1813 (Constant 1988: 114). One cannot simultaneously force subjects to be silent and to speak, or abolish a variety of modern institutions and maintain manipulated and caricatured forms of these. It may be the case that Constant had in mind different stages of Napoleonic rule, beginning as usurpation in a coup and ending up as a despotic empire. The analogy of Caesar, Octavian, and the later Roman emperors speaks for such a view. But Constant also believed that in the modern era despotism cannot be similarly long lived, through several generations of despots. What he seems to have in mind rather is the use of despotism or some of its instruments to try to stabilize usurpation. While this type of strategy is discussed in four chapters (Constant 1988: chs. 5, 15, 18, and 19), we only tend to find out that the reason for usurpation resorting to despotism is that otherwise "all interests would rise against it" (Constant 1988: 143). Thus usurpation can deal with recalcitrant individuals with its own techniques but apparently not with the resistance of factions or parties or interests. Nevertheless, Constant considers the synthesis, whatever its exact nature, to be necessarily unsuccessful in the modern world, because despotism itself cannot last. Since he does not tell us that usurpation is wholly replaced by a despotic system, or if only partially and then in which part, it is hard to know why the argument should apply to the synthesis. Most importantly, he does not face the question of the internal relationship of two systems, between usurpation, based not only on modern institutions but modern dynamism entailed by incessant activity and innovation, and despotism that is still, in his description, a rather traditional formation missing not only significant modern inventions like elections, the press, and the rule of law but also the energy enabling the regime for successful operation in the modern system of states.

Napoleon's state in any case proved itself superior to the motley absolutist states traditionally denounced as despotic, and Constant cannot explain this phenomenon to the extent he assimilates the new, usurpation, to the old regimes of Europe. His second important innovative move, linking usurpation to militarism, helps to account however for the modernity of Napoleonic rule. The causal arrow operates in both directions. First, the system of war or of conquest has a propensity to produce usurpation by military men. The argument is simple, but powerful. In a commercial civilization most people are not warlike. Thus, the stratum that practices the arts of war becomes more differentiated from the social structure than were in earlier ages citizen soldiers or aristocratic warriors. The officer corps becomes a distinct corporate entity, with its own mores, preferences, and prejudices with respect to ordinary life, favoring unanimity, rigid order, and speed over opposition, conflict, and supposedly inefficient procedures (Constant 1988: 60–61). In particular, military men develop a condescending and even contemptuous attitude to civilian methods of dealing with problems of violence, especially the slow mechanisms of the rule of law and legal procedure. Unfortunately however this attitude, which may parallel that of some traditionalists, is in the case of soldiers coupled with the actual possession of the means of violence that can be substituted for legal means. Thus there is a link between the sociological character and social psychology of the modern army and both the application of extra-legal measures dealing with crisis, and the specter of usurpation that would enthrone violence in the place of law.

From the opposite perspective, Constant argues that war is the usurper's most fundamental (inconsistently: sole) resource for his survival (Constant 1988: 163). Eloquence in the modern world supposedly no longer works, thus armed force is the usurper's only secure support (90). Incessant warfare is a good pretext for the usurper's surrounding himself with guards, and by implication to militarize his own society. With his appeal to war, emergency he can substitute military for regular civilian justice, indeed as did Bonaparte, establishing *military commissions* with highly diminished, "expedited" or "curtailed" procedural safeguards (Constant 1988: 61–62, 130). War enables the conqueror at least "to dazzle people's minds" (Constant 1988: 91). Given the threat that free public communication represents to him, he must suppress this also in foreign countries. The only means of doing so is conquest (Constant 1988: 163). In another much less developed epoch of European communication, a usurper like Cromwell, born in war, did not have to resort to ever-new wars. At home, the "something new every three months" that the modern usurper must give to his own institutionalized but manipulated public is military victory.

Thus the usurper needs war, and cannot securely confine himself merely to an occasional just or even rational war. Yet the pretext of pre-emption is almost always available, and can be justified later on by the fact that the attacked defend themselves. Modern, i.e., French Revolutionary militarism has moreover invented according to Constant an entirely new type of pretext: "freeing people from the yoke of governments, which were supposed to be illegitimate and tyrannical" (Constant 1988: 65 fn.2). When liberation takes place the result is often tyrannical rule over the conquered, but as long as conquest is secure, the population of the conquering nation does not seem to mind the contradiction, in other words the fact of being deluded. The patriotic enthusiasm and even intoxication described by Constant finds its limit only in military defeat and the failure of conquest.

We should notice his contradiction: on the one hand usurpation is described as having its own form of self-legitimation, on the other hand, because of its weak symbolic or persuasive power, it is said to be forced to resort to the instruments of despotism. The road to something resembling despotism in the first line of reasoning is not inevitable as in the second, and is based only in the proclivities of the military, and a military usurper. In fact, as the description of usurpation makes clear, modern military government only resembles despotism, and has its own specific organizational forms. Even military justice, parasitic on modern criminal procedure and bureaucratic in nature, is not simply personalistic and voluntaristic *khaddi* justice.

Thus if a modern system of usurpation begins to adopt the instruments of traditional despotism, that according to Constant cannot in any case save it, it must do so because of the failure of its own specific means rooted in successful war. Keeping the Napoleonic experiment in mind, Constant however maintains that such failure is inevitable. The military usurper is a gambler, who stakes his all on successful war. The same public opinion that sustains him would turn against him and his methods with significant defeat. But even when a brilliant general like Bonaparte, sooner or later he will be defeated because of the laws of chance, and because his victories will give rise to more and more powerful alliances of states threatened by the specter of conquest. Unlike a traditional ruler, however, or a popular republic, the system of usurpation cannot survive major military defeat (Constant 1988: 163–164). We are back to fundamental instability. In modern commercial society, neither usurpation nor despotism, nor even their combination can according to him be sustained. All these political forms represent anachronistic atavisms in Constant's thinking.

The idea that in modern society historical forms of despotism and tyranny are obsolete is maintained by Tocqueville much more explicitly than by Constant. He is however equally inconsistent in continually using these terms. Where he differs from Constant is in his much more pessimistic assessment that modern society, based on increasing social equality, is highly prone to its own specific forms of extreme authoritarianism. He tries to explore these in terms of traditional concepts that he is forced however to dramatically alter. As almost universally in the nineteenth century, Tocqueville treats the terms despotism and tyranny as more or less synonyms. But rather uniquely, he breaks the necessary link of these terms to lawless or arbitrary government. Reversing a fundamental premise from Aristotle to Constant (that was rejected by Machiavelli alone, but only in relation to the founding of a new state) arbitrary rule he says may not be tyrannical if it is in the interest of the community. Tyranny or despotism on the other hand can operate within and through despotic *laws*, and indeed by means of procedurally correct, formally general laws that are discriminatory with respect to minority interests. Continuing in this vein, and rejecting Montesquieu's and Kant's approach, the separation of powers turns out to be no guarantee against tyranny if the same power dominates all branches ... the tendency according to him in the United States.[60]

While the idea of a single power acting through a formal separation converges with Constant's notion of modern authoritarian leadership operating through republican institutions, Tocqueville's conception is in fact quite different. Executing a fundamentally sociological turn, the despotic authority he has in mind possesses no political office or holds any formal political powers. The tyranny or despotism of the majority, his famous term, does not even mean that of the electoral majority. The latter can and does act through elected legislatures, and perhaps executives. But juries and the press are not elected in the same way. Yet only when they too are penetrated by the same power as the political branches do minorities lose their protection, turning rule into a tyrannical or despotic one. The reason this happens is because of a social rather than political majority, namely *public opinion* that informs and enforces the conformity of the popular will expressed in all relevant institutions of a democratic political system.

It is thus that Tocqueville radicalizes the views of Madison and Jefferson concerning the dangers of tyranny in republics. He is still ready to seriously entertain their solution: a well-designed system of the separation of powers.[61] But it is no longer clear how such a system, not significantly different than the American one,[62] is really guarded against precisely the phenomenon Tocqueville warns against: the convergence of majority opinion against distinct intellectual, racial, religious, and political minorities. The federal decentralization of the country may produce competing majorities among states and even regions, but does not vitiate the problem *within* them, more relevant in any case in nineteenth century America (see his 260, fn. 7). The resistance of a proto-aristocratic legal profession may inhibit the majorities control of the courts and of judges, but with the interpenetration of lawyers and the political class it is hard to see how the independence of the former can be rigidly maintained. In fact Tocqueville postulates the survival of republican form of life in America as a function above all of two great absences (that will be present in the twentieth century): bureaucratic centralization and militarism.

His critique of administrative centralization is in fact a continuation of the enlightenment identification of absolutist state formation as despotism. What he has in mind however is no longer the absolutist regime; the state he focuses on can exist and develop under different regime forms, including a republican one. His *Old Regime and the French Revolution* (Tocqueville 1955), as it is well known, focuses on the continuity of the bureaucratic state under absolutism, the revolution, Napoleon, and beyond. When fully perfected this state enforces social uniformity and dependence through new financial, administrative, and social scientific methods, without recourse to the violent or arbitrary means traditionally regarded as tyrannical or despotic. But its domination over individuals is all the more effective. And this is doubly so when the state operates in a system of popular sovereignty with all the formal branches of power subordinated to the same will of the people. The bureaucracy on the one hand produces the uniformity of will, on the other hand it is the most efficient instrument possible for harmonizing and extending the effects of a will formally acting through different branches of power.

In America according to Tocqueville administrative centralization did not yet exist. Thus even when there is convergence of national or state branches of power, the administration of decisions will occur locally. He is under no illusions of course concerning the local toleration of minority views and practices. But a locality may have a different majority than the state, or the country, and it seems that the conflict of these different levels can have a restraining effect on each – at least in theory. Tocqueville in fact repeatedly illustrates that this particular version of checks and balances does not work, for example in the area of race relations (Tocqueville 2000: 252, fn. 4) as well as that of intellectual freedom (Tocqueville 2000: 254). With respect to these exceptions, it is unclear whether minorities should fear or favor administrative centralization that was to come to America after the Civil War.

The case is somewhat different with respect to the other significant absence of his own time at least, militarism. There is no greater scourge according to Tocqueville for republics than military glory, manipulated by great generals. It is the influence of glory over a nation's spirit that most easily allows one man to mobilize on behalf of himself the tyranny of the majority. This danger is supposedly absent in the United States because "[t]he Americans have no neighbors and consequently no great wars, financial crises, invasions, or conquests to fear; they need neither heavy taxes nor a numerous army nor great generals ..." (Tocqueville 2000: 278). Paradoxically even Andrew Jackson's presidency is used by Tocqueville to confirm his claim: only in a commercial, prosaic country where military triumphs are irrelevant could a minor triumph like the victory at New Orleans raise a man to the highest office (Tocqueville 2000: 278). This unconvincing argument, whose factual basis could have been used to argue the exact contrary, the vulnerability of Americans to military heroes, is supplemented by a better one. Although often accused of "despotism" and wishing to set up a "dictatorship,"[63] Jackson's politics of states' rights is in fact quite the contrary of what an American despot or dictator would require; political centralization (Tocqueville 2000: 393). In fact Tocqueville is no longer convinced that the Napoleonic paradigm of a great general's glory will remain the modern vehicle of militarism. If because of "the restless spirit of the army" a military oligarchy would be established that would fuse the spirit of bureaucracy with the regimentation of the barracks, its leaders would fuse "the ways of clerks and soldiers" (Tocqueville 2000: note 735). But again the presupposition of such a regime that would be not too different than Tocqueville's bureaucratic model of an authoritarian state whose rulers would be not "tyrants, but rather schoolmasters" (691) is a high level of administrative centralization.

He does not of course exclude the possibility of future military or civilian authoritarianism in America.[64] Indeed he believes that while European militarism and administrative centralization favor these, so does a third trend, American equality. All three are necessary, and they are all depicted as inexorable in the modern world. With respect to the first, militarism, potentially the most violent form, Tocqueville greatly extended Constant's analysis, without the ultimate expectation that a commercial and pacific spirit will necessarily control militarism and the desire for war. The army as a state within the state, or a nation within the nation, plus the desire for promotion more pronounced in an age of equality make the modern military ardently long for war, and for revolutions too when the necessarily pacific spirit of a democratic people counters these ambitions. "Military revolutions ... are always to be feared in democracies." Satisfying the army means increasing its size and/or engaging in actual war, but the danger is only thereby delayed and increased. "War is the surest and shortest means ... to destroy the freedom of democratic nations" (Tocqueville 2000: 650). The only remedy would be to reduce the size of the army, but this option is generally not open in a system of states (Tocqueville 2000: 645–646).

With all this said, Tocqueville considers military tyranny of a victorious general like that of Sulla and Caesar (and Napoleon, too, obviously) only one possible danger in democracies, the less likely one. It is more to be expected he says that war leads not to a military government, but to the continual strengthening of the powers of the civilian one (650). Thus, even as he takes militarism into account, he is able to maintain his general conclusion that "the type of oppression which threatens democracies will be different from anything there has ever been in the world." "It would be more widespread and milder; it would degrade men rather than torment them" (691). He admits that he has himself "vainly searched for a word" to describe this new form, and that "[s]uch old words as 'despotism' and 'tyranny' do not fit ... " (691). In fact he seems to be forced to use the old words continually as in the famous chapters "Tyranny of the Majority" and "What Sort of Despotism Democratic Nations Have to Fear" (250, 690). But the phenomenon he wishes to describe is new.

The new authoritarianism is based on regularity, not arbitrariness. It acts through influence, persuasion, moral compulsion not violence, through the soul and not, like traditional despotism, through the body (255). Thus it is concerned to change motives rather than to sanction acts. While it still needs to separate individuals from one another to destroy the possibility of collective action, the result is achieved not by threats and punishments, but by building on the individualism and privatism of modern life (506ff., 509–510). Thus the new authoritarianism is a sociological and cultural rather than political or legal phenomenon. Its leaders are schoolmasters, clerks, military professionals. While Tocqueville does say that such a system would assume the worst possible form when ruled by one man abandoning all legal forms he is not particularly interested in this possibility (but 539–540).

Constant and Tocqueville thus wind up with very different analyses of modern authoritarian possibilities. Constant focuses on a new political form, misnamed as usurpation, that he does not consider in the long run viable. But his analysis depends on an optimistic philosophy of history, with commercialism replacing militarism. Without that optimism, the conception opens up new political vistas for understanding a new authoritarian form parasitic on republican institutions, whose vehicle is primarily military rule. He is not yet aware of the possibility of one-party regimes. That option does briefly appear in Tocqueville's analysis, when European parties are compared to military organizations (192, 193–195). But the main thrust of his work focuses on oppression and authoritarianism operating through legal and democratic forms, without illegality, usurpation, or personalism. Where in Constant the old terms lose their viability, because they presuppose city states or territorial monarchies, in Tocqueville the same result occurs because modern authoritarianism loses its political form that "despotism' and "tyranny" always presupposed. Only the older forms of despotism are incompatible with a commercial age whose importance Tocqueville too recognizes (539). Where Constant's analysis points to the political form of what the twentieth century will call dictatorship, Tocqueville is a forerunner of the study of the more specific totalitarian phenomenon, understood as an offshoot of mass society.

Nevertheless each shows the obsolescence of the categories of despotism and tyranny, noted by Tocqueville. In Constant's case this happens as he explicitly maintains the incompatibility of the older forms with modern society, and introduces the term usurpation to deal with a new authoritarian pattern. Tocqueville himself manages to water them down beyond recognition by repeatedly applying the traditional terms to countless instances where it is the force of diffuse political opinion or public mores that moves people to abandon or compromise their autonomy. The image of complete cultural un-freedom that is thereby proposed for democratic societies hits the mark only in the rare instances when the conformism of mass culture is intensified and enforced by an extreme political authoritarianism. But for the latter, Tocqueville no longer had a convincing name or category. The gap was to be made up not by Constant's still anachronistic and monarchical term usurpation, overly marked by the specific pattern of

Napoleon's carrier, but by the reinterpreted category of dictatorship with its elective affinity for a republican era.

Dictatorship[65]

The term, as well as the original institution, is Roman, deriving from *dicere*, and *dictare*, and from a political practice of the late sixth or early fifth century BC.[66] Though the date is disputed, it is generally assumed that even this partial, always temporary return to the hated monarchical form[67] occurred under the stress of events, whether or not the precedent of the first dictator Titus Lartius' emergency appointment established the practice or there actually was, prior to this, a *lex de dictatore creando*.[68] What is clear is that unlike tyranny and despotism, and even the partial archaic Greek anticipation of dictatorship, *aisumneteia*, an elective form of "tyranny" (Aristotle *Politics* III. xiv 8), Roman dictatorship comes down to us not as a political ideal type described in detail by philosophers and political thinkers, but as a long-term practice recalled by historical narratives: mainly Titus Livius (Livy 2002) or Plutarchos (Plutarch). Even Polybius pays no attention to dictatorship in the famous systematic section of the *Histories* that treats the highly relevant topic of the stability and longevity of Roman institutions, and mixed government of which dictatorship was evidently an element.[69] Thus the first theoretical treatments we get are early modern: Machiavelli, Bodin, arguably Locke though he does not use the term, Montesquieu, the *Encyclopedia*, and Rousseau, as well as Jefferson in *Notes on Virginia* and Alexander Hamilton in the *Federalist* (70) produced the most famous versions. In view of this state of affairs, or perhaps because they were not treating a living and diverse practice like tyranny in the age of the Socratic philosophers, all the presentations are astonishingly similar, though there are a few differences probably because of the influence of Locke. Even the omissions are the same: chiefly the *dictator rei publicae constituendae*, a permanent and new office given to Sulla in 82 BC (Schmitt 2012) and perhaps proposed for Scipio the younger by Cicero is stressed primarily in the twentieth century, and was apparently earlier considered either the traditional dictatorship legally if not politically speaking (Schmitt 2012) or, in light of the extended time duration, merely a tyrannical form under a misleading name. Thus the two forms[70] of dictatorship all early moderns applaud[71] were the more common type, the *dictatura rei gerunda causa*, meaning getting things done, and always a military dictator appointed in the face of extreme danger in war, and the relatively rare *dictatura seditionis sedandae causa* whose purpose was to suppress civil insurrections, usually plebeian.[72]

The basic practice, as it comes down to us, was the same for both of the two main forms of dictatorship. On the initiative of the Senate, one of the consuls nominated a dictator with a military *imperium* that could be exercised not only in the field, but also within the walls of Rome itself (Bodin, *Six Books* 188). According to Machiavelli this form of nomination was to spare the pride and dignity of the consuls, but that does not seem likely (*Discourses* 204). There was only one case when a dictator was appointed differently, by a popular assembly, namely Fabius Maximus during the wars with Hannibal, but Livy insists that for this very reason he was only "acting dictator" (Livy 2002: XXII. 8 and 31), but Livy admits that nevertheless Fabius was "the all-powerful dictator."[73]

According to Bodin the dictator received a commission in the sense of the later absolutist state, and Rousseau follows him, but the admission that the dictator could neither be recalled, nor, more importantly, his term "prorogued" beyond the maximum of six months (that he himself could reduce) indicates that there was no sovereign in the modern sense to issue a true commission (Bodin 2003: 281 who speaks of a single case of prolongation; Rousseau 1996: 217). Rousseau thinks that it was especially important to have such a short term, because the one-year term of the Decemvirs led or almost led to tyrannical usurpation (218). Machiavelli too repeatedly stresses the Decemvir story as the backdrop against which the powers of dictators could have been defined (chs. xxxv and xl). But the truth of this statement is not supported by the classical sources. What is certain, is that unlike the Decemvirs, dictators could not legislate, and especially change or abolish any of the political institutions (Machiavelli 203; Rousseau 218). He could suspend the powers of command of the Senate and the magistrates, but could not touch their office, nor probably stop the various assemblies from meeting (Bodin 345). Thus according to Bodin the dictator was in no sense sovereign (188), a point contradicted by the *Encyclopedia* (temporary sovereign) without however contesting the definition of sovereignty as legislation, nor asserting that the dictator could legislate (Nolte 1973). All agree that the powers of the dictator were extraordinary, and that he could put people to death without appeal to the popular assembly, but Montesquieu at least says that the point was to intimidate rather than administer punishments (1994: 14).

While Machiavelli debates with unnamed authors who thought that the institution of dictatorship was responsible for its abuse in the permanent "dictatorships" or tyrannies of Sulla and Caesar, until Jefferson who faced the issue in his native Virginia, it is hard to find a modern author representing the contested view.[74] None of the early modern political philosophers – except Hobbes to whom no abuse could be involved, and perhaps Spinoza – agree with this unfavorable judgment. In their case the doctrine of absolute sovereignty may have been responsible for what was long a deviant view. Only the *Encyclopedia* speaks of dictatorship being in the close neighborhood of tyranny (Nolte 1973: 925). According to Machiavelli, Sulla and Caesar would have used other titles or excuses if the dictatorship did not exist (1950: 201–202), and Rousseau argues that the sources of the danger were the external armies and not any internal institution (218). According to these authors, the dictatorship, whether based on external or internal emergency, was based on the strict application of public law, and those who established permanent or legislative dictatorships broke the law (or forced the Romans to adopt illegal laws?) and were therefore tyrants or usurpers but not really dictators whatever their title. Rousseau goes as far as to argue that (internal) dictatorships should have been used against later military usurpers. According to him the sparing use of the term, in due part to its displacement by the more openly anti-popular *senatus consultum ultimum*, that involved the assumption of illegal powers for legal magistrates, was more dangerous for the republic.

The contrast is between legal establishment of an extra-legal magistrate, the dictator, and legal magistrates engaging in illegal or extra-legal activity. The second of these comes closer strictly speaking to Locke's famous prerogative, than to dictatorship proper. Given the separation of powers, the executive power must have the discretion in grave emergencies to act "without the prescription of law, and sometimes even against it." Law cannot foresee all eventualities, and the legislative power is likely to be too slow and certainly too numerous (XIV. 159–160). Yet Locke was not against the people attempting to define and even confine the prerogative by legislation. He only doubts that this can be done effectively precisely because this law too cannot anticipate the conditions under which it too may have to be transgressed. What remains is a popular check, appeal to God, or revolution restricted to extreme circumstances, by Locke. This is a clear difference with classical theory of dictatorship as late as Machiavelli, who insists on the requirement of the strictest legality and delimitation of the dictatorial jurisdiction. On the other hand, Locke probably did not intend the prerogative to mean the suspension of all the laws and the power of the different branches of the separation of powers and their temporary displacement by pure discretion. He implies only that the executive can engage in extra-legal action, and not that he can suspend the whole legal framework.

Authors after Locke, living under monarchies where the establishment of a magistrate even temporarily displacing the king was out of the question, tended to present the two options, executive prerogative and dictatorship, as two more or less equivalent options. Montesquieu (1994: 14) contrasts the Roman dictatorship with the Venetian state inquisitors; while Rousseau (1996: 217) thinks an executive prerogative effects only government, while dictatorship, temporarily, is the exercise of sovereignty (though here he is quite inconsistent since according to him the dictator makes no laws, and all law making is suspended during a dictatorship). The distinction between prerogative and dictatorship was however difficult to sustain if the concept of dictatorship was to be applied to current political realities, that was rarely done (Nolte 1973). Bodin's commissioners were officials of the absolutist monarch, thus under the control of the king as a normal magistrate. Moreover, they were instruments of the destruction of the inherited legal order and did not aim at its preservation or restoration (Friedrich 1968). Quite uniquely, Leibniz spoke of the absolute monarch as a dictator *perpetuus* (Nolte 1973). In that concept, the difference between extraordinary and normal magistracy disappears. Finally, when Lincoln implicitly spoke of his suspension of habeas corpus using Roman justification for dictatorship, and, even more, when he referred to a general's abrogation of property rights as well as the president's (along with the implied usurpation of *legislative* powers) as both "dictatorship," the differences between Locke's prerogative, and the classical Roman concept, was no longer relevant. There was, first probably in the presidential, i.e., the monarchical republic a trend toward the combination of the options: most fatefully, the open-endedness of the prerogative and the immense powers of dictatorship. When that combination acquired its full force, the historically almost unambiguous identification of the category of dictatorship with the Roman model had changed to include dimensions that were traditionally excluded: extra-legality of origin, legislation, and at least relative longevity. In spite of earlier anticipations, as in Lincoln's just cited usage, these accretions led to a generally negative evaluation of dictatorships only in the twentieth century.

The two types of change (expansion and negative evaluation) were anticipated, but did not become definitive during the French Revolution. The term dictatorship was in fact used relatively seldom. Jean-Joseph Mounier, the first leader of the Constitutional Committee of the Constituent Assembly (cited by Carré de Malberg 1920 who cites Thiers' "History of the French Revolution I," appendix) described as "supreme dictatorship" the proposal (in 1789!!!!) *Convention nationale*. Marat (Nolte 1973: 908) apparently called for dictatorship (plebiscitary – Nolte 1973; of the poor, according to Furet 1981 and Lefort 1989: 86) as an emergency measure to save the revolution, but since it is not clear how temporary this proposed solution was meant to be we do not know to what extent the Roman model was adhered to despite the positive connotation. He may have already meant something similar to the non-Roman republican "despotism of liberty against the despotism of kings" (Saint Just) or "against tyranny" (Robespierre) (Lefort 1989: 77–78ff.; Mandt 1973: 170). On the other hand, we know that Robespierre, who suffered under comparisons with Sulla, Catiline, and Cromwell, and was arrested amidst cries of down with and death to the tyrant, spent part of his last speech to the Convention answering the charge that he "sought" a dictatorship (Nolte 1973: 909). These usages may indicate the beginning of a shift toward a polemical, negative usage of the term.

The French Revolution brought only hints of a future change of meaning in a negative direction. More characteristic was the beginning of an expansion that linked the concept to the constituent power (Schmitt 2012). The decisive case was the suspension of the already ratified Constitution of 1793 before its actual coming into effect, and the proclamation of revolutionary government based in the National (Constituent) Convention. Here too the justifications sought to be Roman: an already valid constitution was supposedly interrupted in the name of public safety, during an external and internal war, in the name of the same constitution: "The provisional government of France is revolutionary until the peace … the ministers, the generals, and constituted bodies are placed under the surveillance of the Committee of Public Safety" (Decree on Rev 10 October 1793; Furet and Ozouf 1989: "Revolutionary Government"). The question of the legal validity of this decree was however more than a bit doubtful: the Convention should have been dissolved upon the ratification of the constitution that did not legally provide for emergency government, by its author or any other agency. The idea that a constituent assembly rather than a constitution could be the authority for dictatorship was in any case new, and was to influence both Karl Marx and even more Carl Schmitt. More important in its own context was the change of the interpretation of revolutionary government (dictatorship) from the preservation to creation of a new order of things, as in Robespierre's famous speech "On Revolutionary Government." The Roman dictatorship was not permitted to legislate, but the revolutionary government's task was to establish a constitutional one that cannot exist before it is established. Thus, the model of dictatorship either came to mean a subterfuge for a very different phenomenon, or was already in the process of being redefined, as Schmitt and all who directly follow him (like Bobbio) maintain (Schmitt 2012; Bobbio 1989). Bobbio is torn between the two possibilities: dictatorship meaning not only an interruption within a single legality but a provisional and creative state of affairs between two, old and new constitutions (Bobbio 1989: 162, 163).

It is possible that the association of the expanded model of revolutionary dictatorship with the reign of terror did eventually contribute to the eventual negative connotation for the concept of dictatorship, one that to be sure could be discounted by reference instead to the tyranny or despotism of the Committee of Public Safety. (The reference to the constituted bodies, among them ministries organized around the principle of a separated executive power should have, but apparently did not block the utilization of the traditional categories.) To be sure, even after the fall of Robespierre this association was a badge of honor for the revolutionary left who would reserve the terms tyrant and despot for either the old kings or "the usurper" Bonaparte. The latter however was greeted by the Council of the Five Hundred during his *coup d'état* with both cries of down with the tyrant and down with the dictator (Bobbio 1989 on Babeuf and Buonarotti). Even Nolte who has examined this question in some detail cannot seem to tell for sure whether dictatorship in this context meant the accusation that Bonaparte wanted to exercise extraordinary powers, like the Committee of Public Safety until the achievement of peace, or was the name for a tyrant who grabs power entirely illegally. Since Napoleon, whose dictatorship in the modern sense is beyond much doubt,[75] did not, like the Jacobins, attempt to renew the term or the concept, the decisive change of meanings had to wait until others did. And this happened as I see it mainly because of the efforts of the revolutionary left that were impressed by the radical revolutionary project whatever they thought of the reign of terror in particular.[76]

Undoubtedly, Marx's views of dictatorship had many anticipations among early socialists and radical egalitarians (Bobbio 1989; Nolte 1973). Since however he has brilliantly described the phenomenon itself, in *The Class Struggles in France* and *The Eighteenth Brumaire of Louis Bonaparte*, his initially rather traditional use of the term itself as well as the changes he made are both highly instructive. Simply assuming the rather new idea that a constituent assembly rather than a constitution could supply the authority for dictatorship, Marx has no compunction about applying the classical notion of dictatorship to General Cavaignac who was formally empowered to break the *workers' uprising with a* state of siege in June 1848, by the National Constituent Assembly (Marx 1963: 28–29, 34–35; Napoleon's rule, though described precisely in the modern sense of the term dictatorship, is however called despotism 121). If Cavaignac is described in the most negative terms, this is because Marx detested the state of affairs that the extraordinary measures of the general were able to protect. In fact with such exceptions, having to do with military dictatorship on the right, Marx and Engels did not use "dictatorship" negatively, and at first tended to refer to transitional periods in the classical sense. Even the military authoritarian regimes of both Napoleons are not referred to by this term.[77]

At the same time, the category dictatorship of the proletariat, referring to a more extended period of rule in its final version, an idea that probably appeared in his writings given the negative lesson of the failed Revolutions of 1848,[78] caused his interpreters untold difficulties. Even if continuing a line of leftist and egalitarian proposals (and the analysis of Lorenz von Stein), Marx's idea takes its place in an elaborate and highly influential system. In the same year as his analysis of Louis Bonaparte, he wrote to J. Weydemeyer "that the class struggle necessarily leads to the dictatorship of the proletariat" and "that this dictatorship itself only constitutes the transition to the abolition of all classes and to a classless society" (text: 1852). In the more famous *Critique of the Gotha Program*[79] he then wrote that "the state in the political transition between capitalist and communist society can be nothing but the revolutionary dictatorship of the proletariat" (same page Napoleon's regime: police guarded military despotism in *Gotha Program* 538). Two aspects of the use of the term are new here, or in this tradition. First, dictatorship is depicted as of a class not a single person or even a political group or institution and as a form of the state over an undetermined, probably relatively long period. And second, the same point in effect, the term transition no longer has the sense of temporary or provisional but of a regime. Nevertheless, Marx strongly attacks the charge that this dictatorship would be as Bakunin claimed of a small elite *and* (as all dictatorships according to the anarchist) permanent, if in very unconvincing and mainly rhetorical *ad hominem* terms. We should note that in two respects, by stressing drive to permanence and thus only the negativity of dictatorships, it is the anarchist who is more prophetic in anticipating the future meaning of the term.

Nevertheless, it is Marx who achieves the most important breakthrough to the new meaning by successfully postulating a non-Roman model of revolutionary dictatorship. It is another matter that, as the debate with Bakunin shows, he has left himself and his followers with some explaining to do. Among the latter, two important interrelated answers emerge: (1) the dictatorship of the proletariat is dictatorship only in the sense that all states are repressive apparatuses[80] and (2) the proletariat's dictatorship would be really one only over the minority of previous exploiters, and thus would be the most complete democracy of the immense majority. The first interpretation was absent in the 1848 writings on Paris and Frankfurt. But eventually it may have entered his thought, and was certainly axiomatic for some later advocates of the dictatorship of the proletariat such as Lenin. It represents a partially negative concept of dictatorship, but only to the extent that all states are machines of oppression, and is a positive one to the extent that the dictatorship of the proletariat – unlike right-wing authoritarian regimes – uniquely aims at the abolition of the state, and therefore itself. It preserves the idea of temporary authoritarian rule, but the time limitation now is tied to no purpose that could be accomplished in a relatively short period. Gone too is the idea that dictatorship represents something extraordinary with respect to normal forms of politics. The normal form of the state is dictatorship.

The second Marxian view represents the formulation of a hitherto unparalleled affirmative concept of dictatorship, identifying it with the most complete democracy (modeled by the Paris Commune) before the abolition of the state is possible.[81] No other concept of dictatorship previously understood the form as in itself normatively more desirable than what came before; hitherto dictatorship was only a good in an instrumental sense of serving something that was a genuine value. That instrumental character remains even in the commune model but only to the extent that an even better future is being served. To the extent that democracy is a good, so is perforce the most complete democracy hitherto known.

Neither concept represents much help with understanding modern dictatorships, so well analyzed by Marx himself under different names (mainly: military despotism) that was to come down to us as Bonapartism.[82] But the fact that Marx's followers continued to use the concept of the dictatorship of the proletariat was to be initially more important than his own analysis. The success of revolution in Russia led by a Marxist party allowed the conclusion of an experimental answer to the question concerning dictatorship in the name of the proletariat that divided the German Marx and the Russian Bakunin. Not surprisingly, in the end Lenin preferred Marx's answer in theory and the model of Bakunin's fears in practice. Himself plagued by charges (of Martov, Luxemburg, and the young Trotsky) of seeking one person or small group dictatorship, he resolutely varied the unhelpful and partially inconsistent answers of Marx concerning all states being dictatorships and that of the proletariat (or of the workers and peasants in one version) being actually a democracy. The re-emergence of workers' councils in 1917 allowed him to adopt Marx's commune model, before he was to instrumentalize the soviets (Lenin 1967a).

After the taking of power in November 1917, the dictatorial – i.e., oppressive – character of the Bolsheviks was more and more frankly admitted, as was eventually the substitution of the class by the party as the agent of dictatorship (Lenin 1967c). Trotsky, now the most open in his espousal of terroristic dictatorship (in Trotsky 2007, *Terrorism and Communism*), was to redefine the question of democracy from a focus on participation in the business of rule to the interests represented by the rulers (in Trotsky 1980). With all these changes the positive self-description of the regime as dictatorship over the long haul was preserved, to the satisfaction of the opponents of the Bolsheviks who saw the confirmation of their criticisms in a new oppressive, undemocratic, and arbitrary form of rule. The liberals and democratic socialists among them were happy to concede the term to the heirs of Lenin.[83] Nevertheless, after the dissolution of the Constituent Assembly, the authors of the first post-revolutionary Soviet constitution in 1918 (of the RSFR) still sought to recover the idea of the democracy of the immense majority, and dictatorship over a small minority that was thereby excluded from the franchise. The reality was unfortunately already the reverse, as the destruction of the only democratically elected national legislature in Russian history, until the 1990s, clearly showed (Anweiler 1975).

Astonishingly, as Carl Schmitt was the first to show, a similar, affirmative reconstruction of the concept of dictatorship occurred on the counter-revolutionary right, but, until his own work, without any flirtation with the idea of democracy. With the decline of monarchical legitimacy, authors like Bonald in France and Donoso Cortes in Spain came to represent an anti-liberal and anti-democratic program resting on the pure decision of authoritarian forces for a dictatorship capable of putting an end to the government by discussion and the supposed decline of the political (Schmitt 1985). Whatever his claims on behalf of this doctrine, Schmitt himself, in opposition to what he says about Donoso-Cortes' decisionism, is closer to Marx in understanding at least the genuinely modern form of dictatorship as linked to democratic claims of legitimacy, and even the popular sovereignty detested by the counter-revolution. For the first time, a clear distinction is presented between the Roman model, now called *commissarial* dictatorship, including the commissioners of the absolutist regimes, and modern revolutionary, *sovereign* dictatorship. Both are commissioned by higher authority, for a temporary period and a particular purpose, the former by constituted and the latter by constituent powers, supposedly the sovereign people. The latter idea is equally indebted to Rousseau and to Marx. While *commissarial* dictatorship is to protect an established legal system, sovereign dictatorship is to establish a new constitution (Schmitt 2012). Thus the former is compatible with a liberal democracy, if established, while the latter is a revolutionary dictatorship that can establish only a contradictory rule of law state where conflict between sovereignty and constitution, constituent and constituted powers, legitimacy and legality, plebiscitary and representative forms of democracy seem to be unavoidable. Schmitt assumes that the only source of legitimacy in a modern society is popular sovereignty, but juxtaposing this principle to liberal democratic ones he concludes by 1931–1932 at the latest, with earlier anticipations galore, that a plebiscitary authoritarian regime may be the most consistent claimant of democratic legitimacy (Schmitt 2004). He thus joined the nineteenth century justifications of Caesarism, in particular Émile Ollivier so well described by Rosanvallon (2000: 186ff.).

Interestingly, Schmitt, who clearly utilized the prestige and positive reputation of both the Roman type of dictatorship and French notions of the constituent power, never explicitly draws the conclusion, namely that there is a third type of dictatorship: a permanent revolutionary one (Bobbio 1989). Thus E. Nolte too can point out that it is not plausible to make constituent assemblies rather than single, charismatic individuals the paradigmatic holders of sovereign dictatorship in the name of the people. Schmitt of course rejected the idea that the constituent power of the people needs to be expressed through any particular procedure, and allowed for the possibility that a plebiscitary leader successfully claim identity with the popular sovereign. What he did not see or did not reveal, until 1933 or soon after, was that the two ideas of plebiscitary constitution maker and plebiscitary authoritarian constituted power when taken together can imply the permanence of the condition *ex lex* that he at least considered the hallmark of all dictatorships.[84]

Even if Schmitt did not work out a paradigm that could include the most characteristic forms of twentieth century dictatorships, his two types allow for development that would be able to account for these.[85] Ernst Fraenkel, using the fundamental distinction in the form of commissarial and revolutionary, shows (without making the argument general) how the two forms together led to Hitler's absolute dictatorship (Fraenkel 2006). Under the name of totalitarianism this type was more or less successfully extended to the Soviet Union (by Arendt 1973; and Friedrich and Brzezinski 1965 among many others) and in the process tended to subsume the problem and concept of dictatorship altogether, along with important dimensions of the more traditional concept of despotism and even tyranny (abolition of the public-private distinction; of the separation of powers; link to *coups d'état* – open or hidden). But the analysis of other independent forms (Linz 2000; Linz and Stepan 1978; O'Donnell 1973) under headings like authoritarianism, bureaucratic authoritarianism, and post-totalitarianism came to help us see more differentiation in the forms of dictatorship, the common genus.[86] It remains an important task to analyze the category of dictatorship as indeed the common class concept in the midst of variation, one that can be accomplished because of the overlap of legal form in the context of different forms of legitimacy.

Why dictatorship?

In the historical sociology of knowledge implied here and anticipated by Constant and Tocqueville however inconsistently, tyranny and despotism are forms of government restricted to non-modern forms of politics.[87] *Tyranny* is a typical authoritarian form of small city states where rulers could stay in power through violence, often through foreign troops (Aristotle *Politics*; Renaissance *signorie* with its condottiere; and, used in this way, with a grain of salt – in Colonial America). While republican thinkers continue to utilize it, theoretically at least it is no longer relevant in periods of European state formation in large-scale, heavily populated, multi-ethnic territorial states where hereditary monarchies played the central role. Here, analogies with large, imperial territorial states elsewhere seemed obvious, along with the category available for such states since Aristotle, in one version his seventh governmental form: *despotism*. This "orientalist" conceptual move, actually responded to the Hobbesian complaint concerning the polemical use of the concept of tyranny for some or all monarchies, since in the service of absolutism or enlightened or legal despotism the term could be used and was used by Bodin, Voltaire, and the Physiocrats among others in a descriptive or even positive sense. Nevertheless, the highly polemical original formulation of Aristotle was radicalized by Montesquieu for whom even the Asian prototype, and not only its form applied to the traditional three types of government, represents corrupt political forms based on nothing but fear. The enemies of absolutist state formation tended to assume this polemical version that again tended to violate the norms of a new science of politics as articulated by Machiavelli and Hobbes. In any case, with the end of absolutist state formation, and the decline of monarchical legitimacy linked to the secularization of politics,[88] the concept of despotism, both over-polemical and increasingly obsolete, suffered the fate of its predecessor. Whatever uses historians like Tocqueville and later theorists of Oriental Despotism like Wittfogel would find for the term, despotism no longer played a major role after the Napoleonic period to describe recurring forms of authoritarian rule in the West (Wittfogel 1963). It made sense at best for libertarian critics who – absurdly enough – tended not to distinguish among forms of the state, and thus could denounce even modern liberal democratic states that utilized instruments like taxation, economic regulation, and redistribution (Hayek 2007). For others the concept was now obsolete, at least from the theoretical point of view.

Thus the conceptual obsolescence of the terms tyranny and despotism can be explained. The same is not true for the new choice of dictatorship. In an assessment, Norberto Bobbio helpfully focuses on the similarities and differences of the three terms, at least in their traditional form. Tyranny, despotism, and dictatorship are all forms of absolute rule by monocrats. Where tyranny is neither legitimate nor necessarily temporary, despotism is legitimate and possibly long term. Dictatorship is temporary, and legitimate, and unlike despotism its legitimacy is not traditional but is based on law and appeal to necessity (Bobbio 1989: 160). To the question however why a term denoting legal and temporary authority comes to be used for forms of rule that may be neither, Bobbio points to what he takes to be similar in two forms of dictatorship, traditional and revolutionary, modern: contexts of crisis and temporary character (Bobbio 1989: 162–163). He no longer can seriously add, along with Schmitt, commissioned status (instead: he calls it merely symbolic investiture), and is forced to admit that provisionality may be only a claim, not the reality for modern dictatorships. With this admission and those of other differences (monocratic agent vs. group, non-legislative vs. constituent powers), the argument from mere similarity fails. What we have left is a legitimating claim on behalf of one form that wishes to validate itself by using the name of another. And so reformulated there is much that would be true in this hypothesis, which however does not reveal the whole story and especially the reasons for the adoption of the concept of dictatorship, by both friends and enemies of authoritarianism – to provide a more complex explanation, Bobbio's stresses on the specificity of modern forms of legitimation remain however central.

There are three issues intertwined in this stress: value freedom and self-description, the relationship of legitimacy and legality (and: legitimacy as a legality substitute), and, finally, republican government and popular sovereignty. If anything the problem of value freedom and the suspicion of polemical concepts is stronger in the period when dictatorship becomes a key political category than in Hobbes' time, or during the decline of the category of despotism in the early nineteenth century. Nevertheless, as the history of the other two terms shows, it is difficult to maintain a neutral status for terms concerning the most intense political conflicts. A way of avoiding the distortions due to polemical terms, was to use terms that were really self-descriptions and self-justifications.

As we have seen this was possible in the case of dictatorship, first and foremost because the prestige of the Roman category was mobilized by democratic, socialist, and conservative critics of the liberal era. What "immanent" critics, liberal or anarchists, had to do was point to the contradiction between claim and reality, something they could do on the bases even of Roman experience culminating in the lifetime dictatorships of Sulla and Caesar, or the organizational models of the self-admitted vanguards of future dictatorships. Of course when the future became contemporary, the task of criticism became clearer, with the category of dictatorship however recovering a strongly polemical dimension. To sum up, even though there are important anticipations of a negative turn of the concept of dictatorship during the French Revolution and in the nineteenth century, it is only with the post-World War I dictatorships that the term acquires its primarily negative connotations. To be sure, the dictatorships themselves and their intellectual spokesmen and admirers continue to try to use an affirmative concept of dictatorship, but they fail in the discussions of free publics at least well before the manifest failure of their political projects. Interestingly, the dictatorships themselves eventually come to de-emphasize the term and look for suitable substitutes. But they fail in this attempt as well; the field is delivered to the critics of dictatorship.

Why do the holders of new forms of authoritarian power need to make such strong historical but vulnerable claims, perhaps (though I don't admit this) based only on historical analogies? Here it is important to stress again the insight that under modern conditions of complexity all rule rests on a variety of forms of consent and compliance and has to be legitimated (Weber 1978), and that given the assumption of democratic sovereignty traditional forms of legitimation collapse. Tyranny and despotism, by the time of the emergence of specifically modern form of authoritarian rule, were so negatively loaded that the force of the originally Hobbesian social scientific objection could not be evaded. Not only the authoritarians themselves, but also the analysts of authoritarian rule, considered these forms incapable of legitimation in the *modern* world. Dictatorship however had the positive aura of the Roman republic attached to it at a time when republicanism, rule of law, and mixed governments, in some sense part of the Roman heritage, were on the order of the day. Moreover, as Bobbio argued, unlike tyranny and despotism, dictatorship is linked already in Rome to a specific form of legitimacy based on necessity or emergency (both implying a provisional character, i.e., for the duration of the crisis, emergency or necessity), and even more legality. While necessity implied only an instrumental form of legitimacy (a necessary evil in the service of a high good), the idea of legality contributed a more positive sense of legitimation. In the French Revolution it was these claims that were reattached to a revolutionary form of government, with considerable success, even if the positive understanding of dictatorship was rare.

The Schmittian attempt to apply the Roman idea of "for the sake of legality" to revolutionary dictatorships was not successful. These forms were often introduced by *coups d'état*, which broke with the old law, even if supposedly creating new constitutional orders. As against this exaggeration, his linkage of democratic, popular sovereignty to plebiscitary dictatorships is much more plausible. Dictatorship in this version satisfies the difficult burden of legitimacy, by a combination of arguments from crisis and necessity as well as from democracy, the latter as modern a form of legitimation as the rule of law.

The relationship of dictatorship to modern democracy concerns not only matters of legitimacy or legitimation, but institutions as well. This has been more the concern of those who understood popular sovereignty in terms of republican rather than democratic government. Most obviously, tyranny and despotism, whatever their origins and transferred meanings, are monarchical forms. Tyrants are either kings turned lawless or are new leaders who seek (often successfully in one or two generations) to become kings. Despots are kings as well, of vastly extended households. This is fundamental in spite of the possibility implied already by Aristotle to transfer the meanings of tyranny and tyrannical, despotism and despotic, to democracy as well as oligarchy. Dictatorship however always was and remains a republican form. Even today we do not refer to kings as dictators, however authoritarian they may be. Traditionally, the reference to republics meant only that at least a large and important sector of the subjects has or participates in the supreme power in the polity. As in one interpretation of Aristotle presented here, a *polis* or a republic can be an aristocracy, a polity or even a monarchy, but not formally speaking a tyranny or despotism. Kant, for example, excluded democracy from republican forms, and so did the American framers. In its Roman version, the republican idea is linked with a model of mixed government (partially resembling the Aristotelian *politeia*, the non-corrupt democracy), and in the early modern period republic (vs. democracy) is redefined to mean separation of powers and representative government. As we have seen in Montesquieu, Rousseau, Kant, and Madison it is one or both of these last institutions whose negation is understood as despotism or tyranny.

Dictatorship thus can be seen as compatible with all the relevant meanings of the republic. The classical version was of course an institution of the Roman republic, and could not abolish the popular assemblies and the Senate, the main republican institutions, or the consuls, the executive power of mixed government with a dualistic executive. More deeply, dictatorship could be understood as itself an important feature of mixed government. It is indeed more *mon*archical than the consuls, and implied a temporary reversion to the hated kingship at a time when the safety of the republic could be secured in no other way. But it is a mistake to call it tyrannical, given all the institutional checks the dictator could not remove. In terms of one meaning of tyranny, dictatorship was not an illegal usurpation. And, dictatorship incorporated the learning experience referred to by Polybius (book VI) and Cicero (1943: II. 1–2, 41, 56), and stressed by Machiavelli according to which mixed government was the response to the historical instability of republics. Finally, modern dictatorship did not abolish but sought to use institutions of the separation of powers, legislatures, and courts. This was the insight of Constant, an insight particularly relevant to modern conditions of authoritarian rule. He could have mentioned the interest to produce written constitutions and elaborate legal codes as well. These practices are unknown to classical tyranny or despotism, at least if we mean by the latter the archetype rather than the absolute monarchy that was, especially in its French form, a mixed institutional universe. Again, the Roman category of dictatorship could be relatively easily adapted to an authoritarian option that did not abolish, but coexisted even in the form of revolutionary provisional government with classical and modern republican forms. Augustus, who refused to add the title dictatorship to his many offices, and preferred the term princeps, adhered to this practice most famously.

Of course, under many dictatorships, especially the totalitarian type, criticism could easily point to the death rather than coexistence of republican forms. It could be well asked whether we are still dealing with a learning mechanism of republican politics, or rather a tertiary level learning which the Romans experienced already with Sulla, and then later emperors leading to the abolition and not the preservation of republican forms. The trend under modern dictatorships, interestingly, is not the abolition of republican institutions but in two other directions: instrumentalization and dualization. The type of dual state of prerogative and normal dimensions described by E. Fraenkel for Nazi Germany seems to characterize all modern dictatorships if they survive long enough (see Sharlet on the Soviet Union in Tucker 1977). Crucially, the coexistence and functional complementarity of the two dimensions of the state transforms the diachronic Roman succession of the normal and extraordinary into synchrony. But with one fundamental difference: in Rome the norm was primary, setting out the boundaries and limits between itself and the extraordinary, while the modern forms are based on the primacy of the prerogative state (Fraenkel 2006). This feature alone can be described as the vitiation of the rule of law, and therefore of republican government or their strong subordination at the very least. With popular legitimacy as the standard, dictatorship cannot be maintained under modern conditions as a genuinely republican form. This is one reason (along with the immense powers of the Roman dictator) that constitution makers designing emergency provisions and political theorists (Neumann 1966) no longer wish to describe true commissarial forms as dictatorships. The usage "constitutional dictatorship" suggested by Rossiter and Friedrich never really was established, for obvious reasons. The concept of dictatorship is now a thoroughly polemical concept, almost never used in self-identification. Even Marxist-Leninists rarely stress the dictatorship of the proletariat, and prefer speaking about popular or socialist democracy even as they have not changed their substantive positions.

Alternatives: Bonapartism, autocracy, totalitarianism?

Should "dictatorship" therefore follow tyranny and despotism to the social scientific dustbin of polemical concepts that have become historically obsolete? The case for historical obsolescence could have been certainly made when the term was extended from commissarial to the sovereign type, and from both to permanent types of authoritarian rule. Among these options there were huge differences in spite of some important similarities. How the first of these extensions turned out to be, even before Schmitt's theoretical case for it, can be seen by Marx's simple application, in the path of the National Convention of 1793, of the Roman model of the extraordinary but legal defense of a constitution to the defense, of an also extraordinary, legitimate if not legal process of constitution making under a democratically elected assembly. Nevertheless, the second extension to a permanent authoritarian form in the hands of a man like Louis Bonaparte, or a group, who either carried out an illegal coup or, as Mussolini and Hitler, used a formal legal process as a disguise for an underlying illegality should have been more difficult. Marx therefore has some historical justification as against his posterity when he refused to use dictatorship to describe the results of the two Eighteenth of Brumaires. Nevertheless, the usage was well established in the wake of early twentieth century dictatorships, and was applied even retroactively to Cromwell and Napoleon, so much so that Marx's followers have no qualms describing the rule of either Bonaparte as "military dictatorships." Nevertheless, Marxism did also produce an alternative concept, one that has been regarded within this tradition as more "scientific," the concept of Bonapartism.

Marx at his best, as the author of *The 18th Brumaire* and *The Civil Wars in France* left us a sociological analysis of Bonapartism[89] that served as the theory with which his important followers (Trotsky, Gramsci, Poulantzas, and Vajda among many others) tried to understand the dictatorships of our time. Marx himself saw no need to develop a general theory because he probably believed that he confronted a unique case and saw the next century in any case as that of socialism rather than dictatorships. In spite of this limitation, what he wrote on the *coup d'état* of Louis Bonaparte remains the most influential single source for all Marxists on the problem of "dictatorship." Marx's central point was that the secret of Bonapartism lay in the inability of the modern bourgeoisie, under specific circumstances of crisis or challenge, to rule in the political sense. Accordingly, for the sake of its social-economic domination, it needed to cede political power to an agency capable of exercising the power of the executive independently. Marx assumed that the pure or completed form of bourgeois rule is parliamentary government because only this form allowed the class (as against its mere cliques) to aggregate a common will. As others in the nineteenth century however he believed that universal suffrage along with demographic trends would turn this form, via parliamentary democracy[90] into the instrument (or context) of the evolutionary (or revolutionary) triumph of proletarian power. While the weapons of the bourgeoisie against monarchical absolutism, fundamental rights, public opinion, and majority rule could be given restrictive interpretations that denied these benefits to the subaltern classes, they nevertheless had the potential of turning into popular weapons against bourgeois rule itself (*Eighteenth Brumaire* 29–30, 65–66). Bonapartism and the abandonment of parliamentary government along with "bourgeois" freedoms are needed to forestall this outcome.[91]

The reason why a Bonapartist ruler is capable of resisting popular forces (indeed: history itself) is thoroughly analyzed by Marx. He understands the modern state as structured by two armies, the military proper and, even more important, the political bureaucracy possessing truly immense powers of coercion, surveillance, and control (Marx 1963: 61–62, 121–122). Parliamentary government could ruthlessly suppress all opposition and protest only at the cost of undermining its own presuppositions, the bourgeois freedoms and universal suffrage, leading to immense legitimation problems (Marx 1963: 66). Bureaucratic-military rule had to have no such inhibitions. Moreover in its modern form this latter regime did not have to rely on soldiers and administrators alone. Marx points to the existence of significant social support (the peasantry) and even social mobilization on behalf of the popular ruler who could also rely on his own brand of electoral and plebiscitary forms of democratic legitimacy (Marx 1963: 75ff., 123ff.).

It is difficult not to admire the elegance of this construction, and its powerful depiction of the given case. Its transferability is another issue. For the most part the class-based dimension of its analysis has been applied to cases like Italian and German Fascism where proletarian revolution was not in the cards, and where it was already clear that social democratic reformism did not threaten the capitalist system of property.[92] In the case of Stalinist Russia, brilliantly analyzed by Trotsky (2002: *The Revolution Betrayed*) it was supposedly the immaturity (rather than over-ripeness and decline!) of the new dominant economic class, the proletariat that led to the expropriation (not willing surrender as in the *Eighteenth Brumaire*!) of political power by the bureaucracy and its leader.

If we abstract away from all the relevant differences among the cases to which it has been applied, the Marxist conception is reduced to the premise that dictatorship exists when an economically dominant class is forced, willingly or not, to cede political power to those who control the apparatus of the modern state which means that the state organization becomes independent and dominant over society. But in this form the theory is either a truism or is false. Class is a principle of stratification that represents, unlike cast, order, or estate, inequality within formal legal and political equality. No class is legally empowered to rule; the dominance of a class is rooted in private relations rather than public prerogatives. For this reason, the direct political rule of the bourgeoisie is exceptional in modern society (as the Marx of the *Eighteenth Brumaire* tends to admit, even at the cost of contradicting himself); it is political rule by aristocrats, notables, cliques, or individuals drawn from a variety of classes that is the rule. The idea that the bourgeoisie, in order to preserve its economic status, is forced to cede state power to another actor that relies heavily on the state administration is also a good description of solidly liberal social democracy.[93] I do not wish to claim of course that Marx and all his followers failed to recognize many of the characteristically repressive features of modern dictatorships that distinguish this regime from the liberal rule of notables or social democrats. But they failed to derive these features from the idea of a dominant class under threat and unable to rule. Moreover, tending to identify all states as "dictatorships," and analyzing dictatorship in the narrower sense only sociologically, it became very difficult to determine when Bonapartist rule begins or ends. There was an intense debate for example whether the presidential governments immediately before Hitler's taking power were Bonapartist, or only Fascist regimes qualified for this description. August Thalheimer and Antonio Gramsci claimed that fascism was Bonapartism quite in Marx's sense (Poulantzas 1974: 59–61). Trotsky, who rightly saw fascism as a unique new phenomenon, proceeded to describe Hindenburg's emergency presidential regimes as well as the Nazi regime but only after the demobilization of the specifically Fascist mass movement as Bonapartist (Trotsky 1971: 265ff., 275–280, 438–442). In this case however Trotsky was forced to say that it was the decline of a previous dominant class, as against the weakness of an immature new ruling class as in Russia that brought about the class stalemate that allowed the state bureaucracy under executive leadership to assume power independently of the political representatives of each class. Gramsci, moving consciously beyond Marx, more or less systematized a similar idea and distinguished between progressive (Napoleon I) and regressive forms (Napoleon III, Mussolini), the latter helping a rising class to triumph (Gramsci 1971: 219).

Note that in the case of Trotsky the powers of the political analyst threaten to break through the theoretical straightjacket of class theory. He analyzes the stalemate of the Weimar Republic by focusing on the great strength of the system-hostile parties of the Communists and the Nazis, that made the creation of a pro-Republic coalition impossible. These two *koalitionsunfähige* parties were of course even more hostile to each other, actively and violently so, than to the rest of the political field. "The parliament without a majority, with irreconcilable wings offers an obvious and irrefutable argument in favor of *dictatorship*" (Trotsky 1971: 279). Thus the system became ungovernable, and the executive power around the plebiscitary presidency could step forward as the only possible source of political order. Trotsky papers over the fact that his very incisive political analysis is difficult to reconcile with his sociological theory. The Communists are not the working class, that still voted in larger numbers for the Social Democrats, the Nazis are not the bourgeoisie (nor even the representative of any distinct class) the political stalemate to which the executive responds cannot be described as between two classes, but only in terms of a plurality of polarized parties. Less orthodox, though perhaps less insightful in terms of the negative implications for the theory as a whole, Gramsci made the decline of party and class identification the very condition for the rise of unattached political personalities to the position of "charismatic men of destiny" (Gramsci 1971: 210). In the case of both Trotsky and Gramsci the sociological theory makes them stop too soon, before the political analysis is complete. The presidential-plebiscitary regime that asserts its primacy over the parliamentary forces admittedly resembles the Bonapartism of the nineteenth century. But the same is not true for other efforts of executives in democratic countries to respond to the crisis despite Trotsky's mistaken and absurd attempt to extend the concept to the French government in 1934 that was not even presidentialist and had no plebiscitary leader (Trotsky 1971: 438–439). In a different case, that of the first presidential government in Germany under Chancellor Bruening's leadership in 1930, he was forced to revise his own claim of Bonapartism, and make up a category of pre-Bonapartism to fill the gap (276). When the Stalinist and Hitler governments, in their later stages, are also described as Bonapartist, the confusion seems complete.

Not that Trotsky was unaware of the social character of the totalitarian forms of dictatorships. His knowledge of the Soviet Union, his masterly analyses of its bureaucracy and its leader pointed in the right direction. Thus he had special difficulty to stomach the Stalinist Comintern's identification of fascism and democracy, even if it recalled in a caricatural form his own earlier identification of proletarian dictatorship and democracy. His analysis of the social character of fascism indicates his ambiguity and his methodological limits. From the point of view of the proletariat, he strongly argued for a fundamental difference between parliamentary democracy relying on the organizations of reformist labor, and fascism that smashes the independent organizational and cultural expressions of the working class as a whole (Trotsky 1971: 155, 159; Vajda 1972: 14). He should have seen of course that the same is true for all classes when the total state penetrates and instrumentalizes every sphere of life. But he was prisoner of the theory he postulates – falsely and even contradicting Marx, according to whom, for the bourgeoisie, the question of fascism or social democracy is neutral, of only instrumental significance (Vajda 1972: 18; Trotsky 1971: 155, 158). He does not even go so far as to admit, as does Gramsci, that the form of fascist rule, if not its content, is an imposition by a political actor from the point of view of the dominant class itself (Gramsci 1971: 213).

Since Caesarism and Bonapartism are functional or personalistic relations even in Gramsci, it is not clear what he means by this imposed form. Similarly, Trotsky never asked himself what is common to at least some of these forms, beyond his inconclusive juggling with class categories. Thus he omits the role of presidentialism as a political design problem, analyzed by Marx in the *Eighteenth Brumaire*, common to both the French Constitution of 1848 and the Weimar Republic. In spite of Marx's discussion of the problem of emergency and crisis government, and his own awareness of the role of article 48 (the emergency provision; see 1971: 276) in the demise of Weimar, Trotsky does not consider the emergency form as a clue to the meaning of dictatorship. Indeed, we get no clue to what he means by dictatorship when he uses the term in the context of Hindenburg – in spite of the apparent precision of the usage.

Thus, in the end, Marxist analysis, including the generation of the October Revolution, leaves us with the undesirable alternative that we must either consider all class-based regimes to be dictatorships (as many Marxists in fact do in spite of the *Eighteenth Brumaire*), or we must admit that the argument relying on the linkage of dictatorship to the differentiation of those who rule from the dominant class is at the very least incomplete. If we choose the latter option we must realize that on the given ground it could not even be completed, because Marx's most important followers who came to speak of Bonapartist, fascist, and other dictatorships never attempt to tell us *what* different dictatorships have fundamentally in common, beyond the characteristic of a political stalemate between the main contending classes leading to the "relative independence" of the ruling state apparatus, that apply to the absolute monarchy, social democracy, and even the Nehru governments that no one today would identify as dictatorships (Chatterjee 1998).[94]

Very late in the game, obviously influenced by non-Marxist thinkers and the existence around the world of a variety of dictatorships, Nicos Poulantzas has the merit at least of trying to work out a new conception within the terms of Marxist theory, and, unfortunately, Communist politics in the late 1960s in France. Poulantzas is quite aware of the difficulties of using Bonapartism as the theory for dealing with all modern dictatorships. Thus, helpfully he seeks to distinguish between Bonapartist, military, and fascist dictatorships. Moreover, he postulates that what is common among them is the exceptional state form or the exceptional capitalist state. The forms of dictatorship are the forms of exceptional political regimes dependent on that state (Poulantzas 1974: 11, 16, 312). State in this terminology is not only defined by the monopoly of force, but supposedly by its social and economic role (Poulantzas 1974: 302). Beginning with a clear distinction, Gramsci's domination vs. hegemony, Poulantzas winds up with an incredible muddle.[95] But the idea of an exceptional state as the genus dictatorship to which different regimes belong remains important, and it is worthwhile to note the character of such a state. Poulantzas stresses the renegotiation of the relationship of repressive and ideological apparatuses to the benefit of the latter, the decline of law in favor of arbitrary will, the decline of competitive election and the rise of single-party systems, and the dominance of the political police among the forces of repression. Only one point refers to what was said to be the capitalist character of this exceptional state. The class struggle is said to survive in spite of repression and disorganization, in "the form of behind the scenes wars between 'teams' and 'pressure groups'" (Poulantzas 1974: 329). All these features of politics in fact have something to do with modern dictatorships, indeed not only the capitalist variety. It is certainly not clear why we are being restricted, and how these very categories restrict us, to capitalist states or capitalist dictatorships. Amazingly, in a book entitled *Fascism and Dictatorship* by a Marxist there is one mention and one mention only of the dictatorship of the proletariat, and this in a quotation from Bukharin (Poulantzas 1974: 51). The few discussions of Stalin and the USSR, primarily in an Appendix (Poulantzas 1974: 223–233), have mainly to do with their influence on the analyses of Fascism in the Comintern. While the massacres of the old Bolsheviks are twice mentioned, we are warned that we cannot understand these, or the factional struggles, without understanding the development of class relations and "the real process involving the Soviet bourgeoisie" (Poulantzas 1974: 233) whatever that means. What is never mentioned even once is the possibility that ideological rule, legal voluntarism, police state, and the disorganization of class conflicts, the key features of the exceptional state, may have something to do with the Soviet Union. In this respect the regression vis-à-vis Trotsky is remarkable.[96]

It is however not the political misrepresentations that alone discredit an effort that started out well with respect to a tradition mired in the analysis ultimately of a single case. It is hard to tell what the relationship really is among the plurality of features that are said to be definitive for exceptional states, whether or not some of them constitute threshold or defining characteristics, while others merely dependent ones. The relationship of state and regime is already muddled on the definitional level. Things become far less clear when these terms are applied to a fascist dictatorship. In the end we have neither a clear picture of what ties the various forms of even capitalist dictatorships together, nor what differentiates among them. The increased importance of ideology with respect to repression does not seem to characterize military dictatorship, nor does the primacy of the police over the army. These may indeed be *differentia specifica* of the fascist forms, too bad Poulantzas put them within the state and not the regime where the differences were said to belong.

Thus, ultimately, the principle of identity of political regimes escapes all Marxist conceptions, as it must all purely sociological theories focusing on genesis and supposed function alone. At its best, in Marx's classical analysis of Bonapartism, the conception has been able to give us an analysis of only *one type* of modern authoritarian rule: one that relies on an existing state apparatus as well as a mass movement, containing revolutionary as well as social reformist challenges to an economic status quo, and legitimated by some type of charismatic appeal that is parasitic on the idea of popular sovereignty. (Neumann, actually the most sophisticated follower of Marx, derives one such a type from Marx and the Marxists; on this see below.) Otherwise, the conception suffers from having been tailored too specifically. Indeed, the best analysis, that of Marx himself, deals with only a single case.[97] No one after Marx had the ability to do similar analyses of new forms of dictatorship, and integrate them in a new single conception. With Poulantzas the tradition only moves from genial case study to unclear and one-sided theorizing.

The opposite is the problem with a less influential but more plausible competitor of the category of dictatorship, namely *autocracy*. Norberto Bobbio for example considers only the latter the correct term to deal with modern forms of authoritarianism or non-democratic forms, given the historically specific meaning of dictatorship (Bobbio 1989: 158ff.). It was, in fact, as Bobbio rightly tells us, Hans Kelsen, the proponent of a pure legal theory free of ideological or moralistic or political infusions, who sought to establish the category of autocracy as dealing with all non-democratic forms. Evidently very much disturbed by polemical use of concepts, Kelsen attempted to choose something apparently neutral, at least in contemporary usage, and he chose "autocracy" in opposition to democracy, modeled according to Bobbio on the Kantian distinction between autonomous and heteronymous norms, transformed as autonomous (participatory) vs. heteronymous (imposed) production of norms as the two ways in which a constitution can regulate the production of the legal system (Bobbio 1989: 102; Kelsen 1945: 284, 300ff.).

The term autocracy too has a history, even if not as distinguished as those of the others dealt with here. The Greek terms *auto krator*, *auto kratia* mean "self" or "alone" rule not in the sense of *auto nomia*, giving the law one obeys to oneself, but ruling over others all alone and being accountable for such rule to himself alone (Friedrich and Brzezinski 1965: 4, 15). The term was never a central category of Greek political philosophy. Whatever else it was used for, we know that it was part of the title assumed by Philip and Alexander of Macedon, each of them calling himself *strategos autokrator* (general autocrat), a quasi-imperial title indicating total rule growing out of a military command. In this line of development, Byzantine emperors were to assume the title *basileos autokrator* (king autocrat) and eventually, the tsars of Muscovy and Russia became autocrats. In another line, Greek historians of Rome including Plutarch used the term *autokrator* as the preferred translation for the Latin *dictator*, and thus for the various emergency rulers of the Roman Republic (Schmitt 2012). There was no etymological reason why the term could not be used as a synonym for tyrant or despot, and perhaps it occasionally was though never systematically denoting a particular type of kingship, tyranny or despotism (Aristotle *Politics* iv. par. 27 –1292a; Barker 1969: 168). Aristotle seems to use the term for a democracy that grows despotic; the people as a single composite autocrat (par. 26 1285b). The term was then used by Macedonians to denote their kingship that would be over both Hellenes and Asians, perhaps because they did not wish to represent it to the citizens of the *polis* as either the Asian form of rule, i.e., despotism or a Greek form of limited kingship. Analogously, later Greek historians used autocracy wishing to depict a non-tyrannical, non-despotic, public-interested but still arbitrary form of rule, the Roman dictatorship.

As far as I can tell the same relative neutrality characterizes the only important revival of the category of autocracy in early modern political thought, in Kant's theory of politics, where it is one of the three "forms of government" or *Regierungsarten* (*Autokratie* or *Fürstengewalt* or *Monarchie*: the three terms mean the same thing according to him). Unlike democracy which according to Kant can only be despotic or non-republican as a form of the state (*Staatsform* mistranslated in English as form of sovereignty in "Perpetual Peace," Kant 1963), because of the absence of a separation of powers, autocracy can be either despotic or republican depending on how government and society relations are set up (Kant 1963: 95–97; in German: Kant 1964: 206–208). Kelsen, strongly influenced by Kant, is thus right in his choice of a non-polemical category to denote authoritarian forms of rule. His debt to the specific text of Kant dealing with autocracy goes however no further, because he wishes to definitively leave behind both the three-part model of the forms of government based on number, and, implicitly, the equally Aristotelian, more polemical two-part distinction between republic and despotism. This he does in favor of a new two-term distinction, again: autocracy and democracy. But in fact he cannot fully get away from the three-two problem we have repeatedly seen in the history of thought. The first traditional distinction that leads to three forms, reappears as three ways in which legislation can be organized (Kelsen 1945: 283). The differences here between monarchy, aristocracy, and democracy seem to be real, even if said to be superficial. Kelsen could have said, of course, that despite appearances, actual governing is by ruling elites, and despite appearances, it is never by one man or all. But he did not, probably rightly because a political class can be highly exclusionary or relatively open and inclusive. It can be moreover sociologically representative of society, or highly aristocratic. But if this is true the traditional category referring to the number of governors is not irrelevant, even today. The second distinction Kelsen insists on, that involves two diametrically opposed forms, is also more traditional than he thinks – it is already in Aristotle concerning *polis* and *oikos*, political and despotic forms of rule.[98] Kelsen certainly knew moreover the Kantian adoption of this second Aristotelian distinction renamed as between despotism and republic. Kelsen's is closer to this version, but with respect to Kant at least he is original since here the question is not separation of powers (as it was for the Kant of "Perpetual Peace") but the way the constitution regulates the production of norms.[99] Such production can happen freely or unfreely, autonomously or non-autonomously, from the top down or the bottom up (Bobbio 1989), the subjects of the legal system being also its authors or not – or at least participating or not in its creation. This is how I would interpret the Kelsenian idea that "[d]emocracy means that the 'will' which is represented in the legal order of the State is identical with the will of the subjects" (Kelsen 1945: 284). It would be nonsensical of course for Kelsen to understand this premise in terms of who directly rules or even every single governmental decision, and better to understand his idea of democracy as a constitutional setup involving a variety of political mechanisms (and not just sociological and cultural factors) that guarantee some kind of harmonization between the will of government and the will of its subjects, whereas autocracy has no such political mechanisms. Of course it would be also absurd to postulate an autocracy in which the will of the rulers in no sense corresponds to that of the subjects, or a democracy where the two completely coincide. So what happens between the two extremes? Kelsen actually tells us two different things, one abstractly and one performatively. Abstractly we are told that autocracy and democracy are two ideal types, most of the political world is between them, some forms are closer to one extreme, others are closer to the other one, but at best we can understand most intermediate forms as having no specific designation in terms of fundamental regime types. Kelsen apparently, but only apparently, neglects that last claim when he treats the problem of autocracy. Under democracy to be sure he discusses only mechanisms like elections and electoral systems, representation, parliamentary structures, majority and minority rights, all which play a role, rightly, in providing for participation of the subjects of rule in legislation broadly understood. There is under this heading only one democratic regime type. Under autocracy however we get the following regimes: the absolute monarchy, the constitutional monarchy, the presidential republic, cabinet government, party dictatorship, and the totalitarian state. The curious taxonomy whose members seem to be thrown together pretty haphazardly is immediately corrected by saying that the presidential republic and cabinet government are democracies in which the autocratic element is strong, in the presidential version which he interprets almost as a kind of constitutional monarchy it is stronger. Thus these two types correspond to what he has said about mixed types, and seem to lead to three types of democracies at least. Or perhaps they are two democracies too close to the threshold of authoritarianism to say clearly where they belong. The same cannot be and is not said about clearly autocratic forms, the two forms of monarchy and the one or two modern forms of dictatorship: one-party rule and totalitarianism that may represent one or two regime types in this presentation. In fact the whole taxonomy (including the two democratic types) is presented in order of historical appearance and the major ideal types of autocracy and democracy prove rather useless in distinguishing between them. We should note that without any systematic distinction, monarchies and dictatorships are presented as two fundamental types of autocracy. All we find out about them is that one is an old, the other is a new form. While partially right about the facade character of democratic institutions and procedures under the dictatorships, Kelsen does not note even this difference with traditional monarchies, and only implies the far higher level of social controls under totalitarianism at least than under traditional autocracies. His category of autocracy includes too much, in an undifferentiated manner, and it would be quite wrong, as Bobbio suggests, to replace the supposedly historically inaccurate category of dictatorship with Kelsen's autocracy, especially since he himself seems to use autocracy only as the class concept within which dictatorship, as a modern type, is to be located. The problem is however that whereas we get a systematic presentation of autocracy in Kelsen, the same does not happen for dictatorship that is relegated to a diffuse intermediary space between the democratic and autocratic ideal types. We are not told that dictatorship for example is itself a class concept having different types, and indeed cannot be told this because the nature of such a genus is not explored. Despite the initial reading therefore of Kelsen, it does seem to be true as Bobbio claims that he has replaced dictatorship by autocracy as the fundamental category we should be concerned with. But the cost of this effort is also clear: lack of clarity concerning the distinction between pre-modern and modern forms, as well as difficulty finding the threshold between autocracy and democracy in a framework where all tends to be a matter of degree.

Some of these problems, but only some, are corrected in a second attempt to define autocracy, in part through a reference to the rule of law. Friedrich and Brzezinski (1965) seek to define totalitarian and indeed all dictatorships as species of autocracy. Thus there seems to be a distinct attempt here to understand autocracy as the most general class under which dictatorship is to be located, itself allowing a large variety of types (vs. Kelsen). Just as in the case of the Marxist analysis of Bonapartism, which in its later forms had to be reconciled with the dominant discursive role of the concept of dictatorship, in the case of the initially positivist category of autocracy too the concept of dictatorship had to be accommodated.

Friedrich and Brzezinski understand autocracy as accountability only to oneself. In their view totalitarian dictatorship is mainly the adaptation of autocracy to the conditions of the twentieth century (Friedrich and Brzezinski 1965: 4–5, 15). Since accountability to anyone else must be expressed in rules, autocracy means a "political system in which the rulers are insufficiently or not at all subject to antecedent and enforceable rules of law ... Any self-imposed limits ... do not alter this key criterion, as long as the autocrat retains the power to discard them" (Friedrich and Brzezinski 1965: 5, 8). Note however that while the idea of non-accountability continues the anti-democratic definition of Kelsen, here an anti-rule of law conception is added to that original. (Kelsen does not however appear in their bibliography; nor do the pre-Nazi writings of Schmitt!) Friedrich regards this model of autocracy to be identical to the late sixteenth and seventeenth century conception of absolute sovereignty (Friedrich and Brzezinski 1965; Arato 2000) even if the absolutist regimes never fully achieved the model whose full realization had to wait until twentieth century totalitarian dictatorship, a new form of autocracy.

Friedrich and Brzezinski do not consider totalitarianism the only modern form of either autocracy or dictatorship. Within the large historical variety of autocracy, including despotism, tyranny, absolute monarchy, and types of emergency rule, they are fully aware of the specifically modern forms of military, functional-modernizing, reactionary, and personal autocracies or dictatorships as well. Systematically however they attempt to understand the possibility of only two fundamental modern types, and only in terms of origin rather than structures involving common as well as divergent elements. Thus they are rather ready to dichotomize forms of dictatorship as either revolutionary, generally leading to totalitarianism, or pre-emptive, i.e., to ward off the threat of totalitarian (or revolutionary?) dictatorships. This attempt, which confuses claim and motive in many instances of "pre-emption," does not really work with respect to the variety of dictatorships they themselves point to. Moreover all we find out about the meaning of dictatorship (which semantically seems to be just as much a subtype of autocracy as totalitarianism is said to be its own subtype) is that it has a dictator – i.e., a one-person ruler. But this feature does not even distinguish dictatorship from autocracy in the definition of Friedrich and Brzezinski (1965) since in a group of "autos" the rulers would be minimally accountable, i.e., to each other. The end result, despite its descriptive advantages, does not seem to be so different than Kelsen's. Autocracy here is the only systematic concept under which we can understand authoritarian forms of government, and dictatorship, its various types being concrete species under the genus.[100]

Finally, there is one attempt that I know, and only one, that tries to define autocracy in the path of Kelsen, and separately from dictatorship as a general concept. Giovanni Sartori in effect separates the anti-democratic and anti-constitutionalist dimensions brought together by Friedrich and Brzezinski and makes the first the hallmark of autocracy, the second that of dictatorship.[101] Thus autocracy is defined in effect as the contrary of democracy, as a system in which "[someone] can choose himself, [someone] can invest himself with the power to rule and, therefore, [someone] can arrogate to himself unlimited and unconditional power" (Sartori 1986: 205–206). In an autocracy someone or some ones can rule in his or their own name. Dictatorship on the other hand is seen as the contrary of constitutionalism; it is possible for a dictatorship to be democratic or a democracy dictatorial (Sartori 1986: 205). Sartori tells us little more than the statement that more is involved here than a prince who is *legibus solutus*, i.e., unrestrained by laws because the source of laws – but forgets to reveal what that more is. We can borrow a turn of phrase from Friedrich and Brzezinski, itself borrowed from Ernst Fraenkel who admittedly was relying on Carl Schmitt's theory of dictatorship: the fascist and communist systems "are forms of crisis government." This means in Schmitt's theory that these regimes represent, in terms of their *legitimation* at least, interruptions within or between legal orders, and, in Fraenkel's version (referred to by Friedrich and Brzezinski 1965: 54–55, 120–121) the priority, in terms of *legality*, of extraordinary measures, of the prerogative over the continued if subordinate operation of a normal (traditional in Germany, new under post-Stalinism) legal order. In this correct and traditional interpretation, the absolutist *legibus solutus* represents a normal legal order rooted in his hereditary authority and, sociologically, confined by religious and traditional legal ideologies and practices of all kinds. The ruler is not accountable under such a system and rules in his own name (thus he is an autocrat both in the sense of Friedrich and Brzezinski, as well as Sartori), but is not a dictator. The twentieth century dictator is not accountable (thus an autocrat in one sense) but rules in the name of the class, the people, the nation, or the race (not an autocrat in Sartori's sense). He is a dictator however because the (supreme) law of his regime in reality, and sometimes in ideology, is his word or his command.[102]

In my view[103] the concept of dictatorship is preferable to the sociological concept of Bonapartism, as well as the more plausible rival of autocracy as the genus or class concept of authoritarian forms in the modern period. Bonapartism as developed by the Marxist tradition is both too narrow and too broad. There are authoritarian forms unexplainable by class analysis, for example Stalinism, and the construct includes non-authoritarian forms. Only the Trotskyist use is consistent with Marx's model, but the idea of the Stalinist Soviet Union as a worker's state is absurd. All later neo-Trotskyist (Schachtman, Rizzi, and Castoriadis) models of Soviet society break with the conception: the bureaucracy is both the dominant and the ruling class or stratum or elite. It is best to leave Bonapartism and more accurately Caesarism to its nineteenth century form, recently analyzed by Pierre Rosanvallon (Rosanvallon 2008: ch. V). At best this can be extended to extreme forms of plebiscitary democracy that is indeed an authoritarian form.

Autocracy too includes too much in Kelsen's version, and the attempt to fully differentiate it from dictatorship à la Sartori is extremely artificial. When Friedrich and Brzezinski make autocracy the genus to which despotism, absolute monarchy, modern dictatorship, and totalitarianism all belong, they do come up with a consistent and usable conception. But of these two belong to the modern world only marginally. Moreover, even in their conception dictatorship is the subgenus to which totalitarian dictatorships belong. This corresponds to my conception (Arato 2002) and allows the recovery of the concept of dictatorship even after totalitarian episodes, in whose genesis party or military dictatorships always played a role. But by making autocracy the fundamental category, the link to Roman, classical dictatorship tends to be thereby surrendered, since republican forms are juxtaposed to autocratic ones. As in the work of both Marx and Schmitt that link must be preserved not to insist on the really temporary, transitional character, and even less the reality of emancipatory or constitutionalist promises of revolutionary dictatorship, but to do two other things. First, the classical linkage is easily reinterpreted as diachrony or extraordinary and normal is made into a synchrony of the dual state that corresponds to all modern authoritarian forms. And second, the linkage helps to uncover along with the structure its most important legitimating ideologies. Classical tyrannies, despotisms, or even absolute monarchies were autocracies because they implied neither promise. Thus they did not identify themselves as in any way transitional or temporary. For dictatorships that are ideological systems the revolutionary (or: counter-revolutionary) promise, and hence the claim of transitional status to something better, is constitutive of the identity, if not of the reality. Without it, they could not be established in the modern era or survive for considerable periods. Their paradox is that as against the Roman form, modern dictatorships make transitional claims in order to perpetuate themselves. In this lies their fundamental weakness.

Notes

1 This study is based on drafts concluded in 2003. They were parts of a project that would have included three other studies. Two of them have been published in 2000 and 2002 in *Social Research* under the titles "Good-bye to Dictatorships?" (Arato 2000) and "Dictatorship Before and after Totalitarianism" (Arato 2002). Of a third study on contemporary emergency regimes and presidentialism only fragments have been published, in *Constellations*. The current text leaves the 2003 structure and most of its contents untouched. Here, I mainly supply corrections of the footnotes, and of some of the many unclarities in the text.

2 See E. Nolte's entry on dictatorship in *Geschichtliche Grundbegriffe*, on which I have in part relied (Nolte 1973). I have been influenced by the *Begriffsgeschichte* of Koselleck and his colleagues, but also by Furet and his co-workers in *Critical Dictionary of the French Revolution* (Furet and Ozouf 1989). Unlike Koselleck, I believe that concepts can be present even when the term is absent – and conversely the presence of the term may not indicate a relevant concept.

3 Dictatorship in the modern sense does not become thereby a mere synonym of tyranny in the classical theory of the types of government, as Alfred Cobban (Cobban 1939) maintained. His view, apparently linked to a purely conventional understanding of the link of words and meanings, cannot account for the fact that the concept of tyranny plays a significantly diminished role in modernity as against a variety of ancient categories describing forms of government whose use was uninterrupted and undiminished: democracy, republic, and monarchy among others.

4 Tyranny is one of the three or four forms of rule in Herodotus (Herodotus 2008: 92ff.) since here good vs. bad monarchy – i.e., tyranny – already appears as a problem; or one or two of the six or seven forms (Plato 1930) adds "the best" as a seventh to the standard six that will be revived by Aristotle's *The Politics* and Polybius' *The Histories*. The number of forms will vary in Bodin, Montesquieu, Rousseau, and Kant, but tyranny will be present either identified or differentiated from despotism. Hobbes, as is well known, did not distinguish tyranny and monarchy.

5 I take this highly interesting formulation, originally stemming from Locke's critique of Hobbes, more directly from Vile (Vile 1998: 332), itself dependent on a famous distinction by H. L. A. Hart (Hart 1997).

6 Machiavelli's peerless study of new monarchies in *The Prince* was the first to fully elaborate the reasons why these are likely to be tyrannical and despotic, even if the terms are not used, probably because he did not consider better alternatives, hence relevant contrasts, possible. The same idea however is anticipated by the Plato of the *Statesmen* and the *Laws* (on this see below).

7 See Aristotle's *Politics* III. xiv for the five types of kingship, among which tyranny is included (Barker 1969).

8 *The Histories* III. 80–83; V. 92 (Mandt 1973); similarly Cicero asserts what became the classic "polemical" view among Greek and Roman authors:

> no creature is more vile or horrible than a tyrant...for though he bears a human form, yet he surpasses the most monstrous wild beast in the cruelty of his nature. For how could the name human being be rightly given to a creature who desires no community of justice, no partnership in human life with his fellow citizens...
>
> (Plato 1930: II. 48)

9 See Strauss 2000.

10 This form of typological classification was of course foreign to the ancients. In our time, Hans Kelsen formulated the problem of authoritarian rule in a partially similar way, on a continuum between complete democracy and pure autocracy, neither extreme being more than ideal types unrealizable in reality. This however represented a conscious departure from the ancient classification based in his view on the number of rulers (Kelsen 1945: 283ff.).

11 *The Politics* V. 17–34.

12 *The Social Contract* in Rousseau (1996).

13 *Politics* III. xiv 7–11 (1285a and b). This reference is to *aisumneteia*, an archaic Greek anticipation of the Roman dictatorship (Weber 1978: 442–443 and 1313–1316). Weber identifies this construct with the figure of the lawgiver, an identification that cannot be supported in many famous cases.

14 My interpretation, admittedly contestable, is supported by Aristotle's critique (cf. Barker's interpretation) (Barker 1969: 144) but is opposed by McIlwain who denies that Plato took the idea of a godlike tyrannical ruler(s) seriously (McIlwain 1940: 32–33), and hence came down resolutely on the side of the rule of law. Leo Strauss in *On Tyranny* seemed to represent the first position, but in *Political Philosophy* (Strauss and Cropsey 1987) apparently came around to the second, arguing that the Eleatic Stranger is conducting only a negative argument wishing, by the association with tyranny, to show that both identification of household and *polis*, and the resulting model of the best were wrong or impossible. This second line of interpretation neglects not only the words of Aristotle who carries on a polemic against Plato on the household-*polis* relation, as well as concerning the idea of the best, and the preference of knowledge to law, but also the testimony of the *Laws* that bifurcates the tyrannical and the philosophical personalities (in the formula young tyrant *plus* philosopher) in a way that still seems to support tyrannical, i.e., lawless rule, as well as Plato's own, probably historical, attempt at Syracuse to put this last version into effect.

15 "Tyranny and oligarchy, but different names of monarchy and aristocracy ... the same forms misliked. For those that are discontented under monarchy, call it tyranny ..." (Hobbes 1998: XIX). In the next chapter though, despotism is identified as the acquisition of rule through conquest in war, which nevertheless has the same legitimate status, based ultimately on consent as any other form of sovereignty.

16 See Hobbes 1998; Mandt 1973; Strauss 1995.

17 Bodin 2003.

18 Burckhardt 1954: 7–50. Burckhardt uses the terms despot and tyrant interchangeably, while his sources mostly use the latter along with the non-polemical *signore*, i.e., lord. Similarly, the non-polemical term for tyranny was and is *signoria*. The

feudal origins of *signore* and *signoria* are obvious, and these terms in fact could be applied to hereditary rulers and recipients of fiefs from a theoretical over-lord like the emperor or the pope, as well as usurpers. Burckhardt notes, and probably exaggerates, the disinterest in Renaissance Italy in the legitimacy of origins (Burckhardt 1954: 16–17). Elsewhere he too calls *illegitimacy* a curse that could not be removed (Burckhardt 1954: 14). See also Weber 1978: 1315–1319.

19 Machiavelli *History of Florence* II. viii tells the story of the failed case of the Duke of Athens. See Schevill 1963: 196ff. and more generally Burckhardt 1954.

20 Baron 1955: 161. The "crisis" of Baron is the threat to civic republicanism by the new and emerging tyrannies of the peninsula.

21 Baron 1955.

22 Baron 1955: 5, 134ff., and chapter 7. Defenders of tyranny in general confused, deliberately or not, legitimate rulers and tyrants in the sense of illegitimate ones both in their terminology and their references (e.g., Conversion cited by Baron 1955: 136–144). This is true illogically enough whether or not they tried to distinguish between the two meanings of tyranny. Salutati's motives in defending tyranny along with monarchy are unclear. Possibly, under the spell of medieval monarchical ideas, he was taking the greatest Florentine, Dante's side in the debate concerning the tyranny of Caesar. Having consigned Brutus to the lowest circle of hell, Dante however did not consider Caesar a tyrant, and was a scornful opponent of the Italian tyrannies of his own time (*Purgatorio* VI. 124–127; cited by Schevill 1963).

23 Baron 1955.

24 Boccaccio cited by Burckhardt 1954: 46.; Baron 1955: 48ff. On the medieval origins of both Catholic and Calvinist (Monarchomach) justification of tyrannicide see the outstanding works of Franklin 1981 and especially Skinner 1978: Vol. II.

25 Baron interprets the more important experiments in tyranny as attempts to build a unified North Italian monarchy in the face of the emergence of large, more consolidated territorial states in the further north (Baron 1955: 12–16, 24ff., 28–30 and elsewhere). Many of the defenders of tyranny accordingly were, similarly to Machiavelli in the last chapter of *The Prince*, attracted by the idea of a strong Italian kingdom.

26 La Boetie (2011).

27 See the already cited works of Franklin (1981) and Skinner (1978). I could be mistaken, but it seems to me that the highly influential anti-absolutist thought of the seventeenth century did not innovate regarding the concept of tyranny.

28 Cicero (1943) *De Republica* II. 47, Loeb Classical Library, with the Latin term *dominus* correctly translating the Greek *despotes*, that partially reappears in the English rendering by C. W. Keyes: "a king [Tarquin] was transformed into a despot (*dominus*) … a master (*dominus*) over the people whom the Greeks call a tyrant (*tyrannum*)."

29 *Politics* I. 2. See Mandt 1973: 651ff., 656ff. English renditions of both Plato and Aristotle, sensitive to the immediate context, generally render *despotes* as master or master of the household. This is correct, but loses the thrust of Aristotle's point when he transfers the category to systems of government. See Richter (1968).

30 As suggested by Strauss (2000).

31 *Politics* I. vii 1255; I. xii 1258–1259.

32 See Richter 1968.

33 Richter 1968: 1; Mandt 1973.

34 See Arendt (1998) on isonomy, tyranny, public and private.

35 Figures as different as Jefferson and Robespierre could criticize assembly government by saying that 173 despots would be as bad as one (Lefort 1989: 69).

36 In both terminology and substance *The Prince* and the *Discourses* seem to be on two sides of the early Renaissance debate concerning tyranny. In my view, despite countless brilliant attempts, this contradiction of Machiavelli has never been successfully resolved.

37 Replacing democracy with republic, Machiavelli considers this form to be the best of both the three good and three corrupt forms (I. lviii).

38 Montesquieu 1994. This revision of the Platonic–Aristotelian scheme is more apparent than real, a rearrangement except for the treatment of despotism as a type. Democracy and Aristocracy are presented as one type, the republic, with the same fundamental principle, virtue, but are discussed throughout as quite distinct. Each of them, as well as monarchy, have a degenerate form – it is in this context only that the term tyranny is used by *L'esprit des lois*, but identified with despotism – the latter having no degenerate form.

39 Montesquieu 1999.

40 Fairly uniquely, even with respect to *The Spirit of the Laws* (II. 3), *Considerations* does not treat the permanent, plebiscitary version of dictatorship as in itself a deformation (Montesquieu 1999: 101, 102, 122–123, especially 147), but of course he is aware of the traditional meaning (88).

41 Since he stresses number and relation to law only in the case of monarchy and despotism, but not republics. It is implied of course that these, in their proper form, are under law.

42 See Vile 1998.

43 Today we would say state and regime. See Cardoso (1979).

44 See Vile on Rousseau's version of the separation of powers (Vile 1998).

45 In J. G. A. Pocock's suggestive phrase the colonies "constituted a Country without a Court; they were not face to face with modern government as a force ..." (Pocock 1975: 509). This to be sure led to the well-known American fear of modern government ("Tyranny was indeed to be dreaded 'in every tainted breeze'") but it was articulated in terms of the republican concept of tyranny rather than the anti-absolutist term despotism. However, in spite of the presence of the Court, corruption, and projects of a standing army, the same is true, as Pocock's text shows in the mother country. For this, in both territories, the self-confidence of the Country ideology in limiting absolutist attempts seems to be decisive.

46 Pocock 1975: 401ff., 508.

47 See Jefferson: "The Anas" 118–120; "To John Adams" 438; "To Madison" 438. Even with the end of the immediate threat of monarchy he was to write to Madison: "The tyranny of the legislatures is the most formidable dread at present, and will be for many years. That of the executive will come in its turn; but it will be at a remote period" (464).

48 Ibid.: 120; "To Benjamin Rush" 608–609, where Jefferson tells the two a story that took place during Washington's first administration in his house after dinner with Hamilton pronouncing Julius Caesar as the greatest man who has ever lived.

49 "To Samuel Adams" (557).

50 See Fritz (2008) who explicitly leaves out the secession crisis from his analysis.

51 Op. cit. pp. 156–157; also "Speech on the force bill" (408–409). A remarkable anticipation of this was by "Brutus" in New York (Storing 1981: 162–167), fifty years before Calhoun and before the experience of the Marshall Court of course.

52 More correct in his usage, Lincoln in defending the equality principle of the *Declaration* says that it was irrelevant in the struggle against Great Britain, and put in the text as a moral maxim to guard against future forms of tyranny or despotism. Lincoln 1998: "Speech on Dread Scott" 121.

53 (in Madison's *Notes* 504). Similarly, Jefferson wrote of his fear for his country because "God is just" (Madison: 279).

54 See Rossiter 1948.

55 On vocabulary of the French Revolution see Furet 1981; the entries in Furet and Ozouf 1989 as well as Lefort 1989; Rosanvallon 1998, 2000.

56 He suggests free elections as the way out of the difficulty (158–159), but he was not fully convinced of the empirical viability of this road in a revolution. His reference

to the Americans, Swiss, and Dutch does not reveal a method for establishing a free regime by revolutionary means (166).

57 In Rome he mainly discusses not the classical dictatorship, but the *senatus consultus ultimum* the use of which was extra-legal, in particular in the case of the Gracchi, and was also denounced in Rome itself after Cicero used it in the Catiline conspiracy. Rousseau was to repeat this denunciation in the *Social Contract*, claiming that Cicero should have utilized the classical dictatorship, effectively contradicting the idea (see Andreas Kalyvas) that he opposed the classical dictatorship in its domestic use. Constant has no use for the republican argument of Machiavelli and Rousseau. Since he also criticizes the (so-called) dictatorship law of Valerius Publicola (137), permitting aspirants to tyranny to be put to death without legal formalities, we can assume that he is critical even of the legal emergency regime. The one reference to a Roman dictator of the classical type, Cincinnatus, is positive, but in the same sentence Caesar's soldiers are mentioned who trample on the great republican's grave (63). The point seems to be the Jeffersonian one that even the classical dictatorship led to tyranny, one based on some early Greek criticisms of the Roman dictatorship, namely Dionysius of Halicarnassus (*Roman Antiquities* V. 70–77). This eventually liberal argument, recently revived by Kalyvas (to whom I owe the reference) is also untenable, given the 400-year period separating the establishment and early practice of the Roman dictatorship, and the tyrannical turn (after a period of possible abolition in 202 BC and non-use of 120 years) given to the institution first by Sulla (*legibus faciendis et rei publicae constituendae causa*), and then by Caesar (*perpetuus*). Machiavelli was to give an early critique of this conception, saying that Caesar could have just as easily used a different label. *Discorsi* XXXIV:

> For it was not the name or the rank of Dictator that placed Rome in servitude, but it was the authority taken by the Citizens to perpetuate themselves in the Empire (government): and if the title of Dictator did not exist in Rome, they would have taken another; for it is power that easily acquires a name, not a name power.

58 The historical references too had to be obvious at the time. The revolutionary republic used national emergency as the reason for not putting its own first (1793) constitution into effect, and for repeatedly suspending its second (1795). The latter period, that of the Directory, has even been called government by *coup d'état* (Furet). Thus not only Bonaparte's own coup, but also his permanent "dictatorship" can be said to be prepared for by earlier governmental illegality of the type that Constant condemns.

59 Constant anticipates something like Weber's conception concerning the three types of legitimate authority, but with two differences: for him a purely "individual supremacy" (close to Weber's charismatic type) is illegitimate (Constant 1988: 89–90, 97) and electoral legitimacy, though it can be counterfeited, is possible even when violating existing legal rules (Constant 1988: 158–159).

60

> "When a man or a party suffers an injustice in the United States to whom can he turn? To public opinion? That is what forms the majority. To the legislative body? It represents the majority and obeys it blindly. To the executive power? It is appointed by the majority and serves as its passive instrument. To the police? It is nothing but the majority under arms. A jury? The jury is the majority vested with the right to pronounce judgments; even the judges in certain states are elected by the majority."
>
> (Tocqueville 2000: 252)

61

> "But suppose you were to have a legislative body so composed that it represented the majority without being necessarily the slave of its passions, an executive

power having strength of its own, and a judicial power independent of the other two authorities ... there would be hardly any remaining risk of tyranny."

(253)

62 He believed that the possibility of presidential re-election made the chief executive too much of a docile instrument in the hands of the majority (138). His views on this question were still the same at the Constituent Assembly of 1848, but writing the *Recollections*, when he supported an amendment (and perhaps even an unconstitutional parliamentary statute to that effect) allowing President Louis Napoleon's re-election, he came to recognize the extreme dangers inherent in his earlier views (201, 252).

63 Tocqueville still means by this term some kind of temporary emergency government. See Tocqueville 1970: 162–164, where he however implies the danger of military despotism in the dictatorship of even a staunchly republican general, Cavaignac. He maintains nevertheless that he was, under the circumstances, wrong to oppose the state of siege.

64 He says only that "in America the time for such attempts and the age suited to men of this type have not come yet" (393).

65 In this section, unlike the previous ones, I will avoid trying to fully reconstruct theories of dictatorship, like that of Lenin and Schmitt. Here these authors will be referred to only to indicate the trend of conceptual history toward the contemporary category. Of course, as before, I rely also on existing conceptual histories, in this case Schmitt's own in *Dictatorship* (Schmitt 2012), and Nolte 1973.

66 Schmitt 2012; Rossiter 1948: 17; Livy II. 18; Cicero *De Republica* II. 56 (Cicero 1943).

67 "Now after two hundred and forty years of monarchy ... when Tarquinius [described as a hateful tyrant] had been banished, the title of king came to be as bitterly hated by the Romans as it has been desired after the death ... of Romulus, ... they could not bear even to hear the title of king mentioned ..." (Cicero 1943: *De Republica* II. xxx 52). Livy speaks of a solemn oath by the people "never to allow any man to be king in Rome" (Livy 2002: *Early History of Rome* II. 2.1). However, "[t]he earliest consuls exercised the full powers of kings" (ibid.); and the authority of the dictator Cicero says "was very close to that of a king" (ibid. 56). It is the title of king the Romans banished, says Machiavelli, "not royal power" (*Discourses* I. ii). Here he is speaking of the consuls, but the point applies to what he calls the "quasi regal power" of the dictator (I. xxxiv). The consuls separated the kingly power in space, the dictator in time. Hobbes too argues that sovereign assemblies, in all great dangers and troubles, have need of *custodes libertatis*; that is of dictators ... temporary monarchs" (*Leviathan* second part, ch. 19). According to the terms of his theory of sovereignty and his reading of history, Hobbes argues, contrary to Machiavelli, that the likelihood is that the custodian will deprive the assembly of its powers. He may have had directly Cromwell in mind. Rossiter following Montesquieu (Rossiter 1948: 21–22); but Hamilton also says "against the intrigues of individuals aspiring to tyranny" meaning perhaps the leaders of the plebeian side, as presumably against the followers of Cinna and Marius by Sulla. The institution was in fact not used against the Gracchi brothers when the senate had another method of suppression: the *senatus consultum ultimum* that empowered regular magistrates.

68 See Livy for the circumstances, op. cit. II. 18. He only seems to speak of "the proposal was made of appointing a dictator."

69 When working out his general conception the classical dictatorship was admittedly dormant, thus Polybius may have considered it purely historical, as in the already unorthodox case of Fabius he describes. The same is less true for Cicero's *De Republica*, that introduces this theory (I. 69), and in its separate treatment of

dictatorship treats the consuls and the dictator as interchangeable monarchical elements having the supreme power (*summo imperio*) in an aristocratic government, that had the people's consent (II. 56).

70 There are two other dictatorships as well: one established for ordinary purposes, mainly to conduct electoral rituals, *Comitiorum habendorum causa*, and another the *perpetuus*, used only in the case of Caesar, shortly before his assassination. The Antonine Law of 44BC, introduced by Marcus Antonius, then abolished the dictatorship altogether, perhaps for the second time. Subsequently Ocatavian (Augustus) was to refuse the title, illegally offered to him.

71 And I see no evidence of republican authors accepting one and rejecting the other. For Rousseau, the contrary is explicitly the case as he faults Cicero in the story of the Catiline conspiracy for not having established an internally required dictatorship. What republican authors tended to reject was the *senatus consultus ultimum* used without an impartial dictator being appointed.

72 According to Livy "the appointment of a dictator for the first time in Rome … had the effect of scaring the commons into a more docile frame of mind … from a dictator there was no appeal …" Op. cit. Rossiter in generalizing this point follows Montesquieu (Rossiter 1948: 21–22); but Hamilton also says "against the intrigues of individuals aspiring to tyranny" meaning perhaps the leaders of the plebeian side, as presumably against the followers of Cinna and Marius by Sulla. The institution was in fact not used against the Gracchi brothers when the senate had another method of suppression: the *senatus consultum ultimum* that empowered regular magistrates.

73 The contradiction may be based on the fact that unusually Fabius was not allowed to choose his Master of the horse, but then, subsequently, he rode a horse himself and dismissed the other consul then in office. He did not however violate the restriction on law making nor the limit to a short term of office.

74 Perhaps Machiavelli had primarily Roman and Greek sources in mind, like Livy, who points to the long dormancy of the institution ("a remedy neither wanted nor applied") before it was briefly revived during the Punic Wars (XXII. 9), or Velleius Paterculus, who upon commenting on Sulla's "revival" of the office after 120 years of obsolescence maintains that "the fear which caused the Roman people to feel the need for a dictator was outweighed by the fear of his excessive power" (*The Roman History of C. Velleius Paterculus* II. xxviii). The most important source seems to be the Vth book of the Greek author Dionysius of Halicarnassus' Roman Antiquities on which Kalyvas relies.

75 See Cobban 1939; Furet and Ozouf 1989; Nolte 1973. According to Nolte's version Napoleon was regarded as military dictator probably in the Roman sense still, along with Cromwell, Washington, and Bolivar. Given the imperial construction this is doubtful as a theoretical idea, though could be historically accurate nevertheless.

76 Schmitt describes a parallel development on the right, associated with Donoso Cortes repeatedly (Schmitt 2012, 1985). Even in his treatment this development is much less influential than the one on the left.

77 Indeed in their writings on the Frankfurt Assembly, Marx and Engels heap bitter scorn on those who did not establish a dictatorship for the constituent assembly (e.g., concerning Camphausen's statement that "The Government did not act in a dictatorial way; it could not and *would* not act in such a way" [in Marx and Engels 1978, articles from *Neue Rheinische Zeitung*]). Especially important is Marx's claim that "Every provisional political set-up following a revolution requires a dictatorship, and an energetic dictatorship at that." He goes on to say:

> From the very beginning we blamed Camphausen for not having acted in a dictatorial manner, for not having immediately smashed up and removed the remains of the old institutions. While thus Herr Camphausen indulged in constitutional

dreaming, the defeated party strengthened its positions within the bureaucracy and in the army.

("Herr Camphausen" in *Neue Rheinische Zeitung* No. 102, 14 September 1848, cited by Lenin in 1935 in the chapter "The Vulgar Bourgeois Representation of Dictatorship and Marx's View of It")

The view of military dictatorships remained however entirely negative, even after the affirmation of the revolutionary version. See Engels 1849.

78 See fn. 72.

79 *Marx/Engels Selected Works, Vol. III*, pp. 13–30, Progress Publishers, Moscow, 1970.

80 Nepali Maoist PM Baburam Bhattarai repeated this point at a recent 2011 New School discussion. When I asked him his relation to the ordinary meaning of dictatorship, he answered in terms of the claim that "all states are ..."

81 Engels specifically made this interpretation in his Introduction to *Civil Wars in France* (Marx 1986), which may have facilitated his turn to a democratic (rather than insurrectional) model of transition in his Introduction to the *Class Struggles in France* (Marx 1957). Under Leninism, the claim did not however have any genuinely democratic function.

82 See Gurland (1930) on their influence, and the variety of proposals they inspired.

83 But as Gurland (1930) shows, the self-description among some socialists in terms of Marx formulae continues. Eventually all the Euro Communist parties as well as the socialists and the social democrats formally renounced the dictatorship of the proletariat. This happened after the South European changes of regime, in the 1970s.

84 Verfassungslehre (Schmitt 2008). In a peculiar contrast to Kelsen, for Schmitt dictatorship and rule of law were opposed; while for Kelsen it was dictatorship and democracy. Perhaps Kelsen was trying to deprive his opponent of the stronger principle of legitimation? His view is more attractive, but less rigorous.

85 See Arato 2000.

86 See Arato 2002.

87 This does not mean that in popular literature and journalism the terms are not applied to contemporary regimes. This happens often, but without any clear conceptual guidance.

88 See Casanova (1994) as well as Arendt on the relevant link (Arendt 1981).

89 The term Bonapartism is not that of Marx, but of his followers referring to his theory of this phenomenon, who also used, more or less interchangeably, the category of Bonapartist dictatorship testifying to the power of the increasingly dominant usage of dictatorship for modern authoritarian forms. In light of Marx's own more traditional usage, I here avoid the term dictatorship for Bonapartism, unless quoting from a Marxist author.

90 The *Eighteenth Brumaire* is somewhat unclear on the point, but Marx seemed to think that parliamentary oligarchy, with limited suffrage, represented the "pure form" of bourgeois class rule. The point is unclear, because he also considered limitation of suffrage under parliamentarianism a self-contradiction. On this formal level too we can see therefore why he believed that pure class rule was unstable and pointed beyond itself.

91 Marx did not consider France in 1851, with its defeated proletariat, to be ripe for a socialist revolution. However, pure class rule by the bourgeoisie, "without the concealment afforded by the crown" had in his analysis fatal legitimation problems. This led to the potential tendency of all other classes uniting against this obviously self-serving form of rule (*Eighteenth Brumaire* 48–49). In his genetic explanation of the collapse of the Second Republic he points, à la Tocqueville, to fatal flaws in constitutional design, specifically between a plebiscitary presidency that controlled the army and a single chamber National Assembly claiming to be the repository of

popular sovereignty. These flaws were compounded by a one-term limit on the presidency, and, crucially, an amendment rule that made all these features almost impossible to change *legally* (*Eighteenth Brumaire* 31–33). While for the given case Marx was able to connect the argument focusing on design to his class analysis of the failure of parliamentarianism (since due to its fear of the proletariat the National Assembly abolished, unconstitutionally, universal suffrage, and thereby contributed to both the discredit of the constitution and the popular support of Bonaparte) only the second of these explanatory tracks turned out to be influential among his followers even though many of them like Trotsky (1971: 268–269, 276–279) confronted the transformation of a regime saddled with similar contradictions of the relationship of presidentialism and parliamentarianism becoming a dictatorship, the Weimar Republic.

92 For critiques see Poulantzas 1978 and Vajda 1972.

93 For such an extension of the conception, that leads away from understanding dictatorships (Gramsci 1971: 219–223). Perry Anderson has used exactly the same argument for the absolutist regimes that in his view preserved the economic and social dominance of the landed nobility (Anderson 1996). While the suppression of estate institutions and liberties does suggest an analogy with Bonapartism, Anderson would certainly not consider absolutism any kind of dictatorship. Finally P. Chatterjee applied the concept of Bonapartism to the Nehru government in India (Chatterjee 1998). In the case of Indira Gandhi he had a point.

94 Even here Marx gives us more than most of his followers. He mentions 1) the dominance of the executive power over the legislative (120); 2) the rule of force without phrases (120); 3) the despotism of an individual (without authority!) rather than a class (121); 4) the rule of a caste rather than a class (129). The first of these is important, but also true for the absolute monarchy. The second is false, because most dictatorships do involve legitimation claims and ideologies. The third, the idea of individual rule is not always true as we will see, and is incompatible with the fourth, which is a metaphor at best. The idea of despotism "without authority," though unclear, seems to bring Marx close to the political conceptions discussed below. The idea of the absence of authority, neglected by Marx's followers, would help to distinguish dictatorships from other forms of statism (e.g., the absolute monarchy). However, as my discussion of the "legal theory" will show, the absence of authority, in its two senses of legality and legitimacy, cannot be postulated for most dictatorships.

95 When we get concrete summary of what is entailed by this understanding of state, legal, cultural, and ideological functions are grouped here along with the type of separation of powers, and the role of the state in the economy. Regime on the other hand is, unhelpfully and confusingly, defined as the specific form all the mentioned things take. What were they as parts of the state, without their form?

96 But perhaps I should not be too demanding. The mere fact that Trotsky's analyses of Fascism are treated sympathetically was itself a big departure in the then world of French Communism.

97 Marxists like Trotsky remedy this problem, as I said, by freely using the category of *Bonapartist dictatorship* where the model analyzed by Marx becomes a species of the genus "dictatorship." The genus however remains even here entirely unanalyzed, and probably the purely sociological approach of Marx made this impossible. The only exception I know of is Poulantzas (1974).

98 Sartori is wrong to consider the theory of despotism as never having been elaborated, as we have seen above (Sartori 1986: 203).

99 Between Kant and Kelsen, the biggest difference seems to be the greater importance of the three-part forms of government framework in Kant against the stress on the underlying constitutional form of the state (i.e., the regime) in Kelsen. But he only rejoins Rousseau on this question, to whom sovereignty was more important than form of magistracy.

100 In fact the only general statement concerning what is dictatorship in this book is a quotation from Lenin, from a period when dictatorship (of the Party) as a repressive and violent form was frankly admitted: "Dictatorship is power based upon force and unrestricted by any laws. The revolutionary dictatorship of the proletariat is power won and maintained by the violence of the proletariat against the bourgeoisie, power that is unrestricted by any laws," cited on 110, from 1967 *The Proletarian Revolution and the Renegade Kautsky*. Kautsky held on to the notion that dictatorship of the proletariat was a democracy.

101 This move does occur in the Lenin lines quoted above, but in Friedrich and Brzezinski the definition belongs to all autocracy and not only dictatorship. (See their already cited redefinition of autocracy on pp. 5 and 8). Evidently, however, Lenin's formulation does not apply to the absolute monarchy nor to despotism, both restricted by religious laws and rules. It is however not limited to totalitarianism in its application nor even to one-party dictatorships.

102 I prefer the Friedrich/Brzezinski definition of autocracy in terms of accountability (but not legal voluntarism) to Kelsen's and Sartori's as the genus or class concept for authoritarian forms of rule, but linked to Sartori's definition of dictatorship as legal voluntarism as developed through the concept of crisis government. The question of democratic legitimation for dictatorship and its types, raised by Sartori, belongs to the legitimating ideologies of dictatorships that will help us conceptualize its own subtypes. On this see Arato 2000.

103 These last lines were written in January 2012 for the volume, but they represent what my views were more or less in 2003 as well.

References

Anderson, P. (1996) *Lineages of the Absolute State*, London: Verso.

Anweiler, O. (1975) *The Soviets: The Russian Workers, Peasants, and Soldiers Councils, 1905–1921*, New York: Pantheon Books.

Arato, A. (2000) "Good-bye to Dictatorships?" *Social Research* 67:4, pp. 925–955.

Arato, A. (2002) "Dictatorship Before and After Totalitarianism," *Social Research* 69:2, pp. 473–503.

Arato, A. (2009) *Constitution Making under Occupation: The Politics of Imposed Revolution in Iraq*, New York: Columbia University Press.

Arendt, H. (1973) *The Origins of Totalitarianism*, New York: Harcourt, Brace, Jovanovich.

Arendt, H. (1981) *On Revolution*, New York: Penguin Books.

Arendt, H. (1998) *The Human Condition*, Chicago: University of Chicago Press.

Barker, E. (1969) *The Politics of Aristotle*, Oxford: Oxford University Press.

Baron, H. (1955) *The Crisis of the Early Italian Renaissance*, Princeton: Princeton University Press.

Bensel, R. F. (1991) *Yankee Leviathan: The Origins of Central State Authority in America, 1859–1877*, Cambridge: Cambridge University Press.

Bobbio, N. (1989) *Democracy and Dictatorship: The Nature and Limits of State Power*, Minneapolis: University of Minnesota Press.

Bodin, J. (2003) "Six Books of the Republic," in *On Sovereignty: Six Books of the Republic*, Oxford: Basil Blackwell.

Burckhardt, J. (1954) *The Civilization of Italy in the Renaissance*, New York: Phaidon.

Calhoun, J. (1992) *Union and Liberty: The Political Philosophy of John C. Calhoun*, Indianapolis: Liberty Classics Edition (ed. R. M. Lence).

Cardoso, F. H. (1979) "On the Characteristics of Authoritarian States in Latin America," in D. Collier, *The New Authoritarianism in Latin America*, Princeton: Princeton University Press.

Carré de Malberg (1920) *Théorie générale de l'État*, Paris: Dalloz.

Casanova, J. (1994) *Public Religions in the Modern World*, Chicago: Chicago University Press.

Chatterjee, P. (1998) *A Possible India: Essays in Political Criticism*, Oxford: Oxford University Press.

Cicero (1943) *De Republica*, Loeb Classical Library, Cambridge: Harvard University Press.

Cobban, A. (1939) *Dictatorship: Its History and Theory*, New York: Charles Scribner's Sons.

Collier, D. (1979) *The New Authoritarianism in Latin America*, Princeton: Princeton University Press.

Constant, B. (1988) "The Spirit of Conquest and Usurpation," in B. Fontana (ed.) *Constant: Political Writings*, Cambridge: Cambridge University Press.

Engels, F. (1849) "The Military Dictatorship in Austria," *Neue Rheinische Zeitung* (March 1849).

Fraenkel, E. (2006) *The Dual State: A Contribution to the Theory of Dictatorship*, Clark, NJ: The Lawbook Exchange.

Franklin, J. (1981) *John Locke and the Theory of Sovereignty*, Cambridge: Cambridge University Press.

Freehling, W. W. (1991) *The Road to Disunion, Vol. I: Secessionists at Bay, 1776–1854*, Oxford: Oxford University Press.

Friedrich, C. J. (1968) *Constitutional Government and Democracy*, London: Blaisdell Publisher Co.

Friedrich, C. J. and Brzezinski, Z. (1965) *Totalitarian Dictatorship and Autocracy*, Cambridge, MA: Harvard University Press.

Fritz, C. (2008) *American Sovereigns*, Cambridge: Cambridge University Press.

Furet, F. (1981) *Interpreting the French Revolution*, Cambridge: Cambridge University Press.

Furet, F. and Ozouf, M. (eds.) (1989) *Critical Dictionary of the French Revolution*, Cambridge, MA: Belknap Press of Harvard University Press.

Gramsci, A. (1971) *Selections from Prison Notebooks*, New York: International Publishers.

Gurland, A. (1930) *Marxismus und Diktatur*, Leipzig: Leipziger Buchdruckerei.

Hamilton, A., Madison, J., and Jay, J. (1970) *The Federalist or, the New Constitution*, Dutton, NY: Everyman's Library.

Hart, H. L. A. (1997) *The Concept of Law*, Oxford, Oxford University Press.

Hayek, F. A. (2007) *The Road to Serfdom: The Definitive Edition*, New York: Routledge.

Herodotus (2008) *The Histories*, Oxford: Oxford University Press.

Hobbes, T. (1998) *The Leviathan*, Cambridge: Cambridge University Press.

Jefferson, T. (1984) *Thomas Jefferson: Writings: Autobiography/Notes on the State of Virginia/Public and Private Papers/Addresses/Letters*, Library of America.

Kant, I. (1963) "Perpetual Peace," in *On History*, New York: Bobbs-Merril.

Kant, I. (1964) *Kleinere Schriften*, Frankfurt/M: Suhrkamp.

Kelsen, H. (1945) *General Theory of Law and State*, Cambridge, MA: Harvard University Press.

Koch, A. (1985) *Notes of Debates in the Federal Convention of 1787*, New York: Norton and Ohio University Press.

La Boetie, E. (2011) *Discourse on Voluntary Servitude (The Anti-Dictator)*, Charles River Editions.

Lefort, C. (1989) *Democracy and Political Theory*, Minneapolis: University of Minnesota Press.

Lenin, V. (1967a) *State and Revolution*, Selected Works II, New York: International Publishers.

Lenin, V. (1967b) *Two Tactics of Social-Democracy in the Democratic Revolution*, Selected Works I, New York: International Publishers.

Lenin, V. (1967c) *The Proletarian Revolution and the Renegade Kautsky*, Selected Works III, New York: International Publishers.

Lincoln, A. (1998) *Speeches and Writings: 1859–1865*, New York: Penguin Press.

Linz, J. (2000) *Totalitarian and Authoritarian Regimes*, Boulder, CO: Lynne Rienner Publishers.

Linz, J. and A. Stepan (eds.) (1978) *The Breakdown of Democratic Regimes*, Baltimore: The Johns Hopkins University Press.

Livy, T. (2002) *The Early History of Rome, Books I–V*, New York: Penguin Classics.

Locke, J. (1988) *Two Treaties in Government*, Cambridge: Cambridge University Press.

Lowance, M. (2001) *Against Slavery: An Abolitionist Reader*, New York: Penguin Classics.

Mandt, H. (1973) "Tyrannie, Despotie" in O. Brunner, W. Conze and R. Koselleck (eds.) *Geschichtliche Grundbegriffe, Vol. VI*, Stuttgart: Klett-Cotta, 1972–1997.

Machiavelli, N. (1950) *The Prince and The Discourses*, New York: Modern Library.

Machiavelli, N. (1970) *The Discourses*, New York: Penguin Press.

Marx, K. (1957) *Class Struggles in France*, New York: International Publishers.

Marx, K. (1963) *Eighteenth Brumaire of Louis Bonaparte*, New York: International Publishers.

Marx, K. (1970) "Critique of the Gotha Program," *Marx/Engels Selected Works, Vol. III*, pp. 13–30, Moscow: Progress Publishers.

Marx, K. (1986) *Civil Wars in France*, New York: International Publishers.

Marx, K. and Engels, F. (1978) *Collected Works of Karl Marx and Friedrich Engels, 1848, Vol. VII: Demands of the Communist Party in Germany, Articles, Speeches*, New York: International Publishers.

McIlwain, C. H. (1940) *Constitutionalism Ancient and Modern*, Ithaca, NY: Cornell University Press.

Montesquieu (1994) *The Spirit of the Laws* (1748), Cambridge: Cambridge University Press.

Montesquieu (1999) *Considerations on the Causes of the Greatness of the Romans and their Decline* (1734), Indianapolis: Hackett. Also: www.constitution.org/cm/ccgrd_l.htm.

Neumann, F. (1966) *The Democratic and the Authoritarian State*, Boston: Beacon.

Nolte, E. (1973) "Diktatur" in O. Brunner, W. Conze and R. Koselleck (eds.) *Geschichtliche Grundbegriffe, Vol. I*, Stuttgart: Klett-Cotta.

O'Donnell, G. (1973) *Modernization and Bureaucratic-Authoritarianism: Studies in South American Politics*, Berkeley: University of California Press.

Paine, T. (1984) *Rights of Man*, New York: Penguin Classics.

Plato (1930) *The Republic, Books I–V*, Loeb Classical Library, Cambridge: Harvard University Press.

Pocock, J. G. A. (1975) *The Machiavellian Moment: Florentine Political Thought and the Atlantic Republican Tradition*, Princeton: Princeton University Press.

Poulantzas, N. (1974) *Fascism and Dictatorship*, London: Verso.

Richter, M. (1968) "Despotism," *Dictionary of the History of Ideas*.

Rosanvallon, P. (1998) *Le Peuple Introuvable*, Paris: Gallimard.

Rosanvallon, P. (2000) *La Démocratie Inachevée*, Paris: Gallimard.

Rosanvallon, P. (2008) *Counter-democracy: Politics in an Age of Distrust*, New York: Columbia University Press.

Rossiter, C. (1948) *Constitutional Dictatorship: Crisis Government in the Modern Democracy*, Princeton: Princeton University Press.

Rousseau, J. J. (1996) *Political Writings*, Madison: Wisconsin University Press.

Sartori, G. (1986) *The Theory of Democracy Revisited. Part One: The Contemporary Debate*, Chatham, NJ: Chatham House Publishers.

Schevill, F. (1963) *Medieval and Renaissance Florence, Vol. I*, New York: Harper Torchbooks.

Schmitt, C. (1985) *Political Theology*, Cambridge, MA: The MIT Press.

Schmitt, C. (2004) *Legality and Legitimacy*, Durham: Duke University Press.

Schmitt, C. (2008) *Constitutional Theory*, Durham: Duke University Press.

Schmitt, C. (2012) *Dictatorship*, London: John Wiley and Sons.

Skinner, Q. (1978) *The Foundations of Modern Political Thought*, Cambridge: Cambridge University Press.

Skowronek, S. (1982) *Building a New American State: The Expansion of National Administrative Capacities, 1877–1920*, Cambridge: Cambridge University Press.

Storing, H. (1985) *The Antifederalist: An Abridgement of the Complete Antifederalist*, Chicago: University of Chicago Press.

Strauss, L. (1995) *Thoughts on Machiavelli*, Chicago: University of Chicago Press.

Strauss, L. (2000) *On Tyranny*, Chicago: University of Chicago Press.

Strauss, L. and Cropsey, J. (1987) *History of Political Philosophy*, Chicago: University of Chicago Press.

Tocqueville (1955) *The Old Regime and the French Revolution*, New York: Doubleday.

Tocqueville (1970) *Recollections: The French Revolution of 1848*, New Brunswick: Transaction Publishers.

Tocqueville (2000) *Democracy in America*, New York: Harper Perennial Modern Classics.

Trotsky, L. (1971) *The Struggle Against Fascism in Germany*, New York: Pathfinder Press.

Trotsky, L. (1980) *History of the Russian Revolution*, New York: Pathfinder Press.

Trotsky, L. (2002) *The Revolution Betrayed*, New York: Pathfinder Press.

Trotsky, L. (2007) *Terrorism and Communism*, London: Verso Press.

Tucker, R. C. (ed.) (1977) *Stalinism: Essays in Historical Interpretation*, New York: Norton.

Vajda, M. (1972) "Crisis and the Way Out: The Rise of Fascism in Italy and Germany," *Telos* (Summer 1972).

Vile, J. R. (1998) *Constitutionalism and the Separation of Powers*, Indianapolis: Liberty Fund.

Weber, M. (1978) *Economy and Society*, Berkeley: University of California Press.

Wittfogel, K. (1963) *Oriental Despotism: A Study of Total Power*, New Haven: Yale University Press.

Appendix

Andrew Arato's bibliography

Books

Arato, A. (1993) *From Neo-Marxism to Democratic Theory. Essays on the Critical Theory of Soviet-Type Societies*, Armonk and London: M. E. Sharpe.

Arato, A. (1994d) "Revolution and Restoration: On the Origins of Right-Wing Radical Ideology in Hungary," in Bryant, C. and Mokrzycki, E. (eds.) *The New Great Transformation? Change and Continuity in East-Central Europe*, New York: Routledge, pp. 99–119.

Arato, A. (2000) *Civil Society, Constitution, and Legitimacy*, Lanham: Rowman & Littlefield Publishers.

Arato, A. (2009) *Constitution-Making under Occupation: The Politics of Imposed Revolution in Iraq*, New York: Columbia University Press.

Arato, A. and Breines, P. (1979) *The Young Lukács and the Origins of Western Marxism*, New York: Seabury Press.

Cohen, J. L. and Arato, A. (1992) *Civil Society and Political Theory*, Cambridge, MA: The MIT Press.

Edited volumes

Arato, A. and Gebhardt, E. (eds.) (1982) *The Essential Frankfurt School Reader*, New York: Continuum.

Fehér, F. and Arato, A. (eds.) (1989) *Gorbachev: The Debate*, Atlantic Highlands: Humanities Press International.

Fehér, F. and Arato, A. (eds.) (1991) *Crisis and Reform in Eastern Europe*, New Brunswick: Transaction Publishers.

Rosenfeld, M. and Arato, A. (1998) *Habermas on Law and Democracy: Critical Exchanges*, Berkeley: University of California Press.

Editor of special journal issues

Arato, A. (1978) Guest editor, special issue "Marx Today," *Social Research* 45:4.

Arato, A. (1981) guest editor, special issue "Poland and the Future of Socialism," *Telos* 47.

Arato, A. and Goldfarb, J. (1983) Guest editors, special issue "Democracy," *Social Research* 54:4.

Mack, A. and Arato, A. (1999) Guest editors, special issue "Prospects for Democracy," *Social Research* 66:3.

Book chapters

Arato, A. (1982a) "Critical Sociology and Authoritarian State Socialism," in Held, D. and Thompson, J. B. (eds.) *Habermas: Critical Debates*, London: Macmillan.

Arato, A. (1982b) "Political Sociology and Critique of Politics," in Arato, A. and Gebhardt, E. (eds.) *The Essential Frankfurt School Reader*, New York: Continuum, pp. 3–25.

Arato, A. (1982c) "Aesthetic Theory and Cultural Criticism," in Arato, A. and Gebhardt, E. (eds.) *The Essential Frankfurt School Reader*, New York: Continuum, pp. 185–224.

Arato, A. (1987) "Marxism," in Eatwell, J., Milgate, M., and Newman, P. (eds.) *The New Palgrave: A Dictionary of Economics*, London: Macmillan.

Arato, A. (1989) "Introduction," in Fehér, F. and Arato, A. (eds.) *Gorbachev: The Debate*, Atlantic Highlands: Humanities Press International, pp. 1–19.

Arato, A. (1991a) "Social Theory, Civil Society, and the Transformation of Authoritarian Socialism," in Fehér, F. and Arato, A. (eds.), *Crisis and Reform in Eastern Europe*, New Brunswich: Transaction Publishers.

Arato, A. (1991b) "Revolution, Civil Society and the Problem of Democracy," in Rau, Z. (ed.) *The Reemergence of Civil Society in Eastern Europe and the Soviet Union*, Boulder, CO: Westview Press.

Arato, A. (1991c) "Social Movements and Civil Society in the Soviet Union," in Sedaitis, J. and Butterfield, J. (eds.) *Perestroika from Below. Social Movements in the Soviet Union*, Boulder, CO: Westview Press.

Arato, A. (1992) "Civil Society in the Emerging Democracies: Poland and Hungary," in Nugent, M. L. (ed.) *From Leninism to Freedom: The Challenges of Democratization*, Boulder, CO: Westview Press.

Arato, A. (1994a) "Revolution, Restoration and Legitimation: Ideological Problems of the Transition from State Socialism," in Kennedy, M. (ed.) *Envisioning Eastern Europe*, Ann Arbor: University of Michigan Press.

Arato, A. (1994b) "Dilemmas Arising from the Power to Create Constitutions in East Europe," in Rosenfeld, M. (ed.) *Constitutionalism, Identity, Difference and Legitimacy*, Durham, NC: Duke University Press.

Arato, A. (1994c) "The Rise, Decline and Reconstruction of the Concept of Civil Society, and Directions for Future Research," in Bibic, A. and Graziano, G. (eds.), *Civil Society, Political Society, Democracy*, Ljubljana: Slovenian Political Science Association, pp. 45–56.

Arato, A. (1998a) "Procedural Law and Democracy: Interpreting the Radical Democratic Paradigm," in Rosenfeld, M. and Arato, A. (eds.) *Habermas on Law and Democracy: Critical Exchanges*, Los Angeles: University of California Press, pp. 26–36.

Arato, A. (1998b) "Marxism in Eastern Europe," in Bottomore, T. *A Dictionary of Marxist Thought*, Cambridge, MA: Harvard University Press, pp. 316–320.

Arato, A. (2002) "The Roundtables, Democratic Institutions and the Problem of Justice," in Bozóki, A. (ed.) *The Roundtable Talks of 1989. The Genesis of Hungarian Democracy: Analysis and Documents*, Budapest: CEU Press.

Arato, A. (2004) "The Occupation of Iraq and the Difficult Transition from Dictatorship," in Dworkin, R. *et al.* (eds.) *From Liberal Values to Democratic Transition: Essays in Honor of János Kis*, Budapest: CEU Press.

Arato, A. (2006) "Accountability and Civil Society," in Peruzzotti, E. and Smulovitz, C. (eds.) *Enforcing the Rule of Law: Social Accountability in the New Latin American Democracies*, Pittsburgh: Pittsburgh University Press, pp. 307–322.

Arato, A. (2007a) "Post Sovereign Constitution Making and Democratic Legitimacy," in Stein, T., Buchstein, H., and Offe, C. (eds.), *Souveränität, Recht, Moral*, Berlin: Campus Verlag.

Arato, A. (2007b) "From Interim to Permanent Constitution in Iraq?" in Arjomand, S. A. (ed.) *Constitutional Politics of the Middle East with Special Reference to Turkey, Iraq, Iran, and Afghanistan*, Portland: Hart Publishing, pp. 163–202.

Arato, A. (2010) "Revisiting Civil Society," in Liebert, U. and Trenz, H. J. (eds.), *The New Politics of European Civil Society*, London: Routledge.

Arato, A. (2013) "Conceptual History of Dictatorship (and its Rivals)," in Peruzzotti, E. and Plot, M. (eds.) *Critical Theory and Democracy: Civil Society, Dictatorship, and Constitutionalism in Andrew Arato's Democratic Theory*, London: Routledge.

Arato, A. and Miklósi, Z. (2010) "Constitution Making in Hungary: 1990–1997," in Miller, L. E. and Aucoin, L. (eds.) *Framing the State in Times of Transition: Case Studies in Constitution Making*, Washington: United States Institute of Peace Press, pp. 350–390.

Cohen, J. L. and Arato, A. (1989) "Politics and the Reconstruction of Civil Society," in Honneth, A., McCarthy, T., Wellmer, A., and Offe, C. (eds.) *Cultural-Political Interventions on the Unfinished Project of the Enlightenment*, Cambridge, MA: The MIT Press, pp. 121–144.

Journal articles

Arato, A. (1971) "Lukács' Path to Marxism (1910–1923)," *Telos* 7, pp. 128–136.

Arato, A. (1972) "Lukács' Theory of Reification," *Telos* 11, pp. 25–66.

Arato, A. (1974a) "Re-Examining the Second International," *Telos* 18, pp. 2–52.

Arato, A. (1974b) "The Neo-Idealist Defense of Subjectivity," *Telos* 21, pp. 108–161.

Arato, A. (1974c) "Issues in the Marxian Theory of History," *International Journal of Sociology* 4:1.

Arato, A. (1977) "Introduction: The Antinomies of the Neo-Marxian Theory of Culture," *International Journal of Sociology* 7:1, pp. 3–24.

Arato, A. (1978) "Understanding Bureaucratic Centralism," *Telos* 35, pp. 73–87.

Arato, A. (1981a) "Civil Society vs. the State: Poland 1980–81," *Telos* 47, pp. 23–47.

Arato, A. (1981b) "Rudolf Bahro: Critical Responses," *Telos* 48, pp. 153–168.

Arato, A. (1982a) "Empire vs. Civil Society: Poland 1981–82," *Telos* 50, pp. 19–48.

Arato, A. (1982b) "A Reply to our Non-Critics," *Telos* 53, pp. 188–192.

Arato, A. (1983) "On Cultural Freedom: An Exploration of Public Life in Poland and America," *Telos* 53, pp. 210–213.

Arato, A. (1985a) "Some Perspectives of Democratization in East Central Europe," *Journal of International Affairs* 38, pp. 321–335.

Arato, A. (1985b) "Between Reductionism and Relativism: Soviet Society as a World System," *Telos* 63, pp. 178–187.

Arato, A. (1987) "The Budapest School and Actually Existing Socialism," *Theory and Society* 16:4, pp. 593–619.

Arato, A. (1989a) "A Reconstruction of Hegel's Theory of Civil Society," *Cardoso Law Review* 10, pp. 1363–1388.

Arato, A. (1989b) "Civil Society, History and Socialism: Reply to John Keane," *Praxis International* 9:1.

Arato, A. (1990) "Thinking the Present: Revolution in Eastern Europe, Revolution, Civil Society and Democracy," *Praxis International* 32:1–2, pp. 24–38.

Arato, A. (1991) "Facing Russia: Castoriadis and the Problem of the Soviet Union," *European Journal of Social Science/Revue Europeenne des Sciences Sociales* 37:86, pp. 269–291.

Arato, A. (1992) "Dilemmas Arising from the Power to Create Constitutions in East Europe," *Cardozo Law Review* 14, pp. 661–690.

Arato, A. (1993) "Interpreting 1989," *Social Research* 60:3, pp. 609–646.

Arato, A. (1994a) "Constitution and Continuity in the Eastern European Transitions. Part I: Continuity and its Critics," *Constellations. An International Journal of Critical and Democratic Theory* 1:1, pp. 92–112.

Arato, A. (1994b) "Constitution and Continuity in the Eastern European Transitions. Part II: The Hungarian Case," *Constellations. An International Journal of Critical and Democratic Theory* 1:2, pp. 306–325.

Arato, A. (1994c) "Election, Coalition, and Constitution in Hungary," *East European Constitutional Review* 3, pp. 26–32.

Arato, A. (1994d) "Civil Society and Political Theory in the Work of Niklas Luhmann and Beyond," *New German Critique* 61, pp. 129–142.

Arato, A. (1995a) "Forms of Constitution-Making and Theories of Democracy," *Cardozo Law Review* 17, pp. 191–231.

Arato, A. (1995b) "The Return of the Left in Central Europe?" *Constellations. An International Journal of Critical and Democratic Theory* 2:1, pp. 1–11.

Arato, A. (1995c) "Parliamentary Constitution-making in Hungary," *Eastern European Constitutional Review* 5, pp. 45–51.

Arato, A. (1996a) "Slouching toward Philadelphia?" *Constellations. An International Journal of Critical and Democratic Theory* 3:2, pp. 225–247.

Arato, A. (1996b) "The Constitution-Making End Game in Hungary," *Eastern European Constitutional Review* 5, pp. 31–39.

Arato, A. (1996c) "Reflexive Law, Civil Society and Negative Rights," *Cardoso Law Review* 17, pp. 785–790.

Arato, A. (1999) "Impeachment or Revision of the Constitution," *Constellations. An International Journal of Critical and Democratic Theory* 6:2, pp. 145–156.

Arato, A. (2000a) "The New Democracies and U.S. Institutional Design," *Constellations. An International Journal of Critical and Democratic Theory* 7:3, pp. 316–340.

Arato, A. (2000b) "Good-bye to Dictatorships?" *Social Research* 67:4, pp. 925–955.

Arato, A. (2000c) "Carl Schmitt and the Revival of the Doctrine of Constituent Power in the United States," *Cardozo Law Review* 21, pp. 1739–1747.

Arato, A. (2001) "Congressional or (Weak) Presidential Government: The Results of the Election Crisis of 2000," *Constellations. An International Journal of Critical and Democratic Theory* 8:3, pp. 289–303.

Arato, A. (2002a) "*Minima Politica* after September 2011," *Constellations. An International Journal of Critical and Democratic Theory* 9:1, pp. 46–52.

Arato, A. (2002b) "Dictatorship Before and After Totalitarianism," *Social Research* 69:2, pp. 473–503.

Arato, A. (2002c) "The Bush Tribunals and the Specter of Dictatorship," *Constellations. An International Journal of Critical and Democratic Theory* 9:4, pp. 457–476.

Arato, A. (2003) "The Occupation of Iraq and the Difficult Transition from Dictatorship," *Constellations. An International Journal of Critical and Democratic Theory* 10:3, pp. 408–424.

Arato, A. (2004a) "Sistani vs. Bush: Constitutional Politics in Iraq," *Constellations. An International Journal of Critical and Democratic Theory* 11:2, pp. 174–192.

Arato, A. (2004b) "Interim Imposition," *Ethics and International Affairs* 18:3, pp. 25–50.

Arato, A. (2005a) "Constitutional Learning," *Theoria* 44:106, pp. 1–36.

Arato, A. (2005b) "Post-Election Maxims," *Constellations. An International Journal of Critical and Democratic Theory* 12.2, pp. 182–193.

Arato, A. (2006) "Their Creative Thinking and Ours: Ackerman's Emergency Constitution After Hamdan," *Constellations. An International Journal of Critical and Democratic Theory* 13:4, pp. 546–572.

Arato, A. (2007) "Post-sovereign Constitution Making and Its Pathology in Iraq," *New York Law School Law Review* 51:3.

Arato, A. (2009) "Redeeming the Still Redeemable: Post Sovereign Constitution Making," *International Journal of Politics, Culture, and Society* 22:4, pp. 427–443.

Arato, A. (2010a) "The Constitutional Reform Proposal of the Turkish Government: The Return of Majority Imposition," *Constellations. An International Journal of Critical and Democratic Theory* 17:2, pp. 345–350.

Arato, A. (2010b) "Three Paths of Democratic Transition in Turkey," *Quarterly Bulletin of Third World Studies*.

Arato, A. (2010c) "Democratic Constitution Making and Unfreezing the Turkish Process," *Philosophy and Social Criticism* 36:3–4, pp. 473–487.

Arato, A. (2011) "Multi-track Constitutionalism Beyond Carl Schmitt," *Constellations. An International Journal of Critical and Democratic Theory* 18:3, pp. 324–351.

Arato, A. (2012) "Lefort, the Philosopher of 1989," *Constellations: An International Journal of Critical and Democratic Theory* 19:1, pp. 23–29.

Arato, A. and Cohen, J. L. (1982) "The Peace Movement and Western European Sovereignty," *Telos* 51, pp. 158–171.

Arato, A. and Cohen, J. L. (1984a) "Social Movements, Civil Society and the Problem of Sovereignty," *Praxis International* 4, pp. 266–283.

Arato, A. and Cohen, J. L. (1984b) "The German Green Party," *Dissent*, Summer, pp. 327–333.

Arato, A. and Cohen, J. L. (1988) "Civil Society and Social Theory," *Thesis Eleven* 21:1, pp. 40–64.

Arato, A. and Cohen, J. L. (2009) "Banishing the Sovereign? Internal and External Sovereignty in Arendt," *Constellations. An International Journal of Critical and Democratic Theory* 16:2, pp. 307–330.

Arato, A. and Piccone, P. (1977) "Rethinking Western Marxism: A Reply to Jay," *Telos* 32, pp. 167–174.

Arato, A. and Vajda, M. (1980) "The Limits of the Leninist Opposition: Reply to David Bathrick," *New German Critique* 19:1, pp. 167–175.

Working papers

Arato, A. (1984) "The Democratic Theory of the Polish Opposition: Normative Intentions and Strategic Ambiguities," Working Paper Number 15, Kellogg Institute, University of Notre Dame.

Arato, A. (1990) "Revolution, Civil Society and Democracy," Working Papers on Transitions from State Socialism 90:5, Cornell Project on Comparative Institutional Analysis.

Index